Private Power and Global Authority

Transnational Merchant Law in the Global Political Economy

Claire Cutler offers a critical analysis of the role that international economic law plays in the creation and maintenance of global power relations. By examining the historical and contemporary evolution of merchant law she argues that private interests have governed global economic relations through practices that are little understood. Transnational merchant law, which is mistakenly regarded in purely technical and apolitical terms, is a central mediator of domestic and global political/legal orders. By engaging with literature in International Law, International Relations and International Political Economy, the author develops the conceptual and theoretical foundations for analyzing the political significance of international economic law. In doing so, she illustrates the private nature of the interests that this evolving legal order has served over time. The book makes a sustained and comprehensive analysis of transnational merchant law and offers a radical critique of global capitalism.

A. CLAIRE CUTLER is Associate Professor of International Relations and Law at the University of Victoria, British Columbia. She is joint editor of *Private Authority and International Affairs* (1999) and *Canadian Foreign Policy and International Economic Regimes* (1992).

CAMBRIDGE STUDIES IN INTERNATIONAL RELATIONS: 90

Private Power and Global Authority

Cambridge Studies in International Relations is a joint initiative of Cambridge University Press and the British International Studies Association (BISA). The series will include a wide range of material, from undergraduate textbooks and surveys to research-based monographs and collaborative volumes. The aim of the series is to publish the best new scholarship in International Studies from Europe, North America and the rest of the world.

CAMBRIDGE STUDIES IN INTERNATIONAL RELATIONS

90 *A. Claire Cutler*
Private power and global authority
Transnational merchant law in the global political economy

89 *Patrick M. Morgan*
Deterrence now

88 *Susan Sell*
Private power, public law
The globalization of intellectual property rights

87 *Nina Tannenwald*
The nuclear taboo
The United States and the non-use of nuclear weapons since 1945

86 *Linda Weiss*
States in the global economy
Bringing domestic institutions back in

85 *Rodney Bruce Hall and Thomas J. Biersteker (eds.)*
The emergence of private authority in global governance

84 *Heather Rae*
State identities and the homogenisation of peoples

83 *Maja Zehfuss*
Constructivism in international relations
The politics of reality

82 *Paul K. Huth and Todd Allee*
The democratic peace and territorial conflict in the twentieth century

81 *Neta C. Crawford*
Argument and change in world politics
Ethics, decolonization and humanitarian intervention

80 *Douglas Lemke*
Regions of war and peace

Series list continues after index.

Private Power and Global Authority

Transnational Merchant Law in the Global Political Economy

A. Claire Cutler

University of Victoria, British Columbia

PUBLISHED BY THE PRESS SYNDICATE OF THE UNIVERSITY OF CAMBRIDGE
The Pitt Building, Trumpington Street, Cambridge CB2 1RP, United Kingdom

CAMBRIDGE UNIVERSITY PRESS
The Edinburgh Building, Cambridge, CB2 2RU, UK
40 West 20th Street, New York, NY 10011–4211, USA
477 Williamstown Road, Port Melbourne, VIC 3207, Australia
Ruiz de Alarcón 13, 28014 Madrid, Spain
Dock House, The Waterfront, Cape Town 8001, South Africa

http://www.cambridge.org

First published 2003

Printed in the United Kingdom at the University Press, Cambridge

Typeface Palatino 10/12.5 pt. *System* LaTeX 2_ε [TB]

A catalogue record for this book is available from the British Library

ISBN 0 521 82660 8 hardback
ISBN 0 521 53397 X paperback

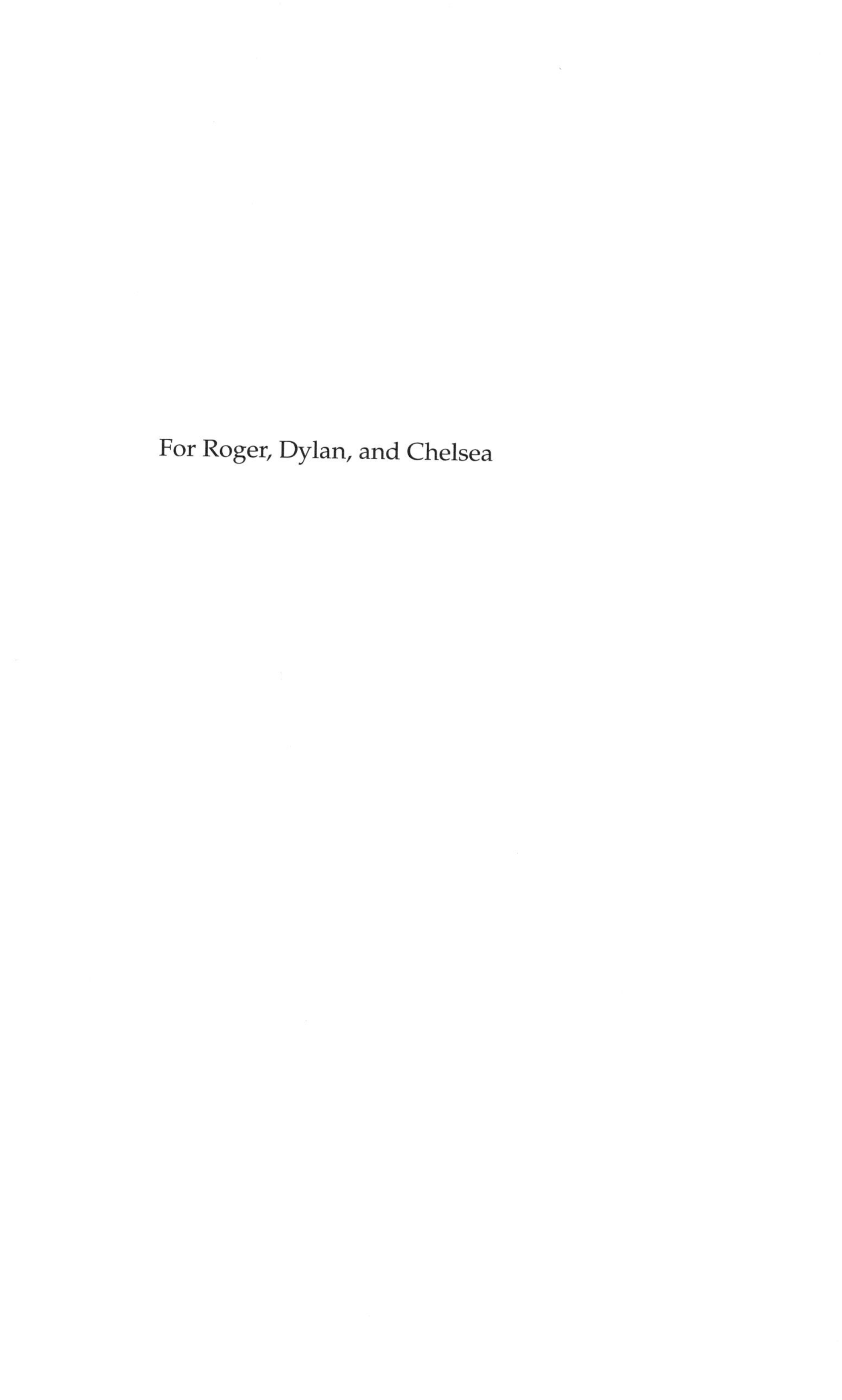

For Roger, Dylan, and Chelsea

Contents

Acknowledgments

A number of people have assisted in the development of the analysis presented here, to whom the author is most grateful. The greatest thanks, however, must go to a few people whose assistance has been crucial. The author owes fond thanks to Mark W. Zacher, whose insistence on developing international relations theory on firm analytical and empirical foundations and whose faith during the author's early years as a scholar continue to provide direction and inspiration. Appreciation must also go to Stephen Gill and to the late Susan Strange for their intellectual guidance and enthusiasm and to the Social Sciences and Humanities Research Council of Canada for its generous research funding. Perhaps the deepest gratitude is deserved by the author's family, Roger, Dylan, and Chelsea, for steadfast support and good cheer, notwithstanding an often distracted partner and mother!

The author would also like to thank the following for granting permission to reproduce parts of previously published material in an expanded and significantly revised form:

Blackwell Publishing for material from "Locating 'Authority' in the Global Political Economy," *International Studies Quarterly* 43 (1999): 59–81, reprinted in part with permission and adapted for use in Chapter 3.

Cambridge University Press for material from "Critical Historical Materialism and International Law: Imagining International Law as Praxis," in Stephen Hobden and John Hobson (eds.) (2002), *Historical Sociology of International Relations*, pp. 181–99, reprinted in part with permission and adapted for use in Chapter 2.

Carfax for material from "Public Meets Private: The Unification and Harmonization of Private International Trade Law," *Global Society* 13 (1) (1999): 25–48, online at http://www.tandf.co.uk, reprinted in part with permission and adapted for use in Chapter 6.

Millennium: Journal of International Studies for material from "Global Capitalism and Liberal Myths: Dispute Settlement in Private International Trade Relations," 24 (3) (1995): 377–97, reprinted in part with permission and adapted for use in Chapter 2.

Thompson Publishing Services Co. (Routledge) for materials from "Law in the Global Polity," in Morten Ougaard and Richard Higgott (eds.) (2002), *Towards a Global Polity,* pp. 58–77 and from "Artifice, Ideology and Paradox: the Public/Private Distinction in International Law," *Review of International Political Economy* 4 (1997): 261–85, online at http://www.tandf.co.uk, both reprinted in part with permission and adapted for use in Chapter 2.

Review of International Studies for material from "Critical Reflections on Westphalian Assumptions of International Law and Organization: A Crisis of Legitimacy," 27 (2001): 133–50, copyright held by the British International Studies Association, reprinted in part with permission and adapted for use in Chapter 7.

In the end, of course, all errors and omissions remain those of the author.

Acronyms and abbreviations

AAA	American Arbitration Association
ASEAN	Association of Southeast Asian Nations
c & f	cost and freight
cif	cost, insurance, and freight
CLOUT	Case Law on UNCITRAL Legal Texts
CMEA	Council for Mutual Economic Assistance
CMI	Comité Maritime International
ECOSOC	Economic and Social Council
EMU	European Monetary Union
EU	European Union
fob	free on board
FTA	Free Trade Agreement (Canada–US)
GATS	General Agreement on Trade in Services
GATT	General Agreement on Tariffs and Trade
IBRD	International Bank for Reconstruction and Development
ICC	International Chamber of Commerce
ICCA	International Council for Commercial Arbitration
ICFTU	International Confederation of Trade Unions
ICJ	International Court of Justice
ICSID	International Centre for the Settlement of Investment Disputes
IDA	International Development Association
ILA	International Law Association
ILM	*International Legal Materials*
IMCO	International Maritime Consultative Organization
IMF	International Monetary Fund

IMO	International Maritime Organization
IOs	International Organizations
LNTS	League of Nations Treaty Series
MAI	Multilateral Agreement on Investment
MITI	Ministry of International Trade and Industry (Japan)
NAFTA	North American Free Trade Agreement
OECD	Organization for Economic Cooperation and Development
TNC	Transnational Corporation
TRIMs	Trade-Related Investment Measures
TRIPs	Trade-Related Intellectual Property Rights
UCC	Uniform Commercial Code (USA)
UNCITRAL	United Nations Commission on International Trade Law
UNCTAD	United Nations Conference on Trade and Development
UNFAO	United National Food and Agriculture Organization
UNIDO	United Nations Industrial Development Organization
UNIDROIT	International Institute for the Unification of Private Law
UNTS	United Nations Treaty Series
WIPO	World Intellectual Property Organization
WOMP	World Order Models Project
WTO	World Trade Organization

1 Introduction

This book explores the historical and contemporary influence of private power in the global political economy. Private commercial actors have over time exercised varying degrees of authority in the generation and enforcement of the laws governing international commercial relations. Today, forces of globalization and privatization are relocating the boundary between private and public authority in international commercial relations and creating new opportunities for private, corporate actors to exercise power and influence. Indeed, this book argues that fundamental transformations in global power and authority are enhancing the significance of the private sphere in both the creation and enforcement of international commercial law. State-based, positivist international law and "public" notions of authority are being combined with or, in some cases, superseded by nonstate law, informal normative structures, and "private" economic power and authority as a new transnational legal order takes shape. Transnational commercial law or the new law merchant is an integral component of this emerging transnational legal order. The new law merchant is variously referred to as transnational economic law (Horn and Schmitthoff, 1982), the law of private international trade (Schmitthoff, 1964a), and international business law (Schmitthoff, 1961). It is regarded by some as a system of "protolaw" that forms the foundation for an emerging transnational lawmaking community (Teubner, 1997 b) and as part of the "transnationalization of the legal field" which is "a constitutive element of the process of globalization" (Santos, 1995: 268). The analytical and theoretical challenges posed by this emergent order resonate powerfully in its description as a "twilight zone" of international law (Bowett, 1986).

The new legal order is working significant transformations in governance arrangements, both locally and globally, suggesting that the distinction between the public and the private realms is becoming increasingly difficult to sustain. Transnational merchant law is implicated in three major trends in governance. These trends are in turn linked to deeper transformations in local and global political economies and are challenging conventional understandings of world order. The first trend is the *juridification* of political, social, and economic life as law is utilized to legitimate increasingly more varied claims to authority. The second is the increasing heterogeneity of, and *pluralism* in, forms of regulation and governance, while the third is the enhanced significance of *privatized* governance arrangements.[1] While more will be said of these trends and their underlying causes in the next chapter, the important point here is that a new transnational legal order is globalizing a corpus of commercial law and practice that derives from increasingly diverse and multiple local, regional, and global locations involving both state and nonstate authorities and state and nonstate law. This order governs a proliferating number and variety of commercial activities and involves increasingly heterogeneous subjects or actors, such as transnational corporations and private business associations, as participants in lawmaking and dispute resolution. We are also experiencing the development and application of novel legal forms and new sources of law that contribute markedly to pluralistic and privatized governance arrangements and which are tailored specifically to meet the demands of business under conditions of late capitalism. These developments are expanding privatized lawmaking and dispute resolution, thereby transforming relations of power and authority in the global political economy.

However, conventional theories of international relations and international law are incapable of capturing these developments. This is due in part to their analytical, theoretical, and ideological orientations that render private and nonstate authority a *non sequitur*. Liberal theories of international relations and international law and state-centric, realist analysis in both fields render the activities of private actors and institutions politically "invisible" as transnational corporations and their law are regarded as part of the realm of "apolitical" and neutral, private economic activity.[2] Notions of liberal, democratic, and

1 See Chapter 2.

2 For analysis of this situation in the context of the governance of maritime transport and for a more general statement of the invisibility of transnational corporations under international law, see Cutler (1999 c).

representative lawmaking and enforcement, and the monopoly held by the state over such processes under both domestic and international law, do not sit well with private lawmaking and private interest governance.

The incapacity of conventional theories to provide a compelling analysis of these fundamental transformations in world order is also due to the more profound inability of the disciplines of both law and politics to adequately account for the role of law in the constitution of local and global political economies. This incapacity, curiously, extends to critical or Marxist-inspired theory as well. Both conventional and unconventional theories in law and politics adopt formalistic conceptions of law which block analyzing and theorizing about the role of law in the constitution of economic, social, and political practices.[3] Formalism treats the law as an external, autonomous, self-sustaining, and independent order, neutralized of the conflict associated with politics, morality, and religion through the liberal separations between public and private authority, economic and political activity, and the state and civil society. As a consequence, neither law nor politics produces meaningful understandings of how law empowers actors as legal subjects or identifies legitimate sources and voices of the law or confers the authority and legitimacy to resolve disputes and determine outcomes or "who gets what" in Harold Lasswell's famous phrase. Conversely, neither law nor politics enables inquiry into the manner in which law disempowers, delegitimizes, and disenfranchises subjects and sources of law. Moreover, in analyzing and theorizing law as an autonomous and self-referential system, legal formalism tends toward a form of historicism that empties the law of a past and a future. Law simply exists "there" (Shklar, 1964: 33) as a body of rules created and applied neutrally by authoritative sources and forming a self-contained, objective, rational order, exhibiting continuity and universalism through time. In a word, neither discipline admits the historical effectivity of the law as a force in the constitution and reconstitution of social, political, and economic practices. Neither captures law as "a constituent of the way in which social relations are lived and experienced" (Hunt, 1993: 121). As a consequence, both disciplines regard law as an inherently conservative force and preclude the possibility of human intervention or agency

[3] Conventional and unconventional theories of international relations and international law are addressed in Chapter 3.

to challenge and change the existing or emerging order, which simply exists out "there."[4]

This book examines the historical evolution of the law merchant over roughly a millennium with a view to illustrating its centrality to the constitution of the global political economy. The law merchant has changed and adapted to transformations in global power and authority, from medieval to modern and postmodern societies and from feudal to capitalist to late capitalist political economies. The analysis illustrates the problematic nature of locating and conceptualizing "authority" in the global political economy and the analytical, theoretical, and normative inadequacies of liberal-inspired theories of international political economy and international law and state-centric theories of international relations that focus on the "public" nature of authority.[5] It is argued that these theories are faced with a legitimacy crisis for they are unable to theorize their subject-matter in any but the most formalistic way, thus obscuring the fundamental transformations in world order that are occurring. Moreover, this crisis is part of a more general crisis experienced by late capitalist societies which involves fundamental transformations in political economies including the movement from the "welfare" to the "competition" state, the advent of flexible patterns of accumulation, the transnationalization of capitalism and the resulting "primacy" of the private sphere.[6]

Transnational merchant law, which is generally and mistakenly regarded in purely technical, functional, and "apolitical" terms, is argued to be a central and crucial mediator of domestic and global political/legal orders in that it enables the extraterritorial application of national laws as well as the domestic application of transnational commercial law. The law merchant provides the basic norms governing property, contract, and dispute resolution, functioning very much in distributional terms as the juridical foundations for global capitalism. Moreover, it provides norms, practices, and a common language that bind and unify a global corporate elite, the "mercatocracy." Derived from the medieval reference to the law merchant, *lex mercatoria*, the mercatocracy is comprised of transnational merchants, private international

[4] This matter will be developed further in pages to come. However, for a slightly different tack on the conservative nature of conventional theory in international relations and law, see Cutler (1991).

[5] See Chapter 3.

[6] These processes are discussed in the next chapter. However, for excellent accounts see Jameson (1991); Cox (1996 a); Gill (1995 a); and Cerny (1990).

lawyers and other professionals and their associations, government officials, and representatives of international organizations. The mercatocracy operates globally and locally to develop new merchant laws governing international commerce and the settlement of international commercial disputes and to universalize the laws through the unification and harmonization of national commercial legal orders. As a complex mix of public and private authority, the mercatocracy blurs the distinction between public and private commercial actors, activities, and law.[7] It exercises near hegemonic influence through its material links to transnational capital and through its monopoly of expert knowledge, thought, and institutional structures. Indeed, the mercatocracy and its law are deeply implicated in the ordering of state–society relations because they operate to recast "public" concerns as "private" and thus are not subject to democratic methods of scrutiny and review. However, this role is obscure and little understood by students of international relations. Prevailing ontological, epistemological, and ideological orientations in the study of international relations and international law obscure the "political" nature of private authority, such as that of the law merchant. The authority of corporate law and transnational corporations, the major agents of corporate power, are minimized by statist political theories that discount the political significance of such corporations and by legal theories that do not regard them as legitimate "subjects" or "sources" of law. These theories thus limit our understanding of the nature of the global political economy by obscuring the nature and significance of private, corporate power and authority. Moreover, the technical and complex nature of merchant law renders its distributional implications intelligible to only highly trained legal specialists. Significantly, these specialists are schooled in a legal science that perpetuates the mythology of the law merchant and the private ordering of international commerce as neutral, apolitical, consensual, and ultimately the most efficient method for regulating international commercial relations (Cutler, 1995). They support the intellectual and ideological hegemony of the mercatocracy and thus are central participants in the juridification, pluralization, and privatization of authority relations. They are also key architects of the legitimacy crisis facing states as the dominant modes of theorizing about political/legal authority are unable to capture the increasing authority of private power in the global political economy.

[7] The historical, material, and ideological dimensions of the mercatocracy are discussed in Chapter 6.

Following on the insight of Robert Cox that "all theories are *for* someone and *for* some purpose" (1996 a: 87), this book aims to displace the dominant theories that view the law merchant as a technical, functional, and apolitical body of law, operating neutrally amongst market participants which are deemed generally to be of equal bargaining power. This is disputed by showing that the law merchant operated historically to serve first private merchant communities and later nation-states in the processes of capital accumulation and state-building. In so doing, it privileged corporate interests. Today, merchant law is integral to the restructuring of the global political economy taking place through deeper transformations in local and global political and economic relations. Transnational merchant law advances what Stephen Gill calls "disciplinary neoliberalism" and a "new constitutionalism" which "confer privileged rights of citizenship and representation on corporate capital, while constraining the democratisation process that has involved struggles for representation for hundreds of years" (1995 a: 413). The book aims to make the central role played by merchant law in the construction and reconstruction of global political and economic authority more visible and hence to displace its characterization as a private, "apolitical" and, thus, politically unimportant domain. It shows how private power has historically been politically determinative and is increasingly significant today with the expansion of corporate power resulting from juridification, pluralization, and privatization. This study is thus concerned with the analytical, theoretical, and normative dimensions of private authority.[8] But it also seeks to clarify the nature of the relationships between international law, international relations, and international political economy. The focus on the historic and contemporary role of transnational merchant law in structuring global material, ideological, and institutional conditions over time it is hoped will illustrate that the law is not an objective force that exists out "there," impacting neutrally on society, economy, and polity, but is in "here," both constituting and constituted by social, economic, and political forces. The law is thus constitutive of capitalist social relations in a most elemental and foundational way.

In exposing the inability of existing theories to account for the nature and scope of private, corporate authority, the book also makes the

[8] There is a burgeoning literature on global governance and private authority. See Cutler, Haufler, and Porter (1999 a); Ronit and Schneider (2000); Hall and Biersteker (2002). For bibliographical references and critical reviews of the literature on global governance, see Cutler (2002 b and forthcoming).

case for developing a new theory of international law. This theory must be capable of analyzing and explaining the role of law in the constitution of the global order. It must be a dynamic theory that comprehends the historical effectivity and inherent normativity of the law: a theory that restores both the theoretical and practical potentialities for human agency to effect change in the law.

Chapter 2 sets the conceptual stage for the analysis of the law merchant by reviewing the three significant trends in local and global governance in which it is implicated. The juridification, pluralization, and privatization of governance arrangements involve both public and private international law, which operate locally, nationally, internationally, and transnationally. However, the significance of private legal ordering in this patchwork of criss-crossing and pluralistic regulation is argued to be obscured by the complex nature of the relationship between private and public international law and the contested status of the law merchant in relation to both bodies of law. These matters are considered in the context of the legal and political distinctions between the private and public spheres, the nature and operation of private international trade law, and the history of the private/public distinction in international law. The chapter argues that four liberal myths provide the ideological and material support for the continuing influence of the conceptual distinction between private and public international law, notwithstanding its declining empirical significance.

Chapter 3 reviews theoretical obstacles to recognizing the historical significance of the law merchant in the constitution of the global political economy. It opens with the more general problems that dominant approaches to international relations and law have in "locating" private authority. Public definitions of authority, state-centric and territorial theories of rule, and positivistic legal ontologies and epistemologies are argued to block recognition of the significance of private law. Conventional and unconventional theories of international relations and law alike obscure the political significance of private authority. Both reproduce problematic distinctions between economics and politics and between domestic and international law and relations and are incapable of theorizing the historical effectivity and inherent normativity of law. Their tendency to analyze law in formalistic and fetishized terms places severe limitations on their theorization of the transformative capacities of the law. In fact, the incapacity of these theories to adequately theorize the juridification, pluralization, and privatization of authority and to account for the enhanced significance of privatized law are linked to a more general incapacity of the broader fields of law and politics to develop a critical understanding of law. The tendency of both fields to analyze law in formalistic and fetishized terms places severe limitations on the transformative capacities of the law. As a consequence, neither discipline is able to engage constructively with the law as a powerful emancipatory force.

A brief overview of the three phases in the historical evolution of the law merchant order, from the medieval, to the modern and then the postmodern law merchant, provides the outline for subsequent chapters. The following chapters illustrate the historical and contemporary significance of the private law merchant order in the constitution and reconstitution of both capitalism and the state, thus challenging conventional understandings of authority. Moreover, the significance of private law in the constitution of the global political economy suggests the need for a new theory of international law. This theory must be able to capture the historical effectivity and normativity of the law and its role in the juridification, pluralization, and privatization of local and global governance over time. A modified form of historical materialism is proposed as the most suitable analytical and theoretical framework for understanding the law merchant order. This modified form recognizes the historical, material, and ideological effectivity of the law and broadens the ambit of historical materialism to embrace nonclass-based claims to identity and inclusion as subjects and sources of law. Most importantly, historical materialism, as here conceived, recognizes the revolutionary potential for a law informed by the reunification of legal theory and practice in emancipatory praxis.[9]

Chapter 4 analyzes the first phase in the development of modern private international trade law and provides an overview of the scope and nature of international commerce from the eleventh to the sixteenth centuries. It reveals that the medieval law merchant operated to support a predominantly private commercial order, generating merchant laws and institutions that operated outside the local political economy of the period. While local transactions were heavily regulated by political authorities, long-distance trade was largely immune to the application of local laws and was governed by the law merchant. The imprecision in the location of authority evident in this dualistic regulatory order reflected ambiguity in the social and political foundations of the period. This is associated more generally with the feudal political economy and

[9] These matters are discussed in Chapters 3 and 7.

the parcelization of sovereignty "in a vertical allocation downwards, at each level of which political and economic relations were . . . integrated," although neither territorially centralized nor fixed (Anderson, 1974 a: 148; 1974 b). Additionally, the predominantly customary nature of the law merchant order reflected the highly personalized nature of feudal authority relations.

The chapter identifies the agents responsible for creating the medieval law merchant. It also describes the merchant court system used to settle commercial disputes and to enforce agreements. What is distinctive about this phase is the essentially self-disciplinary nature of the merchant community in both law-creation and dispute resolution. While there was no distinction yet between private and public international law, the merchant community provides an early hint of what was to become the private realm later with the development of capitalism. Indeed, the absence of a distinction between private and public realms reflects the conditions of the feudal, precapitalist world. Most commercial transactions were local in nature and heavily regulated by local political and religious authorities. Prices were regulated by custom, which involved agreement amongst vendors informed by a notion of the "just price." Quality controls and the prohibition of interest charges were also strictly enforced. Local market activity thus operated within strict guidelines and standards. In contrast, merchants engaged in long-distance trade were not subject to the same kind of discipline, but operated under delocalized customs and practices. However, the freedoms enjoyed by medieval long-distance traders cannot be assimilated to that of later times. It took the emergence of capitalism and the disembedded market and the articulation of liberal political economy to constitute the modern merchant class. These developments served to legitimize commerce and the merchant class by creating a special protected space for international commercial activities.

The chapter shows how merchant laws evolved and achieved considerable universality throughout the European trading world. Their authority is associated with the commercial ascendance of different regions and cities, but their impact was diffuse and universalized throughout the European trading world by consuls who traveled along with merchants to assist in the settlement of their disputes. The first maritime law codes were developed and applied by the Mediterranean trading cities, but as commercial supremacy passed to the Atlantic and northern trading ports and cities, so too did the source of law-creation and enforcement. Many of the laws established in the medieval phase drew upon earlier Phoenician and Roman customs and once received into European law became the foundation for future Anglo-American commercial law. However, what is notable about this phase is the largely autonomous nature of the merchant class and the merchant courts. This was to change as political authorities engaged in processes of state-building came to absorb commercial law-creation and dispute resolution into their local systems of law. The various laws governing sales, insurance, transportation, finance, and dispute resolution were incorporated into domestic commercial laws in the second phase in the development of the law merchant.

Chapter 5 covers the second phase in the evolution of the law merchant order. It reviews the processes by which the merchant class largely disappeared as an autonomous and self-disciplinary order when the law merchant and its courts were nationalized and localized by authorities engaged in state-building projects and in the establishment of nationally-based capital accumulation. The juridification of commercial relations occurred at different times from the seventeenth to nineteenth centuries in Europe and resulted in considerable variation in the degree to which merchant autonomy was displaced by state regulatory controls. The erosion of merchant autonomy was particularly acute for common law jurisdictions, such as the United Kingdom and United States. European, civil law states retained more scope for merchant autonomy. However, in all systems, international commercial law came to be regarded as a matter under domestic governmental authority and positive national legal regulation through increasingly rationalized and systematized legislation. The delocalized, customary order was displaced by localized and nationally-based statutory orders that regulated all commercial transactions through positive law. The important and enduring links between positive local law, capitalism, and rationalized domination were thus established through the increasing juridification of legal commercial disciplines.

Authority structures were reconfigured, territorially, when national legislatures came to displace merchant custom as a source of law and national courts came to replace merchant courts in dispute settlement and enforcement. Moreover, with the articulation of national commercial legal rules and codes, the enforcement of commercial law came to be more generally associated with national public policy processes. Initially mercantilist in orientation, with the birth of liberal political economy and democratic practices of legislative review and accountability, the public sphere was constituted with the enforcement of private commercial relations as an integral component. National systems of law assumed the tasks of resolving private disputes and enforcing private agreements when the jurisdiction of merchant courts was assumed by national courts and when national legislatures replaced commercial custom as a source of law.

Merchant activities were not only legitimized by the state, but reified as political authorities came to appreciate the significance of commerce to state power. This reification took the form of the disembedded, self-regulating market, championed by liberalism as the key to economic performance and success (Polanyi, 1944; Atiyah, 1979). Thus, the private sphere was constructed by disembedding, isolating, and insulating certain aspects of commercial activity from social and political controls. While dispute resolution and the enforcement of private bargains came to be the preserve of state authorities and the public sphere, negotiating the terms of exchange was regarded as a private matter to be governed by individual traders. Liberal mythology provided the ideological framework for this move by articulating a theory of contract law that reified the autonomous "legal subject," "freedom of contract," and the self-disciplining and autonomous nature of private commercial relations. It also provided the foundation for establishing the distinction between public and private international trade law and, ultimately, for the isolation of the latter from democratic scrutiny and review. The laws governing the international sales, transport, insurance, and financial transactions of private traders came to be governed by private international trade law and were neutralized of political content by assumptions concerning the apolitical, neutral, and consensual nature of private economic exchange.

With the proliferation of national legal commercial laws, there was an erosion of the universality of the law merchant, which generated a movement for the unification of private international law in the third phase of the development of the regime.

Chapter 6 reviews the third and contemporary phase in the development of transnational merchant law. This phase is witnessing the intensification of juridified commercial relations and their increasingly pluralistic and privatized character. These changes reflect a more bureaucratic and technocratic form of discipline, both locally and globally, which in turn is linked to a new mode of production in an increasingly globalized political economy. The relationship between law and capitalism is intensifying, both qualitatively and quantitatively as juridified commercial relations deepen their hold on local economies and spread their influence globally. A global mercatocracy or an elite association of transnational merchants, private lawyers, government officials, and representatives of international organizations engaged in the unification and globalization of transnational merchant law is at the center of these developments. This elite association is able to exercise near hegemonic influence through its material links to transnational capital and through its monopoly of expert knowledge, thought, and institutional structures. The mercatocracy is an integral element of a nascent historic bloc associated with neoliberal discipline and the new constitutionalism. The contemporary focal point of the mercatocracy is the unification movement: a movement engaged in harmonizing, unifying, and globalizing merchant law.

The chapter identifies and describes the key public and private authorities in the unification movement that are contributing to considerable pluralism in both sources and subjects of law. The unification movement is argued to be an integral aspect of the social forces that are restructuring global political authority as a result of globalization. The movement is thus placed in the historical contexts of evolving global capitalism and contemporary disciplinary neoliberalism. The chapter argues that the modern unification movement emerged as a cooperative strategy for managing conflicting nationally based commercial laws and thereby facilitated the mobility of capital and national capital accumulation. While originally European and regional in scope, the movement attained global dimensions with the creation of an institutional framework under the auspices of the United Nations and with the leadership of the United States in the post-Second World War years. The initially lukewarm participation of the United States in the unification movement and a radical shift in favor of and, indeed, its acquisition of monopoly over the movement, coincided with the crisis of late capitalism (Jameson, 1991; Cox, 1996 a). The efforts that the United States and other developed states put into unifying commercial law with a renewed neoliberal or "hyperliberal" commitment to the efficacy and inherent superiority of the private and delocalized regulation of commerce reflect attempts by core states to consolidate capitalism and to facilitate the denationalization and transnational expansion of capital (Gill, 1995 b; Held, 1995; Harvey, 1990). This renewed assertion of the "primacy of the private" and the privatization of commercial relations coincided with the advent of the competition state, the advent of patterns of flexible accumulation, and a shift in structural power from nationally to transnationally based interests (Cerny, 1990). These developments are manifested in the growing corporate legal preferences for delocalized merchant customs and nonbinding "soft law" over binding legislation and "hard law." This is part of a corporate strategy to further disembed commercial law and practice from the "public" sphere and to reembed it in the "private" sphere, free from democratic and social control. The devolution of authority to resolve disputes and to enforce agreements to the private sphere through the increasing legitimacy of delocalized private arbitration and the reassertion of merchant autonomy as the substantive norm are perfecting this reconfiguration of political authority. Significantly, this reconfiguration is reordering state/society relations locally and globally. State enforcement of commercial bargains remains crucial to the stability of the system; however, states are recasting their enforcement roles and conferring more powers on corporate actors. Juridified and privatized commercial relations are thus not working a "deregulation" of commerce, but a "re-regulation," casting the state in a different, but still crucial role (Santos, 1985: 324).

Chapter 7 concludes the book with the observation that these reconfigured authority structures portend a crisis of legitimacy for international law and for the global political economy. Positing that all constitutional orders require some degree of fit between their principles and practices, it argues that a legitimacy crisis exists when the lack of fit or asymmetry becomes so great that it strains the foundations of the order. The juridification, pluralization, and privatization of commercial relations are transforming the state system and producing a growing disjunction between the theories and the practices of international society. This disjunction "challenges the old Westphalian assumption that a state is a state is a state" (Cox, 1993 a: 263). The crisis is at once economic, political, sociocultural (Gill, 1993 b: 9), and legal, reflecting profound transformations in structures of local and global authority.

The dominant theories of international relations and international law are revisited and the chapter concludes that the field of international law is experiencing a legitimacy crisis because it is incapable of identifying and theorizing contemporary global authority. It is unable to theorize its "subject," reflecting what is referred to as the "problem of the subject." This problem is generating a growing disjunction between the theory and the practices of the Westphalian state system. The actors, structures, and processes identified and theorized as determinative have ceased to be the only sources of authority or subjects of law and practice. Private actors are increasingly functioning authoritatively. However, this is rendered invisible by an ideology that defines the private sphere in apolitical terms. Liberal mythology makes the political content of the private sphere disappear by defining it out of existence. In so doing, liberalism reifies private commercial activity and effectively insulates it from societal and political controls, contributing further to the denationalization and delocalization of capital. A silencing of potential counterhegemonic voices is achieved through a knowledge structure that privileges expert knowledge. Liberal-inspired contract law provides the ideological foundation for a thought structure that values the private regulation of international commercial relations and thus limits entry to lawyers trained to believe in the superiority of private law. Corporate global hegemony operates ideologically by removing private international law from critical scrutiny and review (Paul, 1988). In this way, private international law has been unable to generate a critical voice. Unlike public international law where critical theory is considerably well developed (see David Kennedy, 1988; Purvis, 1991), private international law remains isolated and is rendered nearly immune to criticism by an ideology that seriously inhibits challenge.

Another aspect of the legitimacy crisis concerns whether the mercatocracy will be able to sustain the internal support and consent necessary to maintain the ideological hold of liberal mythology. Global authority is increasingly based upon fragile foundations as major segments of society are peripheralized and relegated to the margins of the political economy. The possibility that the mercatocracy will be unable to bind these segments by delivering on the rhetoric of globalization and promises of efficiencies and economic development suggests the evolution of hegemony based upon fraud. To Antonio Gramsci, supremacy based on fraud signals a "crisis of authority" and is bound eventually to fail (Augelli and Murphy, 1988: 132).

The chapter argues that the first step is to wage Gramsci's "war of position" and challenge the hold of the mercatocracy by generating a counterhegemonic voice. This involves the critical scrutiny of distinctions that separate domains, such as private/public, apolitical/political, and economic/political. It also involves reconceptualizing global authority through historical materialist analysis that is sensitive to material, ideological, and institutional hegemony and that rejects the separation of existing ontological domains as natural and unconstructed separations. The second step is to rework the relationship between international theory and practice, which requires the development of critical thinking about international law as a form of praxis. This requires taking seriously Robert Cox's view that theory is always "*for* someone and *for* some purpose" and cannot be "divorced from a standpoint in time and space" (1996 a: 87). Imagining international law as praxis promises a new approach that is aware of the dangers of legal formalism and fetishized understandings of law that block the development and recognition of the emancipatory potential of international law. This engagement involves a critical review of the analytical and normative foundations of international law, both in its private and public dimensions. Subjects and sources doctrines must be scrutinized and the interests and values they promote must be laid bare, as too must the remaining doctrinal foundations of both fields. The field of private international trade law is particularly in need of critical examination, especially as regards the theoretical, practical, and normative challenges posed by the expansion of private authority in the global political economy and the centrality of juridified, pluralized, and privatized commercial relations to world order. The book concludes that imagining international law as praxis is not simply a theoretical engagement, but a very practical one with profound normative implications for the future and, indeed, the desirability of the rule of law in international relations.

2 Conceptualizing the role of law in the global political economy

This chapter establishes the analytical foundations for examining the changing nature of authority and law in the regulation of international commerce. It begins by noting the ubiquity of law today regulating local, national, international, and transnational commercial transactions and identifies significant trends in governance that are linked to deeper transformations in the global political economy. The law merchant (*lex mercatoria*), or private international trade law, is argued to play a crucial role in the increasing juridification, pluralization, and privatization of commercial law and practices. However, this role is obscure and little understood by students of international relations for a number of reasons. The centrality of the law merchant to the historical and contemporary constitution of the global political economy is obscured by analytical, theoretical, and normative or ideological orientations in the dominant approaches to the study of international law and international relations. Analytically, the complexity of the way in which the rules of private international trade law operate, the contested nature of the relationship between public and private international trade law, and the location of the law merchant within this legal framework contribute to a lack of understanding of its significance. This problem is compounded by theories of law, politics, and economics that maintain a set of rigid conceptual distinctions, including the distinctions between private and public law, economics and politics, and civil society and the state. The dominant theories of international law, politics, and political economy are premised upon the liberal "art of separation," wherein markets and civil society are regarded as separate and distinct from politics, governments, and the state (Walzer, 1984). Private international trade law is, as a result, isolated from the sphere of politics through a barely perceptible analytical move neutralizing it of political content as part of the private domain of consensual, economic activity (Paul, 1988). This orientation derives as well, as is addressed in Chapter 3, from a more general theoretical inability of the fields of law and politics, in both mainstream and critical approaches, to capture the significance of law as an historically effective social force.

This chapter opens with a discussion of the forces of juridification, pluralization, and privatization, linking these trends in governance arrangements to deeper transformations in the global political economy. It argues that the law merchant is a crucial element of new and changing processes and structures of governance, but that this central role is not well understood by students of international law, international relations, or political economy. While this obscurity is attributed to two reasons, the disputed analytical status of the law merchant order and theoretical uncertainty as to its political significance, the first forms the focus of this chapter. The second reason is addressed in the following chapter. The disputed analytical status of the law merchant order involves analysis of the complex history and nature of the relationship between private and public international trade law, contestation as to the analytical status of the former, and the role played by liberal theory in maintaining the private/public distinction, in the face of its apparent empirical decline.

Juridification, Pluralization, and Privatization

Significant trends in the regulation of the global political economy are transforming the nature of international commercial law.[1] Traditionally, international commercial legal regulation was a matter of national and local legal and regulatory systems (Fried, 1997: 261). When disputes involved commercial transactions between parties from different states they were resolved through the application of national laws or conflict of laws rules, the rules of private international law that constitute the branch of law concerned with private relations containing a foreign element. While this branch of law will be considered in greater detail below, it operates to localize such disputes in one system of national law

[1] The trends addressed here are evident in the findings of many studies of the governance of local and global political, economic, social, and legal relations. For useful bibliographical references to this literature, see Cutler (2000 a and forthcoming). See also Hall and Biersteker (2002).

so as to avoid potential conflict between differing national legal rules. However, the focus remains one of national law. With the expansion of international institutions under the auspices of the United Nations after the Second World War, the regulation of international commercial transactions became increasingly internationalized and transnationalized.[2] In the area of international trade, successive rounds of negotiations under the General Agreement on Tariffs and Trade (GATT) and the more recent institutional innovation of the World Trade Organization (WTO), the negotiation of first a Canada–US Free Trade Agreement (FTA) and then the North American Free Trade Agreement (NAFTA), and other regional legal developments in the European Union, Southeast Asian countries, and Latin American countries are subjecting increasingly more commercial transactions to internationalized and transnationalized legal disciplines. As subsequent chapters will show, the field of private international trade law has expanded in scope with the creation of new kinds of commercial activity and legal regulation and the creation of new subjects and sources of law. The development of new commercial laws and codes and specialized legal processes for dispute settlement under these regimes, as well as legal developments in the areas of investment, finance, and monetary relations, are resulting in the ubiquity of law, domestically, internationally, and transnationally (see generally, Cohn, 2000; Cutler 2001 b). Lawyers tend to analyze these developments in terms of the "globalization of law," while international relations scholars address the "legalization of world politics."[3] Here these general developments are referred to as the increasing *juridification* of commerce as legal and juridical concepts, institutions, and ideologies are used with increasing intensity, in terms of both their expanded scope and their deep penetration into local political/legal/social orders, to substantiate and legitimate claims to political authority.[4] This meaning draws in part on insights from those such as Max Weber, who posit the existence of a natural affinity between capitalism and rationalization through law, and economic historians such as Douglass North, who associate the development of legal institutions with the emergence of

[2] For a good introduction to the institutional developments of international society, see Roberts and Kingsbury (1993) and David Kennedy (1987 b).

[3] See Fried (1997); Twining (1996); the Special Issue on the Legalization of World Politics of *International Organization* (2000) containing articles on the legal regulation of many matters, including the European Union, NAFTA, the Asia-Pacific region, international trade and monetary affairs, and international human rights.

[4] For further discussion of this concept, see Chapter 5.

capitalist economic activity.[5] Both posit the specificity of the association between developments in legal regulation and capitalist business enterprise. The notion of juridification also draws upon the insights of Karl Marx and others that specific forms of economic organization involve very different regulatory orders. For example, Marx showed how the transition from feudalism to capitalism involved an historically specific transformation in regulation from customary norms deriving from status, to legal norms deriving from free exchange and contract (see Cain and Hunt, 1979: ch. 5). Jürgen Habermas (1994) also analyzes the transition from feudalism to capitalism as marked by a growing differentiation in public and private domains and a transition from economic exchange relationships based on estate and birth to relations based upon commodity relations secured by private law. This transformation in the nature of regulation is captured in the famous dictum coined by Henry S. Maine (1885: ch. 1) of the evolution of law "from status to contract." It will become evident in reviewing the historical evolution of the law merchant that feudal economic relations were regulated by society in a qualitatively different manner than were capitalist economic relations. While all social and economic orders give rise to forms of social control and regulation, it is argued here that the juridification of commerce is specific to capitalism. Moreover, contemporary juridification is qualitatively different from earlier forms. The increased salience and intensity of legal regulation that marks the process of juridification is, as Boaventura de Sousa Santos notes, an historically specific characteristic of contemporary capitalism that flows from postmodern conditions of "globalization," "global formation" or "global culture."[6] Such conditions, Anthony Giddens (1990 a: 64) observes, involve "the intensification of worldwide social relations, which link distant localities in such a way that local happenings are shaped by events occurring many miles away and vice versa." To Santos (1995: 268), the development is captured by the idea of the "transnationalization of the legal field," which is a "constitutive element of globalization." Forces of globalization and the privatization and deregulation of industries, sectors, commodities, and services are

[5] See Scheuerman (2000); Max Weber (1966); Beirne (1982); Milgrom, North, and Weingast (1990) and North (1990).

[6] Santos (1995: 252) identifies specifically postmodern developments as the increasing bureaucratization and the enhanced violence of law, and its declining rhetorical significance as modernity's paradigmatic preoccupation with emancipation is replaced by the new paradigm flowing from the postmodern preoccupation with regulation. And see Santos (1985: 307) where he discusses the striking feature of capitalist societies as the degree to which power relations are institutionalized and juridified.

transforming authority relations locally and globally and reconstituting state–society relations.[7] But the juridification of commerce and transnationalization of commercial law are not uniform processes and developments. Like forces of globalization more generally, they are uneven, sometimes discontinuous, and even contradictory for they involve a plurality of regulatory orders, legal forms, and agents or subjects of the law, operating subnationally, nationally, regionally, internationally, and transnationally.[8] Thus Santos identifies different manifestations of globalization and different forms of transnationalized legal relations.[9] The globalization of legal relations may take the forms of *globalized localism*, "when a given local phenomenon is successfully globalized," such as the worldwide adoption of American sales, copyright, or corporate laws (Santos, 1995: 263). Alternatively, they may take the form of *localized globalism*, concerning the "specific impact of transnational practices and imperatives on local conditions that are thereby destructured and restructured in order to respond to transnational imperatives," such as free trade enclaves, the adoption of structural adjustment programs, and deforestation to finance foreign debt (ibid.). As we shall see in the next section, the modern law merchant is a form of transnationalized law embodying both the globalization of local law, as Anglo-American corporate laws are adopted throughout the world, and the localization of global law, as states are subjected to increasing discipline from legal regimes developed by international, transnational, and global organizations. Moreover, forms of transnationalized legal relations are discontinuous and uneven. In some cases, merchant laws operate dialectically, creating deterritorialized transactions and agreements, but then reterritorializing them to facilitate enforcement.[10] Roland Robertson (1992: 15)

[7] There is a growing and vast literature on globalization. Some of the more interesting analyses include: Giddens (1990 a); Held (1995); Hirst and Thompson (1996); Jameson (1991); Robertson (1992); and Bauman (2000).

[8] A number of theorists emphasize the discontinuous and often contradictory nature of globalization, including, Jameson (1991) and Giddens (1990 a).

[9] Santos (1995: 268) identifies seven forms of transnationalized legal relations, including: transnationalized state law, the law of regional integration, *lex mercatoria*, law of people on the move, transnationalized infrastate law (generated by grassroots movements, NGOs, IOs and involving the politics of rights, self-determination, and local self-rule); cosmopolitan law (generated by NGOs, grassroots movements, states, and IOs and involving the politics of rights, international conventions, and tribunals, NGO alternative treaties, international human rights organizations), and *jus humanitas* or the common heritage of mankind (generated by NGOs, grassroots movements, TNCs, and IOs and involving the politics of nature rights and environment rights, international conventions, and NGO alternative treaties).

[10] Santos (1995: 375) identifies dialectical tensions between laws that deterritorialize and reterritorialize, globalize and localize, harmonize and differentiate social relations; that

refers to such phenomena as the "Janus-faced problem of the simultaneity of 'nationalization' and 'globalization'."[11]

In addition, pluralization extends beyond the legal form to include both sources and subjects of legal regulation, which is also a trend that is specific to contemporary capitalism. Subsequent chapters review the historical evolution of international commercial law in detail and reveal that at the time of the creation of the law merchant there was considerable pluralism in the processes of law-creation and enforcement. However, with the emergence of the European state system and the development of modern international law, the state and state-based sources came to dominate analytical and theoretical treatment of the "subjects" and "sources" of international law and national courts became the key agents for its enforcement. Modern international law identifies states as the "subjects" of international law, while international treaties and customary international law, which can be traced to state consent, comprise the legitimate "sources" of law.[12] However, today transnational corporations are significant *de facto* subjects of law, notwithstanding their analytical status as "objects" and not "subjects" of law and their theoretical insignificance or "invisibility" under international law.[13] Indeed, transnational corporations are identified as the "central organizers," the "engines of growth" (Strange, 1996: 45), the "most significant economic players" (Michalet, 1994: 17), the "key agents of the new world economy,"[14] and the "dominant private institutions of the world economy."[15] As we shall see, transnational corporations, most importantly, are crucial participants in the creation and enforcement of merchant laws and seriously challenge the state's monopoly over legislative and

maintain boundaries and transcend boundaries; follow capitalist and anticapitalist logic; regulate socially and emancipate. See Cutler (2002 d) for analysis of these apparently contradictory tendencies in the emerging transnational law governing intellectual property rights as manifestations of the dialectical operation of global capitalism.

11 Another way of seeing this dialectic is as two processes of globalization involving the "universalization of the particular" and the "particularization of the universal" (see Robertson, 1992: 178).

12 The analytical status of subjects and sources of international law is considered later in this chapter. For a good introduction to these matters, see Malanczuk (1997).

13 See below and see Higgins (1985). For the state-centric nature of the analytical foundations of international law see Janis (1984 a: 61–78) and for the analytical and theoretical invisibility of transnational corporations under international law see Johns (1994).

14 See Cutler (2000 a) for the centrality of the transnational corporation to analysts of international political economy. And see Santos (1995: 253).

15 Picciotto (1999 a: 6) citing an UNCTAD *World Investment Report 1997* notes that by 1996 there were about 44,000 TNCs with some 280,000 foreign affiliates, but the top 25 firms controlled over half of outward investment stock, while about one third of interstate trade consists of flows between such affiliates.

adjudicative functions in international commerce.[16] Significant, as well, are the activities of other nonstate agents of law-creation and enforcement, including transnational lawyers and law firms; accountants and transnational accounting firms, insurers, bankers, and their private associations, such as the International Chamber of Commerce.[17] Indeed, later chapters will illustrate that the mercatocracy comprises a curious mix of private and public authority, drawing upon both private corporate and public state offices. The pluralism in subjects has created "a spaghetti bowl or spider's web of intertwined organizations and arrangements, which evade the traditional categories of private and public, national and international law," while "emerging forms of global governance are characterized by the fragmentation of the public sphere into a complex and multilayered network of interacting institutions and bodies" (Picciotto, 1999 a: 9).

Pluralism in contemporary "subjects" of the law is mirrored in the "sources" of law, as well. While customary law created by merchants formed the "source" of law for the early law merchant, the emergence of states and the advent of capitalist business enterprise replaced the customary order with positive law created by state authorities. In international law, "hard law" in the form of international conventions and customary international law formed the definitive sources of the law.[18] Today, they continue to provide the analytical and theoretical foundations for international law. However, new sources of law are emerging which do not emanate from public, state authority, but rather from privatized, nonstate authority. Examples include the legal norms emerging from the dominant legal practices and the contractual activities of transnational corporations and other professionals engaged in international commerce, including bankers, insurers, tax specialists, and the like.[19] Model codes, statements of principle, uniform rules for optional use in commercial contracting, and standardized contracts increasingly

[16] See Chapter 6.

[17] For the growing authority of private institutions and processes in the generation and enforcement of international economic regulation, see Cutler, Haufler, and Porter (1999 a: ch. 6).

[18] While this matter is taken up more fully in the subsequent section, "hard law" consists of binding international conventions and customary international law. "Soft law" may be defined as "guidelines of conduct (such as those formulated by the United Nations concerning the operations of transnational corporations) which are neither strictly binding norms of law, nor completely irrelevant political maxims, and operate in a grey zone between law and politics" and is considered a "special characteristic of international economic law and of international environmental law" (Malanczuk, 1997: 54).

[19] These matters are discussed in Chapter 6.

form the core of transnational business practices. International trade, investment, and finance are increasingly regulated by soft, porous, discretionary standards and procedures. This tendency is associated by many analysts with the increasing complexity of commercial transacting and the resulting enhanced significance of expert knowledge of the fields of law, accounting, and taxation.

In addition, transnational corporate activities are being regulated increasingly by "soft law" in the form of privately created codes governing business practices, such as those governing labor relations, consumer protection, environmental practice, and Memorandums of Understanding between subnational regulatory agencies (Picciotto and Mayne, 1999). This results in "complex and multi-layered interactions between laws, codes and guidelines, operating locally, nationally, transnationally, regionally and internationally" (Picciotto, 1999 a: 17). These developments have significant political and economic implications. For example, while "hard law" reduces transaction costs and strengthens the credibility of commitments, it restricts sovereignty and autonomy and is thus harder to achieve and, initially, very costly to negotiate.[20] Weaker states on the periphery of the global political economy tend to favor hard law because it provides a certain transparency, predictability, and locking-in of commitments that become more difficult for stronger states to renege upon. In addition, hard law, in the form of multilateral treaties, is negotiated in forums that provide rules governing participation and representation, leveling the playing field somewhat for weaker participants.[21] Soft law, in contrast, is cheaper and easier to achieve, but is easier to breach with impunity. It also gives rise to more opportunities for "creative lawyering" and the private shaping of legal regulation (McCahery and Picciotto, 1995). Hard and soft law thus operate differently, give rise to different political economies, and embody different power relations.

[20] See Abbott and Snidal (2000: 421) who define "hard law" as "legally binding obligations that are precise (or can be made precise through adjudication or the issuance of detailed regulations) and that delegate authority for interpreting and implementing the law." However, the terms hard and soft law are not particularly helpful either analytically or theoretically for they beg the question of what it means to be "legally binding," while their association with degrees of precision threatens to lead to legal formalistic analysis that obscures more than it clarifies.

[21] Abbott and Snidal (2000) note, however, that preferences are not necessarily uniform and they cite the preference of Mexican business groups for a hard, legalized NAFTA, that of high-tech corporations for a hard WTO agreement on TRIPS, and workers' preference for hard obligations in the ILO. See also Cutler (2001 a) and Sempasa (1992) for the tendency of developing countries to prefer hard law negotiated in multilateral institutions.

The increasingly heterogeneous nature of subjects and sources of law have important analytical, theoretical, and normative implications.[22] While states are typically regarded as the subjects of international law, the main architects of juridified commercial relations are private individuals and business enterprises, including, for example, transnational lawyers, accountants, bankers and private business associations, and transnational corporations, working in tandem with government officials and representatives of international organizations (Dezalay and Sugarman, 1995). The pluralism of legal subjects or agents contemplated here, however, does not draw on the liberal notion of a world of multiple regulatory orders in which no one order dominates. Nor is it, as Santos (1987) notes:

> the legal pluralism of traditional legal anthropology in which different legal orders are conceived as separate entities coexisting in the same political space, but rather a conception of different legal spaces superimposed, interpenetrated, and mixed in our minds as much as in our actions... We live in a time of porous legality or legal porosity, of multiple networks of legal orders forcing us to constant transitions and trespassing. Our legal life is constituted by an intersection of different legal orders, that is by *interlegality. Interlegality is the key postmodern conception of law.* (297–300)

Whereas contemporary international commercial relations have typically been regulated by states, the new law merchant forms "an enclosure, a new particularism that empties or neutralizes the law of the land" and creates space for personalized and privatized law.[23] It challenges state and national legal orders with a personalized and privatized order comprising private international economic actors, agents, and subjects. Indeed, it operates in a transnational legal space, a space in which "different types of economic agents operate, whose behavior is regulated by new international rules and contractual relations established by dominant multinational corporations, international banks or international associations dominated by both" who have a certain immunity from both national and international law (Santos, 1987: 287). Private authority is exercised through a variety of means from highly informal industry alliances, joint ventures, networks, and business

[22] This argument is developed fully in Chapter 6.
[23] Santos (1987: 293) refers to this law as "egocentric" or highly personalized, as opposed to traditional, geocentric national or state law.

associations to highly institutionalized private international regimes.[24] Significantly, as we shall see, central to the expansion of private legal authority is the movement for the harmonization and unification of private international trade law.[25] The unification movement provides the material, institutional, and ideological framework for the influence exercised by the mercatocracy in the constitution of the law merchant order.

Importantly, notwithstanding the participation of public authorities in this order, the new law merchant constitutes a predominantly privatized legal order. While there is a "new working relationship between corporations and governments," noted by the Secretary-General of the United Nations, it is a relationship structured by the development of a "soft infrastructure" for the orderly conduct of business that is sensitive to the competitive needs of business corporations.[26] As a result, the dominant mode for regulating business corporations in the 1990s was through soft law, voluntary private codes of conduct, and private dispute settlement through international commercial arbitration. These developments are generally regarded to be consistent with privatization and deregulation of corporate activities, what Peter Muchlinski (1995) refers to as the declining "corporate control" function of states[27] and

24 These include multinational law, insurance, management, and consultancy firms, debt-rating agencies, stock exchanges, and financial clearing houses (see Cutler, Haufler, and Porter, 1999 b: 10).

25 See Chapter 6.

26 See UN report: *Development of Guidelines on the Role and Social Responsibilities of the Private Sector, Report of the Secretary General of the United Nations* (2000: 7).

27 See also Muchlinski (1997) where he indicates that efforts to regulate TNCs by protecting investors during the nineteenth century emanated primarily from private sources, such as the International Chamber of Commerce. By the twentieth century, states were engaged in investor protection regulation under arrangements like NAFTA, and the Uruguay Round of the GATT, which produced agreements protecting intellectual property investments (TRIPS), controlling performance requirements (TRIMS) and protecting providers of services (GATS). States also protected investors through bilateral investment treaties entered into under the auspices of the International Centre for the Settlement of Investment Disputes (ICSID) and the World Bank and through World Bank investment guarantee insurance. In contrast, efforts to regulate TNC behavior to protect host state interests have taken place in a multilateral intergovernmental context, such as the United Nations, the International Labour Organization, the World Health Organization, the Organization for Economic Cooperation and Development (OECD), and the World Bank, but neither the OECD Guidelines nor the World Bank Guidelines are legally binding. The recent failed initiative by the OECD to protect investors through the Multilateral Agreement on Investment was severely criticized by many unions, NGOs, and consumer protection groups who argued it favored the private interests of investors over the public interests of the host state. See also Mabey (1999) and Picciotto (1999 b).

their adoption of a regulatory orientation that is facultative, supportive, and more in line with contemporary free-market values.[28]

Analytically and theoretically, the state remains at the center of the international commercial order, but in practice the state-based order is being eclipsed by private subjects and sources of legal regulation. As we shall see, juridification, pluralization, and privatization are also occurring in the area of dispute settlement. Under the GATT, NAFTA, FTA, and through agreements between individual and corporate commercial actors, privatized processes of dispute resolution have eclipsed dispute settlement by national judicial authorities.[29] The proliferation of private institutions and rules for international commercial arbitration evidence remarkable pluralism in privatized methods for settling commercial disputes. In many instances, matters that were formerly regarded as justiciable in national courts of law, such as disputes involving matters relating to securities and antitrust or competition law and regulations, consumer protection and other areas of mandatory law, are being found to be arbitrable subject-matter. This effectively removes such matters from review in public judicial settings and places them in the privatized, closed world of international commercial arbitration (Dezalay and Garth, 1996). As a result, matters once governed by mandatory national law are being found to be arbitrable subject-matter subject to determination in private and closed arbitration proceedings, which are characterized by their informal and discretionary nature. The result is the removal of many politically sensitive matters, such as competition, securities, tax regulation, intellectual property, and consumer protection

28 The free-market orientation is referred to by many as the Washington and post-Washington consensus. Picciotto (1999 a: 4) notes that the Washington consensus of the 1980s "stressed deregulation and the slimming down of the state," but reaction to this emerged from those advocating the success of state-led development and resulted in a "modified Washington consensus" that "now includes the importance of the state and regulation," advocating the "market-friendly state" for developing states.

29 According to a leading practitioner (Aksen, 1990: 287), "in today's world the dispute resolution system will invariably be arbitration." And see Carbonneau (1990). Dezalay and Garth (1996: 6) note that over the past twenty-five to thirty years international commercial arbitration has become "big legal business" and the accepted method for resolving commercial disputes. While they note that there are no global statistics available, they refer to records kept by the leading international commercial centers, such as the International Chamber of Commerce arbitration facilities, which reveal a dramatic increase in arbitration requests (some 3000 requests in its first 50 years of operation compared to 3000 requests over the past decade alone). They also note a 1992 report (cf. 2) that identifies some 120 private arbitration institutions in the world, but they caution that the list is not comprehensive. An indication of the increased recourse to international commercial arbitration is evident in the proliferation of institutions engaged in providing this service. See also Graving (1989) and for a list of arbitration services, see Asser Institute (1988: 713–37).

disputes, from public supervision and control in national courts of law.[30] This undermines the ability of states to regulate many matters that raise national public policy concerns. Moreover, as subsequent chapters will show, governments, at least in the developed world, are participating in limiting their powers of review by providing a hospitable legal and regulatory framework for private, secretive, and closed arbitration proceedings. States are limiting the powers of their national courts to review the decisions of private international commercial arbitrations, while simultaneously committing public offices to the enforcement and execution of foreign and domestic arbitration awards.[31] The world of international commercial arbitration, which is increasingly transnational in its operation, institutional structures, and culture, thus comprises an interesting mixture of private and public authority.[32]

These developments give rise to important normative considerations. Typically, we associate processes of law-creation and dispute resolution with those vested with the authority to legislate and adjudicate.

[30] McConnaughay (1999: 453–4 and 479) argues that the separation between international commercial arbitration and national legal systems is now "complete." He analyzes a number of cases in the US where national courts have permitted the private arbitration of matters under the Securities Exchange Act, the Sherman Act (antitrust), the Carriage of Goods by Sea Act and other regulatory legislation. In each case mandatory law was at issue: "Mandatory national laws share most of the characteristics of that body of law traditionally referred to as 'public law:' they are typically expressed in statutory form, they are regulatory rather than elective, they frequently vary from nation to nation, and they are often enforced directly, although not exclusively, by an agency of government. Traditionally, the freedom of parties to privately arbitrate disputes and to contractually choose applicable law ended when mandatory law began and began when mandatory law ended"(474). In the antitrust case (*Mitsubishi v. Soler Chrysler-Plymouth, Inc.* 473 US 614 (1985)) he notes that the court "effectively transformed arbitral adjudication from an instrument of private contractual autonomy into an exercise of delegated judicial authority from the state." And see Kronstein (1963) for the view that arbitration expands the authority of private interests.

[31] The recourse to private arbitration is being encouraged by states who are participating in creating uniform and mandatory rules that provide for the national recognition and enforcement of foreign arbitral awards. States are adopting legislation that curtails the power of national courts to intervene in private arbitration proceedings and limits judicial authority to set aside awards. The United Nations Convention on the Recognition and Enforcement of Foreign Arbitral Awards (New York Convention), 10 June 1958, UN Doc. A/Conf. 9/22, is in force in some 123 states (as of 4 October 2000) and curtails the power of national courts to intervene in private arbitrations. In addition, states are voluntarily adopting the UNCITRAL Model Law on International Commercial Arbitration (adopted by some thirty-two states as of 4 October 2000) which, in tandem with the New York Convention, provides a comprehensive body of international arbitration law and procedure. For the most current information on the number of states adopting these and other legal instruments, see UNCITRAL Homepage, http://www.UNCITRAL.org/en-index.htm.

[32] For an excellent review of the closed and club-like nature of the international commercial arbitration community see Dezalay and Garth (1996).

In democratic and representative legal systems, legislatures and parliaments create laws, while the judiciary and state enforce them. Under public international law, states are vested with the authority to create and enforce laws in a system in which state consent forms the litmus test of law. Private authority over law-creation and dispute settlement thus raises important concerns about public participation and democratic accountability and legitimacy. As we shall see, the privatization of legal authority is generally inconsistent with conventional notions of the public and nonarbitrary "rule of law." It also challenges the analytical and theoretical foundations of international law as a state-centric and consent-based system of law.

The normative implications of privatized authority take on even greater significance when the juridification, pluralization, and privatization of commercial relations are placed in the context of deeper transformations in the global political economy. These trends in the governance of commercial relations are linked to fundamental transformations in the global political economy associated with postmodernism and late capitalism. While postmodernism suggests "a fluid, 'disorderly' global field of forms of life, identity presentation and consumerism" and parades "heterogeneity and variety" (Robertson, 1992: 178–9), it is as Frederic Jameson (1991: xii) notes, "the reflex and the concomitant of yet another systematic modification of capitalism itself." Late capitalism describes various phenomena relating to "multinational capitalism," new forms of multi- and transnational business enterprises, "the new international division of labour," new dynamics in international banking, stock exchanges, new forms of media interrelationship, computers, automation, the flight of production to advanced Third World economies, the crisis of labor, and global gentrification.[33] The transformations isolated in this analysis relate to the advent of the "competition state," the transnationalization or deterritorialization of capital, and related processes of "flexible accumulation." These transformations provide the ideological, material, and institutional foundations for the juridification, pluralization, and privatization of international commercial law and relations. They also provide insight into the material, institutional, and ideological characteristics of the unification movement and the conditions that secure the dominance of the mercatocracy in processes of law-creation and dispute settlement.

[33] Jameson (1991: xix). He also notes (xvii) that the term "late capitalism" originated in general use in the works of Theodor Adorno and Max Horkheimer of the Frankfurt School in the context of the "administered society."

The first transformation involves the replacement of the welfare state by the competition state in response to enhanced international commercial competition and the imposition of the new constitutionalism of disciplinary neoliberalism (see Gill, 1998; 1995 a; Cerny, 1997). The new constitutionalism legitimizes the increasing juridification of commercial relations as a *grundnorm* of the neoliberal order. It also creates a new ideological context for international and global commerce by providing the theoretical rationale for privileging the expansion of private legal regulation and the subordination of domestic policy concerns to neoliberal market discipline. Stephen Gill (1998: 23) associates the new constitutionalism with the insulation of dominant economic forces, such as transnational corporations, from democratic rule and popular accountability. It "operates in practice to confer privileged rights of citizenship and representation to corporate capital and large investors" subordinating the interests of society and public policy more generally to the interests of capital. The objective is the production of internationally competitive services and industries and the subordination of social welfare concerns of equity and justice to the discipline of market civilization. The goals and interests of competition states are generally consistent with the current deregulatory and privatized business ethos. They also facilitate the activities of the mercatocracy by assisting in creating national and international regulatory orders that minimize barriers to the free flow of trade, services, and capital. The emphasis upon creating regulatory orders that meet the criteria of competitiveness provides a powerful ideological influence, as well, by infusing the unification movement with competitive standards. Legal regulation that enhances global competition by minimizing the costs of negotiating and enforcing agreements, such as privatized standards, soft law, and private dispute settlement through international commercial arbitration, are thus to be preferred over more costly hard laws and public adjudicatory processes.

Relatedly, the transformation of an international political economy based upon patterns of national capital accumulation to a global political economy based upon transnational patterns of capital accumulation is creating new conditions and challenges for both state and nonstate authority and law.[34] Competition states are facilitating transnational trade, production, and finance by undertaking to minimize barriers to

[34] For the transnationalization of capital, see Gill and Law (1993); Robinson (1996 and 1998).

the mobility of goods, services, and capital through entry into hard legal obligations under the World Trade Organization (WTO) and the GATT, NAFTA, the FTA, the Maastricht Treaty and European Monetary Union (EMU), and bilateral investment treaties under the auspices of the International Centre for the Settlement of Investment Disputes (ICSID). These legal arrangements create hard law that bites deeply into the autonomy of national legislative and public policy processes.[35] The law merchant plays a crucial role in harmonizing and unifying legal practices so as to minimize legal barriers to exchange and production, as well. In fact, the international movement for the unification of private law is the major institutional and ideological framework for facilitating legal adjustments to changing terms of global competition.[36]

The third transformation relates to the advent of patterns of "flexible accumulation" associated with post-Fordist production and efforts to improve productivity and competitiveness (Harvey, 1990). Post-Fordism involves enhanced capital mobility and flexibility or "flexible accumulation" and "flexibility with respect to labour processes, labour markets, products, and patterns of consumption;" the emergence of new sectors of production, new financial services and markets; intensified rates of technological, commercial, and organizational innovation; and the resulting time–space compression as the time horizon for decision makers shrinks (ibid., 147). Soft, flexible, discretionary, and *ad hoc* rules that are able to accommodate instantaneous transacting and are responsive to fast-changing economic conditions are mechanisms of flexible accumulation. In some cases the compression of time and distance, associated with advances in technology and communications, renders commercial transactions instantaneous and simultaneous, creating a dynamism that makes traditional forms of unified law quite irrelevant and dated.[37] This is evident in the growing commercial preference for nonbinding soft law in the form of voluntary statements of principle, model laws, and optional codes that provide a certain degree of unification without binding parties whose competitive interests and goals might shift over the course of a transaction. Soft-law agreements are easier to negotiate, require less compromise, are less

[35] For discussion of the impact of these legal agreements on the autonomy of domestic public policy processes and legislative authority, see Twining (1996); Fried (1997); Gill (1998): Cutler (2000 a); Abbott (2000); and Alter (2000).

[36] While this will be clarified in later chapters, for introductions to the institutional and ideological foundations of the unification movement, see David (1972 a).

[37] See Scheuerman (2000). And for a discussion of time–space compression, see Harvey (1990). For the increasing irrelevance of state-based law, see Santos (1993).

restrictive of domestic autonomy, and are easier to breach, if changing market conditions so require (see Abbott and Snidal, 2000; Cutler, 1999 b).

In addition, the privatization of law-creation and dispute resolution and the regulation of corporate conduct through privatized codes that provide a "soft infrastructure" for business are mechanisms of flexible accumulation created by competition states in the quest for enhanced market competitiveness. This "soft infrastructure" is sensitive to corporate interests and the need to facilitate business strategies, such as "cause-related marketing" that "links a company and its product to a social cause, the goal to create relationships with key stakeholders, enhance brand value, increase sales and differentiate similar products in a competitive market place while providing benefit to a cause or issue" (*Development of Guidelines*, 2000: 5 [UN report]).

The trend toward soft regulation appears to be inconsistent with the deepening of hard disciplines under the WTO and NAFTA and suggests, as mentioned earlier, that the juridification, pluralization, and privatization of international commerce are discontinuous and even contradictory processes. However, notwithstanding such apparent discontinuities, it is crucial to recognize that fragmentation occurs in a context marked by deeper sources of unification. The growing legitimacy of privatized lawmaking and dispute resolution is strengthening the material, institutional, and ideological unity and hold of the mercatocracy. As subsequent chapters illustrate, the mercatocracy functions to provide a unity of purpose and a coherence in regulation that is obscured by notions of pluralistic or fragmented governance. Indeed, notions of multiple and plural sources of governance tend to obscure the unity and coherence of contemporary global capitalism and threaten to dissolve "capitalism into an unstructured and undifferentiated plurality of social institutions and relations" (Wood, 1995: 247). Moreover, while the privatized and pluralistic nature of the new law merchant order is said by many to exhibit significant similarities with its medieval ancestor, the contemporary merchant order is here argued to be distinctive and particular to conditions of postmodernity and late capitalism. Notions of multiple and heterogeneous sources of governance also obscure the extent to which state–society relations are being reconfigured by a "privatization of public power" and the creation of an entirely new "'private' realm, with a distinctive 'public' presence and oppression of its own, a unique structure of power and domination, and a ruthless systemic logic" (Wood, 1995: 254; see Cutler, 2001 b). The normative implications of this development are profound in terms of the implications of juridification, pluralization, and privatization of governance for state–society relations, both locally and globally. Privatized legal disciplines are increasingly finding their way into both international and national commercial legal orders, structuring domestic and foreign economic relations in ways that have a significant impact on state–society relations within states and on the political and economic relations between states. However, the centrality of the law merchant to new and changing processes and structures of governance is obscured by the complex relationship between private and public international trade law and the contested nature of the law merchant, to which attention will now turn.

Private and Public International Trade Law

The distinction between private and public international law is of crucial significance in the constitution of identity in the global political economy and subjectivity under international law. Public international law is a state-based order in which the authoritative subjects, actors, and voices in the global polity are more or less confined to states. In contrast, private international law is regarded as an order regulating nonpolitical matters, such as family matters and economic relations involving individuals and private associations. Although we tend to accept the distinction between private and public international law as a natural division, much like that differentiating between private and public law within domestic legal orders, it is important to recognize that it is only an analytical distinction. The distinction between private and public international law is not reflective of an organic, natural or inevitable separation, but is an analytical construct that evolved with the emergence of the bourgeois state (Cutler, 1997). Moreover, as we shall see, the distinction is in empirical decline as processes of juridification, pluralization, and privatization blur the separation between private and public authority. However, while in decline empirically, the distinction continues to hold powerful conceptual and symbolic meaning and is creating a disjuncture between commercial law and commercial practices. Commercial practices are increasingly recognizing the political significance of private actors in the regulation of global commerce, but international law remains steadfastly state-centric.

The distinction between private and public international law operates at multiple levels. It operates, legally, as a separation of academic subjects and as a separation of legal doctrines (Paul, 1988). It also operates materially, as the determinant of political identity and subjectivity in international affairs, and symbolically, as a powerful ideological justification for liberal-inspired theories of international law and international political economy. The discussion will consider the basis for differentiating private and public international law, the subjects and sources of law, the nature and operation of private international trade law, and the history of the private/public distinction in international law.

Differentiating private and public international law

The distinction between private and public international law operates as a distinction between academic subjects and legal doctrine. In terms of subject-matter, public international law deals with matters relating to states, international organizations, and to a very limited extent to corporations and individuals, that raise "an international legal interest."[38] In contrast, private international law deals with matters relating to individuals, and significantly, to corporations, who are assimilated with individuals under legal theory.[39] As a system regulating private relationships, private international law refers to conflict or choice of law principles that determine the appropriate jurisdictional norms to apply to individual claims involving a foreign element or foreign persons (Paul, 1988: 150). It also includes international commercial transactions relating to "domestic and international regulation of foreign investment and the movement of goods and workers across national borders" (ibid., 151). James Fox (1992: 351) defines "private international law" as "rules which govern the choice of law in private matters (such as business contracts, marriage, etc.) when those questions arise in an international context, e.g., will country A enforce the divorce granted under the laws of country B." "Public international law," in contrast, is defined as "law

[38] These include the sources and subjects of international law; the application of international law by domestic and international tribunals; the enforcement of public international law; international organizations; regional associations; dispute settlement; the international law of treaties; the laws of war; the law of the sea and outer space; international protection of the environment and of international human rights; state responsibility for injury to aliens; foreign relations law; diplomatic recognition; diplomatic and sovereign immunities; state responsibility for the acts of nationals; state succession; and the right of states to make claims on behalf of their nationals (see Paul, 1988: 150, n. 50).

[39] See below and see Janis (1984 a); Higgins (1985); Cutler (2000 a and 2001 a) for discussion of the assimilation of transnational corporations and individuals with "objects" and not "subjects" of the international legal order.

dealing with the relationship between states" (ibid., 357). As Joel Paul (1988: 163 and 150) notes, private international law "is about private interests engaged in private transactions (and not about the exercise of public power);" it "excludes questions of international public policy, such as the role of multinationals on social and economic development or the effect of international arbitration clauses on the enforcement of domestic antitrust laws." International public policy concerns are the domain of public international law, for it is states who are deemed to have political identity as legal subjects and authoritative agents in the exercise of public power in international affairs. However, significant analytical and theoretical problems result from associating the subject matter of private international trade law with both *trade* matters and *private* matters. Moreover, these problems shade into the doctrinal nature of the distinction between private and public international law and resulting doubts about the legal status and political significance of private international trade law.

The definition of private international trade law as governing matters of *trade* obscures the scope and nature of legal regulation involved. As a subfield of private international law, private international *trade* law is variously known as international business law (Schmitthoff, 1961), the law of international trade (Schmitthoff, 1964 a), the new law merchant (Schmitthoff, 1961), and the transnational law of international commercial transactions (Horn and Schmitthoff, 1982). It includes matters relating to international trade, such as the international sale of goods and ancillary services including insurance, transportation, financing, and dispute resolution. However, its designation as private international *trade* law is increasingly inaccurate, because it extends well beyond the regulation of exchange to include a full range of international productive relations, including, for example, the regulation of international licensing, distributorships, joint ventures, construction contracts, and the extraterritorial application of tax, antitrust, and securities laws. In fact, the rules of private international trade law establish the fundamental rules governing private property and contractual rights and obligations operative across the full range of international commercial activity, including international trade, investment, finance, transportation, insurance, and dispute settlement (see Horn and Schmitthoff, 1982). In addition to comprehending far more than simple *trade* relations, the rules of private international trade law both connect states and reach inside states. They regulate the "interface" between differing legal and political systems, but also reach inside states to harmonize and unify their policies and laws with those of other states.[40] They function to both *globalize localisms* and *localize globalisms*, mediating local and global political/legal orders by providing juridical links and harmonizing laws that are regarded as essential to the orderly regulation of the global political economy.[41] As such, the rules of private international trade law and the law merchant order are so foundational to the global political economy that they may be usefully regarded as both a constitutive element of global capitalism and an attribute of the capitalist order. This order provides the constitutional foundations of the global political economy through rules governing the protection and enforcement of private property and contractual rights and obligations across a range of international commercial activities that are not limited to cross-border exchanges, but that penetrate into local legal/political orders (Cutler, 1999 a: 6). These rules structure economic relations by providing for stability of possession. Indeed, they articulate the conditions that make economic relations possible in conditions of uncertainty and insecurity generated by nonsimultaneous transactions over time and space. The law merchant provides a common language and business culture, enabling merchants from diverse legal and political systems to speak to one another and to transact in a relatively stable, predictable, and secure environment. The law merchant thus forms part of the juridical foundations of global capitalism and is deeply "imbricated" "within the very basis of productive relations" of global capitalism.[42]

However, and here we come to the second analytical problem, the designation as *private* law obscures its political nature and distributional functions in determining the allocation of risks of international commercial transactions, in regulating the terms of commercial competition and market access, and in enforcing bargains. Most importantly, the way the law merchant assists in the reconfiguration of governance arrangements by deepening, expanding, and legitimizing the privatized regulation of international commercial relations is obscured by public definitions of authority that render privatized authority relations analytical and theoretical impossibilities.[43] As a result, the law merchant works to entrench

[40] See Cutler (1999 b) for analysis of the unification movement as extending beyond the regulation of the "interface" of legal orders.
[41] See Cutler (1995, 1999 a, and forthcoming).
[42] Wood (1995: 74) here cites the words of E. P. Thompson (1975: 260–1) on the untenability of treating law as solely part of the "superstructure" of capitalism. This matter is addressed in the next chapter.
[43] This matter is taken up in the next chapter but the argument is developed most fully in Cutler (1999 a and c).

and deepen the paradoxical exercise of public authority by private agencies who, as putative "objects" of the law, remain invisible as legal "subjects." Understanding this paradox requires a brief excursion into the analytical nature of "subjects" and "sources" of international law, the nature and operation of private international trade law, and the history of the private/public distinction in international law.

Subjects and sources of law

In international law, the public/private distinction forms the foundation for establishing the dominant authority structure as that of the territorial state and the states system, eliminating any potential rival claims to political identity and authority coming from individuals or from corporate entities. Mark Janis (1984 a: 62) notes, "[n]ineteenth century positivists promoted the notion that the individual was not a proper subject of international law ... public international law went to matters affecting states, while private international law concerned matters between individuals." The doctrine of international legal personality forms the analytical core of this statist orientation. This doctrine identifies who or what is a "subject" of the law and, hence, who is politically authoritative. It determines who possesses "rights and duties enforceable at law ... Legal personality is crucial. Without it institutions and groups cannot operate for they need to maintain and enforce claims" (M. N. Shaw, 1991: 135). Shaw elaborates on the doctrine:

> One of the distinguishing characteristics of contemporary international law has been the wide range of participants performing on the international scene. These include states, international organizations, regional organizations, non-governmental organizations, public companies, private companies and individuals. Not all such entities will constitute legal persons, although they may act with some degree of influence upon the international plane. International personality is participation plus some form of community acceptance. (ibid., 137)

The identification of states as the proper "subjects" of international law is generally associated with legal positivism, which attributes the binding force of international law to states and state consent. While we will consider this theory in the next chapter, it contrasts with and followed on from natural law theories,[44] whose assumption of a universal moral order transcending time and place fits more comfortably with a

[44] See Beck, Arend, and Vander Lugt (1996: chs. 2 and 3) for good reviews of natural and positive law theories of international law, respectively.

more inclusive notion of the subjects of international law.[45] Legal positivism developed along with the emergence of the modern states system providing the legal equivalent of the statist political theories advanced by theorists such as Jean Bodin and Thomas Hobbes (see Beck, Arend, and Vander Lugt, 1996). Today, the modern doctrine of international legal personality continues to run parallel to territorial/statist conceptions of international relations.[46] Only states are recognized as full members of the United Nations and the degree of legal personality possessed by international organizations is determined by and derived from their member states.[47] Only states may bring contentious proceedings before the International Court of Justice,[48] declare war, appoint ambassadors or claim the right of diplomatic immunity. Only states are entitled to claim the right of territorial integrity, a basic right recognized in the Charter of the United Nations. The Vienna Convention on the Law of Treaties applies only to treaties entered into by states.[49]

The international legal status of transnational corporations, which are probably the most visible private global actors today, has been likened to the status of the individual under international law.[50] Both are "objects" and not "subjects" of the law: they have no original rights or liabilities at international law; the only rights or liabilities they possess are derivative as nationals of a state, under the principles governing nationality.[51] As "objects" they are devoid of subjectivity: "that is to say, they are like 'boundaries,' or 'rivers,' or 'territory' or any of the other chapter headings found in the traditional textbooks" (Higgins, 1985: 478). Moreover, the rights or liabilities they do possess derivatively can only be asserted

[45] Inclusive of the individual, at least. See Cutler (1991) for the view that natural law theories are more accommodating of the individual as a subject of international law than are positive law theories.

[46] For a very good discussion of the territorial nature of state sovereignty and of contemporary challenges to territorial conceptions of political authority see Agnew (1994).

[47] *Reparations for Injuries Suffered in the Service of the United Nations Case* [1949] ICJ Rep 174, 180.

[48] Statute of the International Court of Justice, Art. 34 (1).

[49] Vienna Convention on the Law of Treaties 1969, 1155 UNTS 331, in force 1980, Arts 2 and 3.

[50] The association of corporations with individuals has been a powerful influence and may be traced to the more general theorization of corporate legal personality in Anglo-American domestic law. See Cutler (2000 a: 57–8) for analysis of the development of corporate legal personality as an integral element of the emergence of market society and capitalist productive relations.

[51] Nationality is defined as "the bond that unites individuals with a given state, that identifies them as members of that entity, that enables them to claim its protection, and that also subjects them to the performance of such duties as their state may impose on them" (Von Glahn, 1996: 147). See also Brownlie (1990: 421–4).

or assumed by the state on behalf of the individual or the transnational corporation.[52] As one legal theorist notes, "[t]he law recognizes as 'international corporations' only those entities which are constructed by international law, that is by treaty . . . This format is not available to the private commercial enterprise which must content itself with stringing together corporations created by the laws of different states" (Vagts, 1970: 740). Another notes that the transnational corporation lacks "concrete presence in international law . . . it is an apparition . . . its actuality sifted through the grid of state sovereignty into an assortment of secondary rights and contingent liabilities" (Johns, 1994: 893). Yet another legal scholar observes the "awkward," but well-established assimilation of corporate nationality to the nationality of individuals (Brownlie, 1990: 421–2. See also, Brownlie, 1998). The result is the "invisibility" of the transnational corporation under international law, as corporate power and responsibility is filtered through the state.

The legal doctrine governing the sources of law mirrors the state-based order governing subjectivity. Article 38 of the Statute of the International Court of Justice is generally regarded as the authoritative statement of the sources of public international law and includes international treaties and customary international law as primary sources and general principles of law, judicial decisions, and the teachings of the most highly qualified publicists as secondary sources. While international treaties and customary law are definitely regarded as "hard law" in the sense of the creation of binding obligations, Article 38 notably does not mention "soft law." Neither are the recommendations of international organizations, such as the United Nations General Assembly, nor the deliberations of international nongovernmental organizations regarded as sources of law. Only states are the authoritative source and "voice" in international affairs, for not even the International Court of Justice (ICJ) can trump state consent as a source of law. Unlike many domestic legal systems where the principle of *stare decisis* applies (by which a precedent or decision of one court binds courts lower in the judicial hierarchy), the decisions of the ICJ are only subsidiary and not primary sources.

[52] There are some exceptions to the limited personality of individuals and private corporations, which might suggest some movement in legal practice that has yet to be reflected in legal theory. Notable exceptions include the status of individuals before the European Court and the status of private transnational corporations that have entered into contracts with states which are "internationalized" by provisions that bring the contract under the purview of public international law. On the individual, see Higgins (1985); Loucaides (1990), and Janis (1984 a). Concerning transnational corporations, see Johns (1994).

In the field of private international law, there is no equivalent to Article 38 as the authoritative statement of the sources of law. Indeed, as the subsequent sections will illustrate, there is considerable disagreement as to the sources of private international law, which derives from its contested status as an autonomous or international legal order. While we will have occasion to revisit the matter of legal subjects and sources in subsequent chapters, for the moment it will suffice to note the state-centric nature of the doctrine governing public international law, and the consequent political invisibility of private, nonstate authority and identities, who as "objects," are simply not accorded legal subjectivity. The differential treatment of state and nonstate subjectivity under law stems, as well, from peculiarities in the nature and operation of private international law.

Nature and operation of private international trade law

While the operation of private international trade law is a complex matter, it may be usefully regarded as functioning in at least three ways.[53] In one way, the rules of private international law operate as a conflict of laws system, providing rules that determine what national law applies to transactions involving persons or corporations from different states when there is uncertainty as to the law that should govern.[54] In this sense, private international law operates as a domestic conflict of laws system and derives its authority from and is an extension of the domestic political/legal order. As a conflict of laws system, the rules of private international law serve to *localize* international transactions in one national system of law, thus linking international and national political/legal arenas.[55] These links derive from the domestic application of foreign law under the rules of private international law and the

[53] In Cutler (1997) only two operations of private international law are identified; there is no differentiation between the second and third operations identified here.

[54] See generally, Baer et al. (1997) and Horn and Schmitthoff (1982).

[55] The rules of private international law operate to identify the national law to be applied in a situation of conflicting jurisdictional options. As noted by Starke (1936: 397), private international law "deals primarily with the application of laws in space" and indicates "the area over which the rule of law extends." Moreover, "the area of recognition, the sphere of authority, the rule of law is wider than the territorial jurisdiction of the sovereign power by which it is enacted." This is because, as Starke notes, the sovereign is in effect applying and upholding the rule of a foreign territorial law in applying the principles of private international law when those rules designate foreign law as the applicable law: "If, for instance, an English Court decides that the capacity of a person who bought the goods in France must be governed by French law, what it decides in effect is that the rule of the French territorial law relating to capacity is effective outside the territorial limits of the French law maker."

extraterritorial application of domestic law under the rules of comity. To the extent that sovereigns came to give effect to foreign laws in deference to the requirements of international comity,[56] private international law, like public international law, was regarded as facilitating relations between independent territorial entities.

However, private international trade law also operates in another way as a more or less independent source of governance through the application of international law generally by domestic and/or international tribunals. In this application, private international trade law operates neither as a conflict of laws system nor as an extension of domestic law, but as a source of governance that may be formulated internationally or transnationally through hard law in the form of international conventions or soft law in the form of model laws, codes, principles, and guidelines that are accepted as law voluntarily by commercial actors (see Cutler, 1997; 1999 a). In this regard, it exhibits some similarities to public international law. In some cases the legal rules are adopted by states into their national legal systems, becoming embedded in national political/legal orders. A good example, discussed later in the book, is the law governing international commercial arbitration that has been formulated multilaterally through both convention and model law and has been adopted by a multiplicity of states into national legal systems, enabling the enforcement of foreign arbitration awards in national courts of law. Globalized international commercial arbitration law illustrates *localized globalism*, as national laws and institutions for the judicial settlement of foreign commercial disputes are replaced by globalized laws and institutions.

There is, however, yet another way in which the laws of private international law operate, which creates considerable analytical uncertainty. Commercial actors may by private agreement adopt rules to govern their foreign contractual relations that form a law between the parties that is enforceable in a court or arbitration. Indeed, the parties may by contract agree to exclude the application of national law and national judicial systems, invoking perhaps the application of general business customs and practices, thus *delocalizing* the transaction and methods for enforcement and dispute resolution. For some, this operation is the essence of

[56] Comity in international law has been variously described or defined in terms of reciprocity, courtesy, politeness, convenience, goodwill between sovereigns, moral necessity, or expediency and is invoked to explain why courts enforce or apply the decisions of foreign courts or limit their own jurisdiction in the face of a competing foreign jurisdiction. See Paul (1991: 2–3).

the law merchant order and is said to give rise to its autonomy from local, national or international law (see Goldman, 1986; Lando, 1985; Paulsson, 1981). In this regard the rules of private international law operate to delocalize rather than to localize transactions, illustrating the dialectical way in which the law operates.

Analysts use a variety of terms to describe and define the law merchant, including "a set of general principles and customary rules" (Goldman, 1986: 116); "the rules of the game of international trade" (Langen, 1973: 21); "common principles in the law relating to international commercial transactions" (Schmitthoff, 1982: 19); "uniform rules accepted in all countries" (Schmitthoff, 1961: 139); "an international body of law, founded on the commercial understandings and contract practices of an international community composed principally of mercantile, shipping, insurance, and banking enterprises of all countries" (Berman and Kaufman, 1978: 272–3). However, these definitions do not disclose the extent to which the analytical status of the law merchant is contested. Some scholars tend to define the law merchant very narrowly, limiting it to harmonized or universalized customs and practices accepted by the merchant community. This book adopts the more expansive approach common in Anglo-American commercial law, regarding the law merchant as coterminous with the law of private international trade (see Schmitthoff, 1982; 1961).

There is, however, another more significant debate regarding the analytical status of the law merchant as an autonomous legal order. In general, European scholars tend to accept the existence of the law merchant as an autonomous legal order much more readily than do Anglo-American scholars. The latter tend to see it as an extension of domestic legal systems, which relates to their more general doubts about the independence of the broader field of private international law (see Cutler, 1997; Stoecker, 1990; Highet, 1989; Delaume, 1989). Doctrinally, private and public international law are treated as separate fields: private international law is regarded as deriving predominantly from municipal legal systems, while public international law derives from international sources.[57] However, although many of the principles of private international law are separate and distinct from those of public international

[57] As noted above, the sources of public international law are generally identified as those listed in Art. 38 of the Statute of the International Court of Justice, two of the most important being international conventions and customs. It should be noted, however, that increasingly private international law is being formulated internationally and embodied in conventions. This complicates the characterization of and distinction between private and public international law, at least as regards their sources.

law, often deriving from domestic or municipal law, the doctrinal status of private international law is contested. Legal theorists disagree about the status of private international law. Anglo-American theorists have traditionally expressed doubts that private international law is anything more than domestic or municipal law. In contrast, European scholars regard private international law as an integral part of public international law. Anglo-American doubts about the independent pedigree of private international law stem from its general isolation from public international law, as the distinction between private and public law emerged historically, as well as from its contested analytical status as an independent legal order.

History of the public/private distinction in international law

It is important to note at the outset that the public/private distinction is an historically specific analytical construct that has undergone revision with changing material, ideological, and institutional conditions.[58] Morton Horwitz (1982: 1,423) argues that the public/private distinction arose out of a "double movement in modern political and legal thought." One movement involved the emergence of the nation-state and theories of sovereignty in the sixteenth and seventeenth centuries in which a distinctly "public realm" began to crystallize. The second movement involved attempts to create "private spheres" free from state regulation. He traces the origins of a distinctively public realm in England to late medieval English law governing property rights in land and taxation laws. With regard to the former, the differentiation between the public and private roles of the monarch as landowner crystallized in the seventeenth-century conflicts over the King's power to alienate certain types of land that came to be regarded as Crown or public land. With regard to the latter, in the seventeenth century taxation came to be regarded as a part of public law, exacted by the state, and not as a private gift, as had been the case before. He notes that "it was only gradually that English and American law came to recognize a public realm distinct from medieval conceptions of property. And equally gradually legal doctrines developed the idea of the separate private realm free from public power" (ibid., 1424).

The public/private distinction was articulated through the emergence of the centralized and absolutist state. In Western Europe, an important

58 See Cutler (1997; 1995; 1999 a) for the history of the private/public distinction in international law.

development was the reception of Roman law and the concept of unconditional and absolute property rights, which replaced the medieval notions of conditional property and parcelized sovereignty. The Roman law distinction between civil law (*jus*), which regulated private and economic relations among citizens, and public law (*lex*), which regulated relations between the state and its subjects, formed part of the foundation for what was to become distinct public and private domains. It also enhanced the concentration of the power of monarchs in centralized state institutions and anticipated the disembedding of economic relations from the sphere of political relations, a move so aptly depicted by Perry Anderson (1974 b: 27) as a "double social movement," wherein the "juridically unconditional character of private property consecrated by the one found its contradictory counterpart in the formally absolute nature of imperial sovereignty exercised by the other."

The separation of the public and private spheres did not occur uniformly throughout Europe. Moreover, the situation was somewhat different for England where Roman law was never received as it was in Europe. In England, the distinction between private and public evolved in the context of class relations attending the emergence of the bourgeois state and the growth of constitutional and responsible government (see generally, Horwitz, 1982; Hanson, 1970). It took the advancement of capitalism and the demise of the feudal order to affect the separation, which was articulated in the separation between politics and economics. Importantly, however, the distinction emerged not as a reflection of separate domains, but as an "evacuation of relations of domination from the realm of production" (Rosenberg, 1994: 84) and the "insulation" of economic relations from political controls (Giddens, 1987: 68). Ellen Meiksins Wood (1995) captures the essential nature of the separation between economics and politics:

> the differentiation of the economic and the political in capitalism is, more precisely, a differentiation of political functions themselves and their separate allocation to the private economic sphere and the public sphere of the state. This allocation reflects the separation of political functions immediately concerned with extraction and appropriation of surplus labour from those with a more general communal purpose ... the differentiation of the economic is in fact a differentiation within the political sphere. (31)

While the emergence of the market as a central legitimating institution placed the public/private distinction at the center of political and legal discourse in the nineteenth century, it is also important to emphasize that the emergence of market society was not an automatic or natural occurrence. Karl Polanyi (1944) shows that the self-regulating market characteristic of modern capitalism did not simply emerge spontaneously, but was the product of a complex set of legislative interventions to remove impediments to the exchange of labor, land, and money. He argues that this demanded "nothing less than the institutional separation of society into an economic and political sphere" (ibid., 71). This development was assisted and legitimized by liberal theories of political economy and law that rationalized the privatization of corporate, contractual, and tortious (wrongful) activities. Indeed, Horwitz (1982) argues that the public/private distinction was central to the development of an "independent" and "neutral" legal science:

> Above all was the effort of orthodox judges and jurists to create a legal science that would sharply separate law from politics. By creating a neutral and apolitical system of legal doctrine and legal reasoning free from what was thought to be dangerous and unstable redistributive tendencies of democratic politics, legal thinkers helped to temper the problem of "tyranny of the majority." Just as nineteenth-century political economy elevated markets to the status of the paramount institution for distributing rewards on a supposedly neutral and apolitical basis, so too private law came to be understood as a neutral system for facilitating voluntary market transactions and vindicating injuries to private rights. (1,425–6)

In domestic law, in the United States, the public/private distinction drew criticism from legal realists in the 1920s and 1930s, in response to growing perceptions of the concentration of capital.[59] They emphasized the coercive and distributive nature of all law and ridiculed the notion

[59] Purvis (1991: 83, n. 10) notes that legal realism emerged in the 1930s primarily at Yale and Columbia and "set itself in opposition to legal formalism," or what is referred to as "classical legal thought." Classicism was formulated during the last third of the nineteenth century and was dominant until the 1930s. According to Fisher, Horwitz, and Reed (1993: xi and xiii–xiv), "[i]ts best-known manifestation was a series of decisions by appellate courts that strengthened the position of business corporations in their struggles with workers and consumers ... The heart of the movement [legal realism] was an effort to define and discredit classical legal theory and practice and to offer in their place a more philosophically and politically enlightened jurisprudence." Horwitz (1982: 1426) identifies the case of *Lochner v. New York* 198 US 45 (1905) in which the Supreme Court enunciated the principle of freedom of contract as a constitutionally protected right as the beginning of attacks launched by Justices Holmes, Brandeis, and Cardozo, and theorists such as Roscoe Pound, Morris Cohen, and Karl Llewelyn on the conservative ideology of the public/private distinction.

of private law as independent, neutral, and apolitical. Of crucial significance to this attack on the distinction was the belief that "so-called private institutions were acquiring coercive power that had formerly been reserved to governments" (Horwitz, 1982: 1,428). By the 1940s Horwitz (ibid.) says it was a "sign of legal sophistication" to recognize the problem of the distinction. Yet, today the distinction is being revived in domestic law and persists virtually unchallenged in international law.

While the conceptual distinction between public and private international law only became clear in the nineteenth century as part of an effort to integrate domestic and international conflict of laws principles (Paul, 1988: 155), it is possible to trace the emergence of the distinction to earlier attempts to reconcile the emerging, individuated, territorial state with a notion of commitment to a broader community of states. The distinction became part of the constitutive separation of the modern state and the international system and was an attempt to address the growing dualism between domestic politics and international relations.[60] In international law, the distinction emerged as part of a twofold process of the emergence of the state system and of capitalism. Curiously though, while the distinction came under attack in domestic law by legal realists who exposed the public and political dimensions of domestic private law, international law largely escaped attack.[61] Paul (1988: 153 n. 12) suggests that the distinction escaped criticism in international law because "most legal realists in international law were too busy defining the field and arguing over the sources of international norms to address private international law issues." He also identifies deeper reasons that are directly relevant to this discussion. These relate to the isolation of private international law stemming from conceptual uncertainty about its status as an autonomous legal order and the belief held by some

[60] Bartelson (1995) provides a good analysis of the process by which the concepts of the state and the international system or society emerged through a process of constitutive separation. And see Steve Smith (1995) for a discussion of this dualism in terms of the tension between international theory and political theory. For a now classic statement of this tension, see Walker (1993).

[61] The public/private distinction came under attack in domestic law, where private laws, like contract law, were exposed to be as much about the exercise of public power as were public laws. However, public international law escaped this exposure. As Paul (1988: 153, n. 12) observes, "[t]he flowering of legal creativity that accompanied the realist attack on the public/private distinction did not directly reach international law, however. One reason for this may be that legal realists were interested in creating a more powerful, centralized administrative state bureaucracy; they were not interested in attacking state sovereignty nor challenging the nascent institutions of international law. After the War, realism was itself suspect as anti-democratic."

that private international law is not really "international law" at all, but as noted by another, has simply been "pompously baptized" as such (David, 1972 a: 209). Paul (1988: 153 n. 120) notes that "Kelsen affirmed that the public/private distinction was inapplicable to international law; private international law is municipal law. Thus, the public/private distinction was not a concern of legal realists in international law." A contemporary statement of this position may be found in one of the most authoritative texts on public international law that "there is no such thing" as "transnational law. No legal order exists above the various national legal systems to deal with transborder interactions between individuals (as distinct from states)" (Malanczuk, 1997: 72). The view that a stateless contract is a "logical impossibility and an intellectual solecism" analogous to "*un marteau sans maître* [a hammer without a master]" (Highet, 1989: 613) reflects the deep connection between law and state territoriality.

Conceptual uncertainty about the status of private international law has contributed to its obscurity and stemmed from obstacles posed by the principles and practices of state sovereignty, which posited the impossibility of an independent body of private international law, and by liberalism, which posited the apolitical nature of private relations. As Paul (1988: 153) observes, the more general distinction between private and public matters "began with the rise of liberal capitalism in the eighteenth century. It was closely associated with the idea that the market was a neutral, apolitical institution for allocating liability and maximizing productivity." In international law, the politics and ideologies associated with the emerging states system, capitalism, and liberal political economy were crucial in the constitution of the public and private spheres.

Although we do not know the specific origins of private international law, it is believed that elements of modern private international law derive from the medieval period and became "a serious question in Europe after the collapse of the Roman Empire and the emergence of city states" (Paul, 1988: 156). Following the collapse of the Roman Empire persons were generally subject to the law of their tribe. As feudalism developed in the tenth through twelfth centuries, persons were subject to the law of the feudal lord. As Paul notes (1988), foreign laws were disregarded and there was no concept of universal personal rights. However, in response to the differentiation in authority structures attending the emergence of city-states, thirteenth- and fourteenth-century Italian authors developed a system comprised of a comprehensive set of categories differentiating local and universal rights.[62] The system was referred to as the doctrine of the statuists and it differentiated between local and universal rights: property rights were subject to local law (*lex loci*), while personal rights (i.e., contract, marriage) were subject to the law of the place of origin. Paul (1988: 157) argues, however, that this separation did not yet reflect the public/private distinction because the statuists presumed the existence of a natural and universal legal order, "so that in theory conflicts principles [governing personal rights] should be uniform everywhere." The emergence of nation-states in the seventeenth century and the articulation of the principle of state sovereignty "challenged the statuists to explain why sovereign states should sometimes apply foreign law in their courts" (Paul 1988: 157). This challenge was an instance of what John Ruggie (1993 a: 164) refers to as the "paradox of absolute individuation:" "Having established territoriality fixed state formations, having insisted that these territorial domains were disjoint and mutually exclusive, and having accepted these conditions as the constitutive bases of international society, what means were left to the new territorial rulers for dealing with problems of that society that could not be reduced to territorial solution?" The Dutch, seeking to limit the application of foreign law in their efforts to gain independence from Spanish hegemony, responded to this challenge with a conflict theory based on the notion of territoriality. They rejected the statuists' appeals to a higher, universal order with a theory of vested rights. According to this theory, the paradox of absolute individuation was in fact nonexistent because courts in applying the rules of private international law were regarded not as applying foreign law, but rather as enforcing rights that had vested in the individual whilst under foreign law. It was left to states to decide whether or not to apply a foreign law within their territory on the basis of international comity and reciprocal sovereignty and not as a necessity dictated by a higher law.

The Dutch thus began the reconciliation of the territorial state with the community of states, but did not yet distinguish between private and public international law. The Dutch view was not very influential in Europe, where natural law theories remained current. However, English and Scottish lawyers who were schooled in Holland in the eighteenth century introduced the vested rights theory to English law, which had no conflict system. Again, however, the theory did not rest on a distinction

[62] Earlier Roman civilization and law, too, differentiated between local and universal rights, but did not differentiate between public and private international law.

between public and private international law. It was Justice Joseph Story who invented the term "private international law" in *Commentaries on the Conflict of Laws*, published in 1834. The *Commentaries* became the foundation for American jurisprudence and were also famous throughout Europe. Story drew on the Dutch vested rights theory, identifying territoriality and comity as the foundations for private international law. The distinction between private and public international law thus evolved in the context of the growing territorial individuation of political and legal authority in the modern state. It became a method of managing conflicting territorialities and of addressing the paradox of absolute individuation. Private international law became the mechanism for the extraterritorial application of the law. It was the means by which states interacted with each other "by tolerating within themselves little islands of alien sovereignty" (Ruggie, 1993 a: 165). Paul (1988) notes in the following passage that in articulating the foundations of private international law, Story identified a basic symmetry in function that gave rise to a unity of the public and private domains. This symmetry lay in the role both systems of law play in facilitating international commerce and cooperation:

> the *Commentaries* reflects a faith in the essential unity of private international law as an integral branch of international law. Story saw conflicts [i.e., private international law] as the cohesive principle to hold together his system of law; public and private law could not be separated. Commerce thrived on political unity and political unity was fostered by commerce. This was as true internationally as it was true domestically ... Like his contemporary Savigny, Story postulated that the goals of private international law were identical to those of public international law, and therefore, conflict of laws also should be resolved based upon the interests of international cooperation and commerce. This sentiment reflected an enlightenment belief in the rationality and science of law, even at the same moment that Story was asserting a more modern view of the state in the guise of the territorial principle. (161)

Despite the unity of the domains postulated in the *Commentaries*, there is no consensus regarding the foundation or status of private international law. Some scholars treat private international norms as municipal or local in origin and status, while others regard them as deriving from and forming an integral part of public international law.[63] Many, as

[63] See, for example, Shaw (1991) and earlier editions of Michael Akehurst's classic, *A Modern Introduction to International Law* (see, for example, Akehurst, 1987: 48–50).

noted earlier, deny the autonomous status of private law norms which are identified with municipal law. This view is associated with A. V. Dicey (1967) whose Hegelian view of the state and Austinian conception of sovereignty were incompatible with the notion of giving effect to the laws of another sovereign (see Starke, 1936). The contrary view, held primarily by European legal scholars, posits that private international law is subsumed by and is an integral part of public international law. This has been referred to as the "law of nations doctrine" and is traced to the work of Savigny in the nineteenth century (Stevenson, 1952: 564–5). According to Savigny, the law of nations, or public international law, developed customs and practices to ensure that private international cases would be decided in the same way regardless of the state within which the case was litigated (ibid.).

Contemporary theorists continue to contest the nature of the relationship between private and public international law, shedding doubt on the conceptual status and autonomy of private international law.[64] However, while private international lawyers were uncertain about the status of their discipline, public international lawyers became increasingly more certain about theirs, distinguishing private international law as a branch of public international law in the latter part of the nineteenth century. By the end of the Second World War, "the division of public and private international law became an article of faith for public international lawyers" (Paul, 1988: 163), as too did the association of private international trade law with apolitical and neutral economic transactions. Liberalism played a crucial role historically, in creating these associations and, contemporarily, in maintaining and deepening them through processes of juridification, pluralization, and privatization. As subsequent chapters illustrate, the public/private distinction is growing increasingly incoherent and may, indeed, be in collapse.[65]

[64] See Horn (1982). For a rejection of the autonomy of the law merchant see Delaume (1989) and for the contrary position see Teubner (1997 a).

[65] As noted in Cutler (1997), Duncan Kennedy (1982: 1,349 and 1,355) argues that for a distinction to be meaningful it must meet two requirements. First, it must make sense intuitively to divide something between its two poles and this sense should be generally shared. Second, the distinction must make a difference in that "it seems plain that situations should be treated differently depending on which category of the distinction they fall into." He identifies the public/private distinction as one of a particular set of distinctions that constitutes "the liberal way of thinking about the social world" that has been in decline since the turn of the century. The distinction is passing through six stages in decline from "robust good health to utter decrepitude." These include: the emergence of *hard cases* that test a distinction; the development of *intermediate terms* in recognition of the inadequacy or indeterminacy of a distinction; the *collapse* of a distinction; the creation of continuums

Moreover, to the extent that the distinction is merely a construct of historical, material, and ideological conditions and reflects no organic or natural differentiation between spheres of activity, one may regard it as having achieved the final stage in its decline. The dissolution of the distinction and the coming together of the private and public institutions and activities are crucial moves in the consolidation of contemporary global capitalism. However, the distinction still operates conceptually and ideologically, serving to conceal the foundational role played by private international law in legitimizing processes of juridification, pluralization, and privatization.

The incoherence of the distinction in international law admits to three explanations that may be referred to as empirical, conceptual, and ideological.[66] The first relates to a blurring of the distinction caused by empirical changes in the nature of the activity constituting the two spheres. This suggests that the distinction may at one time have reflected empirical conditions, but has ceased to do so. Of concern here is the growing interpenetration of the spheres in that private actors are acting publicly and public actors are acting privately. The former is illustrated by the activities of multi- and transnational corporations, private trade associations, and private arbitrations, or cartels that impact on matters of national public policy, eroding the policy-making autonomy of states. The latter is illustrated by state trading and other economic activities in which states engage as private commercial actors. There appears to be much evidence to support this view.[67] Robert Cox (1996 a) argues that the distinction between the polity and economy, between the state and civil society:

> made practical sense in the eighteenth and early nineteenth centuries when it corresponded to two more or less distinct spheres of human activity or practice: to an emergent society of individuals based on contract and market relations which replaced a status-based society, on

(continuumization); the creation of stereotypes *(stereotypification)*, dissolving distinctions; and lastly, *loopification*, whereby the ends of the continuum come together. The final stage of loopification is described thus: "one's consciousness is loopified when one seems to be able to move by a steady series of steps *around* the whole distinction, ending up where one started without even reversing direction." He illustrates this last stage in the decline of the public/private distinction in domestic law with the nature of the market and the family as both parts of the private sector.

66 This discussion further develops the analysis in Cutler (1997).

67 This trend has been noted by a number of people and forms the subject of a collection edited by Cutler, Haufler, and Porter (1999 a). See also, Held (1995); Gill (1997); and Ruggie (1995 a).

> the one hand, and a state with functions limited to maintaining internal peace, external defense, and the requisite conditions for markets, on the other. (86)

He continues that "[T]oday, however, state and civil society are so interpenetrated that the concepts have become almost purely analytical (referring to difficult-to-define aspects of complex reality) and are only very vaguely and imprecisely indicative of distinct spheres of activity" (ibid.). Cox identifies the internationalization of production and finance as central contemporary developments that are reconfiguring state–society relations and recasting the public/private distinction. In a similar vein, Susan Strange (1995 a: 56) emphasizes the increasing porousness of the boundaries between public and private activities, noting the development of the "defective state," wherein "state authority has leaked away, upwards, sideways, and downwards. In some matters, it seems even to have gone nowhere, just evaporated." The growing significance of nonstate authority and the erosion of state authority has been likened to a re-medievalization of the world (Held, 1995: 137; Strange, 1995 b; Cutler, 2001 b). But, as subsequent chapters illustrate, there is a crucial distinction between medieval and modern authority structures. In the medieval period, private authority operated by virtue of the absence of political authorities desirous or capable of disciplining international commerce, whereas in the modern period private authority operates with the full support of state authorities.[68] Indeed, this volume will show that the contemporary period is experiencing a merging of public and private authority in a transnational managerial and commercial elite committed to neoliberalism and the privatization and globalization of authority. To the extent that contemporary incoherence is a result of the interdelegation or merging of public and private authority, one may identify the distinction, empirically, in the final stage of decline. However, it continues to be invoked to justify the private regulation of international commerce, the explanation of which is linked to conceptual and ideological considerations.

Conceptual uncertainty as to the status of private international law as an autonomous legal order, as an entity *sui generis*, contributes to the obscurity of private international trade relations. This in turn leads to the

[68] See also Held (1995) and Perraton et al. (1997) for the continuing role of the state in the face of forces of globalization.

invisibility of the enhanced "political" authority of the private sphere. The sarcastic observation of a leading scholar, René David (1972 a: 209; see p. 46), that private international law has been "pompously baptised international law" by fuzzy-thinking international lawyers, reflects profound doubt as to the conceptual status of the distinction. The view that private international legal norms are no more than municipal law norms reflects a tension between private international law conceived of as the embodiment of national power and sovereignty and the view that it exists as an extension of, or projection beyond, state territoriality. The latter view challenges the territorial foundations of political/legal authority in that it contemplates the extraterritorial application of legal norms. To the extent that this threatens the orthodoxy of the territorial state as "the geopolitical container for human relationships" and as "coterminous with the minimum self-sufficient human reality" (Neufeld, 1995: 11), the autonomy of private international law poses a multifaceted and deeply subversive challenge to territorial conceptions of authority in international relations. Modern textbooks on international law exhibit a subtle imprecision over the status of private international law, which relates very much to conceptual incoherence as to its status as an autonomous legal order.[69]

Arguably, doubts about the autonomy of private international law have been present since the distinction between public and private international law emerged. However, what intensifies the uncertainty today is the reaffirmation of the public/private distinction in assertions of the distinctive nature of private international trade relations as the source of legitimacy for enhancing and deepening the private regulation of international commerce. This raises the ideological nature and role of the public/private distinction. Private international trade law differs from public international trade law, we are told by trade experts, in its essentially "apolitical" nature. (Schmitthoff, 1961; 1982). Private regulatory arrangements are said to be natural, neutral in application, consensual, efficient, and, ultimately, more consistent with globalizing and privatizing trends than are public regulations. Liberalism reaffirms the vitality of the private/public distinction in the face of its decline. The paradoxical nature of the disjunction evident in elite reaffirmations of the analytical vitality of the public/private distinction and empirical evidence of its decline points to the operation of changing ideological conditions. Karl Klare (1982) emphasizes that the ideological function

69 For an illustration of conceptual incoherence see Horn (1982: 12–15).

of the public/private distinction is reflective of the role played more generally by legal discourse:

> The peculiarity of legal discourse is that it tends to constrain the political imagination and to induce belief that our evolving social arrangements and institutions are just and rational, or at least inevitable, and therefore legitimate. The *modus operandi* of law as legitimating ideology is to make the historically contingent appear necessary. The function of legal discourse in our culture is to deny us access to new modes of conceiving of democratic self-governance, of our capacity for and experience of freedom. (1,358)

He describes the "chameleon-like alterations in public/private imagery" that encode ideological messages, suggesting that the distinction operates most significantly at a symbolic level (ibid., 1390). Indeed, the associations of the private realm with civil society and the market and the public realm with the state and government are powerful symbols. However, Antonio Gramsci (1971: 160) observes that the distinction between civil society and the state is not organic, but methodological. *Laissez-faire* liberalism "is a deliberate policy, conscious of its own ends, and not the spontaneous, automatic expression of economic facts." Moreover, liberalism, Klare (1982: 1416) argues, is caught in a dilemma of being incapable of rejecting a distinction that is vested with such ideological significance and yet which cannot capture human experience. Liberalism responds with the "ever-renewed effort to refract the complexities of social life through the basic dualities like public/private . . . liberal discourse has become an intellectual practice designed to generate images of the world conducing to a belief that one can meaningfully conceive of the realm of social and economic intercourse apart from the realm of politics." The "essence" of the public/private distinction is "the conviction that it is possible to conceive of social and economic life apart from government and law, indeed that it is impossible or dangerous to conceive of it any other way" (ibid.). The distinction operates to deny the mutually constitutive nature of the economic and the political domains, thus inhibiting belief that the institutions that order social life are the product of human agency and therefore can be altered. In the context of trade relations, it operates to obscure the political nature of private trade relations and the role of private trade law in the material and ideological constitution of global capitalism.

The artificiality and untenability of the separation of economics and politics in contemporary international relations has been noted by students of international relations and economics alike.[70] The separation, as maintained by the public/private distinction, is reproduced by academic and practical lawyers and by governmental and private elites, obscuring the paradoxical result of private actors legitimately exercising public functions.[71] While the reverse situation of public actors exercising private functions is also the case, it does not raise the same concerns of democratic accountability. The public/private distinction is today maintained by powerful liberal mythology, to which discussion will now turn.

Four Liberal Myths

Four myths form the foundation for the distinction between the public and private spheres. They originate in liberal political economy and posit the natural, neutral, consensual, and efficient nature of private exchange relations (Cutler, 1995).

The first myth is that the private ordering of economic relations is consistent with natural or normal economic processes. In this vein, international trade law distinguishes between normal and deviant trade relations. Private international trade law deals with normal and natural activity, while public international law deals with deviant, unnatural behaviour. As David Kennedy (1991) notes:

> [i]n normal situations, governments adopt a passive *laissez-faire* attitude. The regime of "private international law" sustains trade rules about property and contract, mechanisms to stabilize jurisdictional conflicts while liberating private actors to choose forums, and *ad hoc* mechanisms of dispute resolution. The dominant players are private traders, and to a far greater extent than in even the most *laissez-faire* national system, they legislate the rules that govern their trade through contract. And when governments do participate, they operate "commercially" – as private actors. (380)

In contrast, public international trade law deals with unnatural activities such as dumping, cartels, subsidies, price supports, and the like. The public regime is thus regarded as ancillary or "supplemental" to the

[70] See Strange (1995 a; 1995 b). For a critical evaluation of the distinction in the context of Susan Strange's work, see Cutler (2000 b). And see Heilbroner and Milberg (1995). For what continues to be probably the most thoughtful analysis of the relationship between politics and economics in international relations, see Ashley (1983).

[71] See Held (1995: 133) for a similar identification of paradoxical notions of authority in the global economy generated by the internationalization of production and finance.

private, in that it deals with the reduction or punishment of interventionist abnormalities. In contrast, the private regime constitutes normal and natural economic activities.

The second myth posits the neutral and apolitical nature of the private sphere. Liberalism casts the world in a series of dichotomies: the public/private constituting a central division of authority, and the domestic/international another. Under liberalism, private relations are associated with the domain of neutral economic processes, while public relations are related to the realm of politics. As a political theory, liberalism "purports to be neutral, advancing only the goals of liberty and procedural justice... Liberal ideology provides the mode of governance, based on liberty, and a dispute resolution process, based on the rule of law" (Purvis, 1991: 100–1; see also Kymlicka, 1992). As a legal theory, liberal-inspired contract law embodies and reproduces the separation of the spheres, associating the private sphere with neutral and objective processes of resource allocation and the public sphere with contentious and political processes of resource distribution (Horwitz, 1979–80). Liberalism deems the private sphere to operate according to neutral principles. It does not question the "rightness or propriety of dividing international life into spheres of sovereign authority," but "presenting itself as a neutral and objective system, liberal legality provides no awareness of the political and moral nature of its hidden substantive commitments" (Purvis, 1991: 102). Contract law is endowed with objective foundations and has the "appearance of being self-contained, apolitical, and inexorable" as it regulates transactions amongst market participants who are presumed to be of equal bargaining power (Horwitz, 1975: 252).[72] Its role is to facilitate exchange, ensuring procedural fairness, but it does not inquire into the substantive fairness of a transaction. Thus the law functions as a "mechanism of exclusion," reproducing "the relationship it posited between law and society," in the attempt "to project a stable relationship between spheres it creates to divide" (David Kennedy, 1988: 8).

The identification of certain types of political activity as "private" and thus, apolitical, removes that activity from public scrutiny and review. This process of transforming public and political activity into private and apolitical activity is a central "structural separation" of capitalism

[72] Horwitz (1975: 254) notes that most of the basic dichotomies in legal thought, including that between law and politics and between distributional and allocational goals, "arose to establish the objective nature of the market and to neutralize and hence diffuse the political and redistributional potential of law."

and may be "the most effective defense mechanism available to capital" (Wood, 1995: 20). It also contributes to the third liberal myth concerning the consensual and noncoercive nature of private exchange relations. Mark Rupert (1995: 22–4) cogently illustrates how the coercive aspects of the exchange relationship are obscured by what appear to be impersonal market forces and natural economic laws. "To the extent that capitalism is supported by an explicitly coercive power, that power is situated in the putatively communal sphere occupied by the state, and appears as law and order enforced in the public interest;" the private sphere is "insulated from explicitly communal and political concerns, the 'private' powers of capital are ensconced in the sanctuary of civil society." Similarly, Hazel Smith (1996: 209) reminds us that the depiction of capitalist economic relations as free and just is merely a formalistic move that obscures the fundamental "unfreedom" of capitalist productive relations.

The fourth liberal myth posits the inherent efficiency of the private regulation of commercial relations. This myth also draws upon the other myths, since, for liberals it is not difficult to derive the value of efficiency from allegedly natural, neutral, and consensual processes. Indeed, the proponents of the enhanced private regulation of international commerce invoke precisely these attributes to support liberal-inspired functional and transaction cost analysis of private regulation (see Cremades and Plehn, 1984; Trakman, 1983). Private regulation is thus said to produce greater efficiencies by reducing the costs of doing business and by achieving greater economies. The superiority of the system of private regulation flows as a natural result from the fairness and efficiency of allowing merchants maximum scope for managing their own affairs. The right of freedom of contract becomes the legal equivalent of the liberal principles of freedom of trade, commerce, and markets.[73]

While some legal theorists explicitly engage in transaction cost analysis to explain the origin and continuing influence of law merchant practices (see Benson, 1988–9; William C. Jones, 1958), it is students of

[73] The influence of liberal economic thought on commercial law is profound. For a brilliant discussion of the liberal foundations of modern contract law see Atiyah (1979). Certainly, among Anglo-American scholars the tendency is to assume *a priori* the validity of liberal economic accounts of the efficiency value of the private international trade regime. See generally, Berman, and Kaufman (1978) and Cremades and Plehn (1984). Economic theories of law, such as that developed by R. A. Posner, explicitly develop transaction cost analysis, although it is related to domestic and not international law. Posner's ideas on the evolution of primitive legal orders do, however, provide interesting suggestions for conceptualizing international law. See Posner (1980 a; 1980 b).

"new institutional theory" who develop the approach most fully.[74] The emergence of an institution such as the law merchant is explained as a response to the transaction and information costs and insecurity experienced by merchants engaging in trade over wide geographical regions. It is argued that the merchant courts provided an efficacious system for settling merchant disputes and for enforcing transactions. The self-enforcement actions of merchants included the imposition of the sanctions of market exclusion, bankruptcy, and loss of reputation and provided the foundation for a system of private adjudication suited to the needs of commercial actors. By centralizing enforcement in merchant courts, the system provided invaluable information about the credit-worthiness of those with whom a merchant traded and functioned as a valuable reputation system, enforcing honesty (Milgrom, North, and Weingast, 1990). According to this logic, the system of private enforcement made commercial exchange over time and space possible by lowering the costs of exchange and providing merchants with some security that their agreements would be honored. However, in reviewing the history of the law merchant, subsequent chapters reveal the problems of applying liberal transaction cost analysis to the medieval political economy and then drawing a direct link to modern practices. The problems support the accuracy of charges that new institutionalism has a "need for history" and effectively reduces the political landscape to efficiency arguments (Spruyt, 1994: 532–3). As we will see, the supposed symmetry of the medieval and modern law merchant begins to break down when one considers the absence in the medieval period of a clear conceptual distinction between the public and the private spheres and the shifting boundary between public and private authority structures.

In addition, liberal transaction cost analysis and economic theories of law advance neoliberal discipline by presenting the private ordering of commercial and legal relations as the most effective way of managing interdependence and adjusting to the intensification of global competition. Like the market, private legal ordering is presented as most consistent with freedom and justice.

Michael Walzer (1984: 317 and 319) associates the public/private distinction with the liberal practice of the "art of separation," wherein "political community is separated from the sphere of economic competition and free enterprise." In the private sphere of free economic

[74] A pioneering work in this regard is Milgrom, North, and Weingast (1990). See also North and Thomas (1973); North (1981); and Spruyt (1994).

exchange, there are no restrictions on prices or the quality of goods bought and sold – *caveat emptor* prevails. However, while Walzer justifies the liberal art of separation on the grounds that it is a "necessary adaptation to the complexities of modern life," he recognizes that critics on the left are suspicious of the practice, regarding it as "an ideological rather than a practical enterprise" and "an elaborate exercise in hypocrisy" (ibid.). Indeed, the separation obscures significant temporal differences in the ordering of public and private relations. The conception of a commercial contract founded upon the free will of the parties was an historically specific construct of the bourgeois state and "modelled on the exchange transaction of freely competing owners of commodities" (Habermas, 1994: 75). Private law reduced the relationship of private people to private contracts assuming that the laws of the free market were of a model or natural character. Legal rights ceased to be determined by estate and birth as they had been in the feudal era. Instead, they were determined by "fundamental parity among owners of commodities in the market" (ibid.). The adage "from status to contract" encapsulates the evolution from feudal to capitalist conceptions of property rights. Private law "secured the private sphere in the strict sense, a sense in which private people pursued their affairs with one another free from impositions by estate and state, at least in tendency" (ibid.). As mercantilist regulations more or less disappeared, the private sphere was secured by private law and the force of the state. The law was, in theory at least, supposed to operate amongst equals and in a neutral fashion, protecting commercial freedoms and markets. State intervention was frowned upon as interfering with the "natural" operation of the market, which for merchant law, translated into the ability to predict transaction costs in accordance with rational and calculable expectations.

While liberalism provides a rationale for the distinction between the two spheres, it provides no sense of the historical specificity and the function of their separation. It is simply unhistoric to posit the distinction as a natural division, for it has not always figured as part of the natural world. Moreover, it is reductionist to attribute the complex public–private and state–society relationships to functional efficiency arguments. Transaction cost and efficiency arguments do not capture the complex character of the historical conditions that give rise to different permutations of the private/public distinction. They conflate the modern and medieval periods, missing crucial shifts in the boundary between public and private authority. Nor do they grasp the essentially coercive and political nature of private commercial exchange relations. However, the complexity of the way in which the rules of private international trade law operate, the contested nature of the relationship between private and public international trade law, the location of the law merchant within this legal framework, and liberal mythology contribute to a lack of understanding of the significance of the law merchant order to the constitution of the global political economy. While subsequent chapters will illustrate the historical specificity of relations between public and private authorities in the context of the emergence and ideology of the bourgeois state, consideration will now turn to how dominant theories in both law and politics also contribute to the obscurity of the law merchant order.

3 Theorizing the role of law in the global political economy

In addition to the analytical reasons considered in the last chapter, there are important theoretical factors that contribute to the obscurity of the law merchant order. Dominant approaches to international relations and international law have a problem "locating" private authority and law.[1] They are incapable of theorizing the political significance of nonstate actors and nonstate law. Public definitions of authority and law block the association of politics with private activity and actors, while state-centric and territorial theories of rule confine political activity to the state and create impediments to recognizing the political nature of private international trade law. Thus dominant theories are incapable of theorizing the historical significance and normative force of transnational merchant law. Their fundamentally liberal/realist theoretical origins and legally positivistic epistemologies and ontologies block the association of private, nonstate economic actors and their law with history making and normativity. Such associations threaten to undo the "liberal art of separation." These problems stem, in turn, from a more profound inability of the disciplines of both law and politics to theorize law as an historically effective social force. In other words, neither international relations nor international law is capable of generating a "critical" understanding of international law. As a consequence, they result in theories that are blind to the transformations in global governance associated with the juridification, pluralization, and privatization of international commercial relations. Moreover, limitations in their explanatory capacity, while significant, are eclipsed by an even more pressing limitation. They are unable to transcend the limitations of "problem-solving theory," which "takes the world as it finds it, with the prevailing social and power

[1] This problem is analyzed in Cutler (1999 a).

relationships and the institutions into which they are organized, as the given framework for action" (Cox, 1996 a: 88). In contrast, critical theory "stands apart from the prevailing order of the world and asks how that order came about" and how it might be changed (ibid., 88). While more will be said later of the nature of the theory required to adequately address the significance of transnational merchant law in the political economy, for the moment it is sufficient to note three further characteristics of critical theory. Critical theory is inherently normative and transformative, addressing both the moral dimension of international relations and the promotion of social, political, and economic change.[2] It is informed by the values and goals of human emancipation. In addition, critical theory is characterized by its historicity and its concern "not just with the past but with a continuing process of historical change" (Cox, 1996 a: 89).[3]

This chapter begins by problematizing the nature of authority in the global political economy in a consideration of the dominant tendency of political theory to regard authority as a characteristic of the public and not the private sphere. Consideration will next turn to dominant approaches to theorizing authority and law in international relations and international law. It will be argued that there is remarkable symmetry in conventional theoretical approaches in both fields that limit their utility in capturing significant transformations in global governance. In both law and politics, conventional approaches tend to peripheralize the role of law in the global polity, thus obscuring a critical understanding of law as an historically effective material and ideological force. Both disciplines are dominated by unhistorical and state-centric theories that are incapable of dealing theoretically with contemporary transformations in global power and authority. Moreover, both fail to problematize the nature and origins of international law, treating it as simply and self-evidently "there" by virtue of its treatment as an isolated and "neutral social entity" (Shklar, 1964: 34).

Less conventional approaches are then considered and found to be better at capturing the socially constructed nature of the law, but they too exhibit significant theoretical and transformative limitations. In particular, Marxist-inspired theories of law have experienced problems in

[2] See Brown (1992); Neufeld (1995); Linklater (1990). See also the discussion of critical theory in Cutler (2000 b).

[3] See also Cutler (2000 b and 2002 a) for discussion of critical theory as inspired by the tradition of the Frankfurt School of critical theory and the work of contemporary historical materialists such as Robert Cox and Stephen Gill.

theorizing the significance of law as an historically effective material and ideological or normative force. The chapter provides a brief introduction of historical phases in the development of the law merchant order, which form the foundation for the subsequent chapters. A review of these phases suggests the need for a new theory of international law that is capable of locating the authority and the historical effectivity and normativity of transnational merchant law as it has evolved from medieval to capitalist to late capitalist formations.

Problematic Nature of Locating "Authority"

The location and structure of legitimate authority in the global political economy are neither obvious nor self-evident. When one considers the historical development of the law merchant order, as subsequent chapters do, it becomes quite evident that the constitution of global political authority is an historically specific process involving an array of state and nonstate authorities. An examination of the historical evolution of the law merchant reveals a dialectical movement in the consolidation and expansion of corporate power. This movement parallels the consolidation of state power and capitalism in the nation-state and the subsequent transnational expansion of capitalism beyond the nation-state. A rich and variable array of state and nonstate agents has been involved in this movement and in creating and enforcing the law merchant over its history. We will see that the medieval law merchant supported a predominantly private commercial order, generating merchant laws and institutions that operated outside the local political economy of the period. However, with the establishment of the state system and the gradual emergence of nationally based capitalist activity, the law merchant disappeared, becoming part of states' domestic legal orders. There it was isolated and neutralized of political content by distinctions between "public" and "private" law. As a body of "private" law, the law merchant came to be regarded as apolitical and neutral in operation and in effect. Contemporary developments in the law merchant are both mirroring and structuring developments in global capitalism and are freeing merchant laws and institutions from national controls. Today, the new law merchant is being reconfigured and reconstituted as a "handmaiden" of transnational capitalism. As we saw in the last chapter, it reaches both inside the state and outside to connect local and global political/legal orders and to facilitate both local and global adjustments to the transnational expansion of capitalism. It provides the norms that structure international commercial activities in a manner consistent with "disciplinary neoliberalism" and a "new constitutionalism," which are expanding the market opportunities for corporate capital (Gill, 1995 a). The analysis thus places the law merchant very much at the nexus of private and public activities, of local and global political economies, and of economics and politics. However, recognition of this location of authority is obscured by the dominant tendency in political theory to regard authority as a construct of the public and not the private sphere.

Theorizing "authority"

It has been observed that "authority" is both an elusive and an indispensable concept, linked to central issues of political philosophy and the social sciences:

> The concept of authority is one of the rare ideas that has remained stubbornly central both to political philosophy and to empirical social science in spite of their divergencies in the twentieth century. The highly self-conscious interest that political philosophy has in authority is obvious. For authority is a notion intimately bound up with most, if not all, of the central questions of political philosophy, especially the so-called problem of political obligation. And as for social science, the heavy intellectual burden placed on the notion of authority may be seen in the preeminent role played by the concepts of legitimacy and legitimate power in the study and definition of such "subjects" as the stability of political systems, the transition from traditional to modern society, organizational behaviour, political socialization, etc.
>
> At the same time, the "meaning" of authority has been the subject of ceaseless and acrimonious controversy in both political philosophy and social science. The controversy is invariably cast in the form of a dispute over the relation between the notions of authority, power, and legitimacy; and a large variety of approaches to authority have been forged out of these elements . . . this controversy has come to effect *the very question of what politics is and what the field and scope of political study consists in.* (Friedman, 1990: 56, emphasis added)[4]

Despite the fact that thinking about authority reflects no single view, Friedman isolates its main elements. Two significant elements are the public nature of authority and its identity as a social construction. We will consider each in turn.

The notion of "authority" invokes a sense of "publicness" in that it entails "the surrender of private judgment." "The man who accepts

[4] This analysis follows closely on Cutler (1999 a).

authority is thus said to surrender his private or individual judgment because he does not insist that reasons be given that he can grasp and that satisfy him, as a condition of his obedience" (Friedman, 1990: 64). Authority is distinguished from coercion because it involves "a recognition on the part of the subject that . . . another is entitled to obedience" (ibid.). Such recognition is essential to political authority conceived of as "the right to rule" (ibid., 68 and see Raz, 1990 b: 2). Moreover, the recognition must be public. As Friedman observes, "there must be some public way of identifying the person whose utterances are to be taken as authoritative" (ibid., 69). He notes further that H. L. A. Hart (1961) provides for the public recognition of authority in the notion of "rules of recognition" that enable subjects to identify authority when they give up the right to judge privately. Friedman argues that this public aspect of authority goes right to the essence of the concept and he illustrates how historically the "means" of authority was called the "mark of authority" or a common sign or symbol designating authority for all to see (1990: 69; see also Lincoln, 1991: ch. 1).

Yet another aspect of authority's publicness is its disassociation from private matters, which are deemed to be nonauthoritative judgments. Such judgments are not entitled to prescribe behavior (Friedman, 1990: 79). Significantly, private judgments are not by nature necessarily "apolitical." In fact, they "may be highly political in content but . . . [are] nevertheless not entitled to prescribe behavior. Indeed, it is precisely because of the highly contentious public character of human opinions that from the standpoint of this view of authority it becomes necessary to have a public definition of whose definition is to be designated as merely private" (ibid.). Lincoln (1991: 11 and 116–17) captures the special and public nature of authority in its description as the "privileged sphere" wherein there is a conjunction of certain features that are constitutive of authority, including "the right speaker, the right speech and delivery, the right staging props, the right time and place, and an audience, the historically and culturally conditioned expectations of which establish the parameters of what is judged 'right' in all these instances."

The requirements of the public designation, recognition, and acceptance of authority gives rise to its second characteristic. Authority is a social construct: it derives its meaning from a "normative arrangement" among members of society (Friedman, 1990: 71). As Friedman (ibid.) notes the "concept of authority can thus have application only within the context of certain socially accepted criteria which serve to identify person(s) whose utterances are to count as authoritative." He thus stresses that authority is typically invoked "in political philosophy to help to determine the nature of the cohesion or unity characteristics of human societies" where authority and not coercion or force controls (ibid., 71 and 57).

The social context in which authority is constructed suggests that it is better conceived of as an "effect" rather than as an "entity." Lincoln (1991: 116) disputes its treatment as an entity, noting that authority is an effect of "culturally and historically conditioned expectations" about what constitutes legitimate authority. Stephen Lukes (1990: 209–14) too posits its social construction, noting that the holders, subjects, and observers of authority will each have a different perspective on it. As Lukes observes, mutual recognition of authority by the holder and subject of authority is central to many accounts of authority, while the public or societal aspect is intrinsic to the very notion of authority held by many.

The concept of authority thus involves the surrender of private judgment and a recognition of the right to rule. The existence of a societal context for authority is thus regarded as an essential aspect of its character. In addition, the surrender of private judgment and the recognition of a privileged sphere of authority presuppose the separation of the public and private spheres. Indeed, the "publicness" of authority is constituted by a distinction between private and public activities (Lukes, 1990: 208).

These conditions of authority are problematic, particularly when they are articulated in the context of global political economy. The nature of the social context for global authority is not obvious. Clearly, authority presupposes some sort of "unity of the social sphere." However, the character of this unity is especially troubling in the global context, where "the anarchy problematique:" "the problem of order in the absence of an orderer" has been described as "a perennial problem of modern global politics" (Ashley, 1988: 229). The presumption of social unity slides easily and uncritically into presumptions of societal consensus and/or state consent as prerequisites for constructing authority. The problem lies in identifying the origin and scope of this social unity and the public sphere. This goes to the very heart of what is regarded as the challenge to authority posed by philosophical anarchism: how to reconcile the autonomy of the individual with obedience to authority.[5]

[5] Raz (1990 b: 4) notes concerning the challenge of philosophical anarchism that "[m]uch of the debate about authority in the last two decades is best understood as so many replies to this challenge, even though the authors did not always conceive of the problem in this way." He states the challenge as thus: "The duty to obey conveys an abdication of autonomy, that is, of the right and duty to be responsible for one's action and to conduct

Most theorists begin with the conviction that authority lies somewhere between coercion and persuasion (Friedman, 1990: 63). However, they differ over the nature of the relationship posited to exist between the three conditions. In stating the anarchist's dilemma, R. P. Wolff (1990: 30) distinguishes authority from power and persuasion, but concludes that all authority is illegitimate. Others, in contrast, address the dilemma by positing the legitimacy of authority based upon consent. Indeed, the consent of the governed is deemed to mediate between power and authority and between persuasion and authority, thus reconciling individual autonomy with obedience.[6] This is one liberal solution to political obligation both within the state and under international law. Within the democratic state, authority is traced to the consent of the governed, which is articulated through democratic processes and under a doctrine of limited government.[7] Outside the state, liberal theories of international law craft the basis of obligation or authority upon the express or implied consent of states (see Koskenniemi, 1989; Tesón, 1990; Carty, 1991 a; 1991 b). International legal theory, as "historically no more than a subsystem of the discourse of liberal political theory," is "plagued by the dilemma how autonomous and independent actors can be brought together in support of or under the rubric of some notion of the common good, when authority for a definition of that good must remain with the same autonomous and independent actors" (Carty, 1991 b: 66).

The anarchists' dilemma thus troubles international legal theory as well as domestic political theory.[8] Liberalism, in domestic and international theory, addresses the dilemma by positing a social unity deriving from the consent of the subject. Moreover, this unity is made possible

oneself in the best light of reason. If there is an authority which is legitimate, then its subjects are duty bound to obey it whether they agree with it or not. Such a duty is inconsistent with autonomy, with the right and the duty to act responsibly, in the light of reason."

6 For good discussions of consent-based theories of authority see Greenwalt (1990) and Green (1990). See Finnis (1990) and Linklater (1982: ch. 3) for excellent analysis of contractarian and consent-based theories of both domestic and international political obligation.

7 Raz (1990 b: 11–12) notes that consent-based theories of political obligation require a doctrine of limited and responsible government in order to answer the anarchist's challenge.

8 This suggests that theorizing about "outside" the state is not as different as theorizing about "inside" the state. Both bodies of theory have been overdetermined by extreme individualism and atomism in their treatment of notions of authority and political obligation. See Green (1990: 243) for discussion of communitarian criticism of liberal individualism. Citing Socrates he notes that "the questions that rive our public and private commitments just do not arise for the polis-animal . . . As in marriage, the social relations between individuals and the state should be seen as internal and constitutive, not as external and instrumental."

by the second condition of authority: the public/private distinction. The autonomy of the subject, whether the individual or the state, is reconciled with political obligation:

> by assuming an essential distinction between the "private" and the "public" spheres ("self-regulating" and "other-regarding" actions)... the left side [of the dichotomy] expresses the postulate of subjective freedom while the right has to do with unfreedom and social constraint. In the private sphere, everybody is entitled to pursue happiness according to one's own (private) value-system and desire. In the public sphere, the Government may interfere as provided by objective law.
> (Koskenniemi, 1989: 65)

The private sphere is associated with the individual and freedom of markets and economic exchange, while the public sphere is associated with state authority and legitimate compulsion.

However, there are analytical and normative problems with the presumption of social unity and the public/private distinction.[9] The notion of consent tends, analytically, to equalize the positions of subjects and obscures the asymmetry in power relations between the governed and the governors. The conviction that authority lies somewhere between coercion and persuasion reflects a tension between authority based on power or force and authority based on consent. Neither extreme captures the essence of authority, for as Lincoln (1991) notes, they actually constitute its negation:

> Authority is often considered in connection with two other categories, persuasion and force – the processes through which one wins others over through acts of discourse or bends them to one's will through acts or threats of violence. Persuasion and force have been contrasted to one another since antiquity, persuasion generally being understood as the realm of words and the mind, and force that of deeds and the body. Authority, however, is yet a third entity, which remains distinct from persuasion and coercion alike while being related to them in some very specific and suggestive ways. (4)
>
> ...
>
> Authority is thus related to coercion and persuasion in symmetrical ways. Both of these exist as capacities or potentialities implicit within authority, but are actualized only when those who claim authority sense that they have begun to lose the trust of those over whom they

[9] There are also problems with the assumption of the autonomous subject, which are not pursued here, but will be addressed in the concluding chapter in the context of the "problem of the subject."

> seek to exercise it. In a state of latency or occultation, persuasion and coercion alike are constitutive parts of authority, but once actualized and rendered explicit they signal – indeed, they are, at least temporarily – its negation. (6)

Lincoln's suggestion that coercion and persuasion operate in relationship with authority captures the profound challenge posed by philosophical anarchism to the concept of authority. At root, authority can never be reconciled with the autonomy of the subject because, as Lincoln notes, "force is always implicit in authority." It is implicit in the asymmetry in power relations between the "ruler and ruled, officer and private, teacher and student, parent and child" (ibid., 6). Liberalism obscures this asymmetry by positing a consent-based social unity which tends to equalize relations between members of society.

Furthermore, liberalism also obscures the fact that social unity may be very limited in scope. It may operate only as regards generally accepted procedures for making choices over matters where there is no substantive agreement.[10] The notion that consent somehow creates an equal playing field as between the governors and the governed obscures the fundamental asymmetry in power relations between them and risks overstating the social unity that constitutes political authority.[11] Moreover, the presumed separation of the public and private spheres, the former associated with civil society and economy, while the latter is associated with the state and government, creates the false imagery of a consensual realm of civic and economic freedoms, as distinct from the political and potentially coercive realm of the state. In terms of the global political economy, we have argued that liberal mythology posits the natural, neutral, consensual, and efficient nature of private economic exchange. Private international economic relations are depicted as the apolitical realm of freedom, while the public sphere is depicted as the political realm of necessary unfreedom. But as Antonio Gramsci (1971: 160)

10 Friedman (1990) makes this point. He differentiates between being "in authority" and being "an authority." With regard to the former, there is broad social agreement as to who the authorities are and thus deference to their opinion. With regard to the latter, however, he argues that certain entities are authoritative when there is broad disagreement in society over matters of substantive importance. Authority emerges, thus, as agreement over acceptable procedures to reconcile differences. The unity of the social sphere is thus limited to consensus over procedures. Nardin (1983), Bull (1977), and Franck (1990) have made similar arguments in reference to the foundation of international law and society. For a critical analysis of this view of international society, see Cutler (1999 c).

11 See Linklater (1982: 42) for discussion of the basis of contractarian theories of political obligation in presumptions of the "natural equality and liberty" of individuals.

notes, the distinction between civil society and the state is "not an organic one . . . it is merely methodological:"

> Thus it is asserted [under liberalism] that economic activity belongs to civil society, and that the State must not intervene to regulate it. But since in actual reality civil society and the State are one and the same, it must be clear that *laissez-faire* too is a form of State "regulation," introduced and maintained by legislative and coercive means. It is a deliberate policy, conscious of its own ends, and not the spontaneous, automatic expression of economic facts. Consequently, *laissez-faire* liberalism is a political programme, designed to change – in so far as it is victorious – a state's leading personnel, and to change the economic programme of the State itself – in other words the distribution of the national income.[12]

Liberal mythology thus creates the impression that the private sphere operates neutrally and consensually as a domain of freedom. It functions ideologically and normatively to support the value and superiority of economic liberalism, obscuring the distributional and even coercive foundations of private exchange. We have also noted how the emergence of the public and private spheres and the separation of the economy and the polity did not simply occur spontaneously, as organic and natural developments, but were the products of a complex set of legislative interventions to create a market society by removing impediments to the exchange of labor, land, and money (Polanyi, 1944: 7). The appearance of the separations of the public and private spheres and economics and politics in the nineteenth century suggests that notions of authority that are defined by these separations are of rather limited historical significance. Indeed, the relationship and balance between the public/private spheres and political/economic activity have shifted and the spheres have been given different content at different times in history. The changing nature of public and private authority also suggests that the social sphere has undergone transformation, thus rendering notions of the *unity* of the social sphere problematic. As Michael Mann (1986: 1) observes, societies are never unitary, but are "constituted of multiple overlapping and intersecting sociospatial networks of power." Mann argues that political, economic, and cultural networks "almost never coincide." Anthony Giddens (1981: 44 and 47) too rejects the notion of social unity or totality, observing that societies are constituted by "symbolic, political, economic, and legal/repressive institutional

[12] For a good discussion of Gramsci on this point, see Augelli and Murphy (1993: ch. 6).

elements" that may or may not be localized spatially or territorially (see also Giddens, 1990 a). Indeed, as noted before, one of the most significant transformations in world order today involves a pluralization of authority relations and a multiplicity of cross-cutting and overlapping networks of authority operating subnationally, nationally, regionally, and transnationally.

The problem of social unity becomes even more acute when one considers the historical specificity of different social orders and the gradual articulation of the public/private distinction in the context of different historic conjunctures. The social context of and the balance between public and private authority in the global political economy have changed over time in the context of different configurations of material, ideational, and institutional conditions. However, dominant theories of international relations and international law reproduce the liberal distinctions between private and public authority and between politics and economics, thus obscuring historical differentiation in authority relations and subjects of the global polity.

Theoretical Approaches to International Relations and Law

Students of both international relations and international law are, as noted in the previous chapter, increasingly concerned with the "globalization of law" and "legalization of world politics." This suggests that both disciplines are registering a sense that there has been an intensification in the legal regulation of international relationships that is having an impact on the ways in which states and societies govern themselves. For some, the globalization of the rule of law is a welcome development that is civilizing the globe through uniform laws and practices that replace parochial systems of local and national law (David, 1972 b; Schmitthoff, 1982). Others doubt the "civilizing" role of globalized law and suggest that the transmission of predominantly First World laws throughout the globe engages questionable practices of legal hegemony and colonial domination (Silbey, 1997; Santos, 1995: Cutler, 1995; 1997; 1999 b). For some, the globalization of law signals a loss of national and domestic control over significant policy areas, eroding the foundations for democracy and participatory forms of governance, whilst empowering supranational sites of governance that lack democratic traditions and credentials (Habermas, 1998: 151 and 155; Trimble, 1985). This suggests that juridification and pluralization are thus not necessarily linked with greater democratization. Yet others regard the globalization of law as filling governance gaps created by economic globalization and thus providing much needed public goods in the forms of economic security and certainty (Ruggie, 1993 b; Abbott et al., 2000). Finally, some focus on changes in the nature of global capitalism that are altering the context for international commerce and obviating the need for traditional law. The enhanced significance of soft law, informal, discretionary, *ad hoc*, and private legal regulation is quite inconsistent with and, perhaps, even eroding the foundation of the rule of law as a system of global governance (Scheuerman, 1999; Cutler, 2002 c).

Indeed, students of both international law and international relations contest the precise nature of the role of law in global governance. While international lawyers have long debated the nature and significance of international law, agonizing over the analytical issues of the formal "sources" and proper "subjects" of legal obligation and debating whether international law may be regarded as law "properly so-called," contemporary theorists reflect similar debates over the status of informal or "soft" law sources of law and the authority of nonstate actors, such as transnational corporations, as subjects of law.[13]

International relations scholars also debate the significance of mechanisms of global governance, although in the past the concern has been predominantly with the efficacy of international regimes. While both mainstream and unconventional approaches to the study of international relations are concerned with whether international regimes really influence state behavior or are epiphenomenal and part of the superstructure of the global political economy, they disagree about who makes law and shapes the global polity (see Krasner, 1983 b; Keohane, 1984; Cutler, 2002 c). Mainstream approaches to international law and organization and international political economy posit that states are the main "subjects" and agents or voices of the global polity and that state consent is the prerequisite for a "source" of legal regulation (Franck, 1990; Keohane, 1984). Others challenge this state-centric approach with the increasing authority of transnational corporations, private associations, nongovernmental organizations, global social movements, and transnational class and gender relations and the forms of often "soft" regulation they generate (see Cutler, Haufler, and Porter, 1999 a). In both

[13] For classical statements of the debates, see Austin (1954); Kelsen (1961); and Hart (1961). For a more contemporary example, see Malanczuk (1997: ch. 3).

fields different theoretical approaches or schools of thought contribute often incompatible views to the debate over whether law matters in the regulation of global relations (see generally Beck, Arend, and Vander Lugt, 1996).

This chapter identifies several theoretical approaches to international relations and international law, differentiating between dominant, mainstream, or conventional theories and unconventional or critical theories. In international law, the dominant approach is legal positivism, while in international relations, neorealism and neoliberal institutionalism form the dominant approaches. These will be addressed below, as too will less conventional approaches that draw upon, for example, postmodernism, feminist scholarship, critical theory, historical materialism, and structuralism.[14] Curiously, the review of both conventional and unconventional approaches discloses that neither has generated a critical theory of international law.

Although legal theorists are less inclined than international relations scholars to doubt the efficacy of international law, there is remarkable symmetry in conventional approaches to both fields. In international relations these debates are often framed in terms of the significance of international regimes, institutions, norms, and degrees of legalization (see Krasner, 1983 a; Mearsheimer, 1994–5; Keohane, 1984; Abbott, Keohane et al., 2000), while international lawyers tend to talk about the formal sources and subjects of the law and the problems of legal obligation and compliance (Brownlie, 1998; Shaw, 1997). Many international relations scholars regard international legal regimes to be epiphenomenal and external to the material power relations of states. Susan Strange (1983) probably best articulated this position in her trenchant and now classic critique of regimes analysis. To Strange, the study of regimes was an American fad, conceptually wooly and imprecise, reflecting a value bias in favor of finding order in the world, and producing a static and state-centric view of international relations. The focus on state-led regimes thus obscures rather than clarifies processes of governance in the global polity by ignoring the underlying structures of power and influence, such as production, financial, or knowledge structures. Others too question whether international regimes influence political outcomes autonomously and directly, or are mediated by state interests and goals (Krasner, 1983 b). They question whether regime norms have any compliance-pull or normative influence of their own, or are

[14] This discussion draws in part on Cutler (2002 c; 2002 d).

used instrumentally by states to achieve their particularistic interests (Keohane, 1984).

Similar concerns over the efficacy of legal rules are expressed by legal theorists who adopt conventional approaches to international law (see Franck, 1990; Byers, 2000). This symmetry is due in no small part to three fundamental tendencies shared by conventional approaches in both fields that produce a state-centric view of the global polity, inhibit the recognition of nonstate subjects and sources, and reject the moral foundations of the law (see Cutler, 2002 c). The first tendency is the general application of the domestic analogy and related presumptions of international anarchy to international relations (Suganami, 1989). This involves the application to international relations of a hierarchical model of rule derived from domestic legal orders that precludes conceptualizing pluralism in legal regulation. The second tendency is legal formalism and the association of authority with the formal authority of the state as both the subject and the legitimate source of law (see Cutler, 2001 a). Legal formalism also works against the recognition of nonstate authority. The third tendency is belief in the autonomy of the law as a self-referential and self-contained order that is independent of social, political, economic, moral, and religious influences. Belief in the autonomy of the law is the first principal characteristic of the Western legal tradition (Berman, 1983: 8). It provides the foundation for constructing the rule of law as an objective and neutral operation of the "rule of law and not the rule of man."[15] As the discussion will illustrate, belief in the autonomy of law in combination with legal formalism fetishizes the law by emptying it of historical, social, and moral content, attenuating theoretical links between law and society, law and economy, and law and polity. Fetishized laws take on the "character of active, productive subjects, whilst social relations take on the character of things" (Rose, 1977: 29) inverting the relationship between law and society.[16]

The similarity in approach begins to diminish, however, as analysis moves to less conventional views of international law. These identify increased pluralism in legal governance arrangements, encompass a broader range of legal subjects and sources, and posit the inherent normativity and subjectivity of the law. However, while they are thus more

[15] The classic statement of the "rule of law" may be found in Dicey (1967) first published 1885.

[16] This process will be analyzed further in the context of the Problem of the Subject in the final chapter. For a discussion of Marx's notion of the process of fetishization, see Rose (1977).

theoretically accommodating of contemporary transformations in world order, they too have limitations. These limitations stem from their continuing inability to theorize the transformative capacity of international law. It is argued that the inability of even unconventional theories to engage in critical theorization of law is significant and stems from disciplinary reasons relating to the dominant self-images and professional practices in the fields of international relations and law, as well as from problems in Marxism's theorization of law.[17]

Conventional theoretical approaches

There is a remarkable unity between conventional international legal theory and international relations theory in terms of the tendencies to apply the domestic analogy, to exhibit formalism over the subjects and sources of the law, and to conceive of the law as an external, relatively autonomous, neutral, and objective order.[18]

International legal theories

The conventional approach to international law today is legal positivism (see generally, Beck, Arend, and Vander Lugt, 1996: ch. 3; Malanczuk, 1997: ch. 1; Ago, 1957; D'Amato, 1985). Legal positivism emerged as a reaction to natural law theories that were current during the formative

[17] For the dominant self-images of the field of international relations see Steve Smith (1995) and for the influence of disciplinary and professional considerations on the construction of international relations, see Kahler (1997).

[18] Shklar (1964) notes the ideological affinity between nineteenth-century liberalism, which forms the ideological foundation of modern international law, and legal positivism: "Peace through law is a cherished aspect of liberal ideology. Commercial relations would replace military ones, and law and commerce would go together internationally, as they do within the confines of domestic political society. For a positivist to apply a methodological analysis to this law, however, presupposes that it have at least some existence, that it be 'there' in order to be analyzed in legal terms. The actuality of positive international law must, therefore, simply be posited, its validity simply assumed. This is indeed what happened. Moreover, the contempt for politics inherent in the policy of justice and in legalism has led to a theory of positive international law which regards the latter as not just 'there,' but as a veritable substitute for all other forms of international politics. That is why the modern theory of positive international law, the law of civilized nations, or, as it is now called, world law, is perhaps the most striking manifestation of legalist ideology. Its ideological character is especially discernible because the principles of international law are not supported by effective institutions. As such, it is a program and little else. This has become increasingly evident because it is a declining ideology, challenged openly by rival ideologies. The result is that, in their views on international law, positivists are often close in their approach, though not in their vocabulary or premises, to natural law thinking. They are only less consistent. Ultimately it is the legalist ethos that unites both theories in a common inability to adjust to the historical realities of the present age." (128–9)

time of modern international law. Legal positivists tended to approach the question of whether international law mattered by inquiring into its status as "law properly so called." Proper law was, of course, domestic law. Applying the domestic analogy, John Austin (1832) articulated a hierarchical or "command theory of law" that associated proper law with the command of a sovereign backed by the force of sanctions. Law was theorized to be a body of neutral rules that is applied in an objective manner through adjudication. Thus Austin concluded that international law could be no more than "positive morality" because it lacked the necessary features of an adjudicatory system. Other positivists answered the question of whether law mattered with a qualified "yes." Hans Kelsen (1961; 1952; 1967) theorized that international law was a primitive legal order in which enforcement was achieved through decentralized sanctions (self-help and reprisals), while H. L. A. Hart (1961; 1962) theorized international law to be a primitive system of primary rules (stipulating obligations), but lacking the secondary rules (governing recognition, change, and adjudication) common in advanced legal systems (see generally, Beck, Arend, and Vander Lugt, 1996: 56–9).

Most mainstream contemporary legal scholars, although positivist in approach, tend to impute more efficacy to international law than did the early positivists. The Austinian preoccupation with commands of a sovereign enforced by sanctions has given way to more nuanced understandings of the source of legal obligation and compliance. Compliance is theorized to be related to concerns for reputation, reciprocity, perceptions of legitimacy, trust, and the like, which do not rest on coercion or sanctions (Chayes and Chayes, 1995: Franck, 1990; Cutler, 1999 c). In addition, developments in the institutional foundations of international law in the post-Second World War period make its analytical status as a primitive order lacking secondary rules highly questionable. However, the legal positivist attributions of legal subjectivity to states and the sources of law to products of state consent persist, as too does the presumption that the worlds of law and of morality are separately existing domains. As Judith Shklar (1964: 30) says of legal positivism: "If the core of natural law theory is the proposition that law and morals intersect, positivism lives to deny that proposition" (see also, Hart, 1958). These tendencies are evident in the doubts that many have about the prospects of achieving anything more than procedural, as opposed to substantive, justice in the world comprised of a multiplicity of independent states where normative consensus is fleeting at best. Law thus matters, but only insofar as it regulates procedural and not substantive legal/political matters involving competing normative systems (see Franck, 1990; Nardin, 1983; Oran Young, 1979; Bull, 1977). This is a rather minimalist view of the extent to which law matters.

International relations theories

In international relations the conventional approaches, political realism[19] and neoliberal institutionalism,[20] reproduce many of the reservations expressed by legal positivists about whether law matters. Classical realists, applying the domestic analogy, echoed the Austinian preoccupation with the anarchy problematic and the theoretical impossibility of regarding international law as a "real" binding legal order. The suspicion that it is a dangerous form of "positive morality" is clearly evident in the work of E. H. Carr (1939) and Hans Morgenthau (1948). Neorealists share similar doubts about the efficacy of international law and, with neoliberal institutionalists, are preoccupied with the extent to which cooperation in international regimes is thwarted by cheating, problems of enforcement, and interstate competition (Krasner, 1983 b; Keohane, 1984). Neorealists reproduce many of the classical realist objections, illustrating a continuing debate over the nature and role of law, regimes, and institutions, which concepts tend to be used interchangeably. Stephen Krasner (1983 b) identifies three broad approaches to the significance of international regimes. Structural realism, at one extreme, posits the irrelevance of regimes to state behavior. State action is regarded as interest-based, and not norm-driven. At the other extreme are Grotians who posit the ubiquity of regimes wherever there is regularized state behavior. In the middle lie the modified structuralists who are prepared to accept that regime norms and institutions can influence state actions by intervening between state interests and outcomes. The structural realist position is articulated most powerfully by Joseph Grieco (1988) and John Mearsheimer (1994–5) in the attempt to discredit the position of modified structuralists or neoliberal institutionalists. They argue that legal regimes have a negligible impact on state action for two reasons: states' fear of cheating and competitive concerns about their position *vis-à-vis* other states (relative gains) limit their willingness to cooperate in international institutions. Neoliberal institutionalists, in contrast, believe that cheating and concern over relative

[19] See Morgenthau (1948); Waltz (1979); Grieco (1988); Mearsheimer (1994–5); Krasner (1993 and 1997).
[20] See Keohane (1984); Keohane and Martin (1995); and Oran Young (1979) and see Powell (1994).

gains, while problematic, do not rule out the effectiveness of regimes and institutions. Indeed, neoliberal institutionalists counter that institutions may be even more significant when distributional issues arise for they can assist in balancing unequal gains from cooperation and in mitigating fears of cheating (Keohane and Martin, 1995: 45). Notwithstanding such differences, there is thus a fair degree of unity in the application of both the domestic analogy and the anarchy problematic and in regarding institutional efforts to mitigate the effects of anarchy as the defining conditions of whether law and institutions matter.[21]

In terms of the subjects and sources of international law, legal positivists adopt a state-centric approach that regards states as the only subjects under the law with full and original legal personality and that associates the legitimate sources of law with state consent. Whereas international lawyers talk about subjects and sources, international relations scholars refer to agents or actors, conflating the analytical concepts of source and subject. States as the essential actors in international relations are also the legitimate voices of the global polity. Conventional analysis in international relations mirrors the state-centrism of subject and sources doctrine. Structural realists remain steadfastly committed to the view that states remain the essential actors, notwithstanding what appears to be a proliferation of other entities claiming significance (see Krasner, 1993; 1995: Mearsheimer, 1994–5). Neoliberal institutionalists also continue to regard the state as the main agent of international regimes, despite the fact that the generally accepted definition of international regimes did not limit them to participation by states but to "actors around which expectations converge" (Krasner, 1983 b: 2). The initial promise of regime analysis to include a broader set of actors was not met as regime analysis became progressively more state-centric. This led Miles Kahler (1997: 35) to observe that regimes analysis was "captured" by a neorealist synthesis of realism and neoliberalism. Neoliberals had initially challenged the excessive state-centrism of realism in studies of interdependence and transnational relations that were the precursors to regime analysis. However, over time a synthesis emerged and "[n]eoliberalism was redefined away from complex interdependence toward a state-centric version more compatible with realism."

Structural realists clearly regard states as the legitimate voices, recognizing the authority of the pronouncements of international organizations only insofar as states have empowered them to speak.

[21] See also, Wendt (1995); Ruggie (1995 b); Zacher with Sutton (1996).

Recognizing the voice of individuals is regarded as potentially subversive of the authority of states and is thus discouraged (see Cutler, 1999 c: 290–1), while the activities of transnational corporations are ultimately regarded as conditioned by states (Krasner, 1995: 279). The voices of nonstate actors cannot possibly be regarded as authoritative as that would be inconsistent with the formal logic of state sovereignty. For neorealists, the discourse on sources thus tends to run into and become indistinguishable from the discourse on subjects.

The neoliberal institutionalist treatment of international regimes does raise some of the issues addressed by sources doctrine. The contemporary focus on "explicit" regimes and international treaties reflects a similar preoccupation with formalism. Curiously, an approach that initially embraced the authority of "implicit and explicit principles, norms, rules and decision-making procedures" (Krasner, 1983 b: 2) has become increasingly formalistic in narrowing regimes to explicit acts of state consent. Robert Keohane (1989: 4) defines international regimes as "institutions with explicit rules, agreed upon by governments, that pertain to particular sets of issues in international relations." Andrew Hurrell (1993: 54) notes that the "apparently growing stress on explicit, persistent, and connected sets of rules brings regime theory and international law much closer together." It is most paradoxical that international regimes analysis has moved in the direction of the "formalism" and "legalism" of law, accusations once lobbed with such disdain by classical realists at international lawyers. For both disciplines, formalism concerning subjects and sources precludes theorizing about the authority of nonstate actors and sources of law.[22]

In terms of the autonomy, neutrality, and objectivity of the law, conventional theory in both international law and international relations reflects an *a priori* distinction between the world of state interests and *realpolitik* and the world of morals and normativity. As noted above, for some of the early positivists, the chasm between law and morality, when combined with the application of the domestic analogy, resulted in profound doubt about the status of international law as law "properly so-called" and led to its treatment as "positive morality." In an interesting inversion of this conceptualization, more contemporary legal positivists accept that law is law "properly so-called," but regard it as separate and autonomous from morality, polity, and religion (see Hart, 1958).

[22] But see Abbott et al., (2000) and Abbott and Snidal (2000).

In international relations theory, classical realists shared the early positivist doubts about the legal status of international law. Such doubt is also evident in the work of many structural realists in the context of the efficacy of regime norms and international institutions in regulating state behavior (Mearsheimer, 1994–5). In general, structural realists and neoliberal institutionalists alike have difficulty accepting the binding force of what they regard to be nonmaterial influences such as laws, norms, and ideas (see Goldstein and Keohane, 1993; Krasner 1993 b; 1997. And see Kratochwil, 2000). As will later become evident, it is this position that separates these approaches from more unconventional ones.

In light of this state-centric focus, legal positivism, neorealism, and neoliberal institutionalism are quite clearly theoretically incapable of capturing the significance of nonstate authority and law. They provide theories of law that reinforce the tendency to theorize authority as a construct of both states and the public sphere, ruling *private authority* out theoretically as an analytically significant consideration. Legal formalism and belief in the externality, autonomy, and independence of the law work against a robust recognition of law's nature as a social construct of material and ideological conditions. Neither engages law as a constitutive element of a global order with roots in diverse historical conditions for both regard law instrumentally and unhistorically. Neorealism and neoliberal institutionalism tend to regard international law as an interest-based order that is embedded in a larger anarchical system and is used or neglected by states, instrumentally, in the furtherance of their goals (Waltz, 1979; Keohane, 1984). In international law, liberal theories form the dominant approach and tend to regard law in a similarly interest-based or instrumental and unhistoric way (see Franck, 1990; Slaughter, 1994; Slaughter-Burley, 1993). For the dominant modes of theorizing about international law and international relations, history, if considered at all, provides a "quarry providing materials with which to illustrate variations on always-recurrent themes" (Cox, 1996 a: 92). These themes revolve around a state-centric universe in which international anarchy establishes the foundational historic condition, from which all else flows in recurring patterns. History provides a material context for action, providing certain incentives or disincentives for states who function more or less autonomously, in response to cues from their environment (Krasner, 1993 b). History thus provides a framework or field of action for states who are theorized to function in response to external influences. As Cox (1996 a: 92) notes, "the mode of thought ceases to be historical," even though the materials used are taken from history, and "dictates that the future will always be like the past." The analysis misses the crucial role of states and other entities in the construction of their own history.[23] In addition, historical differentiation in political authority structures is flattened out in theorizing the timelessness of international anarchy and the continuing relevance of state-centric theorization.[24]

Importantly, as Judith Shklar (1964: 123) observes, belief in the "autonomy of law," like belief in the "autonomy of politics," is itself an ideology.[25] It is an ideology that empties international law of history, because "[l]aw is its own creation" it simply exists "there:"[26]

> The possibility of treating law as a conceptual pattern entirely distinct from all political, moral, and social values and institutions is simply taken for granted. The law is something "there" – a discrete entity, however abstract – is assumed to be self-evident.
>
> The idea of treating law as a self-contained system of norms that is "there," identifiable without any reference to the content, aim, and development of the rules that compose it, is the very essence of formalism, for formalism does not involve treating law mechanically as a matter of logical deductions from given premises. It consists rather in treating law as an isolated block of concepts that have no relevant characteristics or functions apart from their possible validity or invalidity within a hypothetical system. But what aim is served by this "homeless ghost"? . . .
>
> This deliberate isolation of the legal system – the treatment of law as a neutral social entity – is itself a refined political ideology, the expression of a preference. As a description of law it does some considerable violence to political actualities.[27]

23 Even "constructivists" embrace the perennial anarchy problematic and state-centrism unhistorically. See Wendt (1992; 1994; 1995); Arend (1998).

24 See Krasner (1993; 1997). For criticism of this unhistoric tendency in dominant approaches to international relations see Amin and Palan (1996); Amoore et al. (2000); Hobden and Hobson (2002).

25 Shklar (1964: 123) further notes that historically, belief in the autonomy of politics was an ideological response to Marxism and to the dominant legal tradition of legal formalism. Belief in the autonomy of politics from economics served to diffuse economic theories of history and their ideology, while belief that politics was separate and autonomous from law, saved *realpolitik* from the idealism and naivete of legal formalism in international affairs.

26 Shklar (ibid., 131) argues that "Kelsen saves himself the trouble of historical reflection by retreating into formalism. 'Law is its own creation,' as rules generate rules, nationally and internationally . . . Not only do rules create each other, they create all political institutions."

27 Shklar (ibid., 33–4) here quotes Cohen (1950: 80).

Legal formalism is an ideology because it depicts the world, not as it *is*, but as it *ought to be*. Legal positivism and formalism depict a world of objective and autonomous legality in the hopes of creating an autonomous analytical legal science by purging law of historical, political, and moral content. But as Shklar notes:

> [n]othing in history is self-evident. Formalism creates this 'thereness' because its promoters think that a legal system *ought* to be 'there' in order to function properly. To be 'there' it must be self-regulating, immune from the unpredictable pressures of politicians and moralists, manned by a judiciary that at least tries to maintain justice's celebrated blindness. That is why it is seen as a series of impersonal rules which fit together neatly. (ibid., 35)

Moreover, legal formalism is a conservative ideology, for its focus is providing "security of established expectations" (Shklar, 1964: 10), which for contemporary international law means the preservation of state-centric and public definitions of authority and law. As the discussion turns to consider more unconventional theoretical approaches to international relations and law, greater recognition of the socially constructed nature of law becomes evident. However, here too legal formalism has left its mark. The constructed nature of law, while recognized, is not internalized so as to overcome analytical and theoretical obstacles to a recognition of the law as a potentially powerful revolutionary force.

Unconventional Theoretical Approaches

The unconventional approaches in international law are numerous and include natural law theory,[28] the New Haven Approach,[29] critical legal studies,[30] feminism[31] and others drawing on critical theory. In general, these approaches contemplate considerable pluralism in both the subjects and sources of legal regulation. As such, they are better positioned to address the processes of pluralization and privatization, as too are unconventional approaches in international relations. However, as shall become evident, they continue to reproduce some of the dominant

[28] See Verdross and Koeck (1983); Bull, Kingsbury, and Roberts (1990); D'Amato (1989); Schall (1991–2).

[29] See Lasswell and McDougal (1943); McDougal (1953); Chen (1989); Falk (1992 and 1970); Mendolvitz (1975); And see Gottlieb (1968) and Trimble (1990).

[30] See Carty (1986 and 1991 b); David Kennedy (1985–6; 1987 a; 1988); Koskenniemi (1989 and 1991); Boyle (1985); Purvis (1991).

[31] See Charlesworth and Chinkin (1993); Chinkin (1991); Gardham (1991); Waring (1991); Wright (1991); Romany (1993).

approaches to theorizing authority and are thus of limited value in theorizing the historical effectivity of the law merchant. Many reproduce the distinctions between private and public spheres and economics and politics, thus obscuring the political significance of transnational economic law.

In international relations, unconventional approaches include feminist[32] and postmodern analysis,[33] as well as work inspired by Marxism, historical materialism,[34] critical theory and Gramscian analysis,[35] and structural analysis, including dependency theory and world-systems theory.[36] However, unconventional approaches to international relations have failed to generate a critical understanding of international law, probably because they too have fallen victim to the "ghost" of legal formalism and a fetishized understanding of international law.

International legal theories

There is something quite odd about referring to natural law as an "unconventional theory," given its historical significance in the articulation of modern international law (see generally, Cutler, 1991; 2002 c). However, to the extent that legal positivism has so thoroughly displaced natural law thinking as the dominant approach, the latter takes on an unconventional character of sorts. Natural law theory predated legal positivism and in many ways precipitated the latter's rise to prominence. For natural lawyers such as the Stoics, Cicero, and Aquinas, there was no question that law mattered. Indeed, belief in the existence of universal transcendent legal principles that could be apprehended through right reason formed the foundations for the earliest forms of international law (*jus gentium*), predating the formation of the state system (see Beck, Arend, and Vander Lugt, 1996: ch. 2). Grotius is probably the best-known natural lawyer, whose work paved the way for legal positivism and an increasingly state-centric view of both the subjects and sources of the law (see Lauterpacht, 1946; Bull, 1966). Grotius theorized law to

32 See Enloe (1989 and 1993); Marchand and Runyan (1999); Peterson and Runyan (1993); Pettman (1996); Steans (1998); Sylvester (1994); Tickner (1992); Whitworth (1994); Zalewski and Parpart (1998).

33 See Ashley and Walker (1990); Campbell (1998); Connolly (1993); Der Derian and Shapiro (1989); Walker (1987; 1993); Weber (1995).

34 See Marx (1976); Marx and Engels (1965); Lenin (1939); Halliday (1994); Rosenberg (1994); Hobson (1965); Brewer (1990); Owen and Sutcliffe (1972).

35 Gramsci (1971); Cox with Sinclair (1996); Gill (1990; 1993 a; 1993 b); Rupert (1995); Murphy (1994); Linklater (1982; 1990); Brown (1992).

36 See Amin (1974 and 1990); Cardoso and Faletto (1979); Chase-Dunn (1989); Frank (1966; 1979); Evans (1979); Wallerstein (1974; 1980; 1989); Galtung (1971).

be based upon both universal principles *and* state consent, anticipating the advent of legal positivism as the theory most consistent with the emerging doctrine of sovereignty (see Bull, Kingsbury, and Roberts, 1990). Early natural law theorists clearly accepted the individual as a subject of international law, although by the time of Grotius the state was clearly beginning to assume greater centrality (see Cutler, 1991). In terms of the sources of law, early naturalists drew upon divine law, transcendental natural law principles, and state-made law, reflecting considerable pluralism in legal regulation. They also regarded law as infused by morality and as an integral element in a larger social totality. Significantly, though, they imputed considerable neutrality and objectivity to its operation by virtue of its link to transcendent and rational principles. Moreover, natural law thinking tended toward a conservative ethos that was inconsistent with revolutionary or transformative impulses.[37]

Although natural law thinking has receded in importance, it continues to influence modern thought. Natural law beliefs in a plurality of legal subjects and sources and the infusion of law with moral values inform international human rights and environmental laws, theories on just war and humanitarian intervention, and the prosecution of war crimes trials, many of which developments are pushing beyond the confines of existing international law.[38] Other approaches, such as New Haven, critical legal studies, and feminism also reproduce significant natural law tendencies (Beck, Arend, and Vander Lugt, 1996: 36). However, most of these approaches developed in response to perceived inadequacies in both natural law and positive law theories. At root was a suspicion that law operated neither neutrally nor as an objective system of rules. Critics emphasized the socially constructed, subjective, and even indeterminate nature of law.

The New Haven approach originated in the work of two Yale professors, Myres McDougal and Harold Lasswell, who sought to develop a "policy-oriented jurisprudence." The approach is interdisciplinary, drawing on law, political science, sociology, and psychology (see generally, Beck, Arend, and Vander Lugt, 1996: ch. 5). It challenges the legal positivist view that law is a body of rules, positing that it

[37] See Cutler (1991: 65) for the insight of Lauterpacht (1946: 14) that the natural law tradition "has served more often than not as the bulwark of the existing order of things than as a lever of progress."

[38] See Cutler (2002 a) for analysis of the revolutionary potential of emerging rules of customary international law that are inspired, at least in part, by natural law thinking.

is an "authoritative decision-making process" involving a multiplicity of participants and choices between competing norms and values (see McDougal and Lasswell, 1959; Lasswell and Reisman, 1968). New Haven scholars thus reject the conventional identification of the state as the only proper subject, arguing that there are many "participants" involved in the process of authoritative decision making (Higgins, 1985; McDougal and Lasswell, 1959; Arzt and Lukashuk, 1998). Rosalyn Higgins (1994: 49) describes the legal distinction between subjects and objects as "an intellectual prison of our own choosing" and advocates a more pluralistic approach that embraces a multiplicity of participants in international law. These participants include states, individuals, groups, and basically any collection of entities seeking to make claims and realize values in the international arena. New Haven scholars thus reflect the natural law position that membership in international society is not limited to states, but extends to individuals as well (Cutler, 1991).

They also reject formalism concerning the sources of the law, asserting the legal status of General Assembly resolutions and arguing that subjects doctrine does not adequately account for the status of individuals under international human rights law (Higgins, 1963). Presumptions of the separation of law from society and morality are also rejected and the law is defined in terms of its normative content.[39] This reflects the natural law position on sources, subjects, and the moral content of law. However, New Haven scholars reject naturalist claims about the objectivity and neutrality of the law. Rather, law is posited to be a construct of states and other participants and is said to promote the values and norms they adopt. Law is thus not an objective and neutral order and its efficacy turns on the extent to which the participants, subjectively, regard it as authoritative and, objectively, behave in accordance with its precepts. Law is clearly regarded as a transformative influence, particularly in the context of the World Order Models Project (WOMP), which attempts to promote international legal values that are consistent with the "basic values of human dignity or a free society."[40] However, critics fault the approach for assuming a unity of the social sphere in the existence

[39] For an interesting discussion of law and policy, see Higgins (1968).

[40] Richard Falk of Princeton University worked with other participants in the World Order Models Project (WOMP), which drew upon the New Haven Approach in order to formulate alternate visions of world order more consistent with the fundamental value of human dignity. See Falk and Kim, (1982: 1–9) for a history of WOMP. See also, Beck, Arend, and Vander Lugt (1996: 142–3) for useful bibliographical references to applications of the New Haven Approach. And see Falk (1992).

of a *single* international community.[41] Moreover, upon close inspection the community values and interests promoted appear to "match closely to the utopian policy prescriptions of American idealists in the post-Second World War era." These were predominantly "Western liberal values" leading to the charge that the "international law enterprise thus becomes a vehicle for Western cultural imperialism" (Trimble, 1990: 815). The New Haven school never did develop a fully critical edge as it was displaced by the emerging critical legal studies movement.[42]

Critical legal studies in international law, also referred to as the "New Stream," adopt the insight that law is constructed by participants in the lawmaking process. Drawing on eclectic and interdisciplinary insights from "normative philosophy, critical theory, structuralism, anthropology, prepositional logic, literature, sociology, politics, and psychiatry" (Purvis, 1991: 88–9), the New Stream is regarded as a "post-modern approach" to international law (Carty, 1991 b: 66), with significant roots in the European critical theory tradition (Purvis, 1991: cf. 89). Critical theory "refers to a particular style of work developed primarily by a group of German intellectuals who saw themselves as the inheritors of a tradition begun by Hegel and Marx . . . [and who were] concerned with overcoming the split between theory and action" (David Kennedy, 1985–6: 216–17). Known generally as the Frankfurt School, they were concerned about making theory an active and liberating force, drawing on Marxist roots in their analysis of class relations. Law was regarded as a mechanism of legitimation, as the institutional manifestation of the dominant ideology.

Critical legal scholars reject the naturalist appeals to transcendental, universal, and neutral legal principles and the positivist premise that law operates as a body of rules. Rather, law is regarded as a "discourse" and as an "ideology" that transmits imagery about the world through legal rhetoric. As such, we can study it through linguistic analysis, focussing "upon the hidden ideologies, attitudes and structures which lie behind discourse, rather than upon the subject matter of the legal talk" (David Kennedy, 1980: 355). Moreover, central to the constructed and ideological nature of law is the dialectical tension between law's role in constituting and empowering the state (through legal doctrines

[41] Trimble (1990: 815) directs this criticism at a specific text, Chen (1989), however, the criticism may be applied to the New Haven Approach more generally.

[42] Contemporary adherents of the New Haven school continue to press for a broadening of the principles governing legal personality to include individuals. See Higgins (1994); Arzt and Lukashuk (1998); and Chen (1989).

associated with state sovereignty including: those governing the use of force; acquisition of territory; sources and subjects of law; and so on) and its role as a regulator and critic of state action. David Kennedy (1988), who first developed this approach, posits that international legal discourse is characterized by the rhetorical movement between these two competing roles (see also, Cutler 2001 a). There is thus no objective content to law; its content is indeterminate and a function of the ideological uses to which it is put.

Central to the New Stream is a critique of the liberal foundations of international law, which posit the nature and role of law to be the impartial settlement of disputes through the application of objective legal principles. The liberal "rule of law" for New Stream scholars is an impossibility given the indeterminacy and ideological nature of legal argument or "rhetoric" (see also, Kratochwil, 2000: 43–51). Critical legal scholars also object to the "exclusionary" nature of state-centric subjects and sources doctrines, which operate as "mechanisms of exclusion" excluding "actual social difference" in the face of the "logic of state orthodoxy" (David Kennedy, 1988: 25). Critical legal theorists reject the state-centricity of international legal doctrine governing subjects, arguing that this simply does not "describe adequately the role of the individual as a subject of international law," particularly in the area of international human rights law (Purvis, 1991: 62).

However, as Beck, Arend, and Vander Lugt (1996: 229) note, there is little constructive role for the law in this view: "because doctrinal arguments merely mask ideological forces, international law is incapable of playing the neutral role traditional approaches prescribe for it. It cannot resolve dilemmas. Instead, it mirrors and reinforces them through its rhetorical structure." Critical legal studies does not make the necessary transformative links between the ideology and materiality of international law or between the theory and practice of the law. As Phillip Trimble (1990: 832) emphasizes, the result of the rhetorical analysis "seems eerily empty" and obscures the pervasive influence and material significance of international law in the promotion of self-interests and the legitimization of actions. Although Trimble (1990: 823–4) recognizes that David Kennedy "clearly is no admirer of positivism," he argues that the latter "projects law and politics as self-contained belief systems, and thus treats international law as an autonomous body" by adopting a structuralist position that excludes the historical and political content of international law and thereby severs law from its "political base." As a result, critical legal analysis empties international law of its historicity and materiality.

The idea that international law does not operate neutrally, but serves to promote particularistic interests and values, is carried forward into other critical approaches. Feminist theorists of international law, however, believe that law matters, not as an autonomous, neutral, or objective legal order (see Charlesworth, Chinkin, and Wright, 1991), but rather, they theorize international law as promoting patriarchal institutions, structures, and methods of legal reasoning.[43] Like the critical legal studies approach, feminist approaches are highly interdisciplinary. However, many feminist scholars focus on both the doctrinal and practical dimensions of patriarchy. The former involves critical analysis of the gendered basis of concepts that regulate the substantive content of international law to exclude matters of particular concern to women. (Charlesworth and Chinkin, 1993; Wright, 1991; Charlesworth 1992 b). The focus on doctrine involves, for example, a critical review of limitations on the scope of legal concepts such as torture, slavery, war crimes, crimes against humanity, and the like, that exclude actions having a disproportionate effect on women, such as rape, forced pregnancy, and prostitution (Byrnes, 1992: 214; Kim, 1993; Gardam, 1991). It also includes a powerful attack on the public/private distinction as a "culturally constructed ideology" that generates real, material injustices (Charlesworth, Chinkin, and Wright, 1991: 627; see also, Bedjaoui, 1979; Charlesworth, 1992 a; Romany, 1993).

The focus on the practical aspects of patriarchy involves analysis of the ways in which lawmaking institutions exclude women. Feminist scholars in both international law and international relations have challenged the state-centricity of conventional approaches and the way in which national governments and international organizations have typically excluded specifically women's issues from emerging human rights norms (see, for example, Chinkin, 2000). Exclusionary hiring and consultation practices of national governments and international organizations and the limitation of conference diplomacy to participation by states and international organizations have generated considerable concern that there should be provision for the inclusion of individual and group participation in international legal forums (Whitworth, 1994;

[43] There are clearly many feminist approaches to law, including liberal, radical, social/psychological, Marxist, socialist, existentialist, and postmodern. See Kim (1993).

Charlesworth, Chinkin, and Wright, 1991). These feminist scholars argue that the increasing participation of women and women's groups in the decision-making structures of national governments and in international governmental and nongovernmental organizations is assisting in the practical inclusion of women in the development of the normative foundations of the global polity. However, until there is a rethinking of the doctrinal foundations of international legal personality, the formal inclusion of women as subjects will not occur. Moreover, the efficacy of the whole human rights regime rests upon developing a sounder foundation for individuals to assert their rights against states under international law by opening up all relevant human rights forums to participation by individual litigants.

For feminists, law matters as a source of both exploitation and potential emancipation. Feminist scholarship rejects legal positivism as a theory of law that is unsuitable for promoting social change. Positive international law is defined and enforced by states whose interests militate against empowering those who might use the law to challenge the conduct of their own state. Natural law theory is faulted as well for its narrow and limited definition of rights drawing upon exclusively Western and male standards (Kim, 1993: 65–6). Feminists thus reject the idea that states are the proper subject or sources of the law and they embrace its socially constructed and potentially emancipatory nature.

Critical legal studies and feminist scholarship go a long way in upsetting the tendencies toward state-centrism and legal formalism that pose theoretical obstacles to analyzing pluralism in authority relations. Both emphasize the inherent normativity, socially constructed, and ideological nature of the law. However, while critical legal scholarship in international law is helpful in displacing legal positivist and natural law fictions about the neutrality and objectivity of law, it does not recognize the centrality of material interests in the formulation of law to enable the construction of an adequate theory or political economy of international law.[44] As Nigel Purvis (1991: 126–7) notes, the commitment of critical legal scholars to modernist criticism and their belief in the predominantly rhetorical and ideological nature of law block the kind of theory construction necessary to contemplating a "more coherent international order. Unfortunately, criticism degenerates into cynicism. It shackles judgment, necessarily separating its critical conception of international

44 Hunt (1993: 180–1) makes this criticism in reference to critical legal studies and domestic law; however, it is equally applicable to international law.

life from an affirmative vision about world order. Criticism cannot actively, programmatically, or normatively participate in the structuring of the international order. It cannot bridge the gap between theory and action."

In addition, as Alan Hunt (1993) observes, many critical legal scholars have been concerned to distance themselves from what they perceived to be crude, economically deterministic, and instrumentalist views of law in their emphasis on disclosing the ideological nature and incoherence of law as a discourse.[45] The discomfort of critical legal theorists with the traditional Marxist distinction between the economic base and the ideological superstructure of capitalism thwarted efforts to theorize the materiality and historical effectivity of law (Purvis, 1991: cf. 89). Efforts to establish the effective role of law as ideology in the creation of relations of dominance and exploitation in the world could not be achieved if law remained merely part of the superstructure. As a result, critical legal studies have not generated a corpus on Marxist theories of international law, although many critical legal scholars are influenced by Marxist analysis.[46] Nor has international law generated analysis that could form a viable alternative to conventional theory.[47] The hold of

[45] According to Hunt (1993): "The influence of Marxist scholarship in the United States has been very limited. It is significant for an understanding of critical legal theory to note that just as Marxism begins to have some influence on radicalized intellectuals during the 1970s, this occurs precisely at the time when the Marxist tradition itself was going through its most significant internal upheaval of recent times. The period in which critical legal studies comes into existence is one in which its radical political perspective encounters a bewildering variety of internal variation, differentiation, and sectarianism within contemporary Marxism. This made the adoption of any single strand of modern Marxist theory unlikely, but more importantly, reduced the general attraction of Marxism as the alternative intellectual paradigm. Second, the strand of Marxism that has had the greatest influence within critical legal theory focuses on the processes of legitimacy and of hegemony. This strand, even in its earliest formulation by Gramsci, and even more clearly in the case of the Frankfurt School of 'critical theory,'was concerned to search for linkages with other intellectual traditions, the most important of those being with European sociology, especially that of Max Weber" (146–7).

[46] But see, Chimni (1993) who attempts to develop a Marxist theory of international law as part of the superstructure of world capitalism. Also, as we shall see in the next section, critical legal studies of domestic law have produced some powerful critiques of law that provide inspiration for the development of critical theory in international law. Here the works of Karl Klare, Isaac Balbus, and Morton Horwitz are significant.

[47] It is curious to note that few international legal texts stray much beyond critical legal studies and feminism in their presentation of alternate views, if they represent such views at all. See Brownlie (1998); Shaw (1997). One of the most significant texts (Malanczuk, 1997: 33) has a scant two pages dedicated to "New developments in theory" and states that theory "has limited relevance for the actual practice of states and the problems that have to be solved in daily life." This reflects belief in a profound gap between the theory and practice of international law. Moreover, Marxist theories of international law are reported

conventional state-centric and public notions of authority remains apparently unassailable. Feminist scholarship alone appears to offer transformative possibilities, linking legal theory with political practices in important ways that require further consideration and examination in the context of developing a program of action. As we turn to consider unconventional approaches to international relations, we will see that significant problems characterize these theoretical approaches to law as well.

International relations theories

The absence of a robust transformative and critical understanding in the field of international law is mirrored in the field of international relations for curiously similar reasons. If international legal scholars are guilty of a legal formalism that fetishizes and, indeed, reifies the law, producing a static and unhistoric concept of law, unconventional international relations scholars are guilty of marginalizing international law as an historically effective material and ideational force. Either through the reproduction of the general skepticism or cynicism about international law expressed by conventional realist and neorealist approaches, or through instrumental analysis that simply equates international law with the interests and ideologies of the dominant actors in the world, the law is similarly robbed of its historicity and transformative capacity. However, this need not be the case and unconventional approaches have much to offer in terms of identifying the material and practical consequences of international legal doctrines.

Unconventional approaches to international relations were identified above with feminist analysis, historical materialism, critical theory, Gramscian analysis, and structural analysis, including dependency theory and world-systems theory. While these approaches challenge the dominance of structures of patriarchy, production, inequality, and underdevelopment, they are not concerned with developing theories of law. The reasons for this are complex and involve more traditional disciplinary and professional considerations flowing from the separate treatment of international law and international relations. They also

to have "vanished from the arena" and to be of "mere historical interest" at "least for the time being." Barker (2000: 54) observes that alternative views tend to be regarded as "deconstructivist" and are consequently "sidelined." It is probably important to note that the critical legal studies movement was founded in the United States, which has never been a hospitable home to critical theory, notwithstanding the brief popularity of the New Left.

involve deeper problems flowing from Marxist theorizations of law more generally. Each will be addressed in turn.

Disciplinary and professional considerations

Skepticism about the transformative capacity of law amongst scholars who make dominant structures and processes of inequality, patriarchy, production, and underdevelopment their focus of study has important disciplinary and professional roots. While the fields of international law and international relations share disciplinary origins, it is hardly obvious today in both conventional and unconventional theory. As Louis Henkin (1968: 6) remarked in his *locus classicus, How Nations Behave*, the "student of law and the student of politics . . . purport to be looking at the same world from the vantage point of important disciplines. It seems unfortunate, indeed destructive, that they should not at least, hear each other." Kenneth Abbott (1992: 167) has similarly observed that it "has been difficult to tell for the last twenty years that the two disciplines were talking about the same world." Indeed, in the words of Anne-Marie Slaughter-Burley (1993: 217), many international relations scholars have "been explicitly distancing themselves from anything called 'law' for twenty years." A number of disciplinary considerations produced the gulf between international relations and international legal scholarship, at least in the United States.[48] As noted earlier, realists such as Hans Morgenthau and George Kennan shared great intolerance if not open contempt for moralistic and legalistic approaches to international affairs. Reasoning that it was faith in international law and institutions that led to the horrors of the Second World War, the postwar generation of scholars were keen not to commit the same mistake again.[49] Hence, international relations came to be framed in terms of politics and not law or morality, which last concepts were used almost interchangeably. Efforts to create a scientific study of international relations also figured prominently in a growing antipathy to historical and textual analysis, in

[48] The situation is quite different in the United Kingdom where the "English School" and students of international society have never fully embraced the disciplinary division. The "English School" of international relations comprises a fast-growing assortment of scholars studying numerous subjects. It is impossible to do justice to the approach in a single note; however, some of the representative texts include Bull (1977); Bull and Watson (1985); Watson (1992); Bull, Kingsbury, and Roberts (1990); Buzan (1993); Buzan, Jones, and Little (1993); Hurrell (1993); Shaw (1994); James (1978); Jackson (2000).

[49] For good reviews of the evolution of the discipline of international relations as it relates to the study of international law and organization, see Rochester (1986 and 1995); Kratochwil and Ruggie (1986); Haggard and Simmons (1987).

favor of quantitative methodologies. These tendencies created a gap between the disciplines, marginalizing what international relations scholars came to see as overly legalistic and formalistic approaches.

While there are numerous attempts today to reunite the two disciplines,[50] the dominant self-images of the discipline of international relations have coalesced in theories, as we have noted earlier, that do not easily embrace international law.[51] Professional practices contribute to this state of affairs, ensuring that the disciplines remain distinct.[52]

Moreover, to the extent that unconventional political theorists do address international law directly, there is a tendency to reproduce many of the orientations of the dominant theories. A good example may be found in the work of David Held (1995), a political theorist who has engaged international law more directly than most international relations theorists. Held accepts many of the criticisms we have noted about the inability of conventional theories to comprehend transformations in global power and authority.

> In an age in which there are many determinants of the distribution of power, many power centres and authority systems operating within and across borders, the bases of politics and of democratic theory have to be recast. The meaning and nature of power, authority and accountability have to be re-examined. In what follows, I seek to do this and to argue that the concept of legitimate political power or authority has to be separated from its exclusive traditional association with states and fixed national borders. (Ibid., 22)

So far so good. Concepts of political authority that are cast in the context of the territorial state need recasting. However, Held (ibid., 227) proceeds to do so by fashioning a notion of "cosmopolitan law:" "a democratic public law entrenched within and across borders." Cosmopolitan democratic law will provide "the international framework for political life" by knitting states together under the umbrella of a Kantian "rule of law." Cosmopolitan law "transcends the particular claims of nations and states and extends to all in the 'universal community'" (ibid., 230). However, the reference to a "universal community" evokes images of public definitions of authority premised upon the presumption of the

50 For a useful bibliography of attempts to reintegrate the disciplines, see Slaughter, Tulumello, and Wood (1998).

51 For the durability of dominant self-images in international relations, see Steve Smith (1995).

52 For professional and disciplinary sources of international relations theory, see Kahler (1997).

unity of the social sphere, which we noted above is deeply problematic in the context of the pluralization and privatization of authority. But Held does not engage in analyzing either this problem or the inconsistency of his supposition of a "universal community" with his recognition of multiple sources of state and nonstate power.[53] Exactly who comprises this "universal community"? Held (ibid.) notes that the decision-making centers of this community:

> need not only be states. Networks of states, that is regions, could in principle assume this form, on the one hand, while sub-national entities or transnational communities, organizations and agencies might do so on the other ... *Sovereignty is an attribute of the basic democratic law, but it could be entrenched and drawn upon in diverse self-regulating associations, from states to cities and corporations.* (234, original emphasis)

Just how universalized sovereignty is to mesh with the foundations of existing international law, in terms of subjects and sources doctrines, is not addressed. Nor are the mechanics of universalized sovereignty considered. But the problem runs even deeper, for the "universal community" is based upon respect for state sovereignty and autonomy. Held (ibid., 231) states that "the idea of cosmopolitan community can be located between the principles of federalism and confederalism:" a "single, unified, international state structure ought not to be regarded as an aim; it is impractical and undesirable for many of the reasons Kant gave." In addition, the community is based upon voluntary, consensual membership (ibid., 231). Cosmopolitan law is beginning to sound here like existing consent-based public international law, while its ill-developed theoretical foundations suggest the application of the domestic analogy, legal formalism, and belief in the autonomy of the law. Just how cosmopolitan law, like the White Knight, is going to revolutionize our understanding and practices of authority remains obscure. International law has not generally been known for its democratic pedigree.[54] As the critical legal scholar David Kennedy (1988) has commented:

> we would find in the origins of international law not a moment of tolerant generality, of liberality, but a well articulated practice of social intolerance. For it was the law of peoples which worked to exclude the

[53] Held (1995: ch. 8) identifies seven sites of power, including: the human body; welfare (the organization of goods and services that provide for community membership); culture; civic association; the economy; the organization of violence; the sphere of legal and regulatory institutions.

[54] See Crawford (1993) and see Picciotto (2001), for a sensitive and insightful analysis of democratizing the changing mechanisms and processes of global governance.

> Jew, the homosexual, the heretic, and perhaps most crucially, worked to suppress the exuberance of spiritual fervour, displacing it with bureaucracy. The suppression of witchcraft, sorcery, but also of ecstatic millenarianism, and their replacement by the logic of state orthodoxy, was a practice of religious inter-sovereign action. (25)

Now, this is not to argue that the law is incapable of promoting democratic ends, just that the association of the "rule of law" and democracy is a presumption that needs to be probed and considered critically in the context of the historicity, materiality, and ideology of international law. This uncritical and unhistorical adoption of the "rule of law" and cosmopolitan law do not assist at all in understanding the significance of law in the global political economy and its implications in the juridification, pluralization, and privatization of global governance. The law is simply assumed to be "there" as an unproblematic and fetishized entity whose operation we need not address, because we all know what law is and does. It is simply assumed that "democratic public law" can deal with the "tension" between liberal democracy and "the existing distribution of resources" (Held, 1995: 265). This is a profoundly apolitical understanding of law.[55] Moreover, once again, the world of private international law and the "private" distribution of resources drops from view, eclipsed by "public" definitions of authority and law.

Marxist theories of law

The inattention of unconventional scholarship to international law is also attributable to a possibly more profound reason than disciplinary and professional practices. If the analytical and theoretical foundations of conventional theories pose problems for capturing contemporary global transformations, Marxist theories are no less troubled. The problem stems in part from ambiguity in Marx's treatment of law and subsequent interpretations that relegated law to the superstructure of capitalism. It also stems from instrumentalist theories that accorded little historical effectivity to the law. As part of the superstructure of capitalism, along with other forms of "social consciousness," such as ideology, law was hard to reconcile with a materialist conception of history.

[55] It is interesting to note that many sociological analyses produce apolitical understandings of law. The great sociologists Emile Durkheim and Max Weber both tended towards apolitical understandings of law. See Hunt (1982 a) and Beirne (1982). This tendency is also evident in the analyses of Gunther Teubner and Pierre Bourdieu who attribute an independence, spontaneity, and automaticity to law that tend towards the externalization and fetishism of law. See McCahery and Picciotto (1995: 238–42). But see Bourdieu (1987).

Neither Marx nor Engels developed a systematic theory of law, although Marx's writings did engage in negative critique of bourgeois law (see Vincent, 1993; Campbell and Wiles, 1980). Marx never succeeded in developing an understanding of the law in relation to the mode of production and commodity form of capitalism (Balbus, 1977). As a result of certain ambiguity in Marx's view of law and notwithstanding the consideration that he neither abandoned law nor declared it to be historically irrelevant, as Andrew Vincent (1993: 378) notes, many subsequent Marxists tended to regard law as part of the superstructure and not the base of capitalism (see also, Fraser, 1978; Balbus, 1977). As such the law was not an effective historical force and as Santos (1982 b) notes, law has no place in revolutionary strategy.

Scholars note that there was an increased interest in the law amongst Western radical scholars in the 1970s that paralleled the more general concern with what was perceived to be a crisis of the capitalist state.[56] Theorization of the "relative autonomy of the law" tended to reproduce debates over the relative autonomy of the state and produced many insights into the extent to which radical legal theories are capable of theorizing the historical effectivity of the law or simply reproduce the tendencies of the dominant approaches toward apolitical and

[56] Holloway and Picciotto (1978: 1–2) associated the crisis of the state with "the urgent need for an adequate understanding of the state and its relations to the process of capitalist accumulation and crisis. In the past, Marxist theory, in so far as it has dealt with the state at all, has too often confined itself to showing that the state acts in the interests of capital and to analysing the correspondence between the *content* of state activity and the interests of the ruling class. For an understanding of political development and the possibilities of political action, however, such an analysis is inadequate. In a period characterized on the one hand by the serious questioning of state interventionist policies and on the other by the rise of communist parties in some countries, the whole question of the limits to state action becomes crucial" (1–2). Beirne and Quinney (1982: 12) associate the revival of Marxist attention to law with the work of Louis Althusser and the insight from his work with Étienne Balibar, *Reading Capital* (1970: 230), that the capitalist mode of production "presupposes the existence of a legal system." They note that a year later Althusser's essay, "Ideology and Ideological State Apparatuses" (1971) was made available in English: "The basis of this article was the seminal – if not entirely original – claim that the distinction between the public and private realms of social life was a distinction formulated by and internal to bourgeois law. The state was therefore every element that contributed to the cohesion of the social formation. In the Althusserian scheme, law occupies a unique role as a state apparatus in that it simultaneously discharges both ideological and repressive functions. Legal ideology lies at the heart of bourgeois individualism ('interpellating the subject'), and the primacy of the juridical subject contributes to the partial neutralization of the class struggle. In other words, for Althusser law is a condition of existence of the capitalist mode of production. Law has its own ('relative autonomous') logic of internal development. No longer could it be reduced to the level of a mere superstructural and passive reflection of economic and other relations." For good reviews of the status of sociological studies of law in the 1970s and 1980s see Feeley (1976) and Spitzer (1983).

unhistoric formalism and positivism.[57] These debates are thus instructive in our inquiry into the nature and operations of law and merit some consideration.

Instrumentalist theories developed an understanding of law as merely the tool or instrument of the dominant class or a reflection of the consciousness and ideology of the dominant class. Accordingly, all that was regarded as analytically or theoretically necessary in order to capture the significance of law was to analyze the law in terms of its role in disciplining and manipulating the subordinate elements of society. However, critics of such thinking argued that instrumentalism reproduces the liberal distinctions between economics and politics, associating law with the political and ideological superstructure.[58] This neglects the economic foundations of law, for it "fails to pose the problem of the specific *form* of the law and the way in which this form articulates with the overall requirements of the capitalist system in which these social actors function" (Balbus, 1977: 571). Moreover, instrumentalism produces an apolitical understanding of law because it regards law as an "expression" of what is, "rather than an arena of struggle, a forum with potential political and economic effects" (Hirst, 1979: 137–8).[59]

[57] See Jessop (1980) for what continues to be an excellent review of different theoretical traditions in Marxist approaches to law. Jessop identifies a dominant tradition in Marxism–Leninism that regarded law as a reflection of the economic base in the private sphere and as an instrument of domination in the public sphere. In the 1960s this view was challenged by the "capital logic" school in Germany, inspired by the work of the Soviet legal theorist Evgenii Pashukanis, and which is evident today in the work of a number of thinkers. This "principle concern has been to derive the necessity of specific forms of law and to reveal the essential class character of the law beneath its appearance of equality, neutrality and universality" (ibid., 341). However, Jessop observes that this approach tends to be ahistorical and to focus on exchange and not productive relations. A second challenge appeared in the form of Althusserian structuralism, evident in the work of Louis Althusser and Nikos Poulantzas, for example, which also rejected crude economic determinism by according law a significant autonomy, but recognizing that economics are determining "in the last instance." Another challenge developed in the adoption of insights from Gramsci concerning the operation of the legal system in securing domination through the constitution of hegemony in different historical conjunctures. See Fraser (1976) for a good discussion of the inadequacies of commodity-form theory in light of changes in the nature of capitalism and the capitalist state.

[58] See Holloway and Picciotto (1978) for the reproduction of the separation between economics and politics in Marxist theories of the state. And see Picciotto (1979).

[59] Hirst argues that Marxist theories of law that rely on Marx's notion of the centrality of the autonomous legal subject, as constituted by private law, assume the distinction of private and public law (because they associate private law with the regulation of the relations of individuals and public law with the state) and tend toward legal formalism by attributing autonomy to the sphere of private relations and their law. Also, in a remarkably prescient observation, Hirst notes how the supposition of the private sphere as a construct of individual subjects excludes from view new corporate legal forms that are not reducible

Thus, like legal positivism, instrumentalist theories fall victim to the tendency to fetishize law by separating it from the "social totality," "disintegrating the unity of law and economic process" and thus obscuring that "law is literally the effected voice of the relations of production" (Gabel, 1977: 622).[60] In the following passage Fraser (1978) captures the problems generated by both instrumentalist and positivist theories of law, which present law divorced from "human subjects in the process of making their own history" (ibid., 160):

> Such an instrumentalist conception of law precludes the possibility of developing a sensitive awareness of the legal process as a form of creative social praxis in its own right. To conceive of law as an inert tool deprives it of any social character and treats it instead as something like a physical fact external to the concrete individuals who create, apply, and are affected by it. Marxist instrumentalism, like bourgeois positivism, conceives the law as only a formal structure of rules, categorically distinct from the social context within which that set of rules is placed. (152)

For Fraser (1978: 160), Marxist instrumentalist theories present law divorced from human agency.

Considerable dissatisfaction with this rather rudimentary and crude understanding of the law has led a number of Marxists to develop the idea of the "relative autonomy of the law." According to this notion, law is autonomous from the will of social actors, but "entails at the same time an essential *identity* or homology between the legal form and the very 'cell' of capitalist society, the commodity form" (Balbus, 1977: 573). Others, such as E. P. Thompson (1975: 261), reject as untenable the distinction between "law, on the one hand, conceived of as an element of 'superstructure', and the actualities of productive forces and relations

to the individual, such as corporate forms of property, and thus is inadequate in the theorization of new and emerging forms of property. The inadequacy of Marx's theorization of the individual as the autonomous subject takes on even greater significance in terms of the "problem of the subject" under international law, which is addressed in the concluding chapter. See also Fraser (1976: 123) for the "intellectual poverty and theoretical sterility" of instrumentalist theories and their incapacity to adequately theorize the contemporary capitalist state.

[60] Sol Picciotto (1979: 622) comments upon the tendency of Marxist analysis to impute an automaticity to law as relatively autonomous from the economy and society, which presents the law "as a neutral and historically unchanging state apparatus," thus masking its relationship to the creation of the material conditions of life. See also Fraser (1976: 129) for criticism of the fundamentally unhistorical tendency to represent "the law as a self-contained, ontologically distinct conceptual universe" and exploration of this tendency in the work of Pashukanis and Poulantzas.

on the other hand" and articulate the view that the law is "deeply imbricated within the very basis of productive relations." Thompson (ibid., 262) submits that law functions in three ways: as an instrument "mediating and reinforcing existent class relations;" as an ideology, legitimating class relations; and as a material expression of class relations through legal forms.[61] He counters superstructural theories of law thus:

> the rules and categories of law penetrate every level of society, effect vertical as well as horizontal definitions of men's rights and status and contribute to men's self-definition or sense of identity. As such law has not only been *imposed* upon men from above: it has also been a medium within which other social conflicts have been fought out. Productive relations themselves are, in part, only meaningful in terms of their definitions at law: the serf; the free labourer; the cottager with common rights, the inhabitant without; the unfree proletarian, the picket conscious of his rights; the landless labourer who may still sue his employer for assault. (Ibid)

Ellen Meiksins Wood (1995: 27) too notes that "relations, of production themselves take the form of particular juridical and political relations – modes of domination and coercion, forms of property and social organization – which are not mere secondary reflexes, nor even just external supports, but *constituents* of the productive relations."

These approaches challenge the continuing relevance of the base-superstructure distinction, purely materialist conceptions of history, and the resulting tendency to peripheralize the significance of law. They

[61] Thompson's analysis of the history of the Black Act in the eighteenth century is instructive as an attempt to capture the materiality and ideology of the law. He illustrates (1975: 260–1) how the law evolved as very much a part of the "ascendancy of the Whig oligarchy, which created new laws and bent old legal forms in order to legitimize its own property and status; this oligarchy employed law, both instrumentally and ideologically, very much as a modern structural Marxist should expect it to do. But this is not the same thing as to say that the rulers had need of law in order to oppress the ruled, while those who were ruled had need of none. What is often at issue was not property, supported by law, against no-property; it was alternative definitions of property-rights: for the landowner, enclosure; for the cottager, common rights; for the forest officialdom, 'preserved grounds' for the deer; for the foresters, the right to take turfs. For as long as it remained possible, the ruled – if they could find a purse and a lawyer – would actually fight for their rights by means of law; occasionally copyholders, resting upon the precedents of sixteenth-century law, could actually win a case. When it ceased to be possible to continue the fight at all, men still felt a sense of legal wrong: the propertied had obtained their power by illegitimate means."

suggest that there is a need to review the analytical foundations of historical materialism, particularly in light of transformations in late capitalism that are rendering the distinction of increasingly dubious analytical and theoretical utility. Karl Klare (1979) argues against the viability of the base-superstructure distinction in the face of changes in capitalist production involving the politicization of the base with government involvement in the economy, the transformation of the superstructure with the increasing infusion of private matters into public affairs (labor, education, welfare), and changes in the nature of the capitalist state in terms of its corporativism, bureaucratization, and the legitimation functions of the state.[62] In a similar vein, Fraser (1978) identifies the need to understand the role of new forms of law that are enabling the fusion of public and private authority and making possible new forms of rationalized and objectified domination. He asserts (ibid., 148) "law must be a central category in any theory of sociality within advanced capitalist societies." However, Marxist instrumentalism has resulted in the disappearance of the human subject, who "has been swallowed up by the capitalist mode of production" (ibid., 167). In an effort to restore human beings as effective agents of historical change, Fraser (ibid., 184–5) thus urges that we "take seriously Gramsci's observation that all people, as political beings, are also legislators in the sense that 'every man, inasmuch as he is active, i.e. living, contributes to modifying the social environment in which he develops . . . in other words, he tends to establish 'norms, rules of living and of behavior' . . . Liberation requires that radical lawyers . . . acknowledge the extent to which we are active participants in our own oppression and alienation."[63]

Marxist instrumentalism thus obscures the extent to which law participates in the constitution of capitalist productive and social relations through moves that, while very distinct from those characterizing conventional theory, nevertheless remove human agency from the picture. A critical understanding of law thus requires a theory that is capable of capturing the connectedness of law, politics, economics, and society. It must be capable of theorizing law as both a material and an ideological force operating with a public and a private face.

[62] See also Roberto Unger (1976).

[63] Fraser (1978: 183) notes how "forms of legality have come themselves to express directly the relations of domination. But that domination is no longer a form of direct personal oppression experienced in the 'private' fields of economic and social relationships" as contemplated under traditional Marxist analysis of the "individual juridical subject." It is now manifest in the "public world of bureaucratic organization" as rationalized domination.

Social Forces, Law, and World Order

A critical understanding of law might begin by accepting the criticisms raised above of the base-superstructure distinction and theorizing law as part of the base of capitalism. This requires investigating the role that law plays in the constitution of the mode of production, the route taken by a number of theorists.[64] Relatedly, we might draw on critical theory and a "looser materialism" that conceptualizes Marxism as a form of "praxis" uniting theory and practice in a symbiotic and reciprocal relationship. This conception denies unidirectional claims of base over superstructure or the material over the ideational.[65]

> The alternative looser materialism can be observed in the elusive Marxist doctrine of 'praxis' (where 'theory' and 'practice' have a symbiotic and reciprocal relation). The basic logic of praxis argument denies the basic premise of the unidirectionality claim [that material conditions causally determine thought and political/legal structures]; that is it asserts that reflective thought and consciousness (as embodied in philosophical, economic, or legal thought) can actually affect our material conditions. We can accommodate our theory to our practices and vice versa. Put simply, human reflective thought has definitive efficacy; it is not just an epiphenomenon of the material conditions of life.
>
> (Vincent, 1993: 379)

Accordingly, one might conceive of law as praxis through analysis of the role of law in constituting the mode of production and the dialectical tension between competing class interests for different historic blocs.[66] Robert Cox (1993 b) has adapted the concept of historic bloc (*blocco storico*) developed by Antonio Gramsci in his analysis of capitalist societies in the 1920s and 1930s, to the study of international relations. Cox (1987: 105) defines an historic bloc as "the configuration of social forces upon which state power ultimately rests" and "the configuration of social classes and ideology that gives content to a historical state"

64 See Balbus (1977); Gabel (1977). And see Cutler (2002 d) where transformations in world order from medieval to capitalist to late capitalist modes of production are analyzed in the context of changing property rights and competing theories of property law that are argued to be constitutive of the mode of production for different historic blocs. The contemporary historical conjuncture is said to reflect a dialectical tension between two conceptions of property. One conception of property as "bundles of rights" works in favor of patterns of transnational capital accumulation. In opposition, the conception of property as "ownership of things" works in favor of patterns of national capital accumulation. See also, Boyle (1996).

65 Vincent (1993); Klare (1979); Cutler (2002 a; 2002 b).

66 Cox (1987); Gramsci (1971); Gill (1993 a); Cutler (1999 b).

(Cox, 1987: 409, n. 10). Social forces are identified as material capabilities, ideas, and institutions (Cox, 1996 a). Material capabilities are "productive and destructive potentials. In their dynamic form these exist as technological and organizational capabilities, and in their accumulated forms as natural resources which technology can transform, stocks of equipment...and the wealth which can command these" (ibid., 98). Ideas consist of intersubjective meanings concerning the nature of social relations that condition behavior and expectations of behavior and the collective images of a social order held by different groups, which may conflict and give rise to new, alternative historic structures (ibid., 98–9). Institutions are amalgams of both ideas and material capabilities and initially reflect the power relations which obtain at their point of creation, but which take on a life of their own and often become the site of conflicting influences (ibid., 99). Indeed, institutions, like international organizations, are important facilitators and legitimators of particular historic blocs (Cox, 1993 b: 138). These social forces are in turn linked to particular state formations and world orders, which may be either hegemonic or nonhegemonic. State formations are determined by the nature of productive relations and are linked to the particular world order prevailing (Cox, 1987: ch. 1). A hegemonic world order is one:

> where the dominant state creates an order based ideologically on a broad measure of consent, functioning according to general principles that in fact ensure the continuing supremacy of the leading state or states and leading social classes but at the same time offer some measure or prospect of satisfaction to the less powerful. In such an order, production in particular countries becomes connected through the mechanisms of a world economy and linked into world systems of production. (ibid., 7)

In contrast, a nonhegemonic world order is a situation where there is no dominant state or world order.[67]

Cox (1987) theorizes that the concept of historic bloc is dialectical in that it contemplates both material and ideational forces that may exist in conflict, giving rise to a crisis of hegemony and representation:

> In such a situation, old and new social forces coexisted, but the old ones had become detached from the political organizations that had formerly represented them, and the new ones had not yet produced

[67] See also, Cox (1996 c: 55–6) for the distinction between hegemonic and nonhegemonic world orders.

> organizations or "organic" intellectuals who could lead them effectively and bring them into coalescence with existing social forces to form a new hegemonic bloc. Two outcomes are possible in an organic crisis: either the constitution of a new hegemony or caesarism, i.e., the freezing of unresolved contradictions. (273)

Like Gramsci, Cox assigns a special role to the "organic intellectuals" who play central roles in the creation of hegemony and consent. They are organically connected to social class and "perform the function of developing and sustaining the mental images, technologies, and organizations which bind together the members of a class and of an historic bloc into a common identity" (Cox, 1993 b: 132). Moreover, law performs a valuable function in establishing the framework for productive relations and is thus a crucial influence in the constitution and reconstitution of state–society relations for different historic blocs (Cox, 1987: 106–7).

Drawing on Gramsci's understanding of hegemony and the ideological mechanisms by which laws become internalized in the consciousness of people, we might thus theorize law as an effective agent in history (see Vincent, 1993: 383–4).[68] Operating predominantly by consent and

[68] Vincent (1993: 374) notes that in the 1970s there was a "surge of interest in the Italian Marxist, Antonio Gramsci" and his "conception of law as ideology and, in consequence, law as a crucial part of the intellectual hegemony of capitalist societies." A number of scholars have engaged in the application of Gramsci to a critical understanding of law. See, for example, those works listed in Jessop (1980) and Benney (1983). And see Hunt (1982 b: 87) for the view that the influence of Gramsci on critical theories of law has been unwarrantedly narrowed by the view of Perry Anderson (1976–7) that Gramsci emphasized the coercive over the consensual operation of law. Rather, Hunt (1982 b: 87) argues that "Gramsci has been the main vehicle that has facilitated the emergence of Marxist analysis of law precisely because it no longer requires an invocation of the primacy of coercion in state and class relations. In this sense, the very existence of Marxist analyses of law owes much to the wider dissemination of Gramsci's writings." These authors clearly disagree with the observation of Bellamy (1990: 336) that Gramsci "showed no awareness of the role the state plays in protecting the diversity of society by upholding the rule of law and the rights of individuals." This latter view shows little sensitivity to the problem Marxist analysts have had in "locating" law in the complexity of relations between the state and civil society and Gramsci's broadened notion of civil society as comprehending material and ideational influences, as well as coercive and consensual relations. For Gramsci's broad notion of civil society see Cox (1993 b; 1999). Nor does Bellamy exhibit an awareness of the challenges that the concept and practice of the "rule of law" pose for critical analysis and emancipatory politics. The belief of many radical theorists that revolutionary societies would have no need for law inhibited historical materialist analysis of law for some time. See Santos (1982 b).

It is also instructive to consider the work of Franz Neumann and Otto Kirchheimer, two critical theorists associated with the Frankfurt School, who engaged in considerable analysis of the political and ideological significance of law. While neither theorized the law as constitutive of the mode of production of capitalism, their work reflects an acute

persuasion, but at the margin by coercion, legal hegemony assists in creating "a social conformism which is useful to the ruling group's line of development" (Gramsci, 1971: 195).[69] Law thus, in addition to creating the material conditions of existence, serves important legitimating functions.[70] But equally important, lawmaking may be regarded as a "form of praxis" and a "constitutive component of the social totality" whose dialectical operations give rise to potentially emancipatory and liberating practices (Klare, 1979: 128).

Drawing upon these insights, we might conceive of international law as a form of praxis involving a dialectical relationship between theory and practice, thought and action, and law and politics. This involves developing a constitutive theory of international law in which the law is understood as operating in a dialectical movement between legal theory and the practices of the actors. Following Gramsci, the philosophy of praxis and the unity of theory and practice is not a "mechanical fact," but a "part of a historical process" (Gramsci, 2000: 334). Theory and practice are not factors that "stand apart from and influence each other in a this-then-that fashion," but "are to be grasped as constituents of living form which are elaborated within the movement of a social totality" (Gabel, 1977: 635–6). The objective is to "free Marxist theory of law from its deterministic integument – i.e., the notion that law is a mere instrument of class power – and to conceive the legal process, at least in part, in a manner in which class relationships are created and articulated, that is, to view lawmaking as a form of praxis" (Klare, 1979: 128). This involves demystifying international law and making its theory relevant to the practices of politics and the lived experiences of people. International lawmaking is thus to be understood in dynamic terms as a process giving rise to material, institutional, and ideological conditions embodying both oppressive and potentially emancipatory social relations. This approach rejects the domestic analogy and embraces the view that law is a social construct with an integral role to play in emancipatory politics. Law exists not as a fixed body of neutral and objectively determinable

awareness of the significance of law in establishing the basic material, institutional, and ideological framework for society (see Scheuerman, 1996). See also Cutler (1999 c) where maritime transport law is analyzed over roughly a millennium as an integral aspect of changing material and ideological conditions.

69 See also Benney (1983) and Cutler (1999 a) on the balance between consent and coercion in Gramsci's notion of hegemony.

70 Benney (1983: 207) notes that the "Gramscian approach to law constitutes a real point of entry into orthodox jurisprudence for Marxist critics of law," notwithstanding the caution of Bellamy (1990) that we must confine Gramsci to his specific historic and political context.

rules, but as a construct of, and thus deeply embedded in, international society. As we turn to briefly review the history of the law merchant it becomes apparent that the law is implicated in the constitution of very distinctive authority structures.

Historical Development of the Law Merchant

It was noted earlier that the historical evolution of the law merchant reveals a dialectical movement in the consolidation and expansion of corporate power. This movement in turn parallels the consolidation of state power and capitalism in the nation-state and the subsequent transnational expansion of capitalism beyond the nation-state and it involves a rich diversity of state and nonstate agents. The law merchant is conventionally regarded as having passed through three phases in its historical development.[71] An examination of these phases illustrates the specificity of the relationship between different forms of authority and different political economies and societies. In particular, the specificity of the relationship between, on the one hand, law and processes of juridification and, on the other, the emergence of capitalist states becomes evident. These phases illustrate the specificity of the relationship between forms of authority and different historic blocs.

The first phase, lasting from the eleventh to sixteenth centuries, is characterized as one of medieval internationalism and the universality of merchant laws and mechanisms for dispute resolution. At this time the law merchant operated as an autonomous system of law, for it was independent of local systems of law. Medieval merchants constituted a separate class with their own law and court system, operating outside the feudal political economy and on the margins of medieval society as a privatized, informal, and discretionary order. The order was first and foremost a customary order, reflecting the state of the medieval and feudal understandings of law and the highly personalized character of feudal authority relations. Processes and institutions of law-creation and dispute resolution formed an autonomous, informal, decentralized, and privatized regulatory order located in pockets throughout the European trading world.

A second phase, lasting from the seventeenth to nineteenth centuries, is marked by the localization and nationalization of the merchant law

[71] While subsequent chapters will review the history of the law merchant, Berman and Kaufman (1978) provide a useful review.

and institutions as modern territorial states developed and assumed greater control over international commercial activities. At this time, merchants disappeared as an autonomous class because their commercial activities and laws were incorporated into national legal systems where they were neutralized of political function as part of the private sphere of civil society. The merchant courts were absorbed into national legal systems, while merchant laws were integrated into national laws governing property, contract, and commercial relations in general. The juridification of commercial relations forged the material and ideological relationship between positive law and capitalism, a relationship that theorists such as Max Weber came to associate specifically with capitalist states. Legislation in the form of systematic, centralized, rationalized regulation replaced decentralized custom and discretion as the mode of governance suitable to the consolidation of power in emerging territorial states and facilitated the emergence of capitalist political economies. At this time there was considerable erosion of the universality of the law merchant as local and national differentiations emerged.

The third phase, from the nineteenth century to the present, is regarded as one of modern internationalism and transnationalism as states move globally to adopt uniform commercial laws and uniform institutions for dispute resolution. Institutionally and normatively, the movement for the unification of international commercial law is at the center of law-creation and dispute settlement. European in origin, the unification movement has expanded to include most regions of the world and most legal and political systems, intensifying legal regulation and the juridification of commerce. Juridified commercial relations are intensifying geographically, as well as in scope, as transformations in local and global political economies create new forms of commercial relations and new claims to identity under commercial law. In addition, there is considerable pluralism in contemporary law-creation and a shift to highly privatized and discretionary dispute resolution. The aspirations from a variety of nonstate subjects and sources for identity, whether through the recognition of women or individuals as subjects of the law, or recognition of new "soft" law sources, or the claims of aboriginal people as bearers of intellectual property rights, are evident. They suggest that the locus of authority is no longer adequately reflected in terms of the public realm of territorial states or understood critically through class relations alone.

As subsequent chapters show, the significant role that private authority has played in the creation and enforcement of merchant law in the medieval and modern phases of the law merchant suggests considerable symmetry and unity between the periods (Cutler, 2001 b). It is thus not difficult to see how the predominantly *private* nature of the medieval law merchant system is suggestive of the contemporary expansion of private authority in the governance of the global political economy. Today, however, merchants operate autonomously and privately with the full sanction and support of political authorities. Moreover, the mercatocracy does not operate outside the contemporary political economy, as did medieval merchants, but in a space that is *insulated within* the global political economy. The shift in the locus of merchant authority is part of a much broader development in the movement from feudal to capitalist and late capitalist political economies and the emergence and transformations in distinctions between the public and private realms, or politics and economics, respectively. However, although the mercatocracy is a central player in the intensification of juridified relations and in the pluralization and privatization of law-creation and dispute settlement, it is not the only active or aspiring player, either materially or ideologically. Contestation over the hegemony of the mercatocracy is evident in the tensions at the margins of the law governing legal sources and subjects, suggesting that its insulation is not a necessary condition of the current global political economy, but is subject to transformative and emancipatory politics.

These developments are central to understanding analytical differences between the medieval and modern law merchant and the historical specificity of structures of global governance. Moreover, they also provide insight into the significance of contemporary transformations in the global political economy that are giving rise to the expansion of juridified, pluralized, and privatized governance in both law-creation and dispute resolution.

The historic specificity of global authority, however, only becomes visible when one departs from the conventional approaches to international relations and adopts a critical approach. A critical approach rejects distinctions between private and public activities, economics and politics, domestic and international affairs and recognizes the political salience of private subnational and transnational socioeconomic forces (see Rosenberg, 1994). It also rejects unhistoric and apolitical theorizations of international anarchy, legal formalism, and belief in the autonomy of the law. To this end, the following chapters examine a range of forces that have defined and redefined the nature of global political authority over time. The study thus draws upon the insights of critical thinkers and "loose" historical materialists such as Robert Cox and Antonio Gramsci, identifying material capabilities, ideology, and institutions as three categories of forces that interact to produce historical structures or blocs that are constitutive of global authority at given times. The study also draws on the insights of a number of scholars who are attempting to historicize and to bring a critical voice to the study of international relations and international law. However, the analysis builds on them in important respects in the attempt to develop a theory of praxis that engages transformatively with the expansion of private transnational corporate power in the constitution of global political authority.

Chapters 4 through 6 will address each historical period in the development of the law merchant order, linking the processes and institutions engaged in law-creation and dispute resolution with the political economies and societies of the day. The objective is to illustrate both the materiality and normativity of the law merchant as a crucial determinant of political, economic, and social relations, locally and globally.

4 Medieval *lex mercatoria*

The law merchant has been described as "a venerable old lady who has twice disappeared from the face of the earth and twice been resuscitated" (Goldman, 1983: 3). Berthold Goldman here refers to the disappearance of the Roman *jus gentium*, occasioned by the breakup of the Roman world and both the disintegration of international economic relations in the Middle Ages and its reappearance in eleventh-century Europe with the rebirth of international commerce. The second disappearance is said to have occurred in the seventeenth century when nation-states localized and nationalized commercial law, resulting in a period of hibernation that lasted until the reappearance of a modern *lex mercatoria* in the twentieth century. Legal theorists generally agree that the law merchant has progressed through three phases in its evolution, although few would agree that it had ever "disappeared from the face of the earth."[1] However, the characterization of its development as a continuous movement or progression from the first phase of medieval internationalism, through the second of localization and nationalization, to the third of modern internationalism and transnationalism misses sharp discontinuities and changes flowing from altered historical, material, ideological, and institutional conditions. The law merchant is implicated in significant changes in society and political economy over its three phases. It has changed in relation to changing social, political, and economic conditions. But it has also contributed to their transformation. This chapter analyzes the first phase in the development of the law merchant. The medieval law merchant order contributed to the expansion

[1] See generally, Schmitthoff (1961; 1964 b; 1981; 1982); Berman and Kaufman (1978): Goldstajn (1981); *Report of the United Nations on the Progressive Development of the Law of International Trade* (1968–70).

of trade and commerce by devising and enforcing commercial transactions that avoided feudal restrictions on the mobility of capital and the transmissibility of property (see North, 1991). These developments contributed to the early articulation of the private sphere of capital accumulation, anticipating what was to become the domain of markets, economics, and civil society. Moreover, they occurred independently of local political authorities and sovereigns. The medieval law merchant system comprised a deterritorialized legal order "that did not derive its normative claims from treaties amongst sovereign states" (Santos, 1995: 289). Indeed, the medieval law merchant supported a predominantly private commercial order, generating merchant laws and institutions that operated *outside* the local political economy of the period. While local transactions were heavily regulated by political authorities, long-distance trade was largely immune to the application of local laws and was governed by the law merchant. Although there was considerable normative and institutional pluralism in the medieval authority structure, including church law, feudal law, manorial law, mercantile law, and urban law,[2] local political and religious authorities were generally incapable of enforcing merchant law and deferred to the merchant courts. The former did not participate in the regulation of international trade, beyond the granting of charters to trade and to hold fairs and markets, the general provision of safe conduct for merchants in their transit to the fairs and markets, and awarding exemptions from local laws in return for the payment of customs and duties.[3] This gave rise to a dualistic system of commercial governance: the regulation of local transaction under the local systems of law and the regulation of wholesale and long-distance transactions under the autonomous law merchant system.

The imprecision in the location of authority evident in this dualistic regulatory order reflects considerable ambiguity in the social and political foundations of the period. This is associated more generally with the feudal organization of society and production. As Perry Anderson (1974 b: 408) observes, it was not the singular nature of class relations alone that constituted the feudal mode of production, but "their specific organization in a vertically articulated system of parcellised sovereignty and scalar property that distinguished the feudal mode of production in Europe." The parcelization of authority relations reflected and

[2] See Berman (1977: 896; 1983).
[3] See generally, Clough and Cole (1946); Pirenne (1937).

embodied specific class relations.[4] Anderson (1974 a) describes the feudal mode of production thus:

> It was a mode of production dominated by the land and a natural economy, in which neither labour nor the products of labour were commodities. The immediate producer – the peasant – was united to the means of production – the soil – by a specific social relationship. The literal formula of this relationship was provided by the legal definition of serfdom – *glebae adscripti* or bound to the earth: serfs had juridically restricted mobility. The peasants who occupied and tilled the land were not its owners. Agrarian property was privately controlled by a class of feudal lords, who extracted a surplus from the peasants by politico-legal relations of compulsion. This extra-economic coercion, taking the form of labour services, rents in kind or customary dues owed to the individual lord by the peasant, was exercised both on the manorial demesne attached directly to the person of the lord, and on strip tenancies or virgates cultivated by the peasant . . . The peasant was subject to the jurisdiction of his lord. At the same time, the property rights of the lord over his land were typically of degree only: he was invested in them by a superior noble (or nobles), to whom he would owe knight-service . . . His estates were, in other words, held as a fief. The liege lord in his turn would often be a vassal of a feudal superior, and the chain of such dependent tenures linked to military service would extend upwards to the highest peak of the system – in most cases, a monarch – of whom all land could in the ultimate instance be in principle the eminent domain. (147)

However, there was little consistency or universality in the incidence of feudal property relations in that there was a "range of juridical, political, and economic institutions – namely fiefdom, vassalage and serfdom – characteristic to a greater or lesser extent of a particular epoch of medieval European history" (Holton, 1985: 27). This in turn reflects pluralism in political authority structures: "[i]n early modern Europe, at least at first, a government could be an Italian city, a feudal principality, the Hanseatic League, or a more familiar empire or kingdom" (Pearson, 1991: 43).

What is distinctive about the medieval law merchant order is the essentially self-regulatory nature of the merchant community in both law-creation (subjects and sources) and dispute resolution. This in turn reflects the more general autonomy of the merchant class from the feudal class system: the law merchant order occupied a space external to

[4] See Wood (1995: 36 –9) for an excellent review of the historical specificity of class and authority relations.

the local political economy and feudal mode of production. Even more importantly, the law merchant created property rights and entitlements that were quite inconsistent with medieval conceptions of property – entitlements that were more consistent with property relations that would later be associated with capitalism. In addition, while there was no distinction yet between public and private international law, the merchant community provides an early hint of what was to become the private realm later with the development of capitalism and the juridification and privatization of commercial relations. Moreover, the dualistic regulation of local and foreign transactions anticipates what was to become a differentiation between domestic and international economic relations. These observations suggest that the notion of "a transition from feudalism to capitalism" really does miss the crucial historical insight that "it is to pre-feudal, or quite simply non-feudal institutions that one must turn in order to locate many of the most significant aspects of the emergence of capitalism" (Holton, 1985: 28).

The analytical focus of this chapter is on two fundamental aspects of the law merchant. The first is law-creation and concerns the subjects and sources involved in creating the medieval law merchant, while the second relates to dispute resolution and enforcement. The pivotal role played by merchant custom as a source of law in the construction of an autonomous merchant regime is highlighted as a defining characteristic of the medieval system of governance, as too is the unique merchant court system that was created to settle commercial disputes and to enforce agreements. As subsequent chapters show, it is the customary character of the medieval regulatory order that differentiates it most acutely from subsequent capitalist and late capitalist orders and suggests that the freedoms enjoyed by medieval long-distance traders cannot be assimilated to that of later times. It took the emergence of capitalism and the private sphere of the disembedded market, along with the articulation of liberal political economy and the juridification of commerce, to constitute the modern merchant class. These developments served to legitimize commercial activity and the merchant class, which had been considered of questionable moral character, to medieval ecclesiastics. These developments occurred within the more general context of the dismantling of the feudal mode of production and associated ideological and institutional developments.

In addition, the law merchant achieved considerable universality throughout the European trading world, which relates to the commercial ascendance of different regions and cities. However, before turning to consider the medieval practices in law-creation and enforcement, it is important to review the historical, material, and ideological context of medieval trade and commerce. The next section reviews the broader context in which the dualistic regulatory order emerged, contrasting the strict disciplinary nature of feudal commercial regulation with the permissive and flexible law merchant order. Although more or less autonomous, the law merchant order intersected at points with the feudal order, resulting in some cross-fertilization of legal conceptions that remain with us today. The discussion next moves to law-creation and enforcement under the law merchant and focusses on the novelty of commercial transactions devised through merchant customs and practices and enforced in merchant courts. Many of these practices were developed to circumvent feudal restrictions on the transmissibility of property and the mobility of capital and they reflected conceptions of property quite at odds with the medieval conception and more consistent with capitalist conceptions of property. The system of enforcement also anticipates more contemporary developments in the privatization of dispute settlement.

Medieval *Jus Commune* and *Jus Gentium*

Europe in the eleventh and twelfth centuries experienced a commercial revival associated with the opening of trade markets in the East and with the economic and political changes brought by the rise in Europe of cities and towns as autonomous political units.[5] The Islamic invasions beginning in the seventh century interrupted merchant commerce and coupled with the advent of feudalism in the ninth century, which occasioned the disappearance of towns and most merchant activity, reduced most of Europe to a "purely agricultural state" (Pirenne, 1937). Henri Pirenne (ibid., 12) observes that "from every point of view, Western Europe, from the ninth century onwards, appears in the light of an essentially rural society, in which exchange and the movement of goods had sunk to the lowest possible ebb. The merchant class had disappeared. A man's condition was now determined by his relation to the land." Pockets of commerce persisted, however, as Venice, Amalfi, Naples, and other Italian cities continued to trade with Byzantium and the Scandinavian countries engaged in trade in the North and Baltic Seas. As Shepard Clough (1959) notes:

[5] See generally, Pirenne (1937); Lopez (1971); Clough (1959).

> Although trade over long distances existed in the Adriatic and in the North and Baltic Seas during the first half of the Middle Ages, most of Western Europe's economy was moribund, based as it was on a rigid land tenure system and upon production for immediate consumption. By the end of the eleventh century, however, there were many signs of economic growth and in the twelfth and thirteenth centuries a revival took place which was to break the older rigidities and greatly extend the range of commercial opportunities. Many forces, such as growth in population, the rise of towns, greater industrial production, and more extensive trade, initiated this change. (77)

While he suggests that to "attribute to any one of them the ultimate cause of what took place is to raise the problem of whether the hen, the egg, or the rooster came first to the poultry kingdom," he identifies the commercial expansion in northern Italy and in the Low Countries as of particular significance (ibid., 77 and 81). The Crusades had freed up the Mediterranean for trade, facilitating the commercial growth of the Italian cities. Venetian and Genoese traders brought goods to the port of Bruges, regarded as the "Venice of the North," which, along with other North and Baltic Sea ports, was experiencing a growth in trade (ibid., 80–2).

It was in the Italian cities and northern port and market towns that the law merchant had its origins. As these trading communities grew and as commerce expanded, merchants created a system of law to govern their commercial activities. This system of law drew initially upon ancient Greek maritime customs, the Roman law of sales, debt, and general civil obligations, as well as the Roman *jus gentium* (law of nations). Then and for some time to come, maritime and commercial law, together, formed the foundation of the law merchant. In a seventeenth-century treatise on the law merchant, Gerard de Malynes (1981: 45) observed the interrelatedness of maritime and commercial law: "[e]ven as the roundness of the globe of the world is composed of the earth and waters; so the body of the *Lex Mercatoria* is made and framed of the Merchant Customs and sea laws, which are involved together as the sea and the earth."

Merchants in ports drew upon the Sea Law of Rhodes, which was received and transmitted to Western Europe by the Greeks and Romans.[6]

[6] There is some disagreement as to the dating and origins of the Sea Law of Rhodes. Most historians date it from 300 BC, although some go back to 900 BC. See Benedict (1909). And see Bewes (1923: ch. 6) for the view that the Rhodian Sea Law is probably not confined to Greek sources, but likely derives from more ancient civilizations. For a review of the historical evolution of maritime transport law, see Cutler (1999 c).

In the eleventh century the Italian Republic of Amalfi produced a collection of maritime laws called the Amalfian Table, which was adopted by all the Italian cities,[7] while the seaport towns of the Atlantic and North Sea and England adopted a collection of maritime judgments of the Court of Oleron on the French coast (Sanborn, 1930; Mitchell, 1904). These laws and customs spread to other commercial centers in Europe as patterns of trade changed creating new centers of commercial activity.[8] In the fourteenth century the Baltic ports adopted the Laws of Wisby, thought to be modelled on the Laws of Oleron, while the Consulato del Mare of Barcelona, consisting of a compilation of the customs of the sea applied in the Consular Courts of Barcelona and based upon the customs of the Italian cities, gained wide currency in the ports of the Mediterranean (Berman and Kaufman, 1978: 253; Pollock, 1901).

Simultaneously, inland towns were developing a body of law to regulate overland trade in the markets and fairs of Europe. In Germany, England, and northern France the law merchant developed in the context of the fair, while in Italy and in southern France it developed in the context of the city-state (Sanborn, 1930: 31). In England, in the thirteenth century the Fair of St. Ives was regarded by English and foreign merchants as "one of the most important in England" (Selden Society, 1908: xxxiii). On the Continent, the fairs and courts of Champagne "had a universal importance" from the twelfth to the fourteenth centuries, while the Fair of Lyon became a major commercial center in the fifteenth and sixteenth centuries (Sanborn, 1930: 157 and 170–1). In Italy, courts held in the commercial cities of Venice, Florence, Genoa, and Pisa were responsible for significant advances in the development of the law merchant (ibid., 137–48). The fair courts developed somewhat later in Germany in the fifteenth, sixteenth, and seventeenth centuries (ibid., 178).

The law governing sales and market transactions drew upon a number of sources, most notably Roman and German sales laws, which were modified by merchant customs, and to a lesser extent, canon law (Mitchell, 1904: ch. 5). The fairs came to play an important role in facilitating the growth of commerce by providing security and safe conduct for merchants, while the fair courts contributed to the universalization of merchant law and custom. Consuls accompanied merchants to the

[7] See generally, Sanborn (1930) and Mitchell (1904).
[8] For discussion of the impact of the shift in commercial power from the Mediterranean to the Atlantic, see Clough and Cole (1946: ch. 6).

fairs and represented them in fair courts. As Wyndam Bewes (1923: vi) observes, the "merchants carried their law, as it were, in the same consignment as their goods, and both law and goods remained in the places where they traded and became part of the general stock of the country." While more will be said shortly of the special role played by merchant courts held in the fairs, cities, and ports of Europe, Frederic Sanborn (1930) underlines their significance in the following observation:

> The privileges and the internal organization of the fairs constituted a very complete and ingenious system, the starting point in the evolution of the special law of the fairs, and all the more important because of the close commercial relations of the fairs with all that part of Europe from Flanders and England to Italy. The fair courts exercised a great influence upon the development of the modern Continental courts of commerce, for they were the first special courts, just as the peace of the fairs was the precursor of the modern peace of commerce. (169)

Merchants came to be accorded a special status in medieval society, as the law merchant emerged as a distinct and autonomous body of law regulating the activities of merchants, who were granted significant immunities from local laws and regulations (Pollock, 1901). The law merchant was regarded as the *jus commune* or common law of the medieval period (David, 1972 a: ch. 5). As Harold Berman and Colin Kaufman (1978) observe:

> The law merchant governed a special class of people (merchants) in special places (fairs, markets, and seaports). It was distinct from local, feudal, royal, and ecclesiastical law. Its special characteristics were that 1) it was transnational; 2) its principal source was mercantile customs; 3) it was administered not by professional judges but by merchants themselves; 4) its procedures were speedy and informal; and 5) it stressed equity, in the medieval sense of fairness, as an overriding principle. (225)

While local variations in the law merchant have been identified, universality in the fundamental principles applied to commercial relations throughout the European trading world have resulted in its characterization as both medieval *jus commune*, or common law, and *jus gentium*, or the law of nations. Indeed, in an authoritative essay on the law merchant Mitchell concludes that the "international nature of the sources from which it drew its rules and of the persons over whom it exercised jurisdiction, combined with the universality of its guiding principles, fairly entitle the Law Merchant to be called 'the private international law of the Middle Ages' " (Mitchell, 1904: 21).[9]

When we turn to consider law-creation and dispute resolution we will see that the medieval law merchant embodied principles that facilitated exchange through informal, expeditious, and flexible standards. It granted significant autonomy to merchants through the independent status accorded to merchants, their customs, and their courts. However, there were also other, at times incompatible, influences at work which gave rise to a dualistic system of economic/legal regulation. Ecclesiastical law also played a part in the development of commercial law in the medieval period.[10] Canon law embodied different notions of equity in commercial relations, stressing the need for fairness and equality in, and the distributional nature of, the exchange relationship. In contrast, the law merchant embodied the Roman law principle of deciding cases *ex aequo et bono*, by what is equal and good. According to this view, equity is less a matter of distribution or redistribution and more a "discretionary corrective" to be applied in specific cases so as to avoid the rigors and potential injustices of formal laws.[11] According to Sanborn:

> the courts of commerce were to proceed according to equity and to examine the truth of the fact itself, without regard to the formal legal rules of evidence and proof. There is nothing more characteristic of the medieval law of commerce than its spirit of equity, its desire for true justice, and its abhorrence of legal technicalities. To express this again we find certain phrases that are commonly used, or their equivalents: *ex aequo et bono, sola veritate rei inspecta, sola facti veritate inspecta*, etc. This principle of substantial equity runs through the *lex mercatoria* in every place at every period [references omitted].[12] (1930: 195)

The merchant courts were to tailor justice to the specific facts of each case, employing standards established by merchant custom and practice. However, canon law presented a different conception of equity. This conception regarded equity as a form of distributive justice, which

[9] Mitchell here quotes Justice Maitland to the effect that the law merchant is the "private international law" of the Middle Ages. See also Pollock and Maitland (1898: 467) for the characterization of the law merchant as "*jus gentium* known to merchants throughout Christendom." For its characterization as *jus commune*, see David and Brierly (1978) and David (1972 a).

[10] See generally, Tawney (1962) and Gilchrist (1969).

[11] This notion of equity came to form the foundation of the common law Court of Equity (or Chancery) and for Anglo-American and Continental civil law notions of equity under international law. For the former, see Scrutton (1907). For the latter, see Janis (1983). The reference to equity as a discretionary corrective is taken from Janis.

[12] See also Sanborn (1930: 143, 162, and 192) and Schmitthoff (1961: 135).

"does not suggest flexible correction of strict rules of law, whether *intra, praeter*, or *contra legem*, but rather suggests a norm correcting existing distributions of wealth" (Janis, 1983: 20).[13] The canonical view of equity was more consistent with the medieval view of society and stood in stark contrast with the view of equity evolving under the law merchant. Medieval ecclesiastics adopted a paternalistic attitude toward commercial relations that was reflective of an organic view of society combined with a general suspicion of material wealth.[14] Indeed, the "medieval thinker had a functional idea of society" (Clough and Cole, 1946: 66) according to which each person as a member of the organic whole belonged to a class and possessed a particular function in society. The accumulation of wealth in the attempt to change one's place in society was held in distrust.

> It was therefore wrong for a man to try to earn more than was necessary to keep him comfortable in the station of life to which he was born . . . The Middle Ages distrusted wealth . . . Of the ways of making money, that of the merchant or trader was to the Middle Ages particularly dangerous and suspect . . . To the strictest view, any profits from pure trade were wrong. (ibid., 67)

Medieval canon law regulated commerce with a view to protecting consumers and the general public from unscrupulous trade practices. "Matters of trade were, by and large, immediate and inter-personal, and therefore, the application of personal morality to personal activity was fairly easy" (ibid., 37). Trade was regarded as an "instrument of social purpose" whereby merchants were required to conform to standards of Christian morality (Hamilton, 1931: 1138). Thus, canon law provided the source for the principle of *pacta sunt servanda*, or the binding force of promises, which were not enforceable under either Roman civil law or the common law of the period.[15] As purely personal agreements, promises were regarded as "private" and thus not appropriate for the King's court. The following passage from Glanvill, a

[13] And see Schachter (1985) for further discussion of the concept of equity as distributive justice.

[14] See generally, Thompson (1971) and Murphy (1961–2).

[15] Bare promises (i.e. not under seal) were not enforceable under either the common law or the civil law. In fact, the history of the common law reveals great difficulty in enforcing bargains that do not meet the formalities required of contracts duly sealed and evidenced through the exchange of some material value. The law merchant drew on the ecclesiastical practice of enforcing such promises, greatly expanding the possibilities for exchange and forming the foundation for modern contract law. This subject is discussed in greater detail in Chapter 5. See also Farnsworth (1969).

twelfth-century text, explains the limited treatment of private agreements on the grounds that the royal court did not deal with such agreements: "We deal briefly with the foregoing contracts which are based on the consent of private persons because ... it is not the custom of the court of the lord king to protect private agreements, nor does it even concern itself with such contracts as can be considered like private agreements."[16] This is a surprising and prescient anticipation of the private/public distinction and illustrates the limited extent to which local legal systems regarded the regulation of commerce as their legitimate domain. The law merchant ultimately adopted the principle of *pacta sunt servanda* and came to enforce private transactions not enforceable in the King's court, thus expanding the scope of commercial exchange and laying the foundation for the modern law of contracts.

Meanwhile, under canon law merchants were required to make confession and to seek absolution before death, which often required making restitution for commercial offences. Excommunication was used by the Church as a means of enforcing the payment of debts and penalizing prohibited practices (Viner, 1978: ch. 2). Canonical notions of equity informed the prohibition of usury, the requirement of "just prices," and the imposition of standards of strict liability for defective goods. A negative attitude toward the taking of profits, a general distaste for men of commerce, and a desire to protect the consumer characterized medieval attitudes towards usury. Gilchrist (1969: 63–4) notes that the prohibition of usury "can be seen as a genuine attempt, somewhat misplaced when applied by rigorists to *all* profits of commercial enterprise, to protect consumer credit in an age when there were few opportunities to save for emergencies provoked by illness, disease, fire, war, alien seizure of one's goods or property, all of which deprived the peasant or the artisan of his means of livelihood and forced him into the hands of the moneylender or pawnbrokers." Others, too, identify consumer protection as the purpose of the prohibition of usury (Tawney, 1962: 45). The idea that fair or just exchange should represent rough equivalence in value, and that the taking of profit in the form of interest constituted the sin of avarice informed the attitudes of early medieval theologians. Thus, the general prohibition of interest charges of the twelfth and thirteenth centuries reflected the canonical conception of equity, emphasizing fairness, equality in exchange, and the distributive nature of commercial relations.

[16] This passage is taken from Simpson (1975: 4).

The requirement of just prices and the imposition of liability for defective goods also reflect canonical conceptions of equity. As Tawney (ibid., 152) notes, the "essence of the medieval scheme of economic ethics had been its insistence on equity in bargaining – a contract is fair, St. Thomas had said, when both parties gained from it equally." The monopolistic raising of prices through the manipulation of supplies, sales at prices that did not reflect equivalent value in exchange, and the taking of excessive profits were regarded as unjust. Malynes (1981), in the seventeenth century, formulated equity in prices in the following way:

> Every man knoweth, that in the Buying and Selling of Commodities there is an estimation and price demanded and agreed upon between both parties, according to a certain equality in the value of things, permuted by a true reason grounded upon the commodious use of things. So that equality is nothing else but a mutual voluntary estimation of things made in good order and true, wherein Inequity is not admitted or known. (67)

For many commodities prices were fixed by local authorities who considered market conditions, the level of necessary supplies, and the labor and costs of the producer (Tawney, 1962: 40–2). According to Gilchrist (1969: 61), "[a]rtificially fixed prices, brought about by base business methods, such as monopoly or price agreement, forestalling, regrating, and engrossing, were considered unjust." Local authorities thus intervened to prevent price manipulation by requiring that all sales take place in open markets (*market ouvert*) and by limiting the activities of middlemen through enforcing the market offences or rules against forestalling, engrossing, and regrating:

> *Forestalling* meant buying up goods before they got to the market, going out to intercept and purchase them on their way into town, or buying grain or produce in the country from the peasants who would normally have brought it into town. *Engrossing* meant trying to corner the market. In the middle ages supplies were limited, transportation was slow and difficult, and famine was usually imminent. By buying up large quantities of goods it was fairly easy to raise the price to the detriment of the townsfolk. *Regrating* was buying to sell again at a profit. It represented the tendency for a middleman to come between the producer and the consumer and was frowned on especially when it was speculative or was done in connection with foodstuffs . . . The prohibition of these practices was designed to protect the consumer as well as members of the gild. Since it had a monopoly of the local trade,

> the gild was forced both by policy and by the teachings of the Church to try to prevent the use of that monopoly to exploit the public.
> (Clough and Cole, 1946: 55)

Max Weber (1978 a: 931) attributes the emergence of market restrictions to the "propertyless" who "protested against monopolies, preemption, forestalling, and the withholding of goods from the market in order to raise prices. Today the central issue is the determination of the price of labour. The transition is represented by the fight for access to the market and for the determination of the price of products."[17] He observes that price controls protected consumers, while quality controls protected the export interests of traders and urban consumers as well.

Merchant guilds, granted legitimate monopolies by local authorities, assisted in the enforcement of market regulations in order to minimize outside competition.[18] When local authorities did not intervene to set prices, prices were established by the *communis estimatio*, or common estimation of the vendors. The individual was to be "guided by a consideration of 'what he must charge in order to maintain his position, and nourish himself suitably in it, and by a reasonable estimate of expenditure and labour' " (Clough and Cole, 1946: 40). The formal theory of the just price went through some modification as fourteenth- and fifteenth-century theologians explored the foundation of the rule of "common estimation" and developed distinctions between different types or grades of price (Tawney, 1962).

As in the case of the just price standard, the standards governing liability for defective goods reflected canon law and the paternalistic and collectivist nature of medieval commercial regulation.

> In medieval society the regulation of trade and commerce was characterized by a strong preference for the rights of the consumer. Extensive regulation sought to insure that all products were the result of good workmanship and proper measure, and that they were sold at a fair price. The community at large was also given preference.
> (Murphy, 1961–2: 3)[19]

[17] See also Weber's discussion (1978 a: 1,328–31) of the political economy of market and urban commercial regulation under feudalism.

[18] See Pirenne (1937: ch. 6) for a discussion of the origin and nature of merchant craft guilds. He argues that guilds performed a public function of consumer protection by enforcing the rules against members. The guilds also provided members with protected markets and were a source of revenue for local authorities who exacted payment in return for the monopoly rights granted to the guild. See also, Clough (1959: 99–103; Weber 1978 a: 1,328– 29).

[19] And see Pirenne (1937: 186).

As Hamilton (1931: 1152) notes, in the "prevailing legal theory it was not so much the buyer who was injured as the commune." Thomas Aquinas had taught that a seller sins and a sale is void if goods are sold containing a defect in kind, quantity, or quality of which the vendor has knowledge. Moreover, the vendor was required to compensate the purchaser for losses sustained by defects of which the vendor had no knowledge (Hamilton, 1931: 1,138). Medieval society adopted this standard of strict liability for defective goods. The vendor was accountable through annulment of the contract, compensation of the buyer, or a reduction in the purchase price. In addition, local authorities established quality control standards. Weights and measures were standardized and for many foodstuffs and manufactured goods, specific rules regulated material content, production methods, and measurement.[20] These regulations were enforced through a variety of means. Local authorities sent inspectors round to insure that artisans and merchants conformed to the rules. In England, the Court of Leet, or view of the frankpledge, was held twice a year at which time the conduct of merchants and tradesmen (e.g. bakers, butchers, tailors, goldsmiths, weavers, etc.) was reviewed. Attendees were expected to report upon the activities of others and records were kept of complaints regarding breaches of content, quality, measurement, and production standards.[21] Merchant guilds assisted in the enforcement of quality controls through the punishment or exclusion of members who breached the rules. "Artisans who broke the rules were severely punished by fines and suspensions; in the case of repeated infractions, they might be subjected to the ignominy of having their shoddy goods exposed before their shops for all to see. Still worse, the artisan might be read out of his guild and hence prevented from practising his trade" (Clough, 1959: 99). In the fairs and markets the rule of open market and the rule requiring "frontage," the open display of wares, contributed to the detection of nonconforming goods.

> The discipline imposed on the artisan naturally aimed at ensuring the irreproachable quality of manufactured products. In this sense it was exercised to the advantage of the consumer. The rigid regulation of the towns made scamped workmanship as impossible, or, at least, as difficult and as dangerous, in industry as was the adulteration in food. The severity of the punishments inflicted for fraud or even more for

[20] See Hamilton (1931) for a very extensive review of the sorts of quality control placed on foodstuffs and manufactured goods.

[21] Hamilton (1931: 1,144) notes that the Court of Leet performed a preventive and not a remedial function for there were no provisions for suits by aggrieved consumers.

> carelessness is astonishing. The artisan was not only subject to the constant control of municipal overseers, who had a right to enter his workshop by day or night, but also to that of the public, under whose eyes he was ordered to work at his window. (Pirenne, 1937: 186)

These practices illustrate the intensity with which both the Church and local or municipal authorities regulated trade and production. They regulated markets to ensure adequate supplies, to control prices, and to collect revenues from merchants who were granted the right to trade in markets and fairs. Local authorities regulated where, when, and what could be sold, in some cases to whom, as well as the administration of markets, in the grant of a right to convene a market or fair. This right could be acquired by prescriptive right or by prerogative grant. The right generally included "the right to police and justice... which had the effect of facilitating the enforcement of summary justice and the law of the market, apart from the ordinary King's jurisdiction and the common law" (Bewes, 1923: 104–5). While the jurisdictional right granted to hold a fair is considered later under the issue of dispute settlement, the grant of a fair specified when the fair could be held, the location, and the goods that could be sold. Local authorities granted merchants safe-conduct during the fair. In England, foreign merchants were granted exemptions from municipal regulations:

> In 1303 the Carta Mercatoria gave to certain foreign merchants, in return for certain customs duties, exemption from certain municipal dues, freedom to deal wholesale in all cities and towns, power to export their merchandise and liberty to dwell where they pleased. They were promised speedy justice "secundum legem mercatoriam" from the officials "feriarum, civitatum, burgorum, et villarum mercatoriariarum;" and any misdoings of these officials were to be punished.
> (Holdsworth, 1907: 301)

Viner (1978: 46) observes that it was not until the seventeenth century and later that there was a "secular literature of economic analysis which could compete with, substitute for, or influence the economic content of scholastic moral theology."[22] Thus it can be said that the

> dominant note of the period was authority. The social organization was a hierarchy of controls: the individual, if such there was, owed allegiance to priest and bishop of Holy Church, to lord and Baron of

[22] Viner defines the term "scholastic" to cover all Catholic moral theologians and canonists who wrote in the tradition of the Church from the late Middle Ages to the end of the sixteenth century.

> Feudal order, to gild and town of a rising third estate. The foundations of obedience, which underlay all human activity, were established by churchmen. The world was the great penitential wherein man was fitted for the Kingdom of heaven; the human being, conceived in iniquity and born in sin, was a depraved person; he must be kept free from the world, the flesh, and the devil; his plans, his actions, and even his thoughts were to be supervised by his betters, – to the great end of the salvation of his mortal soul. The spirit of the age, at least in ideal, imposed a religious purpose upon all human conduct.
>
> (Hamilton, 1931: 1,136–17)

However, religious and municipal discipline was not generally extended to merchants engaged in long-distance and wholesale trade. There was a double standard operating in the Church's attitude towards material wealth, evident in the tolerance of some economic practices and the prohibition of others. This produced a somewhat uneven application of religious sanctions on commercial practices.[23] Moreover, merchants involved in long-distance and wholesale trade were granted immunities from local laws and, as is addressed in the next section, devised unique instruments to evade and avoid religious and municipal regulations. As a general rule, foreign and wholesale trade were not subject to the just price requirement and merchants engaged in such trade were not subject to prosecution for committing market offences.[24] Clough argues that market and price regulations reflected class distinctions.

> Since the city fathers were exclusively consumers of foodstuffs, they wanted adequate and steady supplies at reasonable, if not low prices. To achieve their ends they forced on both peasants and retail food manufacturers all kind of restrictive rules and those people had to submit to them because they depended on cities for markets... no such strict rules were applied to the wholesale business in foods in long-distance trade, for some of the rich merchants were engaged in this activity and they did not want to do anything to curb their opportunities for making a profit.
>
> (1959: 98)

He (ibid., 99) notes that "a kind of a 'deal'" was struck between the municipal authorities and individual, local, and retail trades whereby

[23] Gilchrist (1969: ch. 4) identifies a tension in the Church's permissive attitude toward private property and slavery, but its condemnation of avarice, particularly in trade. He shows how this came to be reflected in the application of dual standards to various commercial activities.

[24] For examples of the enforcement of market offences in the thirteenth and fourteenth centuries, see Selden Society (1892).

the latter would be granted a monopoly of business in return for enforcing the canonical requirement of a just price and market offences. These rules were strictly enforced against local retailers and "had considerable efficacy in maintaining honesty, quality, and fair prices."[25] Ecclesiastical authorities imposed the sanctions of excommunication and refusal of a Christian burial, while the local market and guild courts imposed fines, suspensions, and the sanction of market exclusion. Those trading in wholesale and long-distance trade, however, were not subject to the same discipline. As Pirenne (1937: 176–7) also observes, import trade and large-scale commerce largely escaped these restrictions. The regulations were designed for the municipal market and could not be enforced against "the wholesale merchant, who unloaded on the town quays the cargo of several ships laden with rye, cheese, or casks of wine." Indeed, these merchants were forced by the rule of "going to host," discussed below, to work through the very middlemen or brokers prohibited by the market restrictions. Furthermore, local political authorities were unwilling to impose constraints upon foreign and wholesale merchants as they provided a lucrative source of foreign exchange and revenues in the form of customs duties and taxes (ibid.).

As in the case of the just price requirement and market offences, quality controls were enforced primarily against those engaged in production for local, retail trade. Those producing for wholesale and export trade were not subject to the same degree of discipline. Guild discipline, the inspection procedures of municipal authorities, and the controls exerted by direct and public exchange in the fairs and markets could not extend to cover those working in towns for the wholesale trade. These workers "formed a class apart among the other artisans and bore a pretty close resemblance to the modern proletariat" (Pirenne, 1937: 189). While some were organized into associations, these associations did not exercise the control exercised by the guild system (see Clough, 1959: 101). They worked for merchants for the export or wholesale market and were thus not subject to the controls exerted by direct exchange with consumers in the fairs and markets. Nor did the quality control standards have the same impact on foreign merchants engaged in import trade. Foreign merchants were prohibited from engaging in retail trade and trading with strangers. "During their stay they were to lodge with a

[25] In reviewing the case law dealing with market offences, Thompson (1971; 96, n. 64), observes that it was predominantly local petty traders who were subject to discipline.

'host' appointed by the town or gild magistrates, and the host was held responsible for the behaviour of his guests and expected to see that they did not infringe the rights of the citizen by retail trade or by dealing with other strangers" (Mitchell, 1904: 89). Mitchell notes that while this rule of "going to host" fell into disuse in England in the fifteenth century, it continued to be enforced on the Continent. Foreign merchants thus operated through agents or brokers, who in turn would arrange sales to local retail merchants, rendering direct accountability of the producer to the consumer virtually impossible.

It was amidst this dualistic authority structure that the law merchant took shape, borrowing in some cases from canon law, as regards the principle of the sanctity of agreements, and, in other cases, creating unique mechanisms for evading or circumventing restrictions imposed by religious and local authorities. The discussion will turn now to consider how these various influences and developments were manifested in the creation and enforcement of the law merchant.

Law-Creation and Enforcement under the Medieval Law Merchant

During the medieval phase, private merchants developed trade customs that acquired universal application throughout the European trading world through the activities of consuls and specialized merchant courts that settled disputes in markets, fairs, and ports. Some of the customs came to be codified in merchant laws that operated independently of local legal systems and were enforceable only in merchant courts. Private actors operated more or less autonomously in the regulation of international commercial relations owing to the absence of public authority desirous or capable of exercising a greater role. While local markets and local transactions were heavily regulated by religious and political authorities, international commercial transactions were regulated by the merchants themselves. The primary source of the law was merchant custom, while dispute settlement through private merchant arbitrations was the norm governing enforcement. In both law-creation and enforcement merchant practices emphasized procedural and evidentiary informality and gave rise to transactions that were unique and limited to the merchant community. The discussion will first consider the role of merchant custom in law-creation and then the centrality of private arbitration in dispute settlement.

Law-creation: the role of merchant custom

During the medieval phase merchant customs formed the primary source of law. While local political and religious authorities enacted legislation regulating local transactions and markets, the legislation did not limit international transactions in any significant way. Many merchant transactions were universalized through merchant custom and usage and, moreover, were only recognized by and enforceable under the law merchant and in merchant courts. The laws governing maritime trade formed the foundation for the law merchant and the first instances of international law. The influence of merchant custom is thus most notable in the area of maritime transport (see Cafruny, 1987: Gold, 1981; Cutler 1999 c). Indeed, the various sea laws governing maritime transportation have their origin almost exclusively in commercial custom. Bills of lading, charter-parties, and partnership agreements, though in some instances of ancient origin, were modified by and gained their currency and efficacy through commercial custom. So, too, the principles governing maritime insurance and the range of instruments available to finance commercial transactions were developed and legitimized by merchant custom. The insurance principle of contribution to the general average, the various sea loans utilized, letters of credit, and bills of exchange, used in both maritime and land trade, were widely used and regarded as part of the custom of commerce. Insofar as commercial codes or statutes addressed such transactions, they cannot be assimilated to modern statutory law, for they merely codified existing custom and most often did not emanate from the authority of a sovereign. Most codifications generally provided authoritative statements of commercial custom:

> by far the largest element in the body of the maritime law was either created or modified by custom. Such was the case with the law merchant, which was also mostly customary law . . . in the Middle Ages the words "custom" and "statute" were used quite interchangeably. The very word "statute" may mislead us considerably in the sense in which it was used, say six centuries ago, because many statutes then were just as much a compilation of existing customs as a modern statute may be a compilation of existing case law. And so, although when one examines a statute it may seem to be a new and sweeping code passed by a city or gild, one is much more likely to find that it has been built up almost entirely upon the basis of custom and borrowed bodily from some other place. Custom is . . . the ruling principle and the originating force of the law merchant. (Sanborn, 1930: 182–3, references omitted)

The customary character of the law merchant must be emphasized for it contrasts starkly with contemporary conceptions of positive law associated with conscious legislative enactments of sovereigns. Indeed, Max Weber (1978 a: 1099 and 1105) identifies customary law with premodern and precapitalist law deriving from highly personalized customary relationships based upon "subjective rights" and not "objective laws." To Weber (ibid., 880 and 753–8) customary law is a form of "unconscious" law that departs markedly from "rational and systematic legislation," the latter reflecting "conscious human-lawmaking in conformity with the formal constitutional requirements." The customary character of the sources of the law merchant suggests that the proper subjects of the merchant order were individual merchants. Although the doctrine of international legal personality was not yet in evidence, as was noted in the last chapter, the individual was generally regarded as the proper subject of the law right up to the time of Grotius, whose work even in the seventeenth century exhibited a subtle imprecision concerning the nature of the subjects of the emerging legal order.

Merchants were very ingenious in devising instruments that evaded or avoided the local regulatory controls and facilitated the mobility of capital. For example, despite the general prohibition of the charging of interest on loans, usury was in fact regularly practised. Indeed, "lending at interest continued quite openly in such cities as Venice and Toulouse, and the municipal or state authorities, e.g., in the Low Countries, usually licensed or protected the public usurers" (Gilchrist, 1969: 64–5). The prohibition was generally enforced against local and small lenders and pawnbrokers and did not extend to the activities of the great merchants engaged in wholesale or foreign trade. As Gilchrist (ibid., 48) observes, the canonists "could not get at occult usurers, which included the great merchants, and their profits, for they claimed, and on paper proved, that they took no interest." Bills of exchange, for example, were used as early as the twelfth century and achieved wide currency by the fourteenth century (see Clough and Cole, 1946: 77–9). Douglass North (1991: 27–8) analyzes the evolution of the bill of exchange, particularly the development of instruments and practices that allowed for the negotiability of the bill of exchange and discounting methods, as a significant medieval innovation that affected the mobility of capital. A bill of exchange constituted both an acknowledgment by a purchaser of receipt of the goods from a vendor at a set sum and a promise that a purchaser would pay the vendor for the goods in a certain amount, at a particular place, in the future. The payment of interest on the loan was concealed in the difference between the value of the goods and the sum payable at the future date (Clough, 1959: 106–7). Bills of exchange were probably the most important financial instrument of the period and have their origins in merchant custom.[26] According to Malynes (1981: 269) the "nature of a Bill of Exchange is so noble and excelling all other dealings between merchants, that the proceedings therein are extraordinary and singular, and not subject to any prescription by law or otherwise; but merely subsisting of a revered custom, used and solemnized concerning the same." Bills of exchange were used in the fairs of Champagne, Geneva, Lyons, and Besacon, where a special period was set aside for the settling of debts and the negotiation of loans (Tawney, 1962: 44–5; Clough and Cole, 1946: 78–9). Moreover, they were used by merchants, feudal magnates, the clergy, and even the papacy (see Tawney, 1962: 44–5).

The fair letter or *lettre de foire*, the early precursor of the letter of credit, which developed at the fairs in the twelfth and thirteenth centuries, also provided a mechanism for concealing interest charges. Merchants short of cash would arrange to purchase the goods on credit, payment (including an interest charge) to be made upon resale at the end of the fair or at the next fair (Clough and Cole, 1946: 78–9).[27] Letters of credit came to function like bills of exchange, enabling the clearing of debts without the direct exchange of money. In time, moneylenders became involved in the extension of credit or in the guarantee of the creditworthiness of the purchaser (see Clough, 1959; Clough and Cole, 1946: 79).

The variety of transactions used in maritime trade and finance also provided means for the avoidance of the prohibition of usury. In addition, they facilitated trade relations by enabling the conduct of large maritime ventures through spreading the risks of transacting (North, 1991: 28–9). Maritime transport instruments have their origin in merchant custom and functioned in multiple ways as documents of transport specifying the rights and duties of parties to the maritime adventure and as mechanisms of finance, credit, and insurance. As early as the

[26] Jenks (1909: 50–71) dates bills of exchange from the fourteenth century. However, Bewes (1923: ch. 4) argues that they can be traced to the Arabs in the eighth century who passed them on to the Italian traders who followed the Crusades.

[27] For the history of letters of credit see Ellinger (1970: ch. 2). Ellinger argues that letters of credit were not in general usage on the Continent prior to the fourteenth century and in England prior to the seventeenth century. However, others date their usage from the twelfth and thirteenth centuries in the practices of the great fairs of Europe, in particular those of Champagne, and in the commercial transactions of the English Crown. See Clough and Cole (1946: 79) and Sanborn (1930: 347–8).

thirteenth century bills of lading, transferring to the holder a title to the document and the goods and having the character of negotiable instruments, were in use (Sanborn, 1930: 98). There were numerous ways of determining the freight to be paid and the time at which payment was due under a bill of lading. A merchant could hire a ship by the month or for the entire voyage for a fixed price or at a price reflecting a percentage of the value of the goods. In cases where merchants formed charter-parties, there were a variety of options as to when freight was payable and the proportions owed by the charter-party members. In most cases some proportion of freight was payable at the beginning of the voyage with the balance payable upon completion. The various obligations and risks of the parties concerning unloading, delivery, loss upon jettison of the goods for common safety, shipwreck or collision, or breach of contract by the merchant relating to late loading or of the shipowner for late departure, depended very much on the specific terms of the agreements between merchants. Loans to build or repair ships or to finance a voyage regularly contained hidden interest charges (ibid., 101–2). The medieval *commenda* and *societas*, though forms of maritime loans and partnerships in use from the tenth century, contained specific rules allocating the costs and risks of transportation (see generally, Mitchell, 1909: 103–5). The *commenda* was an early expression of the sorts of risk-sharing arrangements that subsequently took the form of regulated companies and joint-stock companies (North, 1991: 29).[28] The same applied to the bottomry contract, which functioned as a mortgage on a ship given by the shipowner to a financier to pay for the costs of the voyage (the shipowner pledging the keel or bottom of the ship as security for repayment of the loan) (Mitchell, 1909: 103–5). In contrast, for respondentia contracts, the loan was secured by the cargo. In addition to raising capital, these maritime loans functioned to disperse risks amongst lenders, merchants, and shipowners, thus forming the early instances of insurance law (Clough, 1959: 111).[29] In cases where the agreement between the parties was silent as to their respective rights and obligations, the customs of the port applied (Mitchell, 1909: 100). The various maritime codes and customs mentioned earlier addressed these issues comprehensively and articulated principles that continue

[28] See also, Price (1991) and Chaudhuri (1991).

[29] Sanborn (1930: 19) traces the practice of maritime insurance to the early days of Christianity and caravan insurance and the insurance of beasts and ships to the fourth century AD in the Babylonian Talmud. See also Vance (1909: 99); De Roover (1945); and Udovitch (1962)

today to regulate maritime transport.[30] For example, the contemporary rule of contribution to the general average originated in Roman law in the context of sharing responsibility from losses resulting from the needs of common safety. The medieval sea laws varied this rule so that it became a means for:

> mutual insurance of each other by ship and cargo. If the ship is wrecked, dismasted, or loses her tackling, is run into, burnt or attacked by pirates; if the cargo is lost, wetted or plundered, and if no one is to blame for the loss, the Sea Law lays down in many places that ship and cargo, so far as saved, are to contribute to ship and cargo, so far as lost. The common safety resulting from a deliberate sacrifice is not considered, for it is only necessary, in order to have contribution, that there shall have been a loss without the owner's negligence and without the responsibility of any other person in the maritime adventure. The result follows that, by participation in the voyage, one mutually insures, and is insured by, the ship and the property of the other shippers.
>
> (Sanborn, 1930: 38)

Sea loans embodying the rule of contribution to the general average were widely used in the Italian cities in the thirteenth and fourteenth centuries. Vance (1909: 105), upon reviewing records of merchants and financiers of the period, concludes that "as early as 1318 the custom of making insurance upon goods subject to peril of transportation on sea or land became a normal incident of traffic" (ibid., 106).[31] The earliest known insurance policy was made in Genoa in 1347, while a policy issued by a Genoese underwriter is recorded in Bruges in 1370 (ibid., 106). In the fifteenth century, Barcelona passed ordinances regulating marine insurance, which were translated into many languages and "exercised a considerable influence upon the law of insurance by giving precision to the usages and promoting uniformity in the laws of the chief countries of Europe."[32] Italian merchants carried their practices of

[30] The Sea Law of Rhodes is divided into three parts and contains rules governing a variety of risks and obligations, including, for example, the right and result of jettison; the responsibility for ship and cargo upon loss; duty of contribution to the general average; liability upon collision; and salvage. These laws formed the foundation for the Sea Laws of Trani, the Amalfi Table and the decisions from the court at Pisa. Pisa, in particular, is noted for developing a variety of transport documents, including bills of lading, charter-parties, contracts of affreightment, *commenda* (partnerships), and bottomry contracts. Many of the rules embodied in the Sea Law of Rhodes were adopted in the Laws of Oleron, which also include provisions regulating treatment of the ship's crew. Many similar provisions later appeared in the Sea Laws of Wisby. See generally, Sanborn (1930).

[31] Vance, however, cites evidence tracing the rule of contribution to ancient Greece (1909: 100, n. 1).

[32] See Mitchell (1904: 153–5) for the content of these regulations.

insurance to ports and cities throughout Europe and to England in the fourteenth and fifteenth centuries. Mitchell (1904, 141; 155) stresses that these practices were not the "creation of the legislature," but the product of merchant custom. Furthermore, during the medieval period, they were only recognized under the law merchant and in merchant courts. Insofar as legislation regulating insurance existed, it functioned to articulate existing usages and customs. Vance, too, stresses the customary basis of insurance law:

> The usages of insurance . . . readily took on the same character that had already been impressed upon other customs of traders engaged in international mercantile pursuits. The usages governing older forms of commerce, especially maritime usages, had found expression in collections of regulations and ordinances of great antiquity, that came to possess the greatest authority throughout Europe rather by their general acceptance than by the force of authoritative enactment.
>
> (1909: 109)

By the sixteenth century insurance was well established, as is evident in the various treaties on the subject published by Europeans (ibid., 108–9). Insurance was first introduced into England by the Italians and the first record of an insurance transaction dates from 1545 in the Court of Admiralty. As we shall see in the next chapter, as the medieval period of the law merchant drew to a close, state regulation and adjudication of insurance and other commercial matters occurred. However, as Mitchell (1904: 152) notes, "the clauses of the early contracts remain the basis of the modern law of insurance of the civilized world."

This review of merchant practices reveals a variety of instruments used by medieval merchants to structure their transactions. Many were designed to facilitate capital mobility by creating credit, circumventing the general prohibition of usury, and thereby creating greater financial liquidity. In time, as ecclesiastical authorities lost the battle against profit making, attitudes toward usury changed and exceptions to the general prohibition developed. "Gradually the very word *usury* took on its modern meaning of excessive charges for loans, while *interest* or some other pleasing word was used for moderate charges" (Clough and Cole, 1946: 82). Profits on goods purchased for personal use or consumption that later had to be sold (forced sales) and profits on the sale of goods that embodied the labor of craftsmen or the investment of time and money came to be acceptable (Gilchrist, 1969: 53–6). Thus, the taking of profits of a partnership were permitted, provided that the lender assumed the partner's risk (Viner, 1978: 92). Rent charges on the produce from land and interest charges on the late payment of a loan became acceptable.[33] In some cases local authorities intervened to enable the taking of interest. The general prohibition was suspended in order to permit the clearing of accounts during the Fair of Champagne, while in Genoa the authorities prohibited the attempt to use the prohibition as a means for invalidating insurance contracts (Mitchell, 1904: 158).

The Reformation had significant influence on the Church's attitude towards commerce, contributing further to the development of distinctions between permissible and impermissible profit and charges (see generally, Viner, 1978). Toward the close of the medieval phase, though some religious restrictions remained, the charging of interest was widely practised in the world of international finance. Petty, local pawnbrokers were subject to the prohibition, but it was generally inapplicable to larger transactions involving foreign or wholesale trade. As regards the latter, the arrangements adopted by merchants to facilitate the payment and financing of sales transactions in the great fairs and commercial ports avoided or were exempted from the Church's prohibition. These arrangements were utilized with a high degree of uniformity and were enforced under the law merchant and in merchant courts with great success. This led Mitchell (1904: 158–9) to conclude that the impact of the prohibition has been "greatly exaggerated" and did not really impede the development of an autonomous law merchant.

The distinctiveness of medieval practices of customary lawmaking and the commercial and legal innovations to which they gave rise were mirrored in dispute settlement practices. However, before turning to consider the unique nature of the merchant court system, it must be noted that the commercial transactions devised by medieval merchants under the law merchant both embodied and anticipated forms of property and ownership that departed considerably from incidents of property ownership generally associated with the feudal system.[34] The forms of property and commercial relations generated by the variety of sales, financial, transport, and insurance transactions devised by medieval merchants functioned to avoid feudal restrictions on the transmissibility of property and the mobility of capital. The ease and dynamism with

[33] See Gilchrist (1969: 67–70) for a list of transactions that came to be regarded as exceptions to the prohibition of usury.

[34] See Cutler (2002 d) for analysis of the nature of property rights under feudal, capitalist, and late capitalist modes of production in terms of a dialectical tension and competition between property conceptualized alternatively as "bundles of rights" or as "things."

which medieval merchants engaged in long-distance and bulk trade could develop transactions that allowed them to manage risks over time and distance, to create credit, and to evade the local market restrictions and regulations stands in sharp contrast to the intensity and extensity of feudal regulation and the static nature of feudal property law. The "essence of feudal law ... is the inseparable connection between land tenure and personal homage involving often menial services on the part of the tenant" (Cohen, 1927–8: 9). The inseparability of feudal notions of property and ownership with one's association or attachment to land, in a hierarchical and static system based upon birth, estate, and inheritance, worked against the mobility and transmissibility of property rights. Moreover, feudal property relations were clearly inconsistent with the new forms of property being developed as highly mobile interests in commercial paper, joint ownership through abstract associations such as the *commenda* and the creation of new property rights through maritime transactions that operated like modern mortgages.[35] These notions served to sever property from immobile interests in land, paving the way for a new dynamism that characterized capitalist property relations. Moreover, many of these transactions, like those relating to the *commenda*, embodied what Weber (1978 a: 708–9) refers to as "rationally transformed relationships," for they replaced status and familial relationships with business relationships. Such systematic rationality, he observes, is more reflective of legal developments attending the emergence of capitalist business enterprise than of feudal business relations.

Dispute settlement through private arbitration

During the medieval phase, merchants developed a very efficacious system of private adjudication and enforcement. At this time there was considerable normative and institutional pluralism, in that medieval merchants could pursue commercial claims in the royal courts, ecclesiastical courts, common law courts, or law merchant courts (see Benson, 1999: 114 and 120–5; Schmitthoff, 1961). However, the law merchant courts provided the most utilized institutional framework for settling commercial disputes in the medieval period. As was noted earlier, only the law merchant courts enforced the *lex mercatoria* and upheld transactions, such as bare promises or contracts, that were unenforceable in the other courts. The merchant courts operated privately: more like contemporary arbitration tribunals than courts of law. According to the folklore

[35] See Burch (1998) for the association of mobile property rights with capitalism.

of the law merchant, the courts were known for their speed, informality, efficiency, and justice (see Mitchell, 1904; Cutler, 1995; Trakman, 1983). The merchant courts sat in fairs, markets, and seaport towns and enforced unique commercial transactions, such as bare promises, bills of lading, charter-parties, partnership agreements, insurance principles, and financial transactions that were not recognized by other local courts. Juries comprised of merchants sat and arbitrated disputes, applying principles from the law merchant, the latter, as noted above, being predominantly customary in origin (Berman and Kaufman, 1978).

Medieval merchants developed a variety of courts for the settlement of their disputes and these courts achieved a high degree of independence from the local courts and the local legal system. Indeed, they operated more like modern arbitration tribunals than like courts of law. As Clive Schmitthoff (1961: 134) notes, "these commercial courts were unique; they were in the nature of modern conciliation and arbitration tribunals rather than courts in the strict sense of the word." The right to hold a fair court, known also as the court of "pie-powder," formed part of the grant of the right to hold a fair, issued by the king or local lord. The grant established the jurisdiction of the court and provided for its general administration. The following provides an example of a grant from the fifteenth century:

> it hath been all times accustomed, that every person coming to the said fairs, should have lawful remedy of all manner of contracts, trespasses, covenants, debts, and other deeds made or done within any of the same fairs, during the time of the said fair, and within the jurisdiction of the same, and to be tried by the merchants being of the same fair.
>
> (quoted in Holdsworth, 1907: 298)

The origin of the name "pie-powder" ("pieds poudreux" in French) is somewhat in dispute. Some attribute it to the fact that in fair courts justice was administered as "speedily as the dust could fall or be removed from the feet of the litigants," while others attribute it to the fact that "the court was frequented by chapmen with dusty feet, who wandered from mart to mart" (Selden Society, 1908: xiv). Whatever the origin, the courts of "pie-powder" were known for the speed with which disputes were settled and the informality of the procedures adopted. The law applied was the law merchant and the judgments issued from juries of merchants. It has been noted that the important thing about these fair courts was not, however, that they applied the law merchant, although they did, but that their decisions were actually made by merchants.

"[T]he merchants were the suitors or dooms men; they found the judgment or declared the law" (William C. Jones, 1958: 488, quoting the Selden Society). Consequently, the law applied would be the local mercantile understanding of what the law of the particular situation was. Fair courts throughout England and the Continent applied the law merchant, enforcing transactions unenforceable in the local common and civil law courts.[36]

Merchants also had recourse to staple courts held in staple towns. "Justice . . . was to be done to the foreigner from day to day and hour to hour, according to the law of the staple or the law merchant, and not according to the common law or particular burghul usages" (Brodhurst, 1909: 25). Merchants elected a mayor of the staple and officers who were empowered to keep the peace and to enforce or execute judgments of the court. In England, the Statute of the Staples of 1353 granted significant privileges, protections, and independence to the staple courts.[37] Pollock (1901: 239) observes that the statute is "an epitome" of the royal policy whereby foreign merchants were treated tenderly in return for their payment of royal customs duties.

Merchant courts also sat in towns and boroughs applying the law merchant before juries composed of merchants (Holdsworth, 1907: 299–300) and merchant guilds provided facilities for the arbitration of disputes between members. Generally, however, guilds did not exercise a regular jurisdiction (ibid., 300). In the late medieval period, the merchant guilds assisted in the regulation of international commerce by disciplining their members and imposing trade embargoes against political authorities who did not respect the property rights of guild members (Greif, Milgrom, and Weingast, 1994).[38]

In addition, courts in seaport towns applied the law merchant to maritime disputes. In England, the jurisdiction of the Court of Admiralty originated in the fourteenth century (see generally, Mears, 1908) and was established by the fifteenth century:

> It practically comprised all mercantile shipping cases. All contracts made abroad, bills of exchange . . . commercial agencies abroad, charter parties, insurance, average, freight, non-delivery of, damage to,

[36] See generally, Scrutton (1909); Pollock (1901); Selden Society (1908 and 1892); Schmitthoff (1961) for a fuller discussion of jurisdiction, procedures, and administration of the fair courts.

[37] See Holdsworth (1907: 302) and Brodhurst (1909). Similar edicts were promulgated in Paris in 1563 and in Nuremberg in 1508. See Thayer (1936: 141–2).

[38] See also Greif (1993) for discussion of even earlier regulatory associations developed by merchants.

> cargo, negligent navigation by masters, mariners, or pilots, breach of warranty of seaworthiness . . . in short, every kind of shipping business was dealt with by the admiralty court. (Holdsworth, 1907: 313)

It is noteworthy that at the time the common law courts did not have jurisdiction over contracts entered into or torts (civil wrongs) committed abroad. Moreover, common and civil law courts did not recognize or enforce the transactions utilized in maritime trade. Such transactions, along with the various financial instruments discussed above, could only be enforced under the law merchant and its courts. Thus, to the extent that commercial law was applied extraterritorially in the medieval phase, it was in a purely private context. The merchant courts provided an efficacious system for settling disputes and for enforcing commercial transactions. The self-enforcement actions of merchants included the imposition of the sanctions of market exclusion, bankruptcy, and loss of reputation.

The merchant courts are renowned for their informal practices and the absence of formal or rigid procedural constraints on the conditions necessary to create or vary binding obligations. Such informality greatly expanded the range of commercial activities open to medieval merchants, providing further differentiation from local laws and commercial practices. Unlike under the local legal systems, property in goods could pass without delivery, facilitating the expansion of nonsimultaneous exchange over time and distance, while oral evidence was sufficient to vary written agreements and to create partnership agreements, broadening the range of enforceable transactions (Bewes, 1923). Unlike under the common law, bare promises, not supported by consideration or under seal, were regarded by the law merchant as sufficient to create binding obligations, creating new vistas for the development of contractual relations (Pollock, 1901). With regard to the enforcement of agreements, the law merchant provided informal rules of evidence and of proof, obviating the need to meet the formal requirements associated with common and civil law courts. The parties to agreements were regarded as competent and compellable witnesses (ibid., 242–3), journal and ledger accounts were admissible into evidence, and the rules regulating the service of documents were relaxed, all greatly facilitating the enforcement of commercial transactions (Burdick, 1909: 35 et seq.).

This procedural and evidentiary informality, when combined with the flexibility of merchant customs, contributed to the unique and discretionary character of the law merchant and its courts. Indeed, many focus on these characteristics to develop efficiency and transaction-cost explanations that link the emergence and nature of the law merchant and its institutions with the economics of emergent capitalist business enterprise.[39] Customary law is generally regarded as providing greater flexibility and adaptability than legislation (David, 1972 b; 1972 d), while considerable efficiencies are said to flow from custom-based commercial regulation, both in terms of facilitating exchange and in terms of unifying commercial law.[40] Indeed, a distinguishing characteristic of the medieval phase was the general ability of merchants to privately generate, modify, and extinguish legal standards in response to qualitative and quantitative commercial developments through changes in their customs and practices. To the extent that custom did not address an issue, merchant juries were able to fashion remedies drawing upon basic law-merchant principles and their discretion and personal expertise. The development by merchants of uniform commercial practices governing the sale, transportation, financing, and insurance of goods and governing dispute resolution evidences the value they placed on regularizing and standardizing commercial relations. Moreover, despite the proliferation of transportation, financial, and insurance arrangements, commercial practices embodied standards that emphasized the need to avoid formalities and to encourage the expeditious conclusion of commercial agreements. Indeed, the development of customary commercial law and the private enforcement system are described as "feats of coordination" by students of "new institutionalism"(Milgrom, North, and Weingast, 1990: 3). They argue that this system facilitated exchange by lowering transaction costs and by enforcing agreements. As Milgrom et al. contend:

> an enduring pattern of trade over a wide geographical area cannot be sustained if it is profitable for merchants to renege on promises or repudiate agreements. In the larger trading towns and cities of northern Europe in the 10th through 13th centuries, it was not possible for every merchant to know the reputations of all others, so extensive trade required the development of some system like the Law Merchant system to fill the gap.
> (Ibid., 19)

By centralizing enforcement in merchant courts, the system is said to have provided valuable information about the creditworthiness of those

[39] See North (1991); Milgrom, North, and Weingast (1990); Greif, Milgrom, and Weingast (1994); Cremades and Plehn (1984).
[40] See Schmitthoff (1964 b: 20); Trakman (1983); Cremades and Plehn (1984).

with whom a merchant traded.[41] In addition, it is regarded as functioning as a valuable reputation system, enforcing honest behavior:

> The Law Merchant enforcement system . . . restores the equilibrium status of Honest behavior. It succeeds even though there is no state with police power and authority over a wide geographical realm to enforce contracts. Instead, the system works by making the reputation system of enforcement work better. The [law merchant] institutions . . . provide people with the information they need to recognize those who have been cheated to provide evidence of their injuries. Then, the reputation system itself provides the incentives for honest behavior and for payment by those who are found to have violated the code, it encourages traders to boycott those who have flouted the system. Neither the reputation mechanism nor the institutions can be effective by themselves. They are complementary parts of a total system that work together to enforce honest behavior. (Ibid., 19)

According to this analysis, the system of private enforcement made commercial exchange over time and space possible by lowering the costs of exchange and providing the merchants with some security that their agreements would be honored.[42] Medieval merchants, however, were not acting in response to any conscious preference for customary law over statutory law, for the distinction had not yet clearly emerged. Furthermore, they did not have liberal and neoliberal theory to instruct them on transaction-cost economics and the efficiencies of customary law.[43] While medieval merchants clearly valued informal, discretionary, and permissive standards and enforcement procedures that enabled the expeditious conclusion of agreements and settlement of disputes, care must be taken to avoid imputing reasons and rationales from later historical, political, and ideological conditions. Rather, merchant autonomy

[41] See Milgrom, North, and Weingast (1990) for a game theoretic modelling of the law merchant enforcement system that represents "in an uncluttered way the basic facts that traders have opportunities and temptations to cheat and that there are gains possible if the traders can suppress these temptations and find a way to cooperate."

[42] According to Milgrom, et al. (ibid.: 19): "the merchants in Western Europe enhanced and refined their private legal code to serve the needs of the merchant trade – all prior to the rise of the nation-state. Without this code and the system of enforcement, trade among virtual strangers would have been much more cumbersome, or even impossible. Remarkably, the Law Merchant institution appears to have been structured to support trade in a way that minimizes transaction costs, or at least incurs costs only in categories that are indispensable to any system that relies on boycotts and sanctions." See also, Benson (1988–9) for the law merchant as a spontaneous and economically efficient system.

[43] Economic theorists of law, such as R. A. Posner, argue that customary law produces efficiencies because it has evolved over time in response to incentives to structure and adapt rules so as to minimize information costs and reduce uncertainty. See Posner (1980 b and 1986).

in law-creation and in dispute resolution derived from the inability of the "inchoate nation-state system" to regulate the "geographically dynamic" activities of the medieval merchant and from a hands-off approach to foreign merchants who were regarded as providing valuable revenues and supplies of foreign goods (Cremades and Plehn, 1984: 318).[44] As noted earlier, local political, religious, and guild authorities lacked the capacity to regulate international transactions, while the local courts and local legal systems did not recognize law merchant transactions and, thus, were powerless to regulate or to enforce them. The rather sharp contrast between merchant autonomy in international commercial transactions and the intensity with which local commercial exchanges were regulated to protect consumers and regulate markets anticipated what were to become distinctions between domestic/foreign commercial relations and the public/private spheres. The exemption of foreign merchants from market discipline in exchange for foreign exchange and the revenue from the payment of customs duties and taxes suggests that, in addition to simply being unable to regulate international transactions in any significant way, the local authorities were unwilling to do so. Thus, while "[t]he ability of the merchant class to both generate and enforce its own norms of behaviour allowed it to achieve a large degree of independence from these local sovereigns" (Cremades and Plehn, 1984: 319), one must also consider the reluctance of the local authorities to interfere.

The absence of a clear distinction between the public and private spheres and between domestic and international commercial relations reflects medieval political arrangements. The distinguishing feature of medieval Europe was the decentralization of political authority, "overlapping feudal jurisdictions, plural allegiances, and asymmetrical suzerainties" (Holzgrefe, 1989: 11). This diffuse authority structure contributed to the absence of a clear distinction between, and the conflation of, domestic and foreign affairs. "In the Middle Ages, the modern distinction between domestic and international law was therefore unknown. Law was either peculiar to one community (*jus civile*) or common to many (*jus gentium*)" (ibid., 14). Moreover, while ecclesiastical authorities and local political leaders exercised control over local transactions, their ability to discipline international commercial transactions was very limited. Merchant autonomy in law-creation and dispute resolution emerged more as a result of the inability and unwillingness of

44 And see Pirenne (1937) and Clough and Cole (1946).

local authorities to regulate international commercial relations. Thus, the "picture of an authoritarian control is everywhere in evidence; yet the lines of the agencies of supervision are far from clean-cut. The activities of a people passing out of feudalism do not lend themselves to our distinction between public and private" (Hamilton, 1931: 1141). This was to change in the second phase in the development of the law merchant when international commercial relations came to be insulated and isolated in what was to emerge as the private sphere of markets and economic activity. As the discussion now turns to review the second phase, it becomes evident that the emergence of states and their attempts to nationalize and to control foreign commercial activities signaled a change in both the ability and the willingness of political authorities to regulate international transactions. These developments, in combination with emerging capitalism and its ideological foundations, provided powerful rationalizations for the nationalization and political neutralization of international commercial relations as part of the nascent private spheres of law and economy.

5 State-building: constituting the public sphere and disembedding the private sphere

The second phase in the development of the law merchant is characterized by the juridification of international commercial relations as productive and exchange relations were subject to increasing legal discipline. More international commercial activities came to be regulated through law, while legal disciplines were juridified through the creation of national and territorial-based state power, and its association with establishing control over foreign commercial relations through legislative and judicial means. Juridified commercial relations are characterized by rationalized, systematic, and positivist legal regulation and discipline, exhibiting consciousness in planning or design and formalism in operation. Ultimately, juridified commercial relations established the disciplinary link and "natural" affinity between law and capitalism noted, as discussed below, by Max Weber, Karl Polanyi, and others.[1]

With the development of a system of territorial-based sovereign states, and with the movement from feudalism to capitalism, the public/private distinction came to be firmly established. State-building projects involved the nationalization and control of foreign commercial activities, which were increasing in volume. The consolidation of states signaled a change in both the ability and the willingness of political authorities to regulate international commercial transactions. This is evident in the priority given to positive law as the most appropriate mechanism for regulating international commerce and the displacement

[1] Although Michel Foucault cast his concept of disciplinary society much more broadly than a focus on law and legal discipline, John O'Neill (1986) persuasively argues that we might extend Weber's analysis of the nature of rational, bureaucratic-legal discipline under capitalism through Foucault's analysis of knowledge and power in disciplinary society. See, for example, Foucault (1979 a; 1979 b; 1980). See also, Hunt (1993) and Hunt and Wickham (1994) for insightful applications of Foucault to legal analysis.

of custom as a primary source of law. The result was increasing formalism as regards the sources and subjects of law and the development of a tension between the localizing tendencies of national regulation through positive state-based law and the delocalizing and denationalizing tendencies of private, customary regulation. The private sphere contracted as merchant autonomy in law-creation and in private dispute settlement declined. Effective enforcement came to be associated with the state. Any ambiguity that might have been evident in the subjects and sources of law in the earlier phase was settled by the unambiguous formal designation of the state and its positive law (both in the form of domestic law and public international law) as the determinants of subject and sources doctrines. Indeed, the constitutional frameworks established by the principles of territorial sovereignty and legal positivism came to discipline subject and sources doctrines, establishing a state- and consent-based international legal order. In the domestic sphere, as the discussion will illustrate, the liberal ideology of the autonomous "legal subject" exercised similar discipline, creating a consent-based private legal order. As Evgenii Pashukanis (1978: 119) observes about the relation between the state and law, "the impersonal abstraction of state power functioning with ideal stability and continuity in time and space is the equivalent of the impersonal, abstract subject."

Dispute settlement and enforcement became functions of the public sphere as the geographic expansion of commercial relations rendered the self-enforcement system of merchants inadequate. The collection of information regarding the creditworthiness and honesty of merchants became more expensive. The sanctions of market exclusion and loss of reputation became difficult to enforce as markets proliferated in number, as commerce extended to faraway places, and as the practice of simultaneous exchange in markets was replaced by nonsimultaneous exchanges over time and distance. The imposition of the sanction of bankruptcy and the enforcement of agreements became the prerogatives of states and thus contingent upon national intervention as states adopted laws and procedures governing the enforcement and execution of commercial agreements.

During this period, the expansion of trade through colonization, the development of mercantilist doctrine, and the advent of capitalism brought new insights into the role of commerce in determining national power.[2] Political authorities developed a new understanding

[2] See Cox (1987: ch. 5) for a discussion of these developments.

of the importance of regulating international commerce for achieving national welfare goals and political autonomy. This understanding, coupled with the development of the institutional and legal machinery capable of disciplining international transactions, rendered states more willing and more able to regulate international trade.

This chapter reviews the second phase in law-creation and dispute settlement. The discussion illustrates how the balance between public and private authority shifted in favor of the former as state authority replaced the overlapping authority structures of the medieval period. States became the subjects, while their positive law became the primary source of public international law. Moreover, states exercised stronger and more comprehensive control than did the local religious and political authorities of the earlier phase. Notable, however, is the profound change in the nature of public regulation. Medieval paternalistic and religious restraints were replaced by a permissive and facultative approach inspired by liberal political economy, which appeared later in the period. Liberalism sanctioned capitalist business techniques and provided a normative and a theoretical rationale for free-market principles, establishing the basis for the separation between politics and economics. It provided a foundation for assumptions concerning the natural, neutral, consensual, efficient, and apolitical nature of private regulation. The widespread acceptance and legitimacy of prices established under freedom of contract or by the market, the weakening influence of strict liability standards for defective goods, and the growing legitimacy of interest charges show the increased importance of free-market principles and the value of facilitating exchange. However, while establishing the terms of a contract became a private activity, its enforcement became a public, judicial activity.

The trend towards increasing reliance upon national judicial enforcement was bolstered by the incorporation of the jurisdiction of merchant courts into national judicial systems. However, as will become evident, states differed in the extent to which national courts assumed jurisdiction over commercial matters. In addition, significant differences in national regulation eroded the universality of commercial law and generated a movement for its global unification in the next phase in the development of the law merchant.

While there was a profound transformation resulting from the growing territorial individuation of state power and the advent of capitalism and liberal political economy, the conventional view is that the law merchant persisted:

> The Law Merchant did not die. It changed in the seventeenth century, becoming less universal and more localized under state influence; it began to reflect the policies, interests and procedures of kings. Merchant custom remained the underlying source of much commercial law in Europe, and to a lesser degree in England, but it differed from place to place. "National states inevitably required that their indigenous policies and concerns be given direct consideration in the regulation of commerce. As a result, distinctly domestic systems of law evolved as the official regulators of both domestic and international business."[3]

There is much truth to the view that elements of the law merchant persisted beyond the medieval period, but it is important to recognize significant disjunctures and discontinuities. These stem from two central developments: the growing territoriality of state power and the transition to a capitalist mode of production. These developments enabled the articulation of distinctions between domestic and foreign commercial transactions and between private and public international law. Both distinctions were to facilitate the neutralization of many aspects of international commerce as "private" matters, thus insulating them from politics and public regulation. The story of the evolution of the law merchant is as much the story of the construction of public, state authority as it is about the isolation and disembedding of private authority. Before turning to consider the processes of law-creation and dispute settlement it will be useful to provide a sense of the historical, material, and ideological contexts of these developments.

Nationalizing and Localizing the Law Merchant

A number of developments during the second phase changed the environment for international commerce. A shift in commercial power to the Atlantic states, which was related to the establishment of strong nation-states in Western Europe engaged in state-building and in overseas expansion, the universal acceptance of the idea of national sovereignty, the Reformation, the rise of capitalism, the advent of liberal political economy, an increase in the volume of trade, and an enhanced understanding of the economic basis of national power all contributed to an alteration in the material, ideational, and institutional environments for commercial relations. States engaged in the process of state-building sought control over commercial activities. One of the means

[3] Benson (1988–89: 653) quoting Trakman (1983).

adopted to achieve national control was the nationalization and localization of trade law and practice. States came to incorporate the law merchant into their national legal systems. The notion of *jus commune* disappeared as states focused on the creation of national commercial law. This period of codification "engendered an attitude of legal positivism which was further aggravated by nationalist sentiments. Jurists now considered their national law to be the Law" (David and Brierley, 1978: 62).

> The universities in each country no longer taught anything but national law. This gave birth to a new and revolutionary concept. Law came to be regarded as a national phenomenon, controlled by politics and bound up with the existence of the state. The idea of common law disappeared. The existence of natural law, its force drawn purely from the idea of justice, and independent of all state-authority, was challenged: and this idea came to seem more moral than legal, even to those remaining faithful to it. In the eyes of international lawyers, private international law itself ceased to be anything but a regulation of international commercial relations *by the will of the national legislature in a particular state*. It became simply a national system of conflict of laws: its object is and can only be, to say which *national* law governs a particular transaction. (David, 1972 a: 4, original emphasis)

As Harold Berman and Colin Kaufman (1978: 227) observe, "[t]his was an age not only of nationalism but also of positivism." The role of commercial custom declined as states came to regard national legislation and case law as definitive sources of law. The preeminence of custom was challenged "in the West, by philosophy and by lawyers anxious to base law on reason. In the nineteenth century this long struggle terminated. People ceased to believe that wisdom lay in conformity with tradition; they wanted, too, to unify the law at the national level, and to increase the certainty considered indispensable in legal relations. Customary law gave way to law based essentially on legislation in the countries of the European Continent, and on judicial decisions in England" (David, 1972 d: 100–1).

The significance of the movement from a delocalized system of customary merchant law to a localized one of national and positive legal commercial regulation, and the intensification of legal discipline that resulted, are crucial developments in our understanding of the nature and operation of law. Max Weber provides important insight into the "binary relationship between law and the rise of capitalism" for he believed that "only a particular type of legal system is conducive to the growth of capitalism" (Beirne, 1982: 54). A key element of the legal system that differentiates the precapitalist from the modern merchant order is rationality and the dominance of a juridico-political ideology that establishes relationships between law and rationality and between systematic legal regulation and bureaucratic control and efficiency (Weber, 1978 a). This was a first step in the association of (bureaucratic) rationality and (legal) domination that is crucial to the process of juridification and the intensification and deepening of law as a coercive and dominating force. Indeed, Herbert Marcuse (1972 b: 214), in analyzing Weber's conception of rationality, provides the important insight that "in becoming a question of domination, of control, this rationality subordinates itself, by virtue of its own inner dynamic, to another, namely, the rationality of domination." The process of juridification was instrumental in subordinating rationalized and localized legal systems to the broader rationality of domination inherent in capitalism.

The process of legal nationalization and the juridification of commerce "though universal, was carried out in the various countries for different reasons, in different manners and in differing degrees" (Schmitthoff, 1961: 131). Significantly, juridification served particular interests and is linked to specific processes of state-building and national capital accumulation. In England, the nationalization of the law merchant occurred, in part, as a component of the consolidation of the system of the common law and its courts, and in part, as a necessary complement to the country's growing commercial power. In France, nationalization was achieved through various codifications motivated in the early years by concerns of economic state-building, or mercantilism, and in the later years by French revolutionary ideals. In Germany, nationalization occurred through codifications aimed at securing political unification through the creation of uniform laws. In the United States, nationalization was achieved by the adoption of English commercial law and the unification of state commercial law and practices. The following discussion will consider the experiences of each country after reviewing the impact of the most significant developments on the theory and practice of commercial law: the growth of the nation-state, initially in its mercantilist formation and later in its capitalist formation, the reformation, and the advent of liberal political economy.

State formations and the isolation of private international law

It is no accident that the states that were to become the major players in the development of commercial law were those that were the most significant commercial powers. By the beginning of the sixteenth century, Mediterranean trade had declined in importance as Atlantic ports became the major focus of commercial activity. The shift in commercial activity from the Mediterranean to the Atlantic was a result of the discoveries and overseas expansion, undertaken by Western states, and the assistance that their strong national governments gave to the promotion of commerce. Spain and Portugal were the major commercial powers in the sixteenth century, France and Holland in the seventeenth century, France and England in the eighteenth century, and England in the nineteenth century.

> In the Mediterranean, from the central position in Europe, trade sank till it was almost a backwater. In part the change was caused by political factors. The new, strong, national states threw their weight behind their merchants and pushed their trade by force of arms. Lusty young countries like France and Spain made Italy their battleground . . . Spain, Portugal, France and England (and later Holland) – all had governments strong and rich enough to push the explorations and develop the colonies. The very fact that they had not played a major role in medieval commerce made them all the more eager to seize the new opportunities and all the more ready to venture in untried ways. Moreover, in the era that was dawning, the state was to play an active role in commerce. A city which was not part of a big nation state could scarcely hope to compete in naval rivalry, in tariff wars, in the struggle for markets. (Clough and Cole, 1946: 120–1)

Baltic trade, too, declined in importance as commercial opportunities were lost to the newly emerging nation-states and as the Thirty Years' War (1618–48) contributed to the economic decline of Germany.

While the last chapter illustrated that local authorities did regulate local markets and transactions in the medieval phase, state intervention took on new meaning in the second phase as states adopted overtly mercantilist policies for a broad range of commercial activities. This was due, in part, to the tremendous increase in the volume of foreign commercial transactions generated by colonial expansion. It is estimated that British exports and imports increased by 500 percent from the seventeenth to the eighteenth century (Clough and Cole, 1946: 257). The experience in France was similar, with the major commercial expansion occurring in the eighteenth century. In Holland, in contrast, the expansion took place in the seventeenth century.

Mercantilism may be defined as "economic state-building" and involves the use of national policies and practices to achieve a variety of goals (ibid., 257). These goals include securing economic unity through the creation of a national economy, attaining control over domestic economic processes and actors through a weakening of controls exercised by the Church, town, and guild authorities, and enhancing national power through the development of industrial and economic strength (see also, Heckscher, 1955).

It is important here to recall the nature of the relationships between law, the state, and the mercantilist mode of production discussed in Chapter 3. As Robert Cox (1987: 104) notes, "[n]ew modes of social relations of production become established through the exercise of state power." States, or rather the "social forces upon which state power ultimately rests," determine the organization of production by "fixing the framework of laws, institutions, practices, and policies affecting production" (ibid., 106). Moreover, "the legal-institutional framework set up by the autonomous state creates the basis for the social relations of production, laying down the conditions for the development of the dominant mode of social relations of production and for the subordination of other modes to the dominant mode" (ibid., 149). The state's particular orientation to legal regulation is in turn shaped by conditions of world order and the state's "historic bloc" or the "configuration of social forces upon which state power ultimately rests" (ibid., 105). Cox describes the relationship between a state's historic bloc and the conditions of world order thus:

> The novelty of the European developments of the fifteenth and sixteenth centuries was the founding of a state system in a context of economic changes that accumulated wealth in centres that ultimately were able to transform that wealth into a capitalist development process – a process that spread from its points of origin in Europe over the whole world.
>
> The state system provided a framework within which that process engendered a world economy, developing and functioning according to its own dynamic. Initially, during the age of mercantilism, that world economy was constrained within political boundaries laid down by states through national monopolies and trade restrictions. By mid-nineteenth century, with the sponsorship and political support of the most powerful state, the world economy achieved autonomy, such that its own laws began to constrain state policies. (Ibid.: 107)

Mercantilist practices and balance of power politics characterized the particular configuration of social forces and world order throughout the eighteenth century.[4] "Mercantilism varied in every country, according to local conditions and traditions; yet it can be said in a general way that it was the economic counterpart of the political process by which the national states were being built up" (Clough and Cole, 1946: 197). The mercantilism of Portugal and Spain was more protectionist than that of the Dutch, while English and French mercantilism stressed the encouragement of domestic industrial production in addition to the expansion of trade and the accumulation of wealth.[5] However, what united the various approaches was the increased recognition of the role that economic matters played in the determination of national power. This recognition is closely linked to the rise of capitalism and to the economic expansion of Europe.

> It was the increase in capitalist business that turned the attention of people to economic matters as the key to wealth and power. Sometimes the businessmen supported the mercantilist policies; sometimes they opposed them. In a general way, however, mercantilism helped the capitalist by putting the power of the state behind him, even though it hampered and restricted him at the same time. When the businessman had grown strong enough and wealthy enough (by the eighteenth century) he began to think about shaking off the control of the state and using it for his own purposes. The expansion of Europe made the search for national strength in part a competition for commerce, sea power, and colonies and greatly widened the field in which mercantilism could be applied. Furthermore, it brought to the fore just those areas on the Atlantic where the new states were developing national and mercantilist policies. (Clough and Cole, 1946: 198)

The rise in capitalist business techniques and the growth in mercantilist doctrine had a major impact on moral theology and, in effect,

4 It is beyond the scope of this discussion to consider the balance of power system; however, for a good overview see Cox (1987: ch. 5).

5 Portuguese mercantilism focussed almost entirely upon the adoption of policies aimed at securing and maintaining royal control of the spice trade with India. Portuguese policies included exploiting the colonies for the exclusive benefit of the mother country, ensuring an excess of exports over imports, and accumulating bullion. Spain adopted similar policies, imposing considerable controls on colonial trade, while the Dutch adopted more open policies aimed at expanding trade through the imposition of few customs duties and tariffs on imports. England and France, in contrast, emphasized the importance of both domestic production and trade expansion to economic state-building. In England, the guild system and protective tariffs served to encourage domestic industry, while the Navigation Acts and Corn Laws were designed to protect and to enhance national trade. In France, high protective tariffs, policies to encourage exports and to enhance the productive capabilities of domestic producers formed the core of mercantilist practices. For a fuller review of the various forms that mercantilism took in these countries see Clough and Cole (1946: ch. 7); Clough (1959, ch. 2); and North (1981, ch. 11).

sanctioned "a new degree of freedom from religious constraints on individual enterprise and individual aspirations for economic betterment" (Viner, 1978: 113; see also, Weber 1978 b). With the growth of investment practices, capital markets, and new forms of business enterprises the Church had to adapt moral theology to commercial practices. While the impact of such developments was felt more strongly in Protestant theology than in Catholic theology, by the end of the Reformation there was a considerable erosion of the Church's influence on commercial activity.[6] Religious controls on prices, product liability, and usury weakened as states developed different national standards governing commercial transactions. The requirement of just prices and the enforcement of market offences persisted into the seventeenth and eighteenth centuries. However, by the seventeenth century there was an erosion of the just price requirement as the number of permitted exceptions proliferated (Tawney, 1962: 40–1). As Viner (1978: 85) notes "the doctrine of the just price lost most of whatever practical importance it may have had earlier as a justification for state, guild, or ecclesiastical interference" with competitive processes. However, it retained doctrinal and practical significance in cases of monopolies, disputes where there was no ascertainable market price, and where abnormal conditions, such as famine or siege, obtained.

The "paternalist model" of price fixing and the enforcement of market offences continued into the seventeenth and eighteenth centuries. Regulatory statutes continued to be enacted in the eighteenth century controlling prices, but with less frequency.[7] So, too, local authorities continued to enforce the market offences of forestalling, regrating, and engrossing. "Indeed, for most of the eighteenth century the middleman remained legally suspect, and his operations were, in theory, severely restricted."[8] These regulations formed part of the measures adopted by local and state authorities to gain control over economic activities in the era of mercantilism and state building. However, while mercantilist policies assisted states in the accumulation of wealth, as Cox (1987)

[6] Viner (1978: 113) attributes this differential impact to the fact that Protestant churches were more closely tied to the state: "Mercantilism, which was nationalist in essence and stressed national objectives as against the moral claims of individuals or other peoples, found an easier entry into the doctrinal teaching of clergymen belonging to the various state-established, state-supported and largely state-dominated churches of Protestantism than into the corpus of the tradition-bound and supra-national Catholic Church."

[7] See Atiyah (1979: 169). And see Thompson (1971: 109, n. 106) for examples of price regulations enacted in England at this time.

[8] Thompson (1971: 83). See also Thompson (ibid., 84, n. 23 and 6, n. 64) for examples of the enforcement of market offences in the eighteenth century.

notes, the "insular mercantilist state" contained inherent contradictions between social forces aimed at localizing wealth and capital and those aimed at delocalization:

> the commercial interests entrenched in mercantilism, as well as those of the state itself, were resolutely opposed to the further steps necessary to emancipate wealth for capitalist development. These steps would be to transform land and labor power into commodities and to remove mercantilist restrictions on the market when they became an impediment to capital accumulation. (117)

As the rationale for mercantilist regulation came under attack, so too did the foundation for fixed prices and market regulations. The advent of *laissez-faire* theory and the values of economic liberalism in the eighteenth and nineteenth centuries and their adoption by the most powerful commercial states gave new meaning to the idea of merchant autonomy in contract law that reflected more fundamental transitions in world order. The advent of the liberal state marked a transformation in world order and fundamental changes in productive relations: "the liberal state and the liberal world order emerged together, taking shape through the establishment of bourgeois hegemony in Britain and British hegemony in the world economy" (Cox, 1987: 123). Cox (ibid.: 111–12) notes that the "coming of the liberal order was the culmination of the first major transformation in state structures, historic blocs, and modes of social relations of production to have left its traces in the present." Indeed, the advent of the liberal state marked an important development in the juridification of commercial relations by establishing an unequivocal link between law and capitalism and inscribing a tension that persists today between the localizing tendencies of the state system and remnants of feudal and mercantilist legal regulation and the delocalizing tendencies of a world economy and capitalist legal regulation aimed at removing barriers to globalizing economic relations.

Merchant autonomy in commercial law was recast in a manner consistent with the principles of freedom of contract and, in combination with the principle of the sanctity of contract (*pacta sunt servanda*), provided the ideological and theoretical foundations for modern contract theory. The will theory of contract, which stresses the free will of the parties to contract on terms agreeable to themselves, replaced medieval notions of equity in contracting. England played a leading role in changing domestic pricing practices and thus exerted a profound normative influence in terms of the transmission of standards through states that inherited or adopted the common law system through colonial expansion. In 1772 legislation in England against forestalling was repealed, signaling a victory for the "new political economy" of *laissez-faire* and economic liberalism (Thompson, 1971: 89). As E. P. Thompson (ibid., 89) suggests, the "new political economy" involved a "demoralizing of the theory of trade and consumption no less far-reaching than the more widely-debated dissolution of the restrictions upon usury." Demoralization meant that the political economy was "disinfested of intrusive moral imperatives." In the language of Karl Polanyi (1944), this was part of the process by which the economy was progressively disembedded from society. In the context of previous discussions of the origin of the public/private distinction, this move was crucial in the construction of the public sphere and in disembedding and insulating the private sphere of capital accumulation from political or social regulation, thereby neutralizing it of political content. Liberal economists argued that fixed prices distorted markets, which were regarded as organic in origin and operation, and that the marketing offences interfered with natural patterns of exchange. The private sphere was thus infused with an organic and natural character that was embodied in juridico-political understandings of the nature and function of private law. Marketing offences disappeared and the requirement of the just price was superseded by what Adam Smith referred to as the "natural price" (Atiyah, 1979: 299). In law this came to mean the price agreed to by the contracting parties and, in the absence of agreement or in cases of underspecification, the courts implied that the parties intended the current market prices to apply.

The influence of liberal political economy extended beyond the common law family and embraced all Western systems of law in some degree. The principle of freedom of contract became the foundation for contract law on the Continent and beyond.[9] Importantly, legal theory intersected with the dominant social forces of the day. Liberal theory associated contractual freedom with efficiency and the facilitation of exchange. Moreover, freedom of contract was regarded as the necessary corollary of freedom of trade, the growth of commerce, and the accumulation of wealth. "The autonomy or free choice of private parties to make their own contracts on their own terms was a central feature of contract law . . . [and] had a profound effect on the functions of contract law

[9] See David and Brierley (1978) for the foundations of contract law in the different legal systems of the world.

as perceived by the courts . . . [the] primary function [being] facultative" (Atiyah, 1979: 408). The judicial function came to be conceived in terms of facilitating commercial exchange through the enforcement of contracts with minimum intervention into the substantive contractual terms. This might involve the implication of market prices (or other terms) in cases of disagreement or underspecification, but it did not involve reviewing the substantive fairness of the bargain. Indeed, the willingness of the courts to imply a contractual price based on the market price reflected the belief that they had a duty to enforce bargains arrived at by competent and consenting parties and their faith in market mechanisms as the proper arbiter of price disputes. The medieval notion that exchange could be measured by some objective standard of fairness or equivalence in exchange drops from sight and is replaced by the belief that the value of exchange is a matter of subjective choice as articulated through market mechanisms. As Patrick Atiyah (ibid., 167) observes, "[t]he extreme individualism, the belief that all prices are a matter of subjective choice, the stress on the will and intention of the nineteenth century were not found in the law of the eighteenth century in any degree. They only really emerged in the late eighteenth century," marking the birth of Karl Marx's "legal subject." The "legal subject" became the individual bearer of economic rights to the protection of private property through contract in the material and ideological contexts of what C. B. Macpherson (1962) refers to as the property rights associated with the cult of "possessive individualism." The birth of the "legal subject" signaled a fundamental transformation in legal regulation, for it established a legal relationship of "equality" between contracting parties that simply could not exist under feudalism, where birth, inheritance, custom, and legal privileges dominated economic relations. It also legitimized rights to private property, contributing to the transformation from feudal to capitalist conceptions of property.[10] As Evgenii Pashukanis notes:

> [c]ustom or tradition as the supra-individual basis for legal claims, corresponds to the restrictive nature and inertia of the feudal social structure . . . Equality between subjects was assumed only for relations which were confined to a particular narrow sphere. Thus the members of one and the same estate were equal in the realm of the law of that estate, members of a guild were equal in the realm of guild law. At this stage, the legal subject as the universal abstract bearer of

[10] See Cutler (2002 d) for analysis of the transition from feudalism to capitalism as a transition in dominant conceptions of property.

> every conceivable legal claim is in evidence only as a bearer of concrete privileges . . .
>
> Since there was no abstract concept of the legal subject in the Middle Ages, the concept of the objective norm, applicable to a wide indeterminate circle of people, was also connected with the establishment of concrete privileges and freedoms. (1978: 119–20)

For our purposes it is significant to note that Marx's conceptualization of the juridical equality between independent economic subjects is itself a fetishized relationship that reflects the fetishism of the commodity exchange relationship under capitalist production. Moreover, it is a fetishized relationship infused with moral and ethical content.[11] Like the fetishized commodity relationship it, too, obscures the reality of the inequality and dominance of the underlying productive relations. Marx attributed both ideological and coercive roles to law. Ideologically, law establishes the legitimacy of capitalist exchange relations in "idealized form," hiding the fundamentally exploitative character of capitalist production (Young, 1979: 145). For Marx, capitalist exchange relations take the juridical form of the contract between two autonomous and willing individuals:

> [t]his juridical relation, whose form is the contract . . . is a relation between two wills which mirrors the economic relation. The content of this juridical relation (or relation of two wills) is itself determined by the economic relations. Here the persons exist for one another merely as representatives and hence owners, of commodities . . . the characters who appear on the economic stage are merely personifications of economic relations; it is as bearers of these economic relations that they come into contact with one another. (1976: 178–9)

However, the commodity relationship is a fetishized one in which the relationship between the commodity and its producer is inverted so that the producer appears to owe his existence to the commodity rather than the reverse, whereby the commodity owes its existence to its producer. For Marx, the "mystical" and "enigmatic" character of the commodity lies in its assumption of its own objective existence and life-form apart from its creator.[12] In the fetishized commodity relationship, "things take

11 Evgenii Pashukanis (1978, 151–2) identifies the commodity-producing society with the fusion of "man as a moral subject," "man as a legal subject," and "man as an egoistic subject." "All three of these seemingly incompatible stipulations which are not reducible to one and the same thing, express the totality of conditions necessary for the realisation of the value relation, which is a relation in which social relations in the labour process appear as a reified characteristic of the products being exchanged."

12 See Marx (1976: 163 et seq.) for his discussion of the fetishism of commodities.

on the character of active, productive subjects, whilst social relations take on the character of things" (Rose, 1977: 29). This creates a distance between "the visible reality of appearance" and "the invisible reality of essence" (ibid., 38). "Legal fetishism" in turn "complements commodity fetishism"[13] for the relationship between the law and the producer is similarly inverted so that the economic subject appears to owe his existence to the law, rather than the reverse. Accordingly, "individuals affirm that they owe their existence to the law, rather than the reverse, inverting the real causal relationship between themselves and their product" (Balbus, 1977: 583). The law takes on an objective form, obscuring its real essence as a product of human design and choice. The fetishized legal form thus "both produces and reinforces illusory, rather than genuine, forms of equality, individuality, and community" (ibid., 580). As Gary Young (1979: 161) observes, to "go beyond the limits of bourgeois ideology, law would have to acknowledge the existence of capitalist exploitation" by probing the mystification resulting from the commodity form and legal fetishism. This would take one into examining the coercive function of law, illustrated by Marx in his analysis of the role law played in the creation of capitalist productive relations through laws against vagrancy, draconian penalties for theft, maximum wage laws, and minimum workday legislation, and the fundamental transformations affected through the Factory Acts.[14] Juridico-political notions of equal exchange thus obscure the underlying coercive nature of productive relations and mask the crucial role played by liberal theories of contract in the concealment of law's other, coercive face. The "double face of law," as a concealing movement between consent and coercion is nicely captured by Gramsci's insight that law exists at the intersection of hegemony (consent) and coercion.[15]

[13] Pashukanis (1978: 117). Pashukanis's analysis of the commodity and the subject is probably the most developed analysis of the relationship between law and the commodity form under capitalism. Unfortunately, he limits himself to analysis of the exchange relation as definitive of capitalism, thereby obscuring the relationship between law and production. Moreover, he also tends toward a formalistic understanding of law, regarding it as part of the superstructure that would disappear with the disappearance of the capitalist state. See Hirst (1979); Fraser (1978); and Jessop (1980) for excellent reviews and criticisms of Pashukanis's work.

[14] Marx (1976) and see Thompson (1975) for an exhaustive analysis of legislation that transformed the feudal mode of production into the capitalist mode of production. See also O'Neill (1986) for an interesting comparison of factory discipline analyzed by Marx and prison discipline analyzed by Foucault, and see Santos (1985: 313–16) for an excellent analysis of Marx's treatment of the Factory Acts.

[15] See Benney (1983: 205). And see Gramsci (1971: 195–6).

The centrality of the law and increasingly juridified relations to the emergence of capitalism and the liberal state has been noted by many. The tendency of Max Weber to associate capitalism with specifically legal regulation, rationalized and systematized by the development of national legal systems and juridico-political bureaucracies, institutions, and ideologies, has already been noted. Karl Polanyi (1944), too, associates the movement from feudalism to the free-market economy with legislative moves to create free markets in land, labor, and money. Polanyi dispels the misunderstanding that *laissez-faire* means the absence of regulation by documenting in some detail the extensiveness and intensiveness of legislative initiatives involved in the effort to create a free-market civilization. As Boaventura de Sousa Santos (1985: 300 and 307) observes, capitalist societies are specifically "legal formations or configurations" and one of the most striking differences between capitalist and feudal societies is the "extent to which power relations are institutionalized and juridified." However, it is a particular form of legal rationality and juridico-legal ideology that informs the association between law and capitalism: it is the fetishized understanding of law associated with legal formalism. Max Weber (1978 a: 811) captures the relationship between law and capitalism perfectly: "[j]uridical formalism enables the legal system to operate as a technically rational machine," or at least to operate with an appearance of rationality.

Indeed, the juridification of commerce is informed by a juridical ideology that embodies understandings of the proper judicial role that strictly differentiate the legal/judicial function from economics, politics, and morality. These tendencies were addressed in earlier chapters in the context of the legal formalism that characterizes dominant theories of law. Informed by ideological separations between private and public activities and between economics, politics, and law, the common law courts have limited the judicial function. Rules precluding judicial evaluation of the equivalence of exchange or the prudence of bargains, embodied in the legal doctrine of consideration, came to narrowly circumscribe judicial intervention on the grounds of fairness.[16] Morton Horwitz's belief that these developments reflect a decline of the medieval tradition

[16] The doctrine of consideration did not come from the law merchant, but was developed by the common law. Under the common law, an agreement is unenforceable unless it is contained in a sealed instrument or it is supported by valuable consideration. While the origin and evolution of the doctrine of consideration are complex, at the core of the doctrine is the belief that there must be an exchange of value arrived at by way of a bargain in order for a promise to be binding. The doctrine was developed in the late eighteenth century by common law judges. While early statements of the doctrine might suggest

of substantive justice and the equitable conception of contract is worth citing in full:

> Modern contract law is fundamentally a creature of the nineteenth century. It arose both in England and America as a reaction to and criticism of the medieval tradition of substantive justice that, surprisingly, had remained a vital part of eighteenth-century legal thought, especially in America. Only in the nineteenth century did judges and jurists finally reject the longstanding belief that the justification of contractual obligation is derived from the inherent justice or fairness of exchange. In its place, they asserted for the first time that the source of the obligation of contract is the convergence of the wills of the contracting parties... [I]n a society in which value came to be regarded as entirely subjective and in which the only basis for assigning value was the concurrence of arbitrary individual desire, principles of substantive justice were inevitably seen as entailing an 'arbitrary and uncertain' standard of value. Substantive justice, according to the earlier view, existed in order to prevent men from using the legal system in order to exploit each other. But where things have no 'intrinsic value,' there can be no substantive measure of exploitation and the parties are, by definition, equal. *Modern contract law was thus born staunchly proclaiming that all men are equal because all measures of equality are illusory.* (Horwitz, 1974: 917–19, emphasis added)

Whereas the medieval equitable theory of contract limited and defined contractual obligations in terms of the fairness of exchange, under modern contract theory contractual obligation depends upon the convergence of the wills and desires of individuals (ibid., 923): Marx's "juridical subjects." The role of the law was thus to enforce "willed transactions" that the parties believed to be to their mutual interest and advantage (ibid., 947). The law was not to police the equity of the bargain.

that the doctrine was intended to regulate equivalence in exchange, in deference to free-market values and the principle of freedom of contract, the common law adopted the rule that it is not for the courts to enquire into the adequacy of consideration. "A court of equity, for example, should not be permitted to refuse to enforce an agreement for simple 'exorbitancy of price' because 'it is the consent of parties alone, that fixes the price of a thing, without reference to the nature of things themselves, or to their intrinsic value'... 'a man is obliged in conscience to perform a contract which he has entered into, although it be a hard one.'" (Powell, quoted in Horwitz, 1974: 918). For a fuller discussion of the origins of the doctrine of consideration see Farnsworth (1969) and Atiyah (1979).

No similar requirement exists in the civil law. While some civil law countries, such as France, require the existence of a sufficient *causa* to make a contract valid, this concept is not the same as the common law concept of consideration. The modern doctrine of *causa*, rooted in Roman law, was developed in the seventeenth and eighteenth centuries and came to signify a juridical reason, rationale, or purpose for contracting. See Lorenzen (1919).

Indeed, the autonomy of economic and commercial relations was established by "abstracting" them from the "original disciplinary science of government and morals" (O'Neill, 1986: 50). As Horwitz (1974: 952) argues, this vision of contract law gave expression to the ideology of the market economy that dominated the nineteenth century. The development of extensive markets at the turn of the century:

> contributed to a substantial erosion of belief in theories of objective value and just price. Markets for future delivery of goods were difficult to explain within a theory of exchange based on giving and receiving equivalents in value. Futures contracts for fungible commodities could only be understood in terms of a fluctuating conception of expected value radically different from the static notion that lay behind contracts for specific goods; a regime of markets and speculation was simply incompatible with a socially imposed standard of value. (Ibid., 946–7)

Moreover, the modern will theory of contract arose as part of the "procommercial attack on the theory of objective value" (ibid.) in the movement from the feudal to the capitalist mode of production. It both reflected and constituted fetishized understandings of markets and exchange relations. As the legal ideology of the juridical subject, the will theory of contract sealed the separation of economics and politics and neutralized private law by isolating and obscuring socioeconomic processes of capitalist production beneath a "gloss" of individual liberty and freedom of contract (O'Neill, 1986: 46). Nicos Poulantzas (1973: 128 and 284) describes this as the isolating effect of law, while for Nikolas Rose (1977: 37) it is a "movement of concealment," in that productive relations "disappear in the phenomenal forms in which they are manifest" producing a distance between the essential relations of production and the form of their appearance as exchange relations. To Marx, this concealment or isolation is not universal, but is historically specific to the capitalist mode of production. However, the capitalist mode of production is not self-sustaining. Certain conditions have to be met in terms of creating the ideological and technical infrastructure for the practice of fetishized law. These may be found in the legal rules governing contractual and property rights, which constitute the core of private, commercial law.

In domestic commercial law the norm for domestic contracts came to be the determination of prices according to the will of individuals bargaining freely in the exchange relationship and the application of current market prices in cases of underspecification. These norms were evident in both common law and civil law countries, although the zeal with which the common law courts embraced the free-market approach and the peculiarities associated with the common law doctrine of consideration, might suggest that the norm was stronger for common law than for civil law jurisdictions.[17]

The decline in the equitable theory of contract is also evident in the changing standards governing liability for defective goods. While quality controls persisted into the seventeenth and eighteenth centuries, the common law developed the rule of *caveat emptor* or buyer beware. The rule limits the liability of sellers for defective goods to only those instances where the seller provided an express warranty of quality or was guilty of fraud. This rule is said to be an "ancient maxim of the common law," not traceable to Roman law, ecclesiastical law, or to the law merchant (Hamilton, 1931: 1156). In England, it first appeared in print in the sixteenth century and gained acceptance in the seventeenth century. However, it was only widely applied in the eighteenth and nineteenth centuries (ibid., 1164). As the "apotheosis of nineteenth-century individualism," it was consistent with the developing model of contract law which left each party to rely on his own judgment and imposed no duty to volunteer information to the other (Atiyah, 1979: 464). *Caveat emptor* was associated with the ideals of the new political economy. The responsibility to inspect goods was placed upon the purchaser, for it was assumed by the theory that "buyers discounted the prices and were prepared to pay to allow for the risk that the commodity they were buying might prove to be defective" (ibid., 466). According to this rationale, giving the purchaser a statutory protection against defective goods would be to provide a bonus for which he had not paid. The rule came into prominence in England, where Chief Justice Lord Mansfield is credited with stating its definitive application as the common law courts replaced those of the law merchant (see Horwitz, 1974: 945).

In the United States the rule was applied with even more vigor. "In the new republic the tradition of authority did not linger long after the war for independence, the intellectual individualism was reinforced by the spirit of the frontier, an emerging industrial system was not to be shackled by formal control, and the courts were quite loath to take up the shock of business friction" (Hamilton, 1931: 1,178). The rule was

[17] See Atiyah (1979) for a detailed exploration of the particular influence that liberal political economy had on the Bench and Bar in England.

consistent with prevailing views of free-market exchange, for it was felt that the purchaser was in the best position to bear the risk of defective goods through inspecting them upon receipt, refusing to accept defective or nonconforming goods, or negotiating an express warranty of quality.

> The laws contrived for the protection of the consumer were repealed or forgotten; the machinery of law enforcement fell into disuse. The matter of the quality of the ware, passed out of the province of government into the economic order. In the market, as the schoolmen of the day were wont to argue, sellers were balanced against buyers, each was in his mercenary methods checked by the competition of others of his kind, and quality even as price was neatly accommodated to individual want. (Hamilton, 1931: 1,183)

Thus the common law adopted the rule of limiting the seller's liability for defective goods to a narrow set of circumstances (express warranty and fraud). The situation was somewhat different for civil law countries where national commercial codes established rules governing liability for defective goods, carving out a broader scope for liability (see Tallon, 1983).

The disappearance of the prohibition of usury was also consistent with the advent of free-market principles, though, as noted before, exceptions to the prohibition and selective enforcement had been common. Full play was not given to the market for states continued to regulate the rate at which interest could be charged.[18] Moreover, some states established different rates for domestic and international transactions, allowing a higher rate for the latter (Tallon, 1983: 78).

The advent of *laissez-faire* theory and the values of economic liberalism in the eighteenth and nineteenth centuries and their adoption by the important commercial powers thus gave new meaning to the principles of merchant autonomy in contract law. Merchant autonomy was reformulated in the context of the principle of freedom of contract. Together the principles of freedom of contract and the sanctity of contract provided the respective *grundnorms* for the private and the public spheres. Freedom of contract provided the foundation for the construction of the private sphere as an insulated zone of "private" commercial activity secured by the state through the "public" enforcement of contracts. The will theory of contract, which stresses the free will of

[18] In England the Statute of Usury permitted interest charges that did not exceed 10 percent. See Tawney (1962: 180).

parties to contract on terms agreeable to themselves, replaced medieval notions of equity in contracting and articulated the legal framework for the differentiation between private and public activities, which sealed the separation between economics and politics. With the expansion of merchant autonomy in contracting, there was an erosion of the dualistic system of regulation characteristic of the medieval phase. Moreover, now merchant autonomy operated, not by virtue of the absence of political authority, but with the sanction and support of state authorities. In addition, while states limited their regulatory authority concerning the substantive content of commercial agreements, they expanded it in enforcement matters. The concealment of the fundamentally political and coercive nature of capitalism in domestic economic relations spilled over into international economic relations as the law merchant was absorbed into different national systems of law and subjected to the discipline of liberal political economy and ideology and the isolation of private international law.

As noted in Chapter 2, the distinction between public and private international law emerged out of a "double movement," reflecting the emergence of the nation-state and theories of sovereignty and the attempt of newly emerging states to create a private sphere free from regulation and state intervention. Territorially individuated state authority provided material, institutional, and ideological foundations for the separation of public and private international law, reflecting the emerging distinction between international and domestic legal relations. The advent of liberal theory and political economy further refined the distinction by associating private international legal relations with the economic realm of freedom of exchange and markets. The principles of freedom of contract and the protection of private property were thus articulated as the natural and organic conditions of the private sphere and the *grundnorms* for international commercial relations. By the nineteenth century the distinction between public and private international law was clear, although doubts persisted as to the conceptual status of private international law as properly "international" law, particularly in the Anglo-American legal world. By the end of the Second World War, the distinction was an "article of faith" for public international lawyers and the isolation of private international law was complete (Paul, 1988: 163).

However, it will become evident, as the discussion turns to consider the experiences of the key commercial powers, that these developments were experienced rather differently by states.

Law-Creation, Enforcement, and Nation-States

The nationalization, localization, and neutralization of the law merchant proceeded differently and did not produce uniform results in states. The loss of merchant autonomy was more pronounced in common law states, particularly in England, where merchants disappeared as a separate class. In contrast, on the Continent, many countries retained special jurisdictions and courts for commercial actions. Furthermore, national differences emerged in the specific rendering of law merchant norms.

> As national judges and legislators codified commercial law, it tended to lose its cosmopolitan character and outlook. This process of nationalization of commercial law and of its increasing divorce from experience was characteristic of legal development not only in England and in the United States, but also in France, Germany, and the other countries of Europe. When this process was coupled, as it often was, with a hostility toward the proof of mercantile customs, the result was to impede the adaptation of law to new economic circumstances. The tendency of traders to develop new commercial devices thus ran headlong into the tendency of national legal systems to codify, whether through statute or precedent or legal doctrine. (Berman and Kaufman, 1978: 227–8)

Legal developments in England, the United States, and France have been the most significant in the evolution of the law merchant. English commercial law formed the foundation for commercial relations in the common law countries of the world. Laws modeled on British statutes and common law were adopted by countries of the common law tradition. Through colonial expansion and trade relations, the standards embodied in English commercial law have been transmitted throughout the world.[19] While the influence of British law was, arguably, most significant at the height of Britain's hegemony and commercial supremacy in the activities of English traders and the great trading companies, the influence has been even more profound and enduring. The principles embodied in English commercial law established the core for a major part of Western commercial law and, while they have been subject to some modification over time, they have provided much normative consistency. The basic emphasis on freedom of contract and the sanctity of contract has endured.

As British commercial supremacy waned and the United States gained in influence, American commercial standards became more significant.

[19] See David and Brierley (1978) for the transmission and reception of the common law throughout the world.

The United States adopted British commercial law during the formative stages of its municipal legal system, but later came to enact significant reforms under the Uniform Commercial Code (UCC). As shall become evident, the standards embodied in the UCC became influential in establishing global commercial laws in the third and modern phase of the evolution of the law merchant.

Developments in French commercial law, and to a lesser extent in German law, have been significant as sources of civilian commercial law. Civil or Romano-Germanic law developed on the basis of the Roman *jus civile* and has also been transmitted and received throughout the world through the processes of colonization and adoption (see David and Brierley, 1978: 21). Although different in many respects, the common law and civil law share much at the level of guiding principle, thus enabling their classification as one "great family of Western law." "In both, the law has undergone the influence of Christian morality and, since the Renaissance, philosophical teachings have given prominence to individualism, liberalism, and individual rights" (ibid., 24).

Decline of merchant custom

The second phase in the development of the law merchant was marked by a decline in pluralism of both the sources and subjects of the law. Positive law replaced customary law as the primary source of law, though as will become evident, elements of commercial custom persisted. This created a tension between the localizing tendency of national positive law and the delocalizing tendencies of international commercial custom.

As regards subjects of the law, there was also a decline in pluralism. With the articulation of the distinctions between domestic and international law, states replaced individuals as the proper subjects of international law, which was increasingly associated with *public* international law. Here too, however, private associations, corporations, and individuals continued to exercise some influence over law-creation, albeit not as legal "subjects," but as "objects." They too gave rise to delocalizing and globalizing tendencies that conflicted with states' efforts to localize and nationalize international commercial law. With the further articulation of distinctions between public and private international law, the individual and other private entities such as business corporations assumed significance as part of the isolated, concealed, and politically invisible sphere of private international trade law.

In England, nationalization of the law merchant proceeded on two fronts. One involved the disappearance of the specialized courts as their jurisdiction was absorbed by the common law courts. The other involved the absorption of substantive merchant law into the common law (Tallon, 1983: 48–9). While the next section will focus on the disappearance of merchant courts, by the seventeenth century the law merchant "was being gradually absorbed into the general legal system of the country. As in the case of internal trade, so in the case of the foreign trade, the older mercantile courts had ceased to exist. Jurisdiction was therefore assumed by the ordinary courts of law and equity."[20] But the disappearance of commercial courts and the assumption of jurisdiction by the common law courts produced certain anomalies. As previous discussions have shown, the common law courts did not recognize or enforce most transactions and procedures enforceable in the law merchant courts. As a result, merchants were either forced to resort to private arbitration or when possible to the courts of equity.[21] The common law courts responded by absorbing the law merchant into the common law. Under Lord Coke, as Chief Justice in the seventeenth century, this involved the application of the law merchant as custom and not as law, and only to merchants. Merchants had to prove that they were merchants and then prove the customs upon which they relied to the satisfaction of the common law courts. And

> as the Law Merchant was considered as custom, it was the habit to leave the custom and the facts to the jury without any directions in point of law, with a result that cases were rarely reported as laying down any particular rule, because it was almost impossible to separate the custom from the facts; as a result little was done towards building up any system of mercantile Law in England. (Scrutton, 1909: 13)

However, there was considerable discontent with this approach. Berman and Kaufman (1978: 226) note that, as a body of customary law articulated by juries, "the law merchant was hardly suited for a leading

20 Holdsworth (1907: 304). The Admiralty Court survived until the Judicature Acts of 1872–5 and then became a division of the High Court of Justice. See Tallon (1983: 136).

21 The Court of Equity developed alongside the common law courts under the office of the Chancellor. It was also known as the Court of Chancery and was regarded as a court of "conscience" for it dispensed justice when the other courts were incapable of providing the claimant with a remedy. Lord Ellesmere in *Earl of Oxford's Case* (1615) 1 Rep. Ch. 1 at 6 stated the function of the Court of Chancery thus: "men's actions are so diverse and infinite that it is impossible to make a general law which may aptly meet with every particular and not fail in some circumstances. The office of the chancellor is to correct men's consciences for fraud, breaches of trust, wrongs and oppressions of what nature soever they may be, and to soften and mollify the extremity of the law." Quoted in Baker (1990: 122–3).

commercial power, which England had become in the eighteenth century." Moreover, merchants needed the law to be more clearly defined, while "from the point of view of national policy, there was a need for the law to be developed officially and not merely informally by commercial experience" (Honnold, 1964: 75–6). As a result, in the eighteenth century, under the direction of Chief Justice Lord Mansfield, the law merchant was made part of the common law, applicable to all persons.[22] Henceforth, positive law would displace custom as the primary source of law.

The incorporation of the law merchant, however, did not have a uniform influence on different areas of the common law. Merchant custom, formerly an integral component of law-creation, came to be of variable significance in different areas of the law. Merchant customs continued to influence the development of laws governing financial transactions, insurance, and shipping.[23] As a result, these areas remained truer to their law merchant origins. This was not the case for the law governing contracts of sale, which came to adopt distinctively English rules (Honnold, 1964: 72). In some cases, innovations from the law merchant were incorporated into the common law.[24] In other cases, however, incorporation was carried out by modifying the law merchant to suit the common law and its procedures.[25]

> The customary doctrines of the law merchant could not be fitted in all cases into the more rigid framework of the common law without distortion. In more than one direction that was bound to affect its commercial application, the common law had been subjected to backgrounds peculiarly English and divorced from any international influences. With the conclusion of the period of absorption, therefore, the commercial law of England still might be based fundamentally on the customs of merchants, and to that extent might retain a cosmopolitan flavor as its chief distinction; but the direct reflection of former days had become a refraction. (Thayer, 1936: 142–3)

[22] In *Pillans v. van Mierop* 3 Burr. 1663, 97 Eng. Rep. 1035 (KB 1765) Lord Mansfield held that the rules of the law merchant were questions of law to be decided by the courts and not matters of customs to be proved by the parties.

[23] Lord Mansfield is noted for the systematic use of merchant juries to assist in the adjudication of these kinds of commercial dispute. See Honnold (1964: 72).

[24] As in the cases of actions of account, certain rights among partners, and the right of stoppage of goods in transit.

[25] This was the case for the development of many of the doctrines of contract law (i.e., the rules governing formation of contract and consideration) and for the standards of liability for carriers of goods by sea.

During the nineteenth century, significant areas of commercial law were codified on the basis of common law decisions.[26] In some cases, codification contributed to a further decline in the cosmopolitan nature of English commercial law, and ultimately a decline in the universality of the law merchant, by strengthening the national character of the rules.[27] Discontinuities appear, however, in that in other areas codification incorporated merchant custom. Codification of the laws governing bills of exchange, insurance, and maritime matters (e.g. shippers, carriers, general average, and salvage) incorporated international mercantile custom, thus retaining significant universality (Honnold, 1964: 75–6). Moreover, to the extent that these areas of law came to be regarded as strictly private commercial matters, they were insulated and isolated as private international trade law. Indeed, the isolation of private commercial law is most pronounced in the area of maritime law.[28] Increasingly, the laws governing maritime transport and insurance were isolated from public international law as the *commercial* and *industrial* aspects of maritime trade came to be regarded as matters of private international law, while matters of *ocean use* were classified as public international law. Maritime transport and insurance thus evolved as private regulatory regimes, subject to the controls of powerful private associations and organizations, including shipping cartels, shipping or liner conferences, and shipowner, insurance, and other mercantile associations.[29]

In the United States, the law merchant was applied from the eighteenth century. Commercial law was regarded as part of the ordinary law and administered by the ordinary courts (Tallon, 1983: 54). It was only in the nineteenth and twentieth centuries, however, that codification of commercial law occurred. As in England, the common law was codified into and supplemented by commercial statutes governing the sale of goods, bills of lading, negotiable instruments, and other commercial matters.[30] English legislation provided the model and foundation for American legislation in many areas[31] and English law was relied upon extensively in commercial disputes. As a result, commercial law

26 For example, the laws governing the sale of goods, bills of exchange, carriers' liability, marine insurance, merchant shipping, bills of lading, partnerships, and companies.
27 For example, sale of goods law.
28 This argument is developed fully in Cutler (1999 c).
29 See Cafruny (1987) and Gold (1981) for excellent reviews of the history and political economy of the international maritime transport regime.
30 Owing to the federal structure these statutes were enacted at the state level.
31 This is particularly so for the laws governing bills of exchange and negotiable instruments. See Honnold (1964: 74).

in the United States embodied similar reflections of and departures from the medieval law merchant. Moreover, local particularisms emerged in state laws, generating a movement in the twentieth century for the unification of state laws. Unification ultimately took the form of the Uniform Commercial Code (UCC). While the UCC unified domestic commercial laws, it also had an impact on international transactions by rendering American commercial rules more consistent with international usage.[32] This brought American practices somewhat closer to Continental legal theory and practice in several areas (Honnold, 1964: 83).

The nationalization and localization of the law merchant took quite a different course on the Continent. Many European countries retained distinct commercial jurisdictions, specialized commercial courts, and special treatment for merchants and commercial transactions. As Von Caemmerer (1964: 90) observes, "[o]n the continent it was the appearance of national legislation which effectively promoted the commercial law, but which at the same time led to the loss of its universality and to its splitting-up into particular national laws. The leading role here fell to France." There, land-based commerce and maritime trade were codified in the seventeenth century in the legislation of Colbert. The Ordinnance sur le commerce (1673) and the Ordinnance sur la marine (1681) provided the models for the Napoleonic Code de Commerce of the nineteenth century. The Napoleonic commercial code established the pattern of the separate and distinct treatment of commercial matters, a practice subsequently adopted by many civil law countries.[33] However, while this Code established the practice of distinct and separate treatment for commercial matters, it was inspired by French Revolutionary values that stressed the equality of citizens and freedom of commerce. Trade guilds were suppressed and the notion of a distinct status for merchants was replaced with the idea of a distinct status for commercial transactions. This marked a significant move to objectify commercial law through depersonalizing the commercial relationship, a development considered in later chapters to be the *modus operandi* of legal formalism. Tallon (1983: 8–9 and 30) argues that delinking special personal status from the special status accorded to the transaction was more consistent with

[32] This is particularly so for the provisions governing the sale of goods, terms of trade in transport documents, and negotiable instruments. See Honnold (1964: 228). And see Trakman (1983: 35).

[33] Von Caemmerer (1964: 90). The distinction is recognized in the Spanish Commercial Code of 1829, the Portuguese Code of 1833, the Dutch Code of 1838, the Brazilian Code of 1850, the Italian Commercial Codes of 1865 and 1883, and the German codifications of 1861 and 1900.

French Revolutionary emancipatory values. However, there was continuing hostility to the preservation of distinct commercial courts, as will become evident in the next section.[34] As Schmitthoff notes, the:

> Napoleonic codes gave final expression to the political ideals of the philosophy of the French Revolution. The fundamental concepts of the Napoleonic codification are freedom of contract and the assertion of ownership as an absolute right. The Napoleonic codes have been described as ratifying the triumph of the *tiers état* in which, as we know, the *commercants* and the liberal professions were prominent. The French codification is thus the final seal of a victorious political movement. (1961: 136)

The French Commercial Code has been adopted or copied by Belgium, Luxembourg, Greece, and the French colonies.[35] In France, in the nineteenth century, legislation outside the Commercial Code was enacted governing a number of commercial matters, including bills of lading and cheques (Tallon, 1983: 30).

In comparison to the Anglo-American experience, the nationalization of French commercial law has resulted in a decreased loss in universality. French commercial law retains a distinctiveness, more consistent with the medieval law merchant, but lost to the commercial law of the common law countries. Merchants have special rights and duties, the rules of evidence applied to commercial transactions are more liberal, while commercial transactions are subject to special jurisdiction in commercial courts comprised of merchant judges and subject to swifter and simpler procedures (ibid., 36–8).

In Germany, the foundations of commercial law derive from the customs and rules of the merchant guilds. As in France, the separate commercial jurisdiction of the sixteenth century persisted; however, in Germany there were no separate commercial courts. Some commercial legislation was enacted in the eighteenth century,[36] but the multiplicity of German states prevented codification prior to the nineteenth century.[37] The incorporation of the law merchant was largely achieved

34 The distinction Tallon makes between the treatment of merchants and their transactions may be less important than he suggests for he notes (1983: 36) that French commercial law constitutes a "special regime" and confers on merchants a "special status."

35 See Tallon (1983: 41–4) for a discussion of the experiences of these countries.

36 The Prussian Maritime Law of 1727, the Law on Commercial Instruments of 1766, and the General law of Prussia of 1794.

37 Thayer (1936: 144) and see Schmitthoff (1961).

through commercial codifications of the nineteenth century. Schmitthoff (1961: 136) argues that "in Germany the creation of commercial codes was the legal reflection of the struggle for political unity; it was a deliberate attempt to give impetus to the movement for German political unification by means of the creation of a uniform law." The first unitary commercial code was enacted in 1861, while the German Commercial Code became the law of the Confederation of Northern Germany and was extended to the entire German empire in 1871. It was revised in 1897 and, as in the case of France, legislative enactments in the nineteenth and twentieth centuries governing a variety of commercial matters outside the Code have added to German commercial law.[38] The German Commercial Code has been adopted by Austria and forms the basis for Japanese commercial law (see Tallon, 1983: 18–22). While the distinctiveness of merchant law is not as pronounced in the German system as in the French system, it too appears to bear a greater likeness to the medieval law merchant than do its Anglo-American counterparts.

Thus far the discussion has addressed the nationalization and localization of the law merchant through codification. However, it is also important to note that it was at this time that the field of conflict of laws, discussed in earlier chapters, emerged as a means of localizing and nationalizing international commercial transactions and as a mechanism for managing the increasing territoriality of state power. As mentioned before, conflict rules function to localize transactions with a foreign element in a particular national legal system. The proliferation at this time of national systems of conflict rules underscores the importance that states were attaching to the national and local regulation of international commercial relations. The belief that all transactions should be subject to the jurisdiction of one national legal system (i.e., the belief that there are no homeless or stateless contracts) epitomizes the national approach to regulation and is the legal manifestation of the doctrine of sovereignty that was to dominate the nineteenth century:

> Thus, according to the nineteenth-century point of view, efforts must above all be directed to the field of conflict of laws and jurisdictions. The aim is to decide which national legal system of law governs a given legal relationship having international elements, to fix, if possible,

[38] For example, the law on insurance contracts of 1908, the law on credit instruments of 1961, laws on transportation by river of 1895, road of 1952, air of 1922, rail of 1938, and various laws governing competition and industry.

> which national court shall be exclusively competent to take cognizance of it, and, finally, to ensure the international validity of duly executed documents of foreign judgments delivered in accordance with these principles. (David, 1972 a: 45)

Each national legal system developed its own system of conflict of laws, giving rise to significant differences in the rules used to localize international commercial transactions. Important differences emerged both among and between common and civil law jurisdictions. It was thus possible that a particular transaction could be localized in one country under one system of conflict rules, but in another country under a different system of rules. Toward the end of the second phase there were some efforts by states to harmonize national conflict of laws rules so as to produce uniform results. However, these efforts were undertaken by civilian jurisdictions and did not attract the attention or support of the common law jurisdictions. The Hague Conference on Private International Law was the main body that engaged in the harmonization of conflict rules in the late nineteenth century.[39] However, René David (1972 a: 142) observes that obstacles of "a dogmatic nature" inhibited the success of its efforts: the "lawyers from the various countries, delegated by their governments, did not want to abandon, without good reason which was lacking, the positions which their international [conflict] systems of law had adopted for doctrinal reasons or sometimes fortuitously." While these efforts did produce some results, it was only in the third phase, in the twentieth century, that significant efforts were made to unify substantive rules of commercial law.

In addition, while positive law was the dominant source of law, elements of merchant custom persisted. Their persistence created tensions between localizing and delocalizing influences. This is particularly so with regard to maritime law and insurance law where merchant custom remained a significant source of law. The continuing efficacy of merchant custom was linked to the growing significance of private trade and business associations and corporations, who, while not formal "subjects"

[39] The first Hague Conference for the harmonization of conflict rules took place in 1893. Only European states were invited; the United Kingdom was invited but did not attend. Membership in the Hague Conference was limited to Continental states until the twentieth century. The United Kingdom began participating in 1925 and became a member in 1951. The United States sent observers in 1956 and 1960 and became a member in 1963. Other notable efforts to harmonize conflict rules included those of the Latin and South American states, resulting in the Montevideo Convention of 1889 and the Pan-American Conference that first met in that same year and eventually produced the Code Busmante in 1928.

of public international law, were increasingly significant in creating customary private international law. This law was then transmitted globally through their transnational associations.

In the area of maritime transport, the nationalization and localization of the laws were accompanied by progressively more highly organized and institutionalized private arrangements between merchant shippers, marine insurers, underwriters, and financiers. These private groups were key figures in the construction of the mercatocracy, which functioned as the organic intellectuals, forming the core of the social forces that were to define global political/legal relations in the third phase of the law merchant. While more will be said in the next chapter about the role of early mercantile associations, their influence was significant in the area of maritime law. Maritime transport and insurance practices, for example, were generated and transmitted through the activities of a private group of marine underwriters who met regularly at a coffeehouse run by Edward Lloyd and engaged in the practice of underwriting marine risks. Lloyd published the *News* relating to current developments in shipping matters. It was replaced by *Lloyd's List* in 1734 and in 1760 the underwriters began to jointly publish Lloyd's *Register of Shipping*. "From a loose association of men doing business at the same place, the Lloyd's underwriters slowly became a well-organized society, with rules, standard policies, high ethical standards, and a marvelous information service. From the mid-eighteenth century to the present, Lloyd's has dominated the field of marine insurance" (Tetley, 1978). The adoption of standardized contracts of insurance, crystallizing customs and usages, and their widespread use throughout the world contributed to the universalization of insurance practices and the ideological coherence of the industry.

Merchant custom and private actors also figured in the development of "terms of trade" regulating transport agreements which were used routinely, first, in maritime and, later, in other forms of transport. These terms continue to operate today as customary international law and achieved their currency through regular use by shippers, insurers, and financiers.[40] Here, too, national differences began to emerge, generating

[40] Trade terms deal with the transfer of risk, arrangements for insurance and carriage, packing and marking of goods, documentation, inspection, and notifications. The oldest terms are contracts for the sale of goods "free on board" or fob sale or term, under which the seller is responsible for the cost of transport and bears the responsibility for the safety of the goods until the point of their passing the ship's rail. Once delivery is complete, the risk of loss to the goods and further costs of transport are transferred to the buyer. The

a movement for the unification of trade terms in the third phase of the law merchant.

Despite the persistence of merchant custom in some areas, national codification through positive law produced significant differences in commercial laws. In the area of finance, national legal systems came to recognize the various credit instruments formerly recognized under the law merchant. However, significant national differences emerged in the regulation of bills of exchange, promissory notes, and letters of credit.[41] In the area of insurance, states also became involved in the regulation of commercial practices, undermining the universality of law merchant practices. While more will be said about insurance in the next section on dispute settlement, significant national differences emerged in the area of insurance as well.

This review of the experiences of the major commercial states suggests that the process of nationalizing and localizing the law merchant did not produce uniform results and resulted in a tension between localizing and delocalizing tendencies. Common law jurisdictions emerge as more distinctively "national" and localized than do civil law jurisdictions. This tendency is also evident in the development of dispute settlement practices, to which the discussion will now turn.

Dispute settlement: a public affair

In dispute settlement, as well, tensions between the localizing and nationalizing tendencies of national courts of law and the delocalizing and globalizing tendencies of private dispute settlement are evident. An important element in the nationalization and localization of the law merchant involved the incorporation of the jurisdiction of merchant courts

fob term developed to suit the needs of merchants prior to the establishment of regular shipping lines. At the time it was customary for merchants to charter vessels for the transport of their purchases and to accompany the vessel on the voyage. It thus made sense for the buyer to assume responsibility once the goods were on board. However, with the establishment of regular shipping lines and the development of new forms of finance, the buyer was often not present at the point of delivery and payment was often made at a future date. To meet these new conditions, the cif term (cost, insurance, and freight) was developed and gradually replaced the fob term as the most commonly used contract in ocean trade. Under a cif contract the seller is responsible for shipping the goods or furnishing the documentation for goods already seaborne and for tendering the documents to the buyer. The documents include a bill of lading, a policy of insurance covering the goods, and an invoice showing the amount due from the buyer. Delivery and transfer of risk is satisfied upon delivery by the seller of the documents and not upon the physical transfer of the goods. The use of fob term is usually dated to the early nineteenth century. See Sassoon (1975) and Ramberg (1982: 120).

[41] See generally, David (1972 c: 127); Batt (1947); Thayer (1936: 149–50); and Ellinger (1970).

into national judicial systems. While this process occurred in all of the states under consideration, there were distinct differences in the extent to which national courts assumed jurisdiction over commercial matters. England and the United States adopted unitary systems, wherein the national courts assumed jurisdiction for most commercial matters. The specialized merchant courts disappeared, with the exception in England of the Admiralty Court,[42] whose jurisdiction had been severely limited by the common law courts, the rather unsuccessful Commercial Court,[43] and the earlier Insurance Court. During the seventeenth century the staples courts disappeared and the courts of "pie-powder" diminished in importance (Burdick, 1909: 43–4). In a competition for jurisdiction between the common law and Admiralty courts, the former won, with the latter surviving in diminished stature until its absorption by the High Court of Justice in the nineteenth century (Holdsworth, 1907).

In France, special commercial courts and commercial jurisdictions were retained. Tallon (1983: 139) notes that "these courts have retained the greatest importance. Some merchants consider them to be an essential element of their status as merchants. Despite all the criticism directed towards them they have survived a succession of reforms of judicial organization in France." The commercial courts are independent of the regular courts and operate under special rules of procedure, while merchant judges are elected by merchants and by business corporations.

In Germany, the jurisdiction of the merchant courts was assumed by the national courts; however, jurisdiction was retained in a special division for handling commercial matters. The commercial chamber comprises an ordinary civil judge and two commercial judges appointed upon the recommendations of business organizations (ibid.).

While states expanded their controls over dispute settlement, adjudication in national courts of law did not entirely eclipse dispute settlement through private arbitration. This created a tension between the national outlook of courts of law and the anational, delocalized nature of private arbitration panels. Indeed, for England and the United States, private mechanisms for dispute resolution persisted through the period of the nationalization of the law merchant and judicial system. The

42 See generally, Mears (1908) and Holdsworth (1907).

43 While the Commercial Court was created in 1895 and recognized in 1970 by the Administration of Justice Act as a specialized division of the Queen's Bench of the High Court, it does not operate as an independent court with a separate, fixed jurisdiction and has not been very successful. See Tallon (1983: 51–2); Devlin (1961: 8–11); and Lord McNair (1970).

sanction of market exclusion continued to be utilized by private trade associations to discipline their members and merchants turned to private arbitration when the national court systems were unable to settle disputes in an expeditious and satisfactory manner (William C. Jones, 1958). In England, for instance, for some time insurance disputes continued to be settled in private arbitrations owing to dissatisfaction with the abilities of the common law courts (Vance, 1909: 115). The experiences of these courts is instructive of the changing balance between private and public authority. In England, marine insurance had become highly specialized by the seventeenth century. The first English insurance act was enacted in 1601 at the instance of marine underwriters who were dissatisfied with the ability of the existing courts to adjudicate maritime insurance disputes. Prior to the accession of Lord Mansfield to the bench, insurance disputes were handled by merchant courts and private arbitration. "It was generally understood that the common law courts, which did not recognize the quasi-international customs of merchants, afforded no fit forum for the determination of causes among merchants" (ibid., 111). However, merchants were unable to enforce the judgments of the private courts and private arbitrators and so they turned to the courts of Admiralty and common law. These courts, too, proved inadequate:

> [T]he common law courts of that day, with their highly technical and tedious rules of procedure, as governed by precedents of agricultural rather than mercantile origin, were ill adapted for the settlement of merchant disputes. Thus it appears that at the beginning of the seventeenth century persons having insurance causes were without a satisfactory tribunal for their determination. The conventional [merchant] courts could not enforce their judgments, the courts of admiralty had proved inadequate, possibly because of the vexatious jealousy of the common law courts in unreasonably restricting their jurisdiction, while the common law courts were wholly unfit. (Ibid., 113)

The Insurance Act of 1601 established a special court of insurance commissioners, comprised of an admiralty judge, civil law and common law lawyers, and merchants, to hear insurance cases. However, the court was not successful because of its limited jurisdiction and it lapsed into disuse by the end of the century.[44] As a result, merchants continued to pursue private means to settle insurance disputes. With the accession

[44] Its jurisdiction applied only to policies issued in London and to insurance on goods. Only the insured and not underwriters could take actions and its judgments were not a bar to actions in other courts. Vance (1909: 114).

of Lord Mansfield to the bench in the eighteenth century, the incorporation of insurance principles from the law merchant into the common law began. He is famous for impaneling juries of merchants and often cited the Sea Laws of Rhodes, the Consulato del Mare of Barcelona, and the Laws of Oleron and Wisby in his decisions (Vance, 1909: 116). The common law courts adopted the law merchant principles governing sea loans and recognized the principle of the general average (Scrutton, 1907: 242–3).

The practice of arbitration came to be bolstered by state intervention in the form of legislation providing for the enforcement of arbitration agreements. In England, an arbitration act was enacted in 1697 providing for the state enforcement of private arbitration awards and was amended in 1889 to provide for the enforcement of agreements to arbitrate future disputes. William Jones (1958: 462) observes that by the end of the nineteenth century in England it was estimated that "almost all mercantile cases, even those that eventually came to the courts, went to arbitration. Exchanges such as the Liverpool Cotton Exchange, the London Stock Exchange, the London Corn Trade Exchange, and the Coffee Trade Association, had machinery for arbitration."

In the United States, private arbitration persisted until the end of the eighteenth century. The state courts were avoided as too costly, unjust in outcome, and resistant to rapidly changing commercial practices (Benson, 1988–9: 655). Bruce Benson (ibid., 655) observes that "it was not until the end of the eighteenth century that public judges began to convince merchants that they could understand complex business issues and practices, and that they accepted as law, agreements established to facilitate the reciprocal self-interest motives of traders." It was then that the private arbitration system began to disappear. Indeed, courts in the United States came to regularly invalidate arbitration clauses and agreements and evidenced considerable judicial hostility to the practice of arbitration. In England, courts likewise deemed arbitration agreements to be against public policy because they ousted the jurisdiction of the courts of law and the procedural justice afforded only in courts of law (see generally, Carbonneau, 1984: 39).

At the end of the nineteenth century there was a change in judicial attitude in the United States brought about by national policies and legislative changes creating a more hospitable environment for arbitration. What was regarded by many as overly intrusive state intervention into commercial disputes was limited by restrictions on the abilities of courts to interfere in arbitration proceedings (Benson, 1988–9: 656). The practice of arbitration thus became more common again. Exchanges and mercantile associations proliferated at this time, providing arbitration facilities for their members.[45] A number of other trade associations were formed towards the end of the nineteenth century, providing for the arbitration of disputes.[46] Legislation was passed in New York in 1791 providing for the enforcement of arbitration awards and agreements by state courts. In England, as well, judicial hostility toward arbitration began to weaken as national arbitration legislation was enacted (see Carbonneau, 1984: 40–5). In France, judicial attitudes toward arbitration exhibited similar hostility, but later underwent similar revision (ibid., 53–7).

William Jones (1958: 463) concludes that in England and the United States in the nineteenth century "there was a development of private mercantile tribunals in which the bulk of mercantile disputes was settled entirely outside the state judicial system. The indications are that this trend has continued and exists today in a strengthened form." Indeed, as will be illustrated in the next chapter, private arbitration has eclipsed adjudication in national courts of law as the preferred method of settling international commercial disputes. The balance between private and public regulatory authority in dispute settlement appears to be shifting over time to the private sphere. However, the increasing prominence of private arbitration has been a result of the juridification of dispute settlement relations as state policy initiatives and legislative changes limited state/judicial intervention into the arbitration process. Private authority over dispute settlement thus exists with the support of the state and in a political and legal climate created by public authorities through the juridification of commercial relations. This is quite distinct from the autonomy of the dispute settlement system of the medieval merchants, whose autonomy flowed from the incapacity and general unwillingness of the local legal systems to enforce merchant laws.

Moreover, and of great significance, public authority continues to play an absolutely crucial role in the *enforcement* of commercial agreements. Only public state officials may make declarations of bankruptcy, order the execution of judgments through the seizure of assets, and generally enforce contractual performance or payment. Another way of framing

45 These included the New York Stock, Produce, Mercantile, Cotton, and Coffee and Sugar Exchanges, the Chicago Board of Trade, the St. Louis Merchants' Exchange, the Philadelphia Commercial Exchange, the Kansas City Board of Trade and the Milwaukee Grain Exchange. See William C. Jones (1958: 462).

46 The Grain and Feed Dealers Association, the National Hay Association, the National Cotton Seed Products Association, and the American Seed Trade Association. See William C. Jones (1958: 462–3).

the centrality of state enforcement is to consider that delocalized transactions must ultimately be localized in a system of legitimate legal compulsion in order to be enforced.[47] Indeed, as a review of the third phase in the development of the law merchant will reveal, it became increasingly more apparent that mechanisms were necessary to facilitate the recognition and enforcement of foreign arbitral awards. States came to be intimately involved in the practice of arbitration by recognizing and enforcing both domestic and foreign agreements and awards. National differences emerged in the treatment and status accorded to private arbitration by various legal systems, generating a movement for the unification of arbitration law in the third phase.

This review of the second phase in the evolution of the law merchant reveals that states came to assume a central role in the juridification of international commercial relations. Juridification forged links between law, capitalism, and rationalized domination – links that would come to be associated specifically with the capitalist mode of production. State authority replaced the overlapping authority structures of the medieval period. The dualistic system of regulation characteristic of the medieval phase was in many jurisdictions replaced by unitary systems of state control. Furthermore, states exercised stronger and more comprehensive discipline than did the local religious and political authorities of the earlier phase. State authorities engaged in state-building sought greater control over international commercial transactions and public authority largely eclipsed private authority in creating and enforcing international commercial laws. Merchant custom virtually disappeared as a source of commercial norms as positive law became the mark of state authority and legal codification a method of state-building. In the area of enforcement, private merchant arbitrations were replaced by adjudication in national courts of law under national commercial codes. However, the practice of arbitration persisted, anticipating a major expansion of private regulatory authority at the end of the period.

Merchant autonomy in law-creation and in enforcement contracted, while state authority expanded. During the early part of this phase, mercantilist principles informed state regulation of commerce, but later the advent of liberal political economy marked a shift in favor of a more permissive and facultative approach that stressed free-market principles. Public authorities thus generated laws and enforced disputes

[47] This factor is a significant influence in the conclusion drawn by Highet (1989: 616) that the law merchant might in fact be like the "Emperor's clothes."

consistent with private law principles stressing freedom of contract, the sanctity of agreements, and the facilitation of exchange. Freedom of contract became the *grundnorm* for the private sphere, while the sanctity of agreements formed the normative foundation for the public sphere. Both principles were linked through liberal political economy to greater efficiencies and to the generation of wealth and happiness. Significantly, liberal political economy and ideology gave rise to the distinction between public and private international law. In the commercial sphere, the relationships between individuals and private associations and corporations were juridified as part of the private sphere of capital accumulation. There they were neutralized from political control as the separation between economics and politics sealed their status as apolitical and neutral, economic transactions. Through distinctions between private and public international law and the rules governing international legal personality, individuals and business corporations were rendered "invisible" as "subjects" of the law, for legal theory and formalism recognized them only as "objects." The influence of liberal ideology was profound in terms of mystifying and fetishizing the emerging understanding of law, concealing its coercive face:

> [T]he separation of the economic from the political made possible both the naturalisation of capitalist economic exploitation and the neutralisation of the revolutionary potential of liberal politics – two processes that converge to consolidate the capitalist model of social relations.
>
> . . .
>
> Confined to the public place, the democratic ideal was neutralised or strongly limited in its emancipatory potential. On the other hand, the conversion of the public place into the exclusive site of law and politics performed a crucial legitimation function in that it convincingly obscured the fact that the law and the politics of the capitalist state could only operate as part of a broader political and legal configuration in which other contrasting forms of law and politics were included. (Santos, 1985: 306–7)

Over time, differences emerged in the way national legal systems regulated many private law transactions, bringing private international trade law greater visibility. National differences appeared in the legal interpretation and effect of trade terms, bills of lading, and liability standards in transportation. In the area of marine insurance, national distinctions also became evident. Differences in the interpretation and legal consequences of financial instruments, including bills of exchange and letters of credit, also developed. In the area of law-creation, while national positive law replaced merchant custom as the primary source of commercial law, national systems became increasingly inflexible, differences in the legal weight to be given to newly developing customs emerged, and incompatibilities in national conflict of laws systems appeared. Finally, the expansion of public regulatory authority in the enforcement of commercial agreements reinforced national particularisms. These developments were all more or less consistent with the acceptance of national sovereignty and political autonomy as the fundamental ordering principles in international relations. Legal positivism articulated these principles by elevating positive law over customary law and by generating nationally-based conflict of laws systems to regulate international transactions. Many of these developments generated efforts to regain the lost universality and distinctiveness of the law merchant in its third phase.

6 The modern law merchant and the *mercatocracy*

The third phase in the evolution of the law merchant, the twentieth century, is said to be witnessing a revival of the law merchant and the "medieval internationalism" of the first phase (Schmitthoff, 1961: 139–40). Known as "global capital's own law" (Santos, 1995: 288), the law merchant is being revived as an integral force in the "hyperliberalization" of the state and world order. The "hyperliberal" state, "reasserts the separation of the state and economy" (Cox, 1996 b: 201), reinscribing distinctions between politics and economics and the public and private spheres through an intensification of juridified, privatized, and pluralized commercial relations. However, this marks a qualitatively new process of juridification because it is associated with transnationalized social forces (Cox, 1987: 357–9) and the "transnationalization of the legal field" (Santos, 1995: 276). Whereas earlier juridification occurred through the processes of state-building and national capital accumulation, contemporary juridified relations are being deepened and intensified through delocalizing and transnationalizing legal disciplines that both reflect and facilitate the transnational expansion of capitalism and related practices of competition states and patterns of flexible accumulation.[1] Moreover, contemporary juridification is intensifying the relationship between law and capitalism through processes that are more aptly described as "reregulatory" rather than "deregulatory,"[2] for the state plays an integral although different role in regulating international commerce.

At the heart of these transformations is the global mercatocracy, an elite association of public and private organizations engaged in

1 See Chapter 2 for discussion of these concepts.

2 Santos (1985: 324) argues that law has never been so hegemonic, especially in developed, core states.

the unification and globalization of transnational merchant law. This elite association exercises near hegemonial influence as the "organic intellectuals" of the transnational capitalist class, materially, ideologically, and institutionally.[3] Robert Cox (1999: 12) refers to a "nascent global historic bloc consisting of the most powerful corporate economic forces, their allies in government, and the variety of networks that evolve policy guidelines and propagate the ideology of globalization." The mercatocracy is an integral component of this nascent historic bloc. As "organic intellectuals," the mercatocracy provides a "general conception of life, a philosophy" and performs an educative role which assists in replacing coercive class relations with consensual relations (Gramsci, 1971: 103–4). Leslie Sklair (2001) describes this emerging historic bloc and the role of the transnational capitalist class:

> The transnational capitalist class is the main driver of a series of globalizing practices in the global economy. It is, therefore, the leading force in the creation of a global capitalist system. The *global* is the goal, while the *transnational*, transcending nation-states in an international system is in some respects still having to cope with them in others, is the reality. The global capitalist system and the global economy exist to the extent that private rather than national interests prevail across borders. (3)

The goals of this nascent historic bloc are consistent with the ends to which processes of globalization are leading: "the establishment of a borderless global economy, the complete denationalization of all corporate procedures and activities, and the eradication of economic nationalism" (ibid., 3). The mercatocracy plays a very significant role in the furtherance of these goals. Its contemporary focal point is the unification movement: a movement engaged in harmonizing, unifying, and globalizing merchant law. The decline in the universality of the law merchant, caused by the proliferation of national differences in the period of nationalization, generated efforts to unify commercial law. The unification movement is being advanced by social forces committed to

3 See Kees van der Pijl (1998: ch. 4) for analysis of historical transnational class formation in the associations of Freemasons in the late seventeenth century. Merchants, the clergy, and royalty formed transnational links through the masonic institutions. Later in the nineteenth century he notes that bourgeois class formation tended to focus nationally, not transnationally. But elements of transnationalism were evident in the associations of international investment bankers or "haute finance" based mostly in London. He associates the transnational capitalist class in the twentieth century with the operations of the International Chamber of Commerce, a private organization that is argued here to be a central player in the constitution of private international trade law.

facilitating the transnational expansion of capitalism. The unification of commercial law facilitates exchange and the transnational mobility of capital by reducing national and territorial legal barriers to exchange through delocalized laws, procedures, and dispute settlement mechanisms. Transnationalized merchant laws are generating greater pluralism in law-creation, as new sources of law are legitimated and new subjects of law emerge to challenge conventional legal sources and subjects doctrines. Transnational merchant law is also blurring the boundary between the public and private domains as state elites participate in delocalizing law and dispute settlement, thus narrowing the jurisdiction and powers of the public sphere and broadening those of the private sphere.

This chapter reviews the third and contemporary phase in the development of the law merchant. Again the analytical focus is on law-creation, and dispute settlement. However, the context for these processes is increasingly transnational and global. The laws governing private international trade are increasingly being generated through multilateral initiatives to unify and harmonize divergent trade laws. In addition, a revival of private arbitration as the preferred method for settling international commercial disputes is sweeping the globe as an integral element of the unification movement. The mercatocracy is comprised of a diversity of public and private participants and is driving these developments in response to local and global conditions that are changing the terms of international commercial competition. Indeed, the chapter places the unification movement in the historical contexts of evolving global capitalism and contemporary disciplinary neoliberalism. It argues that the modern unification movement emerged as a cooperative strategy for managing conflicting nationally-based com--mercial laws and, thereby, facilitated the mobility of capital and the expansion of capitalism. While originally European and regional in scope, the movement attained global dimensions with the creation of an institutional framework under the auspices of the United Nations and under the leadership of the United States after the Second World War years. The initial disinterest of the United States in the unification movement and the radical shift in support of, and, indeed, its acquisition of monopoly over, the movement coincided with the crisis of late capitalism. Robert Cox (1987: ch. 8) associates the crisis with the disintegration of the post-Second World War neoliberal historic bloc and the decline of US hegemony, which became apparent in the economic turmoil of the 1970s.[4] The efforts that the United States and other developed states put into unifying commercial law with a renewed neoliberal or, in fact, "hyperliberal"commitment to the efficacy and inherent superiority of the private regulation of commerce reflect attempts by core states to consolidate capitalism and to facilitate the denationalization and further expansion of capital.[5] This renewed assertion of the "primacy of the private" also coincided with the advent of the competition state and a shift in structural power from nationally to transnationally based interests.[6] This structural shift is argued to be manifested in the growing pluralism of sources of law, evident in the corporate legal preference for nonbinding "soft law" over binding "hard law," and a renewed emphasis on merchant custom as a source of law. It is also evident in increased pluralism in the subjects of law, with transnational corporations and private business associations functioning as *de facto* legal "subjects" and with a host of other identities aspiring to status as "subjects" of law. The expansion of privatized dispute settlement through private, delocalized, and transnationalized international commercial arbitration is also part of a corporate strategy to further disembed commercial law and practice from the "public" sphere and to reembed them in the "private" sphere, free from democratic and social control. The devolution of authority to resolve disputes and to enforce agreements to the private sphere through the increasing legitimacy of private arbitration, and the reassertion of merchant autonomy as the substantive norm are perfecting this reconfiguration of political authority. This is reordering state–society relations both locally and globally. While state enforcement of commercial bargains remains crucial to the stability of the system, states are recasting their enforcement roles and conferring more powers on corporate actors. Recalling the earlier discussion of stages in the decline of the public/private distinction, the meeting of public and private authority in the unification movement represents the final stage in its decline. However, the influence of the mercatocracy is neither complete nor hegemonic in the Gramscian sense, for the crisis also involves a crisis of representation and legitimacy. Indeed, competing social forces articulating new claims to subjectivity under international law are emerging

[4] See also, Fredric Jameson (1991).

[5] For developments in contemporary capitalism, see Gill (1995 a); Harvey (1990); and Held (1995).

[6] See Cerny (1990: 233–4 and 1997) and Gill (1998 and 1995 a) for discussion of the competition state. For the transnationalization of capital, see Gill and Law (1993) and Robinson (1996 and 1998).

from those of formerly marginalized and legally "invisible"status. They are pressing beyond the formal reaches of international law, suggesting potential sites for transformative and emancipatory politics.

Before turning to modern developments in law-creation and dispute resolution, the discussion will review the historical, material, ideological, and institutional contexts of the unification movement.

The Unification Movement and World Order

The modern unification movement seeks to recreate the medieval tradition of *jus commune*, which disappeared as international commercial law was assimilated by national legal systems in the second phase of the development of the law merchant.

> The legal process in general was characterised in the nineteenth century by a disappearance of the traditional *jus commune* which had developed in the field of international commercial law over centuries; the engine behind this process was the drive toward the nationalisation of the law, an outcome of converging political, philosophical and cultural developments dominant in this period . . . [T]his nationalisation of international commercial law has in its core been preserved ever since, and the past and current efforts at unification by international agencies may, in the historical context, be seen as attempts to modify, in a limited manner, the adverse affects which the extreme emphasis upon national laws in international commercial legal relations has had upon the flow of trade between states. (Dolzer, 1982: 62)

These initiatives form part of what is referred to in international legal literature as the "unification movement," although, as will be discussed, both unification and harmonization are involved (David, 1972 a). The unification movement is an integral although neglected aspect of the juridification of commerce and the globalizing processes that are reconfiguring state–society relations both locally and globally. Legal unification is part of world order and global structuration processes in that it is an essential aspect of "*how* the global system has been and continues to be *made*" (Robertson, 1992: 53). It is a constitutive element of what Roland Robertson (ibid., 54) refers to as "movements and organizations concerned with the patterning and/or the unification of the world as a whole." Initially conceived of as a strategy of international cooperation in the late nineteenth century, unification is evolving into a strategy of international competition consistent with the move from the welfare to the competition state. As Philip Cerny observes:

> [t]he state is no longer in a position anywhere to pursue the general welfare as if it were a domestic problem. As the world economy is characterized by increasing interpenetration and the crystallization of transnational markets and structures, the state itself is having to act more and more like a market player, that shapes its policies to promote, control, and maximize returns from market forces in an international setting. (1990: 230)

The movement is blurring the distinction between public and private authority because states in their public capacities are negotiating laws that govern commercial transactions which have traditionally been regarded as private by liberal theories of international political economy and of international law, while private actors are increasingly participating in the settlement of matters that were previously regarded as part of the public domain.[7] The blurring of the public/private distinction has important implications for understanding the relationship between the new law merchant and world order. Indeed, the growing ambiguity of regulatory authority over international trade is an integral aspect of the reconfiguration of political authority that is accompanying the crisis of late capitalist societies. As Robert Cox notes:

> [t]he key criterion today is competitiveness; and derived from that are universal imperatives of deregulation, privatization, and the restriction of public intervention in economic processes. Neoliberalism is transforming states from being buffers between external economic forces and the domestic economy into agencies for adapting domestic economies to the global economy. (1995: 39)

Today, law-creation, dispute resolution, and enforcement in international commerce are regulated by the mercatocracy. This elite association of transnational merchants, private lawyers and their associations, government officials, and representatives of international organizations are engaged in unifying, harmonizing, and, importantly, globalizing private international trade law. The mercatocracy constitutes a transnationalized social force, what Cox (1987: 359) describes as a "transnational

[7] For example, states are engaged in unifying the laws governing the international sale of goods, agency relations, banking and financial documents, transport documents, insurance documents and practices, and a growing list of "private" law matters. Inversely, private actors are increasingly engaged in the settlement through privatized international commercial arbitration of disputes that were formerly regarded as matters of mandatory national law, justiciable in national courts of law. See Cutler (2002 b).

managerial class" that is characterized by "awareness of a common concern to maintain the system that enables the class to remain dominant." As he further (ibid., 359–60) notes, this class is not limited to the managers of multi- and transnational corporations, but also includes government officials and representatives of international organizations and specialized business groups and experts. The mercatocracy is able to exercise near hegemonic influence through its material links to transnational capital, its monopoly of expert knowledge and thought structures, and its controlling influence in the institutional framework of the new law merchant order.[8] The influence is thus material, ideological, and institutional and provides an instance of what Stephen Gill (1995 a) refers to as "disciplinary neoliberalism" and a "new constitutionalism." As he notes, this

> [n]ew constitutionalism confers privileged rights of citizenship and representation on corporate capital, whilst constraining the democratisation process that has involved struggles for representation for hundreds of years. Central, therefore, to new constitutionalism is the imposition of discipline on public institutions, partly to prevent national interference with the property rights and entry and exit options of holders of mobile capital with regard to particular political jurisdictions. (ibid., 413)

Moreover, this new constitutionalism is unfolding in the context of the "hyperliberal state" which is "an ally of capital" (Cox, 1987: 347) and is taking the "neo" out of liberalism, in "that it seems to envisage a return to nineteenth-century economic liberalism and a rejection of the neoliberal attempt to adapt economic liberalism to the sociopolitical reactions that classical liberalism produced" (Cox, 1996 b: 199). The hyperliberal state assists in the restructuring of productive relations by creating the conditions that make possible the further expansion of capital through the disciplining of societies into the acceptance of market ideology and the primacy of the private sphere.

This renewed assertion of the "primacy of the private" coincided with the advent of the competition state and a "shift in structural power from national political actors to those state actors and nonstate actors who might be described as *gatekeepers* of the interface between transnational markets and structures, on the one hand, and 'nationalized social identity' (and nation-state resources), on the other" (Cerny, 1990: 233–4;

[8] For hegemonic knowledge structures see Gramsci (1971); Cox (1996 a); and Strange (1995 a).

see also, Cox, 1996 b: 201). As is addressed below, this structural shift is manifested in corporate legal preferences for nonbinding "soft law" over binding "hard law," the devolution of the authority to create and to enforce commercial norms on the private sphere (through the increasing emphasis on merchant autonomy as the operative substantive norm), and the increasing legitimacy of private arbitration. Soft law provides normative guidance, but remains largely optional, while private arbitration offers the security of enforceable agreements and avoids interference from national courts or policy makers. These preferences are expressed in the modern unification movement and form essential components of disciplinary neoliberal restructuring.

As part of the effort to create a modern *jus commune*, the unification movement originated during what Roland Robertson (1992) refers to as the "take-off" period of globalization from 1870–1925:

> "Take-off" here refers to a period during which the increasingly manifest globalizing tendencies of previous periods and places gave way to a single, inexorable form centred upon the four reference points, and thus constraints, of national societies, generic individuals (but with a masculine bias), a single "international society," an increasingly singular, but not unified conception of humankind. (59)

The discourse of the unification movement echoes the views of those who like Robertson regard globalization as operating not just materially, but ideologically, at the level of culture, civilization, and international society. For legal scholars such as René David (1972 a), the restoration of the tradition of the *jus commune* was regarded very much as a civilizing and globalizing antidote to the vagaries of legal positivism and legal nationalism. The global unification of commercial law came to signify progress to higher and better forms of business civilization. Moreover, the expansion of the movement beyond its European origins to embrace the Anglo-American business communities and, ultimately, to include African, Asian, and other non-Western states was heralded as portentous of great things. The ultimate achievement would be the creation of an international commercial code replacing national standards with a global common law.

The unification movement has made significant progress in restoring the universality of international commercial law and practice. Indeed, it has been observed that "we are discovering the international horizon" in commercial law and furnishing the basis for the "first common law of the world" (Schmitthoff, 1961: 152–3). Others note that it "may be said without exaggeration that the revitalization of the ancient *lex mercatoria* in the process of creating a new uniform commercial code for world trade should be recognized as a major accomplishment in this century" (Gabor, 1986: 697). Significantly, unification efforts are reasserting many of the values embodied in the medieval law merchant. Substantive norms emphasize merchant autonomy in creating contractual rights and duties, while procedural norms emphasize speed and informality. In addition, today a renewed emphasis is placed on the primacy of liberal, capitalist values. Proponents of the new law merchant, predominantly representatives of Western industrialized state and corporate interests, stress the self-disciplining abilities and capacities of merchants (see Trakman, 1983; Benson 1988–89; Cremades and Plehn, 1984). In asserting, either explicitly or implicitly, that the purpose of commercial regulation is to facilitate economic exchange, they believe that the best way to achieve efficiency and certainty is to give maximum scope to the principles of merchant autonomy, freedom of contract, and private dispute settlement (arbitration) and to recognize the fundamental role played by commercial custom. The following justification of merchant autonomy as the operative principle in the legal regulation of international commercial transactions is fairly representative of the views of proponents of the new law merchant:

> What merchants do in international trade is the result of what they have learned to do, what other merchants in similar positions have done in the past and what merchants should continue to do in the future in the interests of economic survival and the just allocation of resources. The legal regulation of such business activity can only truly advance when the law reflects upon, indeed embodies, merchant values. To create law in disregard of the context in which international commerce operates is to deplete the self-sufficiency of the merchant regime; it is to create a legal system in a vacuum at the expense of the practical necessities of business.
>
> Freedom to transact is a necessary component in the evolution of international business. Merchants engaged in world trade do have the facilities to overcome trade barriers threatening their business affairs. Commercial practices facilitate their daily enterprises. Trade conventions delineate the permissibility of their business habits; while customs codify their trade adventures. (Trakman, 1983: 97)

This position is advanced with about as much evangelical zeal as the "new political economy" and utilitarianism were advanced by their proponents in the nineteenth century. While recognizing the legitimate interests that states have in regulating international commercial activities, they emphasize that such regulation should be permissive, suppletive, and facultative. Moreover, although national public policy concerns are recognized as establishing valid limits to the principle of freedom of contract, it is argued that such limits should be sensitive to the international dimension of transactions (Sono, 1988: 485) and the furtherance of international comity.[9] As mandatory rules, they should be regarded as "exceptions from and restrictions of the general principle which is still that of freedom of contracting, i.e., optional law" (ibid.). Proponents emphasize the ability of merchants to manage their own affairs under self-regulating and delocalized contracts that establish the rights, obligations, and remedies of the parties and that designate the applicable law and dispute settlement procedures. They argue that freedom of contract is "a delegation by the state to the individual of the power to enter into binding contracts" wherein "parties are free to define their contractual relationship subject to certain limits and procedures" and they assert the need to maximize and expand this freedom as "essential" to the development of a "non-national New Lex Mercatoria" (Cremades and Plehn, 1984: 328). Central to this expansion of merchant autonomy are self-regulating contracts and merchant custom. Private arbitration is equally important for independent dispute settlement.

The expansion of merchant autonomy is presented as fully consistent with maximizing efficiencies and competitiveness in the face of globalization. It is also an essential aspect of disciplinary neoliberalism and the new constitutionalism of the primacy of the private sphere:

> The age of independence, or even interdependence, has already gone and we are now in the age of interpenetration, where national boundaries lose their meaning. For a global legal order to be established to govern business transactions "ignorant" of national boundaries, such a legal order must first free the business world from the dogmas that heretofore have shaped the traditional local orders. This is the road for the restoration of *lex mercatoria*, in the same manner as it existed in the medieval age, at a global dimension in relation to the so-called "international" transactions. (Sono, 1988: 485)

[9] Comity in international law has been defined in terms of reciprocity, courtesy, politeness, goodwill between sovereigns, moral necessity, or expediency and is invoked to explain why courts enforce or apply the decisions of foreign courts or limit their own jurisdiction in the face of a competing foreign jurisdiction. See Paul (1991: 2–3). For an excellent review of the role of public policy in the application of conflict of laws rules in common and civil law jurisdictions and the view that national courts should exercise restraint in rejecting foreign law on public policy grounds see Murphy (1981).

However, although proponents of the new law merchant invoke images of the medieval trading world in order to sustain their faith in the self-regulating abilities of the merchant community, as we have seen, there are crucial distinctions between the contemporary and the medieval orders. Clearly, in terms of the sheer volume of overseas transactions alone we are talking about profoundly different conditions. More to the point, however, are the differences in the political economies of the two periods. As has been emphasized before, in the medieval trading world merchants engaged in foreign trade were autonomous by virtue of the absence of political authorities desirous or capable of disciplining their activities. Local political authorities did exercise very general control in granting trade charters, providing for the safe-conduct of merchants, and securing the peace of the markets and fairs. However, the laws governing commercial exchange emerged from the customs generated by the merchant community, while dispute settlement was an entirely private engagement amongst merchants. In contrast, today merchant autonomy operates with the full support of state authorities. The privileging of private commercial regulation is being promoted and enforced by states, which function in an alliance with corporate actors as a part of the broader mercatocracy. The privileging of the private sphere is thus also an integral part of the process whereby the state is reemerging as a "commodifying agent," "a role which it was often seen to play in the emergence of capitalism itself in the postfeudal period and the years of mercantilism" (Cerny, 1990: 23). In efforts to adjust to conditions of late capitalism, political authorities are reconfiguring the relationships between politics and economics; between the public and the private spheres. National regulatory authority is being delegated to or being assumed by private groups and institutions. In some cases, national governments are delegating authority to intergovernmental institutions. These diverse actors constitute a mercatocracy: a relatively autonomous business class that operates nationally and transnationally within a framework of shared language and norms. The emergence of this transnational mercatocracy is linked to contemporary developments that are more generally associated with transformations in the capitalist mode of production. The globalization and transnationalization of productive relations and advent of flexible patterns of accumulation are contributing to significant restructuring in state–society relations. The restructuring of production processes, associated with new patterns of accumulation, brings "an end to the social contract that was the linchpin of postwar historic blocs" (Cox, 1989: 47). In some instances national regulatory authority is weakening as decisions over the disposition of capital resources are made increasingly by transnational corporate actors.[10] The discipline exercised by domestic public policy processes and by organized labor is eroding as capital goes global (Gill, 1995 a and b; Gill and Law, 1988). Instead, disciplinary neoliberalism holds out the private regulation of commerce as the most progressive method for managing globalization, for achieving international competitiveness, and for securing justice in international commercial relations. The mercatocracy unites private and public authorities committed to the expansion of capitalism through further disembedding international commerce from national, social, and democratic controls and reembedding it in the private sphere. It advances neoliberal ideology and contributes to a blurring of the distinction between public and private authority. The alliance of public and private actors reasserts the efficacy of merchant custom as a source of legal norms, favors the adoption of soft over hard law and private arbitration over adjudication in national courts of law. Moreover, belief in the self-sufficiency and autonomy of the law merchant system reinscribes the autonomous "legal subject" and the tendency to legal formalism, identified in earlier chapters with the dominant theories of international relations and law, as the dominant ideological and juridical underpinnings of the emerging world order. Treating law as an objectified system that exists out "there" thus embodies important ideological commitments and profound normative implications. The discussion will now consider law-creation and the alliance between public and private authorities in the unification movement, before reviewing the history of the unification movement.

Law-Creation: Unification Through Public and Private Authorities

The contemporary phase in the development of the law merchant exhibits considerable pluralism in law-creation, both as to the subjects and the sources of law. A multiplicity of actors, public and private, individual, institutional, and corporate are involved in the creation and unification of private international trade law. In addition, a plurality of new sources of law are emerging. Before considering new developments in law-creation, it will be helpful to consider very briefly the nature of legal

[10] See generally, Ruggie (1994; 1995 a); Strange (1995 a); and Picciotto (1988).

unification undertakings, for this relates to the role that legal unification plays in establishing the juridical conditions for global capitalism.

While the terms unification and harmonization are used almost interchangeably by trade experts, they do have different meanings. A review of these differences reveals that unification and harmonization represent different strategies pursued by public and private actors for the purpose of facilitating the expansion of capitalism. They also represent varying degrees of juridification and legal discipline.

The unification of trade law may be defined as "the process by which conflicting rules of two or more systems of national laws applicable to the same international legal transaction are replaced by a single rule."[11] Unification differs from harmonization in that "the 'unification' of law, or the adoption of uniform laws, is harmonization with a zero margin" of difference (Leebron, 1995: 7–8). Whereas unification contemplates the replacement of multiple and different rules with a single uniform rule, harmonization contemplates the move to greater similarity, but not necessarily to unity or identity. The margin of harmonized laws can therefore range from a zero margin of complete unification, which admits no differentiation from agreed-upon standards, to broad and tolerated deviations from the norm. Viewed this way, unification is simply a subset or type of harmonization that has no margin of difference in law. Harmonization thus suggests the possibility of different degrees of similarity.[12] This view also suggests that as a strategy of cooperation, harmonization may be less ambitious and potentially less limiting on the domestic autonomy of the participants, be they states or merchants:

> Harmonization can be loosely defined as making the regulatory requirements or governmental policies of different jurisdictions identical, or at least more similar. It is one response to the problems arising from regulatory differences among political units, and potentially one

[11] See the United Nations Report, "Unification of the Law of International Trade: Note by the Secretariat" (1968–73: 13); and see Cutler (1999 b).

[12] Leebron (1995: 8) identifies different forms of harmonization, including the harmonization of rules, of governmental policy objectives, of principles, and of institutional structures and procedures. He also notes that even unification may not achieve a zero margin of difference if it is not accompanied by institutional and procedural unification: "Zero margin harmonization has been adopted only in certain regulatory and political contexts. Even uniform laws, if they are not accompanied by harmonization of institutions, effectively allow differences in implementation and effects. One can reject the idea that all countries must adopt the same standards while still seeking to narrow differences. Thus in many instances margins of tolerance are implicitly or explicitly allowed. In the latter case both a 'ceiling' and a 'floor' might be set, but more often harmonization programs only require that all countries accept some minimum."

> form of inter-governmental co-operation. The term harmonization is often used not only to refer to this result, but also to the process for achieving greater similarity.
>
> ...
>
> a particular harmonization claim might require one or more of these forms of harmonization [rules, government policy objectives, principles, institutions, and procedures] or be addressed by alternative forms. These forms entail different types of compromise, and at different governmental or inter-governmental levels. They vary in their continued tolerance of difference, and hence in allowing societies to reflect their own social choices. (Leebron, 1995: 3–4 and 7)

Both unification and harmonization may be achieved through the adoption of hard law sources in the form of multilateral agreements or soft law sources, including model law, standard contracts, and contract guides, or general statements of principles. The legal status of unified law therefore turns upon the legal status of the unifier, as well as upon the method of unification chosen, and involves both subjects and sources doctrines.

Subjects of transnational merchant law

Today a multiplicity of organizations and actors are participants in the unification of commercial law.[13] The diversity of agencies involved in law-creation is so significant that as Rudolph Dolzer (1982: 62) observes, "so far no scheme of scientific classification has been found which would allow classification of all existing bodies into a few categories." It is, however, common to differentiate between intergovernmental, or public, and nongovernmental, or private, agencies and organizations (Schmitthoff, 1982: 27–9). The main intergovernmental organizations are the United Nations Commission on International Trade Law (UNCITRAL), the International Institute for the Unification of Private Law (UNIDROIT), the Hague Conference on Private International Law and the International Maritime Organization (IMO). The main nongovernmental organizations are the International Chamber of Commerce (ICC), the International Law Association (ILA), and the Comité Maritime International (CMI).[14]

13 For a full discussion of these various agencies see Cutler (1992).

14 This list of formulating agencies is not exhaustive. The United Nations Conference on International Trade and Development (UNCTAD) has adopted codes of relevance to international commercial law, including the Multilaterally Agreed Equitable Principles and Rules for the Control of Restrictive Business Practices, the UNCTAD Code of Conduct for Liner Conferences. UNCTAD is also working on a Code of Conduct on

It is important to recall our discussion of the doctrine of international legal personality and the differing capacities of participants in the creation of international law. As Hugh Kindred et al. (1993) note:

> [i]nternational law applies to certain entities as "subjects" of international law. These entities have legal personality – that is, a capacity similar to an individual person in domestic law, to enter into legal relations and to create the consequent rights and duties attached to that capacity. Without this capacity an entity will be unable to maintain any claims. International law itself determines who shall have legal personality and not all entities possess the same personality. (11)

They further note that:

> [u]ntil the twentieth century the prevailing view was that only states could possess international legal personality. This view was due mainly to the fact that the concept of the state had predominated in the international system and the question of personality had been regarded as belonging exclusively to this domain. Thus, entities other than states could have no standing on the international scene. (Ibid.)

The general rule that only states have full and original personality as subjects under the law has already been discussed. This means that only states, in their capacity as legitimate public authorities, may generate binding hard law. While a number of developments in the areas of international human rights law, the law governing international organizations, and international economic law have carved out some space for nonstate entities such as individuals, international organizations, and transnational corporations to function under international law, their formal capacities in law-creation remain severely limited in comparison to those of states (see Cutler, 2001 a). However, upon closer inspection of the participants involved in the unification movement and in creating merchant law, it becomes evident that the formal incapacity of private individuals and corporations has not actually limited their active participation in law-creation. In fact, as will become evident, the

the Transfer of Technology, a model contract for marine hull insurance, and rules protecting industrial property (for an overview of UNCTAD's continuing work, see online http://www.unctad.org/). The United Nations Industrial Development Organization (UNIDO), established in 1966 as an organ of the General Assembly, is working on the development of model contracts for specific industries, while the World Bank and the International Monetary Fund (IMF) have established Guidelines for Procurement under World Bank Loans and IDA Credits that establish standards for contracting. The International Maritime Organization (IMO), formerly the International Maritime Consultative Organization (IMCO), has also been active in the unification of maritime law. For fuller discussion of these agencies, see Dolzer (1982) and David (1972 a).

growing asymmetry or disjuncture between the formal legal status of private participants and their actual, political significance is growing more acute, portending a crisis of legitimacy. In order to develop this analysis it is first necessary to consider the lawmaking process in greater detail.

The doctrine of international legal personality confines the lawmaking role to states and their representatives. Accordingly, when a private organization such as the International Chamber of Commerce (ICC) undertakes a unification initiative, it must turn to national governments to formulate its work into law. States must either convene an international conference to conduct negotiations on a multilateral treaty on the subject or otherwise give legal effect to the unification initiative developed by the private organization. Typically, national members of the ICC will brief their governments on the nature of the unification initiative and the latter will then turn to consult with both public and private domestic interests that are affected by the initiative. These interested parties undertake research into the matter, consult with other professionals, and provide their governments with their views on the rules, treaties, or laws they prefer to have implemented. In many cases, their views are directly adopted by their governments. Indeed, a review of the major unification initiatives undertaken to date discloses the absolute centrality of private business associations, banks, insurance companies, accountants, and international lawyers in the formulation of unified commercial law.[15] This suggests that while private associations may lack formal legal personality as subjects of the law *(de jure)*, they do in fact exercise considerable influence and operate as *de facto* subjects of the law (see Cutler, 2001 a). Moreover, this influence is growing with the deepening of juridified, pluralized, and privatized commercial relations and thus merits closer examination.

As noted in Chapter 2, the international legal status of transnational corporations, which are probably the most visible private global actors today, has been likened to the status of the individual under international law. Both are "objects" and not "subjects" of the law: they have no original rights or liabilities at international law; the only rights or

[15] Canadian unification efforts in the areas of international commercial arbitration were driven by the private sector and aided by government bureaucrats who favored legal unification. In the United States, the unification of international sales law was pursued after successful national unification efforts and was spearheaded by lawyers, the American Bar Association, and other professionals who had supported national efforts to remove barriers to the mobility of capital. See Cutler (1992; 1999 b; 2001 b).

liabilities they possess are derivative as nationals of a state, under the principles governing nationality.[16] Moreover, such rights or liabilities can only be asserted or assumed by the state on behalf of the individual or the transnational corporation.[17] The result is the "invisibility" of the transnational corporation under international law, as corporate power and responsibility is filtered through the authority of the state.

Notwithstanding their legal "invisibility," transnational corporations and private business associations are exercising significant influence on the creation of international commercial law through a variety of means. The influence exercised by lawyers, bankers, accountants, and other business professionals on the development of transnational legal norms through "the routine repetition of myriads of transnational contractual relations" is one such example (Santos, 1995: 290).[18] The harmonization and unification resulting from standardized contractual relationships and from general principles established through mercantile customs are major contributors to the unification movement and form an increasingly important aspect of the juridification of international commercial relations as well.[19] They are also a significant source of privatized legal relations, for these contracts and principles are most often created and articulated in a delocalized legal setting where privately negotiated arrangements obtain.[20]

Relatedly, private actors participate in the creation of international law in the establishment of customs that subsequently acquire the status of customary law through repeat usage. Very important unification initiatives have emerged this way. The ICC's success in unifying

[16] As noted in Chapter 2, n. 51, nationality is defined by Gerhard von Glahn (1996: 147) as "the bond that unites individuals with a given state, that identifies them as members of that entity, that enables them to claim its protection, and that also subjects them to the performance of such duties as their state may impose on them."

[17] There are some exceptions to the limited personality of individuals and private corporations, which might suggest some movement in legal practice that has yet to be reflected in legal theory. Notable exceptions include the status of individuals before the European Court and the status of private transnational corporations that have entered into contracts with states which are 'internationalized' by provisions that bring the contract under the purview of public international law. On the individual, see the references cited in Chapter 2, n. 52. Concerning transnational corporations, see Johns (1994).

[18] For the lawmaking role of transnational corporations, see Muchlinski (1997) and Robé (1997). For the specialized role of corporate contractual networks in the regulation of business, see Picciotto (1999 a) and for the significance of corporate regulatory networks, see Picciotto (1996) and Braithwaite and Drahos (2000).

[19] See Schmitthoff (1968) and Wiener (1999: ch. 7).

[20] Indeed, this attribute is often what leads legal theorists to conclude that the law merchant is an autonomous and self-sufficient order. See Wiener (1999: ch. 7).

the terms of trade (*Incoterms*) and the development of widely accepted customs governing Documentary Credits are initiatives that emerged as customary international law (see Rowe, 1982).

Another important example of corporate subjectivity lies in the role that business enterprises, banks, insurance companies, and the like play in international unification negotiations. As a general rule, only states are the formal participants in international negotiations. However, there has been considerable expansion of corporate representation, particularly in the United Nations system regarding the creation of public international law (Charney, 1983: 750–1). In the International Labour Organization, representatives of business and labor participate and vote independently of national governments, while in the Organization for Cooperation and Economic Development (OECD) business and labor are able to enter into formal negotiations (ibid.). A similar trend is evident in the negotiation of private international law, where often the highly technical nature of the negotiations dictate considerable input from lawyers, accountants, bankers, insurers, and the like. As Allan Farnsworth (1995), a trade lawyer assisting the United States at UNCITRAL and at UNIDROIT, has observed about the role of technical expertise:

> [t]o a considerable extent, the representative often has to rely on his or her own understanding of the subject matter. I recall once being told by the State Department that I should have "instructions" from the Department for an UNCITRAL meeting. When I asked who would provide them, I was told to my surprise that I would. So I prepared a draft and sent it to Washington. As I sat in my assigned place at UNCITRAL's opening session, an attendant handed me an important-looking envelope. It contained my instructions – my draft verbatim signed "Kissinger." (93–4)

Indeed, Yves Dezalay (1995: 2) argues that the "market for expertise in national and international regulation is . . . going through an unquestionable boom. These experts have never been so much in demand: whether to circumvent existing devices or to build new ones. This dual role gives them a strategic position" in the competition amongst regulators for control over regulatory processes.

Relatedly, as discussed in Chapter 2, the proliferation of privatized domestic regulatory regimes amongst business enterprises constitutes a potentially very significant source of privatized international legal regulation, particularly if they are adopted by national legislatures as self-regulatory regimes often are.[21] National regulatory standards can be important in determining the outcomes of international regulatory efforts, as is evident in the influence that nationally unified sales law in the United States had on the global unification of sales law. The influence of privatized regimes can, of course, flow the other way, as in the case of the Concordats of the Basle Committee on Banking Regulation and Supervisory Practices, which provided the basis for the harmonization of domestic banking laws in Europe and the United States (Wiener, 1999: ch. 2).

Possibly the most significant accretion of corporate personality, however, is evident in the area of dispute resolution. While the doctrine of international legal personality identifies states as the proper subjects of legal rights and duties, thus forcing private actors to work through the agency of the state in the pursuit of claims under international law, increasingly corporations are being granted direct access to forums for dispute settlement (see Cutler, 2001 a; 2000 a; Tollefson, 2002). Corporations have legal standing to pursue claims in the European Economic Community and the European Coal and Steel Community (Arzt and Lukashak, 1998: 167). The International Bank for Reconstruction and Development (World Bank) has created an international tribunal, the International Centre for the Settlement of Investment Disputes (ICSID), that hears investment disputes between states and foreign corporations. The proliferation of bilateral investment treaties that provide access to dispute settlement in the delocalized setting of ICSID (see Cutler 2000 a: 60) and that expand corporate rights by prescribing standards of treatment of corporations, protecting them from expropriation without compensation, and granting corporations the right to take legal actions against states, constitute significant accretions of corporate legal personality.[22] Both corporations and individuals have legal standing in the Iran–United States Claims Tribunal, which was created to hear disputes arising from the Gulf War, while the Hague Permanent Court of Arbitration has amended its rules to attract more business by hearing claims of nonstate parties (Malanczuk, 1997: 101 and 294).

[21] See the UN report, *Development of Guidelines on the Role and Social Responsibilities of the Private Sector* (2000).

[22] Bilateral investment treaties create legal agreements between two states whereby each promises to observe a certain set of standards of treatment in dealings with foreign investors. They are intended to protect foreign investors and, when they are used in conjunction with an agreement to submit disputes to ICSID, provide corporations with significant authority to enforce their legal rights against host states. See generally, Muchlinski (1995: 617).

Significant, as well, are the Canada–US Free Trade Agreement (FTA) and the North American Free Trade Agreement (NAFTA), both of which provide binding dispute settlement for corporations in delocalized settings (see Castel, 1989: Eden, 1996; Malanczuk, 1997; Tollefson, 2002). It is noteworthy that the OECD's failed initiative to create a Multilateral Agreement on Investment (MAI) also would have provided direct legal access for private parties (Engering, 1996: 156–7).

These examples of *de facto* corporate subjectivity reflect an expansion of corporate authority in law-creation that is consistent with the more general trend in business culture and ideology. Changes in national business culture and ideology are emphasizing the deregulation and reregulation of corporate activity and the declining "corporate control" function of states that characterized earlier efforts to regulate transnational corporations (Muchlinski, 1995: 9–11). As Jan Scholte (1997: 442–3) notes: "states have played an indispensable enabling role in the globalization of capital . . . governments have facilitated global firms' operations and profits with suitably constructed property guarantees, currency regulations, tax regimes, labour laws and police protection." Moreover, corporations are gaining important rights under innovative uses of domestic human rights legislation, such as the Canadian Charter of Rights and Freedoms and the United States Bill of Rights (Tollefson, 1993; Mayer, 1990).

Stephen Gill (1995 a: 413) places these developments in the context of "disciplinary neoliberalism" and a "new constitutionalism" that expand the rights of capital while constraining democratic elements. However, international legal theory appears to be slow to react to the expansion of corporate authority. This development is effecting a shift in authority structures, recasting state and corporate authority and control. In some cases the political authority of states is being challenged and modified in a manner that enhances corporate power. This is evident in the broadly permissive nature of the principles that are being articulated as the *grundnorms* for commercial law and in the unprecedented expansion of private international commercial arbitration. In other cases, corporations are working with states in corporatist associations and enhancing state authority and control.[23] This reflects the dialectical nature of the localizing and delocalizing roles of law and the tensions between social

[23] The working relationship between national courts and nationally-based corporations that do business or have subsidiaries abroad is evident in their efforts to limit the rights of foreign litigants, seeking to take advantage of liberal American products liability laws, to litigate in the United States. See Ismail (1991). For a disturbing view of the appropriateness

forces committed to national capital accumulation and those committed to transnational capital accumulation.

While there appears to be a great deal of recognition of the enhanced power and authority of transnational corporations, it is unaccompanied by commensurate efforts to regulate them:

> The obvious importance of private corporate activities to the international legal system is yet to be accommodated in legal theory, which still equates them with the individual. As participants, certain multinational enterprises control resources more extensive than many states, and their decisions contribute to the shaping of the political structure of national and international regimes. As put by one observer, "the international combine has wrested the substance of sovereignty from the so-called sovereign state." Their effective power permits them to negotiate and agree as equals with governments.
>
> (Kindred, et al., 1993, 50, notes omitted)

In many matters, international law is silent. There is no binding and general international commercial code governing the practices of transnational corporations. Most matters are dealt with under national systems of corporate and conflict of laws principles, which even corporate lawyers agree are inadequate (Notes of Cases, 1984).

Numerous efforts by international organizations, regional organizations, and business and industry associations have produced guidelines, codes, recommendations, and other "soft law" norms in the attempt to regulate the activities of transnational corporations.[24] It was hoped that the Draft Code of Conduct produced by the Commission on Transnational Corporations[25] would be a major contribution to the development of a regulatory framework, but a consensus over the Draft was never achieved. Other failed efforts "affirm rather than challenge the assumption that it is a state's prerogative to deal with TNCs

of the decision to deny the litigants in the Bhopal disaster their day in a US court, see Seward (1987).

24 Johns (1994: 897, nn. 21 and 22) identifies ECOSOC (Economic and Social Council), the European Union, the ICC, the World Bank, OECD, UNCTAD, UNFAO (UN Food and Agriculture Organization), ICFTU (International Confederation of Trade Unions), Japanese Business Council, and the Japanese MITI (Ministry of International Trade and Industry) Council on Industrial Structure as institutions that have attempted to regulate TNCs (transnational corporations).

25 The Commission was created in 1974 by ECOSOC and given the mandate to prepare a code of conduct for governments and TNCs. Drafts were produced in 1978, 1983, 1988, and 1990. Consensus over the draft was never achieved and in 1992 the United Nations Centre on Transnational Corporations, Secretariat to the Commission, was dismantled and its functions were transferred to a new Transnational Corporations Management Division within ECOSOC.

[transnational corporations] through its national legal systems" (Johns, 1994: 899).

This state of affairs poses a major normative problem of ensuring corporate accountability, for accountability, like subjectivity, is filtered through the lens of state sovereignty. There is no guarantee that a state will assume responsibility for the actions of corporations having its nationality. Often the place of nationality is only remotely connected to corporate operations, functioning in many cases as a tax haven.[26] As the United Nations Centre on Transnational Corporations observed: "[a] number of factors... conspire to make purely national control systems variously evadible, inefficient, incomplete, unenforceable, exploitable, or negotiable... with respect to transnational corporations."[27] One solution is the recognition of the transnational corporation as a legal subject, bearing rights and responsibilities directly under international law. However, this faces major problems in states' unwillingness to "relinquish their traditionally dominant position in international law, or to acknowledge the effectiveness of law in the absence of a sovereign" (Johns, 1994: 900).[28]

Arguably, students of international political economy are more tuned into the increasing significance of transnational corporations. However, while few analysts would go so far as to declare transnational corporations to be "invisible" in terms of their political significance, there is a dominant tendency to regard corporate power as ultimately linked to and conditioned by state power. This is particularly evident in the comment by Stephen Krasner (1995: 279) that "it is states or polities that structure the basic environment within which transnationals must function: the nature of the legal system; the specification of legitimate organizational forms... the determination of acceptable modes of political action."[29]

Some analysts address the question of the significance of transnational corporations in terms of their relative autonomy of state influence and control, arguing that the "footloose and fancy-free" corporation is

[26] For an interesting analysis of measures taken by the Australian authorities to prevent the manipulation of the Australian tax system so as to shield corporate profits from taxation by integrating the profits of offshore subsidiary corporations with the profits of the Australian-based parent company, see Azzi (1994).

[27] Quoted in Johns (1994: 896).

[28] See Cutler (1999 c and 2001 a) for fuller discussions of the problems in recognizing corporate personality under international law.

[29] Note, however, as does the volume's editor (Risse-Kappen, 1995 a: 281), that the various selections in the volume illustrate the oversimplification of the "state-centred" versus "society-centred" approach to the significance of transnational corporations.

but a myth. They focus on the continuing influence of national business culture and ideology on transnational corporate behavior[30] and the continuing links to states through incorporation, taxation, corporate filing and reporting requirements, securities regulation, and the like. Indeed, Detlev Vagts (1970: 787–8) argues that for a "truly non-national, autonomous entity" a corporation would have to meet five requirements: no country of incorporation; widely dispersed business activities across different states; multinational distribution of shareholders; internationalization of management; and declining national claims to the extraterritorial application of domestic laws. Arguably, many corporations meet the second, third, and fourth criteria. However, there is no mechanism for international incorporation and the extraterritorial application of laws continues to be practiced by states such as the United States. It must be noted, though, that the emphasis on the formal legal links between corporations and states overlooks the extent to which corporations can be operating *de facto* more autonomously through manipulating the laws governing nationality of corporations, through the reluctance of states to take on their claims, and through novel corporate arrangements that do not involve incorporation of the transnational enterprise (e.g., contractual arrangements) (see generally, Muchlinski, 1995). In some cases, new corporate forms are emerging as a response to processes of economic globalization. Susan Strange (1994: 26) observes that the proliferation of interfirm relationships, such as "partnerships, production-sharing arrangements, collaborative research and networking . . . have begun to blur the identity and indirectly undermine the authority of the state." Corporate mergers, acquisitions, strategic alliances, and networking between firms add further complexities. She notes that when "partners in the network operate and are registered in several countries, it is impossible even to guess the 'nationality' of the whole network. Yet much media comment and much academic analysis still assume that each transnational corporation has a national identity and that governments can identify and then support their own national champion."[31]

We have seen that, in theory, corporations cannot be authoritative because, as private actors, they lack international legal personality. They do not possess identity as "subjects" of the law. Under international law, their activities are by definition nonauthoritative; they only become so

[30] See Keller and Pauly (1997); Pauly and Reich (1997); and Hirst (1997).
[31] Strange here cites the work of Michalet (1991).

when a state assumes responsibility for their actions or enforces their claims. However, emphasis on the legal aspects of corporate personality risks a formalism that mistakes the legal form for the actual conduct and practices of corporations and of states. It also risks obscuring how corporations use their nationality to avoid or evade responsibility. For example, corporations can manipulate the rules governing nationality and use their corporate status strategically to shield themselves against liability coming from the actions of foreign subsidiaries, foreign shareholders and creditors, and injured third parties, such as consumers. The intensification of interjurisdictional competition for incorporations is producing a "race to the bottom" as jurisdictions engage in the competitive deregulation of corporate standards (Blackburn, 1994; D. Charny, 1991) and narrow the scope of state responsibility. The problem is particularly acute in the case of rules of corporate nationality and conflict of laws that allow corporations to use their subsidiaries as shields against liability for environmental disasters, hazardous waste disposal, or wrongs suffered by foreign shareholders (Notes, 1986; Ismail, 1991).

In terms of enforcing corporate claims, states are not compelled to take on the claims of their national corporations. The problem of statelessness is very real when a state is unwilling to intervene on behalf of a corporation or when a state is unable to act for a corporation because the rules governing nationality have not been met (Staker, 1990: 159). The latter situation arises when business enterprises incorporate in jurisdictions for tax or other reasons of convenience but the rules of nationality require a *genuine link* between the corporation and the place of incorporation. In such cases, the incorporating state would not be in a position to protect the corporation (ibid.).

In addition, emphasis on the continuing influence of national corporate culture and ideology overlooks the extent to which these norms are changing in response to a globalizing corporate ideology and business culture. As the discussion has argued, this ideology and culture is being advanced by a global mercatocracy through the principles and practices of the modern law merchant. The modern law merchant is a central mechanism for the globalization of disciplinary neoliberal norms. Moreover, it is also a significant element in the pluralization of authority relations as a variety of nonstate actors, the most visible being transnational corporations, participates in the creation of international commercial law.

These considerations suggest that it is too simplistic to frame the problem in terms of corporate autonomy versus state control. The relationships between states and corporations are very complex and are deeply implicated in more general processes of juridification, pluralization, and privatization. These processes are restructuring state–society relations through the general decline in the corporate control functions of states and the expansion of their role in facilitating and enabling corporate activities (see Muchlinski, 1995). In some instances, states are experiencing a loss of control in relation to corporations, whereas in others state enforcement of property and contract rights and the ability of states to shield corporations from liability are strengthening the enforcement powers of states. Indeed, corporations are clamoring to litigate in state jurisdictions, such as that of the United States, which offer handsome damage awards and well-developed procedural protections. Paradoxically, while corporations are central players in this restructuring process, linking global and local political economies, they remain invisible as "subjects." This *de jure* insignificance of corporations in the face of their *de facto* significance reflects a disjunction between legal theory and state practice, and raises the "problem of the subject," which is pursued in the final chapter after considering the sources of law and the history of the unification movement.

Sources of transnational merchant law

The enhanced privatization and pluralization of the legal practices surrounding subjects doctrine is also evident in the practices surrounding sources doctrine. The contemporary phase in the development of the law merchant is experiencing a proliferation of new legal sources. The highly personalized nature of legal regulation emanating from law firms and other professional associations, such as tax and accounting firms, is captured in the significance of their members as "merchants of norms" who are causing a "revolution from above" in their influence upon business regulation (Dezalay and Sugarman, 1995).[32] These professionals are able to shape and reregulate economic transactions in response to challenges posed by economic globalization, highlighting the enhanced significance of expert knowledge in the creation of business law.[33] This is also evident in the notable trend toward the increasing privatization of business regulation through transnational corporate networks,

32 See also Bratton, McCahery, Picciotto, and Scott (1996).

33 For the significance of expert knowledge in the expansion of privatized business regulation, see Dezalay and Sugarman (1995); Picciotto and Mayne (1999); and Cutler, Haufler, and Porter (1999 c: 333–76).

private corporate codes of conduct, and voluntary approaches to regulating corporations.[34]

A very significant development is the increasing reliance on "soft law," nonbinding, informal, and discretionary standards in the unification of international commercial law. It will be recalled that soft law consists of "instruments that are not legally binding though they affect the conduct of international relations by states and may lead to the development of new international law" and are called "soft" because "they are not directly enforceable in domestic courts or international tribunals" (Kindred, et al., 1993: 78).[35] "Soft law" contrasts with "hard law," such as treaties and customary international law, which were noted in Chapter 2 to constitute the primary sources of international law. The differentiation between hard and soft law suggests different degrees in the juridification of commerce that are associated with the legal status of the entity engaged in law-creation. Clearly, private organizations, such as the ICC, the CMI, and the ILA lack the requisite international legal personality to create hard law in the form of legally binding international conventions. They must rely on states to adopt their unification efforts in order to create binding laws. However, they can create soft law and influential norms that, though legally nonbinding, acquire binding force through the voluntary adoption by parties in their contracts or by their evolution into customary international law.[36] They thus can and do have a significant role in the creation of soft law and merchant custom. The ICC Incoterms, discussed below, are a good example of formally nonbinding model terms that have over time and through customary usage acquired the status of customary international law (Rowe, 1982).

[34] For an excellent overview of the nature and scope of private corporate codes of conduct utilized today to regulate corporate labor relations, environmental and social policies, human rights, pricing, fair trade, corruption, bribery, tobacco use, and animal welfare policies and practices see the UN report, *Development of Guidelines on the Role and Social Responsibilities of the Private Sector* (1999). See also, Kearney (1999) and Mayne (1999).
[35] An example of soft law is the UNCITRAL (United Nations Commission on International Trade) Model Law on International Commercial Arbitration, which has been voluntarily adopted by many states. Canada, for example, has implemented its terms in national law, affecting its transformation from soft to hard law. Other examples of soft law include the ICC (International Chamber of Commerce) trading terms, known as Incoterms that are given legal force by the voluntary incorporation in private contracts; the Helsinki Accords; and the OECD *Guidelines for Multinational Enterprises*. See also Seidl-Hohenveldern (1979). And see Schachter (1977) for a discussion of the influence that soft law can have, despite its legally nonbinding nature, and see Kennedy (1987 c) for a suggestive analysis of the nature of customary law.
[36] For a very good discussion of the role played by intentions in the creation of soft discipline, see Schachter (1977).

However, the private/soft and public/hard associations are imperfect. As mentioned above, privately generated soft laws may be transformed into hard law through the instrumentality of state practice and public entities such as states and international organizations do engage in the creation of soft law. Organizations with formal authority to bind member states sometimes opt for unification through voluntary codes and rules. Examples of this approach are the UNCITRAL Model Law on International Commercial Arbitration (see Hoellering, 1986) and UNIDROIT's Principles of International Commercial Contracts which unify the basic principles governing international commercial contracts (see Bonell, 1995; Farnsworth, 1995). The unification method chosen depends as much on the nature of the interests to be served through unification as it does on the legal capacities of the entities involved in the process. There is a tendency to associate harmonization with soft law and with less ambitious undertakings where agreement over harmonized standards comes relatively easily. In contrast, unification tends to be associated with hard law and with comprehensive and more exacting undertakings that are much harder to achieve. These tendencies are evident in the observation of one trade law expert that "[i]t is generally agreed that there is a need for harmonization of the private law rules that govern international transactions. There is less agreement as to the need for unification by means of multilateral treaties . . . [which will] be subject to only a single system" (Farnsworth, 1995: 83–4). These tendencies also reflect important assumptions about the objectives and purposes of unification. Most trade experts identify the objectives of unification and harmonization as the achievement of uniformity in commercial laws. The general presumption is that commercial activity will expand as a result of removing barriers generated by the legal uncertainty produced by multiple and different national standards (see Patterson, 1986: 266 n. 7). The unpredictability, inconvenience, and costs generated by uncertainty as to the legal rules that will be applied under different national systems of commercial and conflict laws are most commonly cited as the practical reasons for unification (Sturley, 1987: 731 nn. 7–11). Unification of commercial law is regarded as contributing to reduction of the costs of doing business.

> Non-uniformity of substantive legal rules imposes transaction costs on businesses engaged in international trade. A business that wishes to know if it has entered into an enforceable contract with a foreign trading partner, for example, must first go through a choice-of-law analysis [i.e., conflict of laws analysis] to determine which country's laws

> govern contract formation. The business must then construe the applicable substantive legal rules, which well may be the rules of the foreign legal system. Both steps in this analysis are difficult and may involve greater risk of error than is present in a purely domestic transaction.
>
> To reduce these transaction costs one could unify either the choice-of-law rules [conflict rules] or the substantive legal rules themselves. (Winship, 1988: 533–4)

Unification is said to produce important efficiencies. The unification of private international trade law is referred to by some students of harmonization as the harmonization of "jurisdictional interface," which enables those from multiple jurisdictions to communicate with each other. This makes international contracting easier and helps to avoid uncertainty and to reduce transactions costs. "Multilateral interface regimes reduce the costs of international transactions in many cases by achieving economies of scale for all transactions" (Leebron, 1995: 15). A review of the history of the unification movement reveals the importance that participants have attached to efficiency concerns. It also illustrates the trend away from unification through binding international treaties and towards unification through "soft law," voluntary statements of principle, model laws, and rules.

History of the Unification Movement

As noted in Chapter 4, during the medieval phase of the law merchant uniformity was achieved through the universality of merchant customs and the unifying influence of private dispute settlement norms and procedures. Merchants devised instruments and transactions that were enforceable only in private merchant courts, which operated more like private arbitrations than like courts of law. Justice was administered swiftly; procedural and evidentiary informality were the rule; and juries of merchants sat in judgment on the cases. Merchant customs could be used to prove the law before the merchant jurors, who issued judgments and even imposed penalties on the spot in the form of declarations of bankruptcy and market exclusion. During the second period of nationalization, there was a substantial erosion of uniformity as states became involved in the regulation of international commerce. Indeed, the consolidation of states marked a change in both the ability and the willingness of political authorities to regulate international commercial transactions. States engaged in state building expanded their authority over international commerce and incorporated the law merchant into domestic commercial law, juridifying commercial relations. By the end of this phase, significant differences in national commercial laws emerged, giving rise to contemporary efforts to unify national commercial and conflict laws.

It is important to note that the earliest modern unification efforts were self-regulatory initiatives undertaken almost exclusively by private merchant associations in the late nineteenth century. For example, the Hamburg Bourse for Corn Traders, the Bremen Cotton Bourse, the Silk Association of America, and the London Corn Trade Association were important in generating uniform commercial norms. These associations "were initiated by the business communities themselves with the aim of establishing norms to be adopted voluntarily by all members" (Dolzer, 1982: 62). At about the same time, the International Law Association (ILA),[37] a private body created in 1873, was founded for the purpose of unifying private and public international law. Another private body, the Comité Maritime International, was created in 1897 for the purpose of unifying private maritime law. Later, in the twentieth century, the International Chamber of Commerce (ICC) was founded as a private French association of national chambers of commerce and engaged in a number of projects aimed at unifying international commercial law. These associations have been generally very successful in articulating standards of broad application. Indeed, private associations have initiated some of the most significant unification efforts. However, as we noted earlier, their status as private associations limits their unification efforts to the creation of nonbinding and soft law, unless the laws develop into customary international law or are subsequently codified by states into binding conventions or adopted as law by the contracting parties.

The ICC undertook the unification of trade terms in the 1920s and produced a set of rules in 1936. They were revised in 1953, 1980, 1990, and 2000 in response to technological changes in transportation and changes in documentary procedures. Incoterms are designed as a set of uniform rules governing transportation costs and liabilities that may be adopted by parties through incorporation into their contracts. They are designed to facilitate exchange by providing greater certainty as to the parties' rights and obligations under the different terms. The voluntary application of Incoterms reflects the principle of freedom of contract,

[37] The ILA was originally named "The institution for the reform and codification of the *jus gentium*," but its name was changed in 1895 to reflect its involvement in private, as well as, public international law. See David (1972 a: 151– 2) and Dolzer (1982).

for the parties are free to select the term deemed appropriate in the circumstances. As a private association, the ICC clearly lacks international legal personality and is thus incapable of creating norms of a mandatory nature. However, reliance on Incoterms has become so common and generalized that many regard them as having acquired the status of customary international law (see Ramberg, 1982: 146; Rowe, 1982). This is particularly so for European trade where they are applied to sales transactions in the absence of voluntary incorporation by contracting parties.[38]

In contrast to the work of the ICC and Incoterms, unification efforts for bills of lading, bills of exchange, promissory notes, and letters of credit, while initiated by private associations were subsequently taken over by intergovernmental associations, which produced binding laws in the form of international conventions. The ILA undertook the unification of bills of lading and bills of exchange, while the ICC initiated efforts to unify letters of credit. These initiatives were later taken up by intergovernmental organizations and formed the basis for the negotiation of binding international conventions, which will be considered shortly.

Governments became involved in the unification movement late in the nineteenth century, primarily through the Hague Conference on Private International Law, which although created in 1893, only attained status as an international organization in 1955. This was the first intergovernmental body to undertake the unification of commercial law and its main focus has been unifying conflict of laws rules.[39] It has been

[38] Incoterms 1980 provided rules for fourteen trade terms. Uniform rules are provided for the more traditional trade terms, such as cif (cost, insurance, and freight), fob (free on board), and c & f (cost and freight), and new additions have been made to reflect container and multimodal transport techniques and new forms for documenting sales transactions, such as the shipped-on-board bill of lading. Subsequent revisions of Incoterms in 1990 and 2000 have further adapted them to modern trade (see Ramberg, 1982: 146; 2000; Honnold, 1982). While Incoterms go a long way in unifying the standards governing transport costs and liabilities, their usage is not yet universal. In the United States, for example, many merchants continue to rely on the American Foreign Trade Definitions, which, though substantially similar to the Incoterms, are regarded as generally more favorable to exporters. There does, however, appear to be some movement in the United States towards reliance on Incoterms. See Berman and Kaufman (1978: 229), Ramberg (1982: 151) and see the ICC web page http://www.iccwbo.org/ for its contemporary areas of work, including regulating corruption, arbitration, banking, competition, intellectual property, taxation, trade, investment, and E-business.

[39] The Hague Conference on Private International Law is an intergovernmental organization established by treaty to "work for the progressive unification of the rules of private international law." It has forty-three members, predominantly industrialized states, including Canada, and most European states, the United States, Australia, Japan, China,

active in unifying trade law in areas relating to conflict rules and procedural matters, but has not made much contribution to the unification of substantive rules of law. Moreover, in its early days, the Hague Conference functioned more as a regional than a global organization. Membership was largely confined to European states and the texts it produced reflected civilian legal traditions.

During the interwar period, the Economic Committee of the League of Nations undertook the unification of limited commercial subjects, mainly dealing with financial and credit transactions. Government involvement in unification increased with the creation of the International Institute for the Unification of Private Law (UNIDROIT), which was formed in 1926 within the framework of the League of Nations and engaged in the unification of certain areas of commercial law.[40] However, as in the case of the Hague Conference, unification undertakings were

Argentina, and Venezuela, and meets in plenary sessions every four years to prepare conventions and to establish future work. Between sessions, Special Commissions meet to prepare draft conventions. The Hague Conference works toward the unification of the conflict of laws rules relating to a number of commercial law matters. With regard to international trade law its main unification efforts concern the enforcement of foreign judgments, the international sale of goods, and procedural matters. See Reese (1985); Droz and Dyer (1981); Gabor (1986). For a review of the methods, objectives, and early work of the Hague Conference, see Castel (1967) and also Dolzer (1982) and Honnold (1995) for its more recent initiatives. See the Hague Conference on Private International Law's web page http://hcch.net/e/ where the following areas of work are identified: jurisdiction and foreign judgments relating to civil and commercial matters, indirectly held securities, and E-commerce.

[40] UNIDROIT was established in 1926 on the basis of a bilateral agreement between the Italian government and the League of Nations. UNIDROIT separated from the League in 1935, following the withdrawal of Italy from the League. In 1940 it was reestablished as an independent intergovernmental organization by a multilateral treaty, the UNIDROIT Statute. Since then it has entered into cooperation with a number of international organizations, including the United Nations. UNIDROIT has a membership of some fifty-seven countries, including most Western European states, some Eastern European states, and a number of African and Asian states. UNIDROIT has worked on the unification of a number of commercial law subjects, including the international sale of goods, international agency, validity of sales contracts, rules of road and waterway, recognition and enforcement of arbitral awards, bills of exchange, intellectual property, leasing, factoring, warehousing, garaging, the law of contract and powers of attorney, a code on international trade law, the law of franchising, security interests in mobile equipment, and the regulation of stolen and illegally exported cultural objects. UNIDROIT is presently working on a revision of the Principles of International Commercial Contracts, extending them to additional topics, including agency, assignment of debts, and limitation of actions. Recent initiatives are discussed in a regular publication prepared by UNIDROIT, *UNIDROIT Proceedings and Papers*. See also the UNIDROIT web page http://www.unidroit.org/ where the following areas of work are identified: international interests in mobile equipment, franchising, transnational civil procedure, and transnational capital market transactions. For the history of the organization and its work, see generally, Monaco (1977); Bonell (1978); Matteucci (1977).

primarily regional in scope and civilian in character and did not attract broad support outside Europe.

Significant global intergovernmental involvement in the unification of commercial law really only occurred after the Second World War. Indeed, one of the distinguishing characteristics of the modern law merchant is the proliferation of intergovernmental agencies involved in the unification of commercial law and claiming the representation of most of the economic and legal systems of the world. It is central to consider the context in which global intergovernmental cooperation emerged.

As noted above, a significant limitation to the success of early unification efforts was their regional and civil law character. The Hague Conference on Private International Law and UNIDROIT were for some time limited in membership to European states and to those who shared the civil law tradition. As a result, their early unification projects were not greeted with much enthusiasm by common law jurisdictions. The United States, for example, only became involved in both organizations in the 1960s. Because of the essentially European and civilian nature of their unification efforts, their texts and conventions did not receive broad acceptance outside Europe. Common law states, less developed states, and states with centrally planned economies objected that their interests and legal systems were not adequately represented.

The creation of the United Nations and its network of specialized agencies after the Second World War provided the first truly global institutional context for the unification movement. In addition, the principles and practices of "embedded liberalism," under the leadership of the United States, provided the broader normative framework for the movement (Ruggie, 1982). This involved the preference for rules that facilitate international commercial activity through the reduction of transaction costs, but that provide necessary protections for domestic commercial interests. Such rules inform the various organs engaged in unification under the auspices of the United Nations. The mandate of the UN General Assembly includes the unification of commercial law under its duties regarding the progressive development and codification of international law and under its competence to promote international economic cooperation.[41] The General Assembly established a number of bodies and specialized agencies engaged directly or indirectly in the unification of commercial law. The International Maritime Organization (IMO), created as a specialized agency in 1948, but entering into force in

41 The Charter of the United Nations, Articles 13. 1 (a) and (b).

1958, has engaged in a number of projects unifying private maritime law. The United Nations Conference on Trade and Development (UNCTAD) was created as an organ of the General Assembly in 1964 and has engaged in a number of projects involving the unification of law, as too has the United Nations Industrial Development Organization (UNIDO), which was established in 1966 as an organ of the General Assembly and acquired status as a specialized agency in 1983.

However, the main global forum for the unification of commercial law was provided with the creation of the United Nations Commission on International Trade Law (UNCITRAL) in 1966.[42] UNCITRAL was given a mandate to "further the progressive harmonization and unification of the law of international trade" (ibid.). This mandate includes, *inter alia*, the preparation or promotion of international conventions, model laws, and uniform laws, and the promotion of codification and wider acceptance of international trade terms, customs, and practices.[43] UNCITRAL was created in response to observations made in a report to the General Assembly by Clive Schmitthoff, who is regarded as the "conceptual father" of UNCITRAL (Herrmann, 1982: 36), concerning the lack of coordination amongst organizations engaged in unifying trade law. Schmitthoff also observed that unification efforts failed to achieve universal application owing to both the lack of participation of the developing and centrally planned economies and the European and civil law basis of earlier initiatives. UNCITRAL was thus created with a view to representing the principal economic and legal systems of the world and the developed and developing countries. Membership in the organization is designed to represent all major legal systems in the world and states of various levels of development, including both planned and market economies.[44]

[42] UNCITRAL was established by the General Assembly Resolution 2205 (21) (1966) and became operative in 1968.

[43] UNCITRAL has engaged in a number of unification efforts, including the unification of the laws governing: the international sale of goods and related transactions; the international transport of goods; international commercial arbitration and conciliation; public procurement; construction contracts; international payments; electronic commerce; and cross-border insolvency. UNCITRAL publishes the *UNCITRAL Yearbook* annually which provides a good source for information on its unification efforts. See also Cutler (1992). See UNCITRAL's web page http://www.uncitral.org/ for a good summary of contemporary areas of work, including privately financed infrastructure projects, arbitration, transport law, insolvency law, security interests, and electronic commerce.

[44] The membership scheme is regional and membership rotates. Initially, UNCITRAL membership included twenty-nine states: seven African; five Asian; four Eastern European; five Latin American; eight Western European, and "other states." Canada, Australia,

The attempt to broaden participation in legal unification beyond its original European basis reflects a number of important developments. UNCITRAL was created at a time when demands for a New International Economic Order were being articulated by the countries emerging out of colonial pasts. Calls from the less developed world and also from socialist countries for a greater voice in the creation of international economic law, while dominant in UNCTAD, were also heard in UNCITRAL. As part of its program of work, UNCITRAL inherited some unification efforts that had previously not met with great success. For example, the laws governing maritime transport had been identified by UNCTAD when it initially convened in 1964, prior to the creation of UNCITRAL, as in need of significant reform by developing states who claimed that the existing laws favored powerful private associations of marine insurers and underwriters, shipping liner conferences, and cartels.[45] While UNCTAD was given the mandate of addressing the international trade concerns of the developing countries and had identified a number of areas in need of reform,[46] it had not been terribly successful in generating texts that were acceptable to most developed states. Indeed, as Edgar Gold (1981: 28) notes, the demand in UNCTAD for international regulation of bills of lading, marine insurance, charter-parties, shipowners' liabilities, and flags of convenience, all parts of what was generally regarded as a "private industry," "astonished" the major maritime states, who perceived it as a direct attack on the " 'law merchant,' Adam Smith, the Protestant ethic, and free enterprise." The leading maritime states were successful in blocking significant developments in UNCTAD and as part of a renewed effort to further isolate what they regarded as the domain of private authority, had the matter of shipping legislation deftly transferred to the newly created UNCITRAL, a body heralded as appropriately technical, neutral, and apolitical in operation and thus more appropriate for the resolution of deeply divisive issues in shipping legislation. The developing states opposed this transfer, but were unsuccessful. UNCITRAL, in consultation with UNCTAD, produced a

and the United States qualify as other states. In 1973 membership expanded to thirty-six states with the addition of: two African; two Asian; and one additional Eastern European, Western European, and Latin American state. See "Working Methods of the Commission: Note by the Secretariat" (1988).

45 See generally, Cutler (1999 c) for a detailed examination of the private interests that have historically defined maritime transport laws and for the conflicting interests of less developed and other states.

46 For example, the unilateral fixing of freight rates, discriminatory practices of shipping conferences, inadequacy of existing shipping services, and inequities in existing shipping legislation.

set of rules governing bills of lading that are more accommodating of states' development concerns than were either of the earlier unification initiatives (the Hague Rules and the Hague–Visby Rules). However, so few states have adopted the new rules that most of world trade continues to be governed by the earlier rules that are said to favor the interests of shipowners.[47]

The creation of UNCITRAL thus marked the attempt to create a global trade organization that would be both representative in nature and integrative of the previously fragmentary and unsuccessful, largely regional unification efforts. It also marked the real beginnings of the involvement of the United States in the unification movement. Indeed, the United States has become a leader in the movement and today exercises considerable influence over the nature and content of regime standards. Prior to the creation of UNCITRAL, the attitude of the United States was "one of indifference towards all efforts at international cooperation in private commercial matters" (Lansing, 1980: 270–1). This indifference was born out of a preference for judge-made or common law, ignorance of the civil law, and the belief that civilian efforts at unification could not accommodate common law conceptions and theories. In addition, the perception that the unification of private law was unnecessary and the existence of limitations on the treaty-making power of the executive in matters of private law also posed obstacles to the cooperation of the United States (ibid.).

Success in domestic unification efforts undertaken in the creation of the US Uniform Commercial Code (UCC) generated a change in attitude in the United States regarding the merits and possibilities of unifying commercial law. In 1963 the US Congress authorized the executive to join international organizations engaged in the harmonization and unification of private law and membership in the Hague Conference, and UNIDROIT followed (see Pfund and Taft, 1986). Congress was responding to a recognition of extraordinary increases in the volume of world trade and commerce and to the concern that unification efforts in Europe would proceed with or without the participation of the United States. As one Commissioner on Uniform State Laws said in a statement before Congress:

> [w]e must enter into the problems of great unification in fields of law touching social intercourse and business activity at a time when we can get the viewpoint of the United States heard in the original drafting,

[47] See generally, Cutler (1999 c) and Gold (1981).

> not at the time it is considered for final adoption. It is in the preparatory stages that there is an opportunity to weave into it the basic problems that we face in the United States and upon which the commissioners [on Uniform State Laws] have been working for years.[48]

Moreover, with the creation of UNCITRAL and the adoption of its program of work that spanned significant and varied areas of commercial activity, the United States was prompted to reassess its attitude towards international unification. Concern was expressed that if American representatives did not take the work of UNCITRAL seriously, they would be faced with the development of standards that were unrepresentative of their interests. The United States thus began participating in UNCITRAL in earnest, adopting a leadership and, in some cases, a dominant role. Other states, including Great Britain and Canada, also began to take greater interest in the unification movement with the creation of UNCITRAL.

The significant influence of the United States on the unification movement is particularly evident in the unification of international sales law. The United Nations Convention on Contracts for the International Sale of Goods (Vienna Sales Convention), negotiated under the auspices of UNCITRAL and which came into effect in 1988, is generally regarded as one of the most "successful" unification initiatives ever undertaken.[49] By 1992 the Vienna Sales Convention was in force in thirty-four states from every region in the world, indicating "substantially world-wide acceptance" (Honnold, 1995: 1038). By 1997, it was in force in forty-nine states and described as "a hallmark in international law" (Giannuzzi, 1997: 991). Moreover, the Vienna Sales Convention is regarded as very much a replica of the domestic commercial law of the United States Uniform Commercial Code. The United States not only exercised leadership in the negotiation of the Vienna Sales Convention, but was able to tailor the provisions to US commercial norms and practices. American trade experts Allan Farnsworth and John Honnold both exercised leadership roles in the negotiations. Honnold represented the United States at the Vienna Sales Conference where the Convention was negotiated and was head of the UNCITRAL Secretariat during the drafting of the Vienna Sales Convention. The success of the United States delegation led a US State Department official to conclude that the Vienna Sales Convention "resembles [the UCC] more than the law of

48 Joe Barrett, Commissioner for Arkansas, cited in Pfund and Taft (1986: 671, n. 1).
49 For this assessment see Farnsworth (1995); Bonell (1995); Honnold (1995).

any other country."[50] While developing states did articulate demands for a more development-oriented sales law, they were generally unsuccessful in promoting notions of substantive equity in contracting. They were successful in blunting, though not displacing the rule of "open price" in cases of contractual underspecification, which they argued favored exporters and worked against them in rising markets.[51] "Such contract prices would tend to be the sellers' prices and, as is well known, while the prices of raw materials exported by the developing countries are generally fixed in the commodity markets of the developed world, the prices of manufactured goods are usually determined by the manufacturers themselves" (Date-Bah, 1981: 28).[52] Developing countries were also able to negotiate extended time periods for rejecting defective goods. Developed countries wanted strict treatment of the notice periods for rejecting defective goods, while developing countries wanted accommodating standards that were more sensitive to their development needs. Here too developing countries managed to soften, but not displace the rules promoted by the developed world.[53]

Another area dividing states in the negotiation of the Vienna Sales Convention was the status to be accorded merchant customs and trade usages. While more will be said on this issue below, socialist and developing states opposed the inclusion of trade usages and customs because "those usages were settled primarily by industrialized nations and [were] likely to reflect the interests of those countries. In contrast, countries like the United States and Great Britain place[d] prime emphasis on regularly observed trade usages, which are said to increase mercantile flexibility, and thereby, economic efficiency" (Garro, 1989: 476–7). As the trade expert Allan Farnsworth (1979: 465–6) comments, "[g]enerally, developed countries like usages. Most usages seem to be made in London, whether in the grain or cocoa trade, for example. Developing countries, on the other hand, tend to regard usages as neocolonialist. They cannot understand why usages of, let us say, the cocoa trade should be made

50 Peter Pfund, Assistant Legal Advisor for Private International Law, US Department of State, cited in Patterson (1986: n. 55) and see Honnold (1984).

51 Developing countries, socialist countries, and some civil law countries opposed the practice of open price contracts, while the United States favored a minimum regulation of price specificity. Developing states argued that open price contracts work against their interests in light of the unfavorable terms of trade for raw materials, in contrast with the rising prices of manufactured goods. See Garro (1989: 463).

52 See also, Rosett (1984).

53 See Goldstajn (1981: 76); Jones (1989: 497–500); Patterson (1986: 283–94); and Garro (1989: 469–73) for fuller discussion of the conflicting interests of developed and developing states.

in London."[54] The Soviet delegate to the Vienna Conference objected that "usages [are] often devices established by monopolies and it would be wrong to recognize their priority over the law," while the delegate from Yugoslavia stated that trade usage "has been formed by a restricted group of countries... whose position did not express worldwide opinion" (Bainbridge, 1984: 641). Despite these objections, the Vienna Sales Convention recognizes the binding force of commercial custom.[55]

A review of UNCITRAL's most significant unification efforts reflects a tendency in the early years to unify through binding international treaties, such as the Convention on the Limitation Period in the International Sale of Goods (New York, 1974); the United Nations Convention on the Carriage of Goods by Sea (Hamburg, 1978); the United Nations Convention on Contracts for the International Sale of Goods (Vienna Sales Convention, Vienna, 1980); the United Nations Convention on International Bills of Exchange and International Promissory Notes (New York, 1988) and the United Nations Convention on the Liability of Operators of Transport Terminals in International Trade (Vienna, 1991).

Recent unification efforts have focussed more on unification through model laws, such as the Model Law on Procurement of Goods, Construction, and Services (1993), Model Law on International Commercial Arbitration (1985), and Model Law on Electronic Commerce (1996). UNIDROIT's very successful Principles of International Commercial Contracts also reflect the trend to unify through voluntary, soft law.[56]

While trade experts offer practical and efficiency-related considerations to account for the preference for voluntary soft unification efforts,[57] deeper structural and distributional influences are also at work. These influences stem from attempts by states and private commercial actors to adjust to changing terms of international competition which are generated by contemporary developments in the capitalist mode of

[54] See also, Boka (1964: 227–40).

[55] The Vienna Sales Convention embodies a compromise on the legal status of commercial usage which goes part way in recognizing the objections of socialist and developing states. However, it clearly indicates the growing legitimacy of unformulated custom as a source of law and adopts a test of custom very close to that adopted in the Uniform Commercial Code (UCC) of the United States, which emphasizes behavior over intent and arguably works in favor of the major trading states and corporations. See Garro (1989: 479–80) and Date-Bah (1981: 45) for discussion of the debates over the legal status of usage. See also Farnsworth (1984: 81–9) for a good comparison of the Vienna Sales Convention and the UCC.

[56] See also the unification initiatives listed in note 60 below.

[57] See the Introduction to UNIDROIT's Principles of International Commercial Contracts for the stated preference for unification through less exacting and less time-consuming soft law.

production. The globalization of production and finance and privatization of many economic sectors and activities have created new opportunities and incentives, influencing the terms of commercial competition. States are responding in a variety of ways. Cerny (1990: 205) notes that the social and economic roles of states are changing "in the attempt to respond to, and to shape and control, growing international economic interpenetration and the transnational structures to which it gives rise." States have shifted from macroeconomic to microeconomic interventionism, which is reflected in deregulation, and have altered the focus of their industrial policies in the pursuit of "competitive advantage"over "comparative advantage." The policy shift also translates into politics that no longer revolve around national welfare concerns, but that are increasingly geared to "the promotion of enterprise, innovation and profitability in both private and public sectors" (ibid., 205; and see Cerny, 1997: 260).

The shift in focus from comparative to competitive advantage is evident in contemporary developments in the unification movement.[58] As Leebron notes:

> [r]ecently, claims for harmonization of national laws and policies have been closely linked to claims for "fair trade." The scholarly literature has begun to embrace the notion that harmonization is the mechanism by which unfair differences in legal and other regimes are eliminated, and the level playing field, the metaphoric symbol of fairness, is restored. Harmonization in this sense is the Procrustean response to international trade, a response fundamentally at odds with the theory of comparative advantage that has justified liberal trading policies since the early nineteenth century. (1995: 1)

Leebron here recollects the myth of Procrustes. This classical figure was known to tie to his bed errant travelers crossing his path. Measuring the wanderers, he would stretch those too short and cut bits off those too long. Leebron vividly depicts the potential artificiality and problematic nature of standards. More to the point, though, is that contemporary harmonization and unification represent part of the compromise of embedded liberalism struck by states to secure domestic welfare in the face of the exigencies of increasing globalization. This compromise has, however, come undone. This is reflected in the shift in emphasis from unification policies aimed at creating binding, comprehensive, and equitable

58 For an interesting exploration of "unification as a product of competition and conflict," see Dezalay and Garth (1996: vii).

terms of competition to those aimed at leaving the terms of competition to private negotiation and agreement. It is also evident in the reassertions of merchant custom as the preeminent method for creating law and of arbitration as the preferred method of dispute resolution. While the first unification efforts were regional and in some cases sectorally specific, later activities involving UNCITRAL and other actors were more global, multilateral, and comprehensive. The Vienna Sales Convention probably represents the high watermark for comprehensive global unification. Since then, however, initiatives are increasingly fragmented, sectorally focussed, and soft in application. The growing trend in the use of soft law sources and voluntary or nonbinding arrangements, such as UNIDROIT's recent restatement of Principles of International Commercial Contracts, signals the increasing salience of the private ordering of commercial relations that grants maximum scope to merchant autonomy and flexibility. The drafters of the Principles addressed their underlying rationale:

> Efforts towards the international unification of law have hitherto essentially taken the form of binding instruments, such as supranational legislation or international conventions, or of model laws. Since these instruments often risk remaining little more than dead letter and tend to be fragmentary in character, calls are increasingly being made for recourse to non-legislative means of unification or harmonisation of law.
>
> Some of these calls are for the further development of what is termed "international commercial custom," for example, through model clauses and contracts formulated by the interested business circles on the basis of current trade practices and relating to specific types of transactions or particular aspects thereof.
>
> Others go even further and advocate the elaboration of an international statement of general principles of contract law.
>
> UNIDROIT's initiative for the elaboration of "Principles of International Commercial Contracts" goes in that direction.
>
> (UNIDROIT, 1994, Introduction)

This initiative was premised upon great faith in the ability of private ordering to solve many of the problems facing international commercial actors. Indeed, the Principles are recognized as embodying a "change in paradigm in international commercial law" in the "privatization" of legal unification and harmonization (Berger, 1997: 951). The international business community has enthusiastically embraced the Principles, which have been translated into eight languages in addition to the five official versions and have already been referred to in international arbitral awards (Bonell, 1995: 62).

Merchant custom is being held out as the source of law most consistent with the goal of private ordering. Important efficiencies and economies are said to flow from the adoption of merchant custom as a source of law in comparison to negotiated international conventions:[59]

> Experience has shown that the development of uniform rules of international trade by practice is much more efficient and far-reaching than the unification of commercial law by means of international conventions. The technical process of the formation of a custom is already in itself more flexible and easier to carry out than the conclusion of an international convention which in this domain – where necessarily a modification of national law is involved – is inconceivable outside the context of ratification procedures . . . And since the modification of particular legal rules which one wants to alter in order to achieve uniformity in the law of international trade, in many instances, involves an attack on some general principles of national law of which the rules form part, the already considerable obstacles become insurmountable because, although one is only concerned with commercial law, one must rise from the level of particular rules to that of the general theory of law. (Kopelmanas, 1964: 118–26)

As noted above, Western developed states tend to favor unification through custom for it is regarded as more flexible, adaptable, easier to achieve, and, ultimately, more efficient.[60] However, not all are in

59 Schmitthoff (1964 a: 16) identifies legislation and custom as the two main sources of international economic law. International legislation may be created by the adoption by states of a multilateral convention or the formulation of a model law, which is then adopted by states through the enactment of municipal legislation fashioned upon the model law. In contrast, international commercial custom "consists of commercial practices, usages or standards which are so widely used that businessmen engaged in international trade expect their contracting parties to conform with them and which are formulated by international agencies . . . or international trade associations." Schmitthoff (ibid.) further notes that the main difference between the two sources is that international legislation applies "by virtue of the authority of the national sovereign," while international custom is "founded on the autonomy of the will of the parties who adopt it as the regime applicable to the individual transaction in hand."

60 There is a distinction between formulated and unformulated customary law. Formulated customary law comprises customs that have been formally and deliberately articulated by formulating agencies such as the ICC. Examples are the ICC Incoterms, the ICC Uniform Customs and Practice for Documentary Credits, the Code of International Factoring Customs, the ICC Uniform Rules for a Combined Transport Document, and the York–Antwerp Rules in the General Average. Unformulated custom, in contrast, is constituted by practices that are in common usage, such as marine insurance certificates, but that have not been deliberately or formally articulated by formulating agencies. Schmitthoff (1964 a: 23) refers to the former as formulated international custom and the latter as unformulated commercial usage. While formulated international custom has unquestionably gained legitimacy as a source of law, as is evidenced by the widespread use of Incoterms and other standards developed by nongovernmental formulating agencies, the

agreement about the merits of customary law and the sufficiency of private ordering in achieving efficiencies or fairness in international commercial relations. Developing states tend to prefer unification through hard law, for the convention process at least guarantees some rules governing access and transparency (Sempasa, 1992). Moreover, while customary law is arguably more adaptable, its distributional impact often remains obscure. For example, Alan Cafruny (1987: 58 and 261) argues that certain trade terms have functioned for developing states as barriers to entry into the bulk trading market, but there has been little challenge to the distributional consequences of the terms of trade because of their highly technical nature. The United Kingdom was able to build its merchant marine through an informed and selective use of different trade terms that were then dictated to trade partners on the basis of commercial power and influence.[61] This suggests that the distributional consequences can be very significant. It also raises a related problem of long-term contracting and standard form contracts whose distributional consequences may be obscure to the parties who must deal on a take-it-or-leave-it basis.[62] Typically, asymmetrical relations are built right into such contracts, but this is obscured by their technical nature, their general acceptance, and the frequency of their use.

There are also important distributional consequences flowing from soft law.[63] Soft law norms respond to perceptions of intensified competition and the sense that some players are cheating and that the playing field is not so level. They allow room to move and to cheat if necessary.[64] However, soft law norms probably benefit only those businesses that are

legitimacy of unformulated custom remains controversial. As Honnold (1991: 147) observes, "[g]overnments have sometimes viewed such custom as inconsistent with their sovereignty and with principles on which their regimes were based." Garro (1989: 476–7) notes that this controversy emerged over the status of custom in the Vienna Sales Convention, where developed states, such as the United States and the United Kingdom, placed "prime emphasis on regularly observed trade usages, which are said thereby to increase mercantile flexibility, and thereby, efficiency."

61 Cafruny argues that the trade term fob (free on board) creates a barrier to the entry of developing countries into bulk trading. Under this term, the importer chooses the shipowner to transport the goods. In contrast, under the cif term (cost, insurance, and freight) the exporter selects the vessel. Britain expanded its merchant marine by contracting the sale of coal cif and the import of cotton, fob. In both cases, British shipowners were selected.

62 Standard form contracts are also known as contracts of adhesion and are widely used in international commerce, particularly in maritime transport and insurance. See Eörsi (1977).

63 See generally, Abbott and Snidal (2000).

64 Cutler (1999 b). Scheuerman (1999 and 2001) notes how discretionary law serves the more powerful social and economic interests which are in a position to exploit vague and open-ended norms.

large and dispersed enough to carry the risks generated by uncertain standards. Hard law norms, in contrast, regulate the terms of competition more closely and visibly, probably benefiting smaller businesses which face high transaction costs in collecting information about national rule differences. This suggests that there are distributional consequences to the method of unification or harmonization chosen.

Significantly, the distributional consequences of different sources of law transcend private commercial interests and impact on state interests and competitiveness. Arguably, the ability of the United States to tailor international sales law to its liking gives US-based traders a competitive edge over other less influential states. It also suggests that transaction-cost analysis of the incentives to unify potentially obscures the distributional issues involved and overstates the mutuality of benefits flowing from the unification process.

Santos (1995: 290) associates hard legal regulation or the "iron cage mode" with legal relations where there is a great asymmetry in power relations because coercive regulation is needed to temper the overwhelming power differentials of the parties. In contrast, he notes that the soft "rubber cage mode" of legal regulation tends to characterize relations between relatively equal parties where there is less need of the coercive function of the law. However, he also identifies a trend in the development of capitalist legality in peripheral states toward the increasing soft, voluntary, informal, and discretionary regulation of legal relations. This informality creates the appearance of consensual legal relations but, in actuality, represses dissent. The appearance of mutually agreed outcomes through informal arbitration and conciliation both "disarm and neutralize" dissent "through mechanisms of trivialization and integration" (Santos, 1982 a: 253).

> Informalization thus means powerlessness. It will help to stabilize social relations since no dramatic changes can be expected from institutions or settings that must be oriented to consensus and harmony because of the limits on their coercive powers.
>
> Many disputes that are intended to be processed by the new informal settings share two characteristics: There are structural differences in the social power of the parties, and they occur repeatedly. Landlord–tenant and merchant–consumer disputes are examples. In such cases mediation or arbitration becomes repressive because the setting lacks coercive power to neutralize the power differences between the parties. Repressive mediation leads to repressive consensus, which, I submit, will more and more characterize the exercise of capitalist state power. (Ibid., 260–1)

In a similar vein, the increasing informality and personalized nature of law merchant discipline assists in locking peripheral states into neoliberal market disciplines by disarming them and neutralizing their dissent. Arguably, major conflicts of interest are much more visible in formal negotiations of hard treaty law where the scope of concessions granted by the more powerful states are obvious. In contrast, soft discipline is by definition unenforceable and, as a result, even the most generous concessions may in actuality be quite meaningless.

Criticisms of private initiatives to unify and harmonize international commercial law are being voiced by those who question how representational private initiatives can be.[65] Some challenge the dominant view that UNCITRAL's success in unifying a number of areas of law can be attributed to its ability to accommodate a variety of different interests and to arrive at acceptable compromises between often incompatible rules (Garro, 1989: Patterson, 1986). For example, concessions made to less-developing states in the negotiation of the Vienna Sales Convention were marginal (Patterson, 1986). Michael Bonell (1995), a legal consultant to UNIDROIT, in evaluating the success of the negotiations over the Vienna Sales Convention notes that:

> due to the differences in legal tradition and at times, even more significantly, in the social and economic structure prevalent in the States participating in the negotiations, some issues had to be excluded at the outset from the scope of the envisaged instrument, while with respect to a number of other items the conflicting views could only be overcome by compromise solutions leaving matters more or less undecided.
>
> (64)

The sales regime emerged very much a product of the developed world with a strong American imprint. Bonell contrasts the outcome of the unification of sales law with unification efforts leading to UNIDROIT's Principles. He observes (ibid., 66) that "it was precisely because the negotiations leading up to CISG [Vienna Sales Convention] had so amply demonstrated that this Convention was the maximum that could be achieved at the legislative level," that UNIDROIT abandoned "the idea of a binding instrument" and decided instead "to take another road for its own project." The road they chose was unification through soft law. While the drafters of UNIDROIT's Principles pride themselves on the incorporation of norms reflecting the needs of less-developed states, one must bear in mind the status of the Principles as soft law. As Ignaz

[65] See Farnsworth (1995) for a review of some of these criticisms.

Seidl-Hohenveldern (1979: 193) observes "the market-economy industrialized States have shown their willingness to accept a good number of the Third World demands on principle, provided that these rules merely become 'soft law.'" Critics of the soft law approach argue that conventions of mandatory application offer better protection for parties with weaker bargaining power. While recognizing that merchant autonomy and freedom of contract remain "articles of faith" for merchants, there are those who identify a growing need to protect weaker parties from those exercising monopolistic or quasi-monopolistic economic power (Matteucci, 1960: 138). Some argue that unrestricted reliance on merchant autonomy and freedom of contract are unacceptable foundations for the unification of commercial law.

> Many vital questions are at stake, ranging from the reconciliation of common and continental law to the protection of the weaker party and the satisfactory regulation of transactions between parties from different social and economic systems or from developed and underdeveloped countries, and it would be irrational madness to leave the legal responses to these problems to an uncontrolled *laissez-faire* in a world of perpetual strife. It is a fact that the economic and political matters involved in international trade transactions considerably exceed the narrow margins of private interests which are often – and mistakenly – understood to be the only concerns in the private law regulation of international commercial issues. (Naón, 1982: 91)

Moreover, the distinctions between accommodation, compromise, and domination are often difficult to draw when the disputes turn on legal technicalities whose greater political and distributional significance probably escape all save for commercial law experts. The significance of legal expertise in the unification movement was noted earlier. While legal experts played a central role in the negotiation and drafting of UNIDROIT's Principles,[66] they too dispute the political or distributional significance of commercial law. A number of such experts attribute the success of the unification movement to precisely the "apolitical" nature of international commercial law. Clive Schmitthoff (1982), a leading scholar of international commercial law, has argued that the success of the unification movement turns on its apolitical nature and the resulting appeal of its laws to all parties involved in international commerce. Others, who refer to the harmonization of private commercial law as "jurisdictional interface harmonization," question the normative

[66] See Bonell (1995: 66) and see above.

content and distributional impact of the unification movement (Leebron, 1995: 3, n. 10). They regard the process as a "value-neutral" engagement and, thus, of unquestionable suitability for private regulation. The view that privatized law-creation is the most appropriate means to regulate international commerce is also evident in the matter of dispute settlement. Significant, as well, is a related trend toward the increasing informal, personalized, and discretionary nature of dispute resolution.

Dispute Settlement: The Privileging of the Private

The commitment to the privatization of international commercial transactions is most pronounced in the preeminence of private methods of dispute resolution. Today the settlement of commercial disputes through private arbitration is the norm. Indeed, there has been such a tremendous expansion in both institutional and normative structures facilitating arbitration that most trade experts would agree that private arbitration has eclipsed national adjudication as the preferred method for resolving international commercial disputes.[67] This is resulting in considerable pluralism in dispute settlement mechanisms, as well:[68]

> For many years it was fashionable to say that international commercial arbitration had come of age. That is no longer an appropriate observation. By now it has entered a mature and sophisticated middle age. Both the crises and illusions of youth are past, and in the eyes of businessmen (although not necessarily their lawyers) the creature has developed an identity and ability to solve problems that match the needs of the critical role it plays in world commerce today.
>
> (Graving, 1989: 319–20)

The trend towards increased recourse to private arbitration is being encouraged by states which are participating as part of the mercatocracy in creating uniform and mandatory rules that provide for the recognition and enforcement of foreign arbitral awards. States are adopting

[67] See Berman and Kaufman (1978); Carbonneau (1984 and 1990); Aksen (1984 and 1990); Dezalay and Garth (1996).

[68] According to Aksen (1990: 287) "in today's world dispute resolution will invariably be arbitration." Dezalay and Garth (1996: 6) note that over the past twenty-five years or so international commercial arbitration has become the accepted method for resolving international commercial disputes and they note the dramatic increase in the caseload of arbitration institutions, such as the ICC facilities. According to a 1992 report they cite (ibid., 6, n. 2), some 120 arbitration institutions are identified in the world. For a list of arbitration services, see Asser Institute (1988).

legislation that curtails the power of national courts and policy makers to intervene in private arbitrations and that limits the ability of judicial authorities to set aside arbitration awards. This is expanding and privileging private methods of dispute resolution. Curiously, national government officials are participating in the expansion of the private sphere and the neutralization and insulation of international commercial concerns from public policy review. However, this insulation is incomplete, for state authority over the enforcement of private settlements has been strengthened as states undertake the binding commitment to enforce foreign arbitral awards. State authority has thus been curtailed in the settlement of substantive commercial legal issues and disputes, but expanded in the enforcement of the final awards. Indeed, state intervention to legitimize and to expand the practice of private arbitration has been instrumental in bringing about the growth of private dispute settlement. This intervention is, in turn, consistent with neoliberal discipline and the new constitutionalism that are recreating states as market participants. The move to the competition state and policies aimed at securing a competitive advantage in international commercial relations is evident in state support for the creation of a multilateral framework creating a mandatory regime for the recognition and enforcement of foreign arbitral awards. It is also evident in state adoption of national legislation that creates the necessary institutional structures and procedural rules for the conduct of international arbitrations. The underlying rationale is clearly the perception that arbitration is more efficient, more neutral, and more reliable than adjudication in national courts. Indeed, the arbitration community is like a private "club" that prides itself on its efficiency and its unique ability to deal with the exigencies of international commercial competition (Dezalay and Garth, 1996) and to relieve the burdens of increasingly overloaded national judicial systems. Central to the success of this "club" is the operation of large law firms and lawyers trained in the "virtue" of arbitration.[69] They are the "organic intellectuals" who work to disseminate the arbitration ethos locally, through national government and business circles, and globally, through the operations of multinational law firms, international business associations, such as the ICC, and globalized arbitration practices. Even developing states, although initially wary of liberalizing their dispute resolution processes through the adoption of denationalized

[69] See Dezalay and Garth (1996) for the role of lawyers and huge law firms in internationalizing the rule of law through the practice of arbitration.

arbitration law and services, are joining the club, albeit as junior and not quite equal members.[70]

The reassertion of arbitration as the preferred method for settling commercial disputes reflects the growing importance that is being given to the privatization of commercial relations, reinscribing in the very fabric of national and global laws liberal mythology concerning the natural or organic, neutral or apolitical, consensual, efficient, and, hence, superior nature of private regulation. Private arbitration is regarded as the most natural means for resolving international commercial disputes for it gives maximum scope to the autonomous "legal subject" through the principles of freedom of contract and the autonomy of the contracting parties. "Arbitration is almost exclusively a creature of contract. The parties determine the content of the contractual agreement, and any requirement to arbitrate is dependent upon and subject to the will of the parties in almost all respects" (Buchanan, 1988: 512). The parties to the arbitration agreement are free to choose the law to be applied and the procedures to be adopted in the settlement of disputes and to designate the arbitrator.[71] It is generally believed that the informality in the procedures adopted by arbitrations and the ability to select arbitrators with technical expertise contribute to more expeditious and less expensive dispute settlement. This is said to produce significant efficiencies over adjudication in national courts of law.[72] Moreover, as agreements to arbitrate are based on the consent of the parties, it is believed that they are more likely to be respected than judgments imposed by national courts (Smit, 1986). Merchants who have agreed to binding arbitration are unlikely to refuse to accept the arbitral award.

The neoliberal commitment to the privatization of dispute settlement procedures is being embraced by developed and developing states alike and by formerly planned economies that are participating in the

[70] For a positive evaluation of the impact of ICC arbitration on developing countries, see Naón (1993). For a less sanguine view, see Dezalay and Garth (1996: chs. 11, 12, and 13) where it is argued that the reception of international commercial arbitration law and practices reproduces core–periphery relations in developing countries. De Enterría (1990: 391, n. 5) notes the reluctance of many Latin American states to open up commercial dispute resolution processes to international standards. And see Sempasa (1992) for the concerns that African states have with international commercial arbitration.

[71] In a survey conducted by the American Arbitration Association respondents indicated that the identity of the arbitrator was the most important factor in arbitration. The integrity, impartiality, linguistic ability, and technical knowledge of the arbitrator were regarded as critical considerations in the choice of arbitrators. See Coulson (1982).

[72] For discussion of the greater efficiency of arbitration in dispute settlement see Bagner (1982); Smit (1986); Graving (1989).

globalization of arbitration law and practices.[73] This is facilitated by the operation of multinational law firms operating globally in the transmission of the arbitration ethos throughout the world. Moreover, the compelling practical incentives for private arbitration become even more so when they are combined with the development of an institutional and procedural context for facilitating arbitration proceedings and enforcing their awards. This institutional context is generally regarded to be a result of efforts undertaken to unify arbitration law so as to address the uncertainty, inefficiency, and parochialism produced by national adjudication in the second phase in the development of the law merchant. It was noted earlier in this chapter that there was a proliferation of private associations engaged in international arbitration in the early part of the twentieth century. While there are "literally hundreds of institutions" engaged in commercial arbitration throughout the world, the ICC Court of Arbitration, created in 1923, is today the most successful of the arbitration associations (Graving, 1989: 328).[74] In terms of the volume of cases it hears and its use by states with different legal traditions, of various levels of development, and with both market and nonmarket economies it is considered the "premier institution" for international arbitration in the world. Developed and developing states and market and nonmarket economies have regular recourse to ICC arbitration.[75] The ICC Court of Arbitration developed from a predominantly Western institution in the 1920s to one of worldwide scope.[76]

The American Arbitration Association, formed in 1926, is the second most heavily utilized institution for international arbitration and it utilizes a number of different rules governing different types of commercial transaction (Graving, 1989: 336–42). The London Court of Arbitration, originally the London Chamber of Arbitration, was founded in the late nineteenth century and operates under its own set of rules. Though it was once a popular venue for arbitration, it declined in popularity in the late 1970s as a result of the imposition by the courts of procedural obstacles to arbitration. Legislative reforms have since increased its popularity and today it hears about one-half of the cases heard by the American Arbitration Association and about one-tenth of those heard

[73] See Naón (1993); Craig (1995); Yakovlev (1996); Liu and Lourie (1995).
[74] For a comprehensive list of arbitration institutions, see Asser Institute (1988); and McClendon (1993).
[75] See Derains (1981); Bannicke (1985); and Naón (1993).
[76] In 1987 one-third of ICC arbitrations involved developing states, while one-sixth were state-controlled entities (Graving 1989: 331).

by the ICC Court of Arbitration (ibid., 344). The efforts of these and other arbitration institutions[77] did not, however, displace adjudication by national courts. Nor did they offset the trend toward the increasing fragmentation and diversity of national commercial arbitration laws, which generated efforts to unify arbitration law.

Intergovernmental efforts to unify arbitration law began under the League of Nations, producing two largely unsuccessful conventions.[78] These conventions did not attract much support outside Europe for it was felt that they were too limited in aim and objective (see David, 1972 a: 130–3). The ICC produced a draft convention on arbitration in 1954, but work was subsequently taken over by the Economic and Social Council of the United Nations, which produced the United Nations Convention on the Recognition and Enforcement of Foreign Arbitral Awards (New York Convention). The New York Convention imposes on states party to the convention the mandatory obligation of enforcing arbitral awards and recognizing and enforcing foreign awards. It is in force in some 119 states, including the major trading states.[79] The New York Convention assists in the settlement of international commercial disputes by placing mandatory enforcement obligations on states. In theory, states retain some control over the arbitration process in that they can affect procedures and substantive law through the imposition of public policy considerations. However, in practice, the courts are interpreting such limitations very liberally in deference to the principles of international comity.[80] As Mark Buchanan (1988: 513) notes, while "public policy provides states with a tool for external constraint upon the relative freedom of the members of the international business

[77] Other notable arbitration institutions include the Stockholm Chamber of Commerce, which provides the venue for the settlement of East–West commercial disputes. Switzerland, as well, provided the locale for many arbitrations. Other institutions that engage in international commercial arbitration include the International Centre for the Settlement of Investment Disputes, the Indian Council of Arbitrators, the Japanese Commercial Arbitration Association, the CMEA (Council for Mutual Economic Assistance), the EU, the China International Economic and Trade Arbitration Commission, and the Inter-American Commercial Arbitration Commission. See Sauders (1979) for a more extensive list of arbitration institutions. It should also be noted that arbitrations are conducted under the dispute settlement procedures of the North American Free Trade Agreement (NAFTA), the Free Trade Agreement (Can–US) (FTA), and the World Intellectual Property Organization (WIPO).

[78] The Protocol on Arbitration Clauses (1923), while the Convention on the Execution of Foreign Arbitral Awards (1927) provided conditions governing the enforcement of awards.

[79] Adherents include the United States, Japan, Great Britain, Germany, Canada, the Russian Federation, France, Monaco, India, Israel, and Egypt.

[80] See the discussion of comity in this chapter, n. 9.

community," "it can also provide the mechanism for freeing international commercial transactions from the stringent requirements of the domestic law of the forum state or foreign states."[81] Others, too, note that the public policy exception to the enforcement of awards is significant only in theory and not in practice.[82]

Indeed, there has been a general decline in judicial hostility to arbitration, initiated by developments in domestic dispute settlement practices. In the United States a shift in the court's attitude towards arbitration occurred after the enactment of domestic arbitration law in the 1920s. This marked a change in public policy concerning arbitration. The courts came to differentiate between domestic and international arbitrations, applying considerably more restraint in intervening into the latter (Buchanan, 1988). In the United Kingdom judicial attitudes also shifted in response to domestic legislation that imposed limits to judicial intervention in arbitral proceedings; however, there is still resistance to the complete acceptance of arbitration.[83] Similar developments occurred in France, although the policy shift was initiated by the courts and not the legislature (Carbonneau, 1984: 53–7). Carbonneau elsewhere observes that subsequent legislative enactments have rendered France one of the most hospitable forums for enforcing arbitration awards (Buchanan, 1988: 528).

> Developments in the legal systems of England, the United States, and France evidence a clear "rehabilitation" of arbitration as a parallel process of resolving domestic disputes. The redefinition of the judicial role in arbitration was central to the reevaluation in each country. Rather than a competitive relationship, the various domestic arbitration laws mandated collaboration between the judicial arbitral processes, with the public process lending its assistance of its coercive jurisdictional authority where necessary. In England, this phenomenon principally involved a lessening of judicial review powers . . . In the United States

81 Buchanan (1988) notes that public policy considerations may include matters of morality, conscionability, economic policy, and professional conduct. He reviews the domestic treatment of international arbitration in a number of countries and finds a liberal approach to the recognition and enforcement of international arbitral awards in the United States, Argentina, and France. This is less so for Egypt, where traditional values and legal rules provide obstacles to arbitration. Brazil, not a party to the New York Convention, has not been a hospitable forum for enforcing awards. He was unable to assess the situation in the former Soviet Union, which, though a party to the convention, had entertained no judicial proceedings to enforce foreign awards. For a contrary view on the situation in Egypt, see Enein (1986).

82 So concludes De Enterría (1990) in a survey of US and Spanish practices.

83 See Carbonneau (1984: 40–5) for a review of the English position.

> and France, the legislation expressly established a cooperative interrelationship between the courts and the arbitral tribunals.
>
> (Carbonneau, 1984: 57–8)

A number of other countries are showing a greater willingness to recognize and enforce foreign arbitral awards. The New York Convention was brought into force in the People's Republic of China in 1987, in Algeria in 1989, and in Canada in 1986.[84] Many other states modernized their arbitration laws in the 1980s, creating legal environments that are more hospitable to arbitration.[85]

The shifts in domestic policies concerning arbitration clearly were a response to the tremendous growth in commercial transactions and the unprecedented expansion in commercial litigation (see generally, Carbonneau, 1984; 1990). Domestic courts were simply unable to respond adequately to the increased volume of commercial cases and to the increasing complexity of commercial transactions. In addition, most states recognized the economic benefits that would flow from improved enforcement. For many states modernization was also prompted by unification initiatives undertaken by UNCITRAL. The unification of arbitration law was made part of UNCITRAL's program of work when the Commission was initially created. The Commission adopted the UNCITRAL Arbitration Rules in 1976 after "extensive consultation with arbitral institutions and centres of international arbitration."[86] These rules have achieved "world-wide recognition and application, primarily due to the text's reliance upon the principle of party autonomy and purposeful consideration and incorporation of international consensus and opinion" (Weiss, 1986: 372). The rules may be invoked in arbitrations held by the ICC Court of Arbitration, the London Court of Arbitration, and the American Arbitration Association. UNCITRAL also produced uniform rules on conciliation after consultation with the ICC and the International Council for Commercial Arbitration (ICCA), which is a private association of arbitration experts from some thirty countries (Dore, 1983: 340).[87] Like the arbitration rules, the conciliation rules are voluntary in application. However, the conciliation rules

84 See Lecuyer-Thieffry and Thieffry (1990: 578–9). And see Graving (1989: 373–6).
85 Including, Italy, Belgium, the Netherlands, Switzerland, Australia, Nigeria, Cyprus, Dijibouti, and Spain. See Lecuyer-Thieffry (1990: 579).
86 *Report of the United Nations Commission on International Trade Law on the Work of its Ninth Session*, UN Doc. A/Conf. 31/17.
87 And see Freedberg (1995).

do not involve adversarial proceedings and do not produce binding awards.[88]

UNCITRAL's most ambitious undertaking in the area of arbitration, however, is the Model Law on International Commercial Arbitration, adopted in 1985.[89] The model law embodies the principle of merchant autonomy in the freedom it accords parties to "tailor the 'rules of the game' to their specific needs" (Hoellering, 1986: 327). For example, the parties are free to specify arbitrable subject-matter and to choose institutionalized arbitration and rules, the procedures governing the conduct of arbitrations, and the applicable law. Party autonomy is also reflected in the strict limits placed on judicial intervention into the arbitration process. The "approach of the model law, which allows limited prompt recourse to the court during arbitral proceedings, but simultaneously permits the arbitration to go forward, represents a balance between the potential for delay through dilatory tactics of a recalcitrant party, and the futility and high costs of arbitral proceedings in which the award is ultimately set aside by the court" (ibid., 331). In tandem with the New York Convention, the model law provides a comprehensive regime for the settlement and enforcement of international commercial disputes.[90]

This regime expands the private sphere considerably, delocalizing transactions by narrowing the potential for judicial and public policy interventions. This is effecting a profound transformation of relations between public and private regulatory authority. In the United States, for example, disputes governed by mandatory legislation, such as disputes over antitrust and competition laws and policies, consumer and environmental protection laws, and intellectual property and securities laws and regulations, are being held to be arbitrable subject-matter, thus removing their resolution from the judicial realm and placing it in the privatized and delocalized realm of international commercial

88 UNCITRAL Conciliation Rules, UN Doc. A/Conf. 35/' 17, reprinted in *International Legal Materials* (*ILM*) 20 (1981), pp. 300–6.

89 UN Doc. A/ Conf. A/40/17. For the background to the drafting of the arbitration rules and the model law see Broches (1987).

90 Many states have adopted or are considering the adoption of the UNCITRAL Arbitration Rules and the Model Law. Canadian jurisdictions have enacted legislation bringing the rules and model law into effect, while some states in the United States have enacted the Model Law. Bulgaria, Cyprus, Egypt, Hong Kong, Hungary, Germany, India, Singapore, Great Britain, Kenya, Mexico, and New Zealand have brought the Model Law into effect, while the Netherlands has enacted legislation based upon the Model Law. See Cutler (1992); Potter (1989). UNCITRAL produces case law involving the Model Law called Case Law on UNCITRAL Legal Texts (CLOUT).

arbitration. This expansion of arbitrable subject-matter, when combined with the secretive, closed, and highly discretionary and informal nature of international commercial arbitration, forms a powerful challenge to democratically accountable institutions. Unlike in judicial proceedings where judges are bound to produce judgments and reasons and have a duty to admit interested parties as interveners, private arbitrations are conducted in secret with no publication requirement or rights of public access. This privacy is fundamentally antithetical to the rule of law (Scheuerman, 1999 and 2000) and marks a substantial departure from the judicialized nature of dispute settlement in the second phase in the development of the law merchant. The ability of private parties to evade the application of mandatory national antitrust, taxation, securities, consumer protection, environmental, and intellectual property legislation or to have their rights and duties determined in private, when combined with the general problem of holding transnational corporations accountable under international law, are formidable accretions of corporate power and authority (see Tollefson, 2002). Moreover, "the very purpose of most mandatory economic regulation legislation is to constrain private commercial activity in ways believed to be essential to the greater public good" (McConnaughay, 1999: 495). The private arbitration of such mandatory regulations infuses the private sphere with public functions, raising crucial problems of the distinction between judicial and arbitral functions and important concerns about democratic accountability. While judges operate as part of the public sphere and are duty-bound to protect unrepresented public interests, private arbitrators are not: their duties go to resolving the differences of the parties before them. As one international arbitration lawyer notes:

> [t]he object of a modern, progressive arbitral regime is to minimize judicial interference with the arbitral process. But a municipal system is the means by which any given polity implements its rules in the context of private disputes. If those disputes are taken out of the judicial system and the courts are commanded not to interfere with the process or results unless there are fundamental departures from fair process, how may the polity ensure adherence to applicable private and public law? Furthermore, how can the municipal polity monitor the formation and execution of legal rules affecting its economic, social, and political interests? A private forum whose rulings will be enforced by municipal courts without substantive review may result in some loss of control over the implementation of private and public rules of law.
>
> (Donovan, 1995: 649)

He notes that many Latin American states reluctantly adopted modern arbitration laws and practices in the 1980s and 1990s as a component of economic liberalization and argues that developments in legal practice threaten to compromise their regulatory abilities in the areas of competition and securities laws.[91] Paradoxically, these are states who once resisted international commercial arbitration as "one element of a broader program of European and American economic imperialism."[92] African states have also reluctantly adopted modern arbitration law but have taken exception to the formulation of arbitration law through model law as opposed to through the negotiation of an international convention. They argue that the treaty-making process provides for transparency and participation in lawmaking, leveling the playing field somewhat for less powerful African states (Sempasa, 1992).

Concerns over the limited representation of weaker trading partners in the creation of international commercial law also extend into the institutional practices of international commercial arbitration. Commercial participants from developing states characterize international commercial arbitration as a private club that limits entry to participants from the developed world, raising concerns about legal imperialism and neocolonialism (Silbey, 1997; Sempasa, 1992; Abbott; 1976). Moreover, privatized dispute settlement is a highly informalized, discretionary, and personalized system that relies primarily upon the judgment of private arbitrators. The emphasis on procedural informality and the ability of arbitrators to remain flexible and responsive to changing economic conditions and mercantile practices widens the possibilities for discretionary decision making by replacing rules and procedures with personalized judgment. To the extent that the commercial customs and practices invoked represent those of the dominant Western trading states, the problems of legal imperialism are intensified. For example, transnational corporations had an overwhelming influence on the creation of international commercial arbitration law and institutions, while "[e]ssentially, the Western industrialized world's view of the arbitral process is embodied in the rules of practice of arbitral institutions, nongovernmental organizations such as the ICC, national nongovernmental arbitral

[91] Canadians became acutely aware of the abilities of foreign corporations to undermine domestic legislative and policy measures to protect the environment when the Canadian Government was ordered to pay $19.5 million to settle a claim brought by Ethyl Corp. in 1998 and arbitrated privately under chapter 11 of NAFTA. See Tollefson (2002) for the impact of NAFTA disciplines on domestic public policy processes.

[92] Donovan (1995: 650); Abbott (1976).

agencies like the AAA [American Arbitration Association] and the various national and transnational trade systems."[93] Indeed, Santos (1995: 292–3) argues that the modern law merchant does not represent a globalization of legal culture, at all, but rather a *globalization of localized* US commercial culture and practices through the dominance of US-based multinational corporate practices and law.[94]

The integration of peripheral and semiperipheral states into the arbitration world is recasting them as competition states as well. They too exhibit the curious mix of private and public authority: private authority settles substantive disputes, but public authorities undertake to enforce their settlements. In some cases this produces rather anomalous results, as in the case of China where the law merchant is mixing with two very localizing influences: Chinese capitalism and Chinese modernization. Both give priority to state policy, tradition, culture, and *quanxi* relationships over legality. *Quanxi* is a highly personalized system of familial, clan, and friendship networks regulating social and economic relations and mediates the interface of foreign and domestic practices. As Santos (1995: 294) notes, "[t]o the extent that partners in international transactions resort to *quanxi* to obtain or intensify business predictability and security, we may say the *lex mercatoria* is being quanxified. In other words, in China *lex mercatoria* and the old Confucian dimensions of Chinese legal culture interpenetrate."

The reinscription of free-market principles as the norms for dispute settlement and enforcement is an integral component of global disciplinary neoliberal restructuring. Indeed, the increasing reliance on soft, discretionary standards and privatized international commercial arbitration is strengthening private institutions and processes, whilst weakening mechanisms that work toward participation and democratic accountability. These transformations in law-creation and dispute settlement are in turn linked to transformations in both global and local political economies associated with the advent of the "competition state," the transnationalization of capital, and processes of flexible accumulation. These transformations are crucial to the juridification of commerce and the expansion of privatized commercial law for they provide the ideological and material foundations for the unification movement and for the increasing plurality of law-creating sources and subjects and of

93 Professor Wilner, quoted in Sempasa (1992: 392, n. 17).

94 See also Sempasa (1992: 407–9) for the rejection by the African countries of the modern law merchant as a neutral and universal legal order.

dispute settlement processes. The privatization of law-creation and dispute settlement, in turn, rests upon a set of assumptions concerning the apolitical nature of private international trade law. It also reflects the operation of liberal mythology concerning the natural, neutral, consensual, efficient, and just nature of private regulation. This embodies a particular understanding of the conditions of political authority in the global political economy, to which attention will now turn.

Unification and global authority

On the one hand, the increasing reliance on soft, discretionary, informal, and highly personalized systems of justice in international commerce characterizes juridified, pluralized, and privatized international commercial relations. On the other, juridified commercial relations also take the form of hard law, such as the FTA, NAFTA, and GATT/WTO disciplines, that bite deeply into domestic social, political, and legal orders. This illustrates the dialectical nature of juridification, pluralization, and privatization. These processes are fueled by the mythological notion that private international trade is an apolitical domain and they embody an understanding of political authority premised upon distinctions between public and private authority, politics and economics, and domestic and international law. While the privileging of private regulation under the new law merchant is politicizing private law by infusing it with public purposes, its proponents still cling to the public/private law distinction as a natural and inevitable state of affairs.[95] However, this book has argued that the distinction is not reflective of either an organic or an inevitable separation, but is an analytical construct that evolved with the emergence of the bourgeois state as an essential component of its material, ideological, and institutional foundations. Indeed, as noted earlier, the separations of public and private domains and of political and economic activities are central to the constitution of capitalist productive relations and are "structural requirement[s] for the reproduction of capitalist societies" (Hirsch, 1995: 271; Wood, 1995). These separations are premised upon liberal mythology about the natural, neutral, consensual, and efficient nature of private regulatory arrangements (Cutler, 1995). It will be recalled that the first myth is that the private ordering of economic relations is consistent with natural and normal economic processes and draws on the liberal belief and faith in the natural and organic character of market behavior. The second

95 See Chapters 2 and 3 and Cutler (2000 b).

myth posits the neutral and apolitical nature of private activity. Under liberalism, private relations are associated with the domain of neutral economic activities, while the public activities are associated with the domain of politics. Liberal-inspired contract law embodies and reproduces the public/private separation by associating the private sphere with neutral and objective processes of resource allocation. Contract law is endowed with objective foundations and "has the appearance of being self-contained, apolitical, and inexorable" (Horwitz, 1975: 252) as it regulates transactions among participants – autonomous "legal subjects" – who are deemed to be of equal bargaining power. The law of the self-regulating contract facilitates exchange and ensures procedural fairness, but does not question the substantive fairness of a transaction, for that would impair its self-regulating characteristics. Moreover, inquiry into the substantive fairness of a contract is precisely what the distinction ensures will not take place, because it "arose to establish the objective nature of the market and to neutralize and hence diffuse the political and redistributional potential of the law" (ibid.: 254). The third liberal myth concerns the consensual and noncoercive nature of private exchange and flows directly from the view that markets are natural in origin, neutral in result, and, hence, consensual in operation. The fourth myth posits the inherent efficiency of private regulatory arrangements. Private regulation is regarded as producing greater efficiencies by reducing transaction costs and achieving greater economies. Liberal myths thus present the private regulation and ordering of international commerce as producing the best-of-all-possible-worlds.

These myths are today being revived by public and private authorities who together form a global mercatocracy united by its commitment to the superiority of privatization through merchant law and practice. Merchant autonomy in establishing the terms of self-regulating contracts and private dispute settlement through arbitration directly links global competitiveness with the enhanced power of the private sphere. Disciplinary neoliberalism assists in the growth of private power and authority through commitments to deregulation and privatization. The growing efficacy of private ordering is regarded by trade experts as the most appropriate and successful way to compete globally. Interestingly, state authority remains essential for the enforcement of commercial agreements. However, this is achieved in a hands-off way by enforcing the awards and judgments of private arbitral authorities. State authority remains central, but its role has changed, confirming the view that globalization "does not involve some sort of linear process of the withering away of the state as a bureaucratic power structure; indeed, paradoxically, in a globalizing world states play a crucial role as stabilizers and enforcers of the rules and practices of 'global' society" (Cerny, 1997: 257–8).

The unification movement is an integral element of the reconfiguration of public and private authorities that is resulting from these developments. Critics have condemned legal unification efforts for privileging First World, private, corporate interests (Scheuerman, 1999; Sempasa, 1992; Eörsi, 1977; Patterson, 1986; Santos, 1995; McConnaughay, 1999). These criticisms echo those made about the growing power of private lawmaking groups evident in the unification of domestic commercial law in the United States (Patchel, 1993; Schwartz and Scott, 1995; Kronstein, 1963). The underrepresentation of the interests of domestic consumer groups and the lack of concern for smaller businesses raise many of the same distributional and market-access concerns identified by critics of international unification who document the underrepresentation of the interests of less-developed states (Patterson, 1986). The global unification movement privileges the private sphere, delocalizing and privatizing law and justice. In so doing, it facilitates the further denationalization of capital and the disembedding of commercial activities from governmental and social controls.

Unification thus operates as a corporate strategy designed to assist the reconfiguration of authority in the global political economy in line with the disciplinary neoliberal agenda. This agenda functions to secure the interests of transnational corporations and associated governmental interests, whilst eroding protections for locally based domestic corporations and states on the periphery of the global economy. The unification movement is an integral and an important aspect of globalization. Its significance confirms that globalization "is not a single process, but a complex mixture of processes, which often act in contradictory ways, producing conflicts, disjunctures and new forms of stratification" (Giddens, 1994 b: 22). But the rhetoric of unification represents these processes as progressive in terms of efficiency concerns and value-neutral in terms of normative or distributional concerns. Crucially, unification is described as "a significant step forward in the globalization of legal thinking."[96] A generous and benign interpretation of this description requires that one assume the existence of the underlying unity, stability, and neutrality

[96] This was said by Joseph Perillo (1994: 282) with specific reference to UNIDROIT's Principles.

of legal thought and practice. A more critical understanding recognizes that "law is nothing but a repetition of the relationship it posits between law and society. Rather than a stable domain which *relates* in some complicated way *to* society or political economy or class structure, law is simply the practice and argument about the relationship between something posited as law and something posited as society" (David Kennedy, 1988: 8). Legal unification, thus, repeats key movements in the global political economy and, in so doing, lends a sense of legitimacy to these processes as natural, progressive, and ultimately good.

The tendencies to legal formalism and to treating the law merchant as an autonomous and neutral legal order that simply exists out "there," disciplining international commercial relations, obscure the fundamentally political nature of legal discipline and its imbrication in the very fabric of productive relations. Legal formalism also obscures the ambiguity of both subject and sources doctrines. Doctrinally, both identify subjects and sources that cease to adequately define the fields of legal and political practice. Transnational corporations and other private business associations in fact function as legal subjects, while legal doctrine pronounces their "invisibility" as "subjects." Sources doctrine is similarly obfuscatory in its identification of legal sources that are in practice being eclipsed in significance by sources that are not recognized as instruments of law-creation. Privatized dispute settlement, in turn, infuses private activity with public purposes, eroding the foundations for accountability under the rule of law but, by virtue of self-disciplining distinctions between public and private activities and politics and economics, is neutralized or sanitized of public content and function. These tendencies reflect a profound disjunction and asymmetry between legal theory and state practice. While international legal doctrines identify and empower the state as the legal "subject" and state-based law as the legitimate source of law, practices in law-creation and dispute settlement are challenging this state-based order. New sources of nonstate law are emerging, while nonstate actors, such as transnational corporations, function as *de facto* subjects. Clearly, subject and sources doctrines are incoherent insofar as they bear only remote relevance to actual practices.

More significant than incoherence, however, is the legitimacy crisis facing international law. The disjunction between theory and practice is in actuality a reflection of a deeper disjunction between law and society that goes to the very heart of the constitution of political identity, subjectivity, and legitimacy in the global political economy. International law is facing a profound legitimacy crisis, because its theory is so out of keeping with its practices. As is argued in the next chapter, all constitutional orders require some measure of correspondence between their theories and their practices and a profound disjunction of the two portends a crisis of legitimacy.

However, the hegemony of the mercatocracy is incomplete. The dialectical nature of processes of juridification, pluralization, and privatization, which is evident in tensions between globalizing and localizing tendencies, hard and soft regulation, and state and nonstate authority, suggest that there is room for contestation of the law merchant order. Indeed, social forces that are contesting the state-based order provide hope that the legitimacy crisis might be resolved in favor of a union of participatory and emancipatory legal practices and theories. Santos's (1995) insight that in China local cultural and religious practices are localizing or "quanxifying" the reception of the law merchant reveals cracks or holes in the hegemony of the law merchant and the mercatocracy. Competing claims to subjectivity coming from nonstate subjects and sources of law, moreover, suggest that there is room for progressive and emancipatory versions of the law. Claims to legal status from "invisibles," such as women, individuals, aboriginal, and indigenous people, reflect tension at the borders of legal subjectivity. Such claims raise the "problem of the subject" and hold promise for a new theory of international law. This new theory seeks to unify theory and practice through emancipatory praxis so as to better address the analytical, theoretical, and normative problems attending private power and global authority.

7 Conclusion
Transnational merchant law and global authority: a crisis of legitimacy

This chapter argues that fundamental reconfigurations of global power and authority are creating a legitimacy crisis in the global political economy. It makes the case for a new theory of international law that is both capable of addressing the analytical, theoretical, and ideological dimensions of this crisis and working towards its resolution. The chapter begins by positing the existence of a global constitutional order centered on Westphalian conceptions of authority and rule and argues that all such orders require some degree of fit between their principles and practices. A legitimacy crisis exists when there is a disjunction or asymmetry between theory and practice that becomes so great that it strains the foundations of the order. Processes of juridification, pluralization, and privatization are transforming structures of authority, "which implicitly challenges the old Westphalian assumption that a state is a state is a state" (Cox, 1993 a: 263) and related understandings about the "public" nature of authority that we have discussed. Traditional Westphalian-inspired assumptions about power and authority are argued to be incapable of providing contemporary understanding or locating the authority and historical effectivity of transnational merchant law. This is producing a growing disjunction between the theory and the practices of the Westphalian system. This disjunction suggests that the fields of international law and organization, which are generally regarded as repositories of our theoretical and empirical understanding about global authority and rule, are experiencing a crisis. This is particularly so with regard to dominant understandings of the nature of the relationship or nexus between international law and international relations. In both law and politics, conventional approaches tend to peripheralize the role of law in the global political order, thus obscuring a critical understanding of the contribution that transnational merchant law makes to the constitution of political practices.[1] Moreover, both disciplines are dominated by unhistorical and state-centric theories that are incapable of dealing analytically, theoretically, and normatively with contemporary transformations in global power and authority. Dominant theories are incapable of theorizing contemporary developments that do not fit within the Westphalian paradigm of authority and rule. Indeed, a critical analysis of the Westphalian model of rule illustrates that it has never adequately captured international practice. However, the chapter argues that the lack of fit or asymmetry between theory and practice is becoming more acute, portending a crisis of legitimacy. The actors, structures, and processes identified and theorized as determinative by the dominant approaches to the study of international law and organization have ceased to be of singular importance. Westphalian-inspired notions of state-centricity, positivist international law, and "public" definitions of authority are incapable of capturing the significance of nonstate actors, informal normative structures, and private, economic power in the global political economy. Moreover, as previous chapters have argued, liberal mythology makes the content of the private sphere disappear by defining it out of existence as a political domain. In so doing, liberalism effectively insulates private activity from social and political controls. As a result, as part of the private sphere, neither transnational corporations nor individuals are regarded as authoritative legally or politically. This produces some rather bizarre results. When placed in the context of the expansion of corporate power resulting from the juridification, pluralization, and privatization of commercial relations, the legal invisibility of the transnational corporation enhances its influence, whilst the invisibility of the individual seriously inhibits individual challenges to corporate power.[2]

The chapter revisits the dominant theories of international relations and international law, noting that they are incapable of identifying and theorizing contemporary global authority and are thus unable to theorize their "subject" in any meaningful way. Private actors, such as transnational corporations and private business associations, are increasingly functioning authoritatively, but this is rendered invisible by an ideology that defines the private sphere in apolitical terms. Liberal mythology makes the political content of the private sphere disappear

[1] See Chapter 3 and see Cutler (2002 a).

[2] For a collection of papers that explores the dimensions of private, corporate power and authority in the global political economy see Cutler, Haufler, and Porter (1999 a).

by defining it out of existence and, in so doing, isolates and insulates private commercial activity. A knowledge structure that privileges expert knowledge through the juridification, pluralization, and privatization of international commercial relations and the operation of liberal-inspired commercial laws that reify the autonomous "legal subject" provide the ideological foundation for assumptions concerning the inherent superiority of private legal ordering in the regulation of international commerce. A mercatocracy of lawyers, merchants, corporations, and governments maintains this thought structure by limiting entry to lawyers trained to believe in the superiority of private law. It works through both consensual and coercive methods to silence voices of dissent. Corporate global hegemony operates ideologically by removing private international law from critical scrutiny and review, producing apparently consensual private arrangements. However, these arrangements, in fact, operate coercively in that they reinscribe asymmetrical power relations between buyers and sellers, employers and workers, insurers and insured, lenders and borrowers, shipowners and cargo in their contractual arrangements and in the very fabric of the law. The apparent consensual nature of these "private" relationships contributes to their characterization as neutral and apolitical, inhibiting the development of a critical understanding of private international law. Unlike public international law where critical theory is considerably well developed, private international law remains isolated and is rendered relatively immune to criticism by an ideology that appears to permit little challenge. However, it is questionable whether the mercatocracy will be able to sustain the internal support and seeming consent necessary to maintain the ideological hold of liberal mythology. Global authority is increasingly resting upon fragile foundations as competing social forces contest their peripheralization and marginalization in the global political economy. The inability of the mercatocracy to bind these segments by delivering on the rhetoric of globalization and promises of efficiencies, economic development, and justice suggests the emergence of an historic bloc based upon fraud. To Gramsci, supremacy based on fraud signals a "crisis of authority" and is bound eventually to fail (Augelli and Murphy, 1993: 132).

The chapter first articulates the "problem of the subject" and the inability of Westphalian assumptions of power and authority to capture the activities of corporations and of individuals as subjects or sources of the law. It then examines the dialectical operation of international legal doctrines governing subjects and sources as a prelude to developing a new constitutive theory of international law. This theory imagines international law as the union of theory and practice through emancipatory human praxis.

The "Problem of the Subject"

While much divides theorists of domestic and international politics, many are united in the treatment of their subject-matter as a constitutional order.[3] As theorists of international society have shown, the domain of international relations is characterized by principles and rules that provide a normative framework for action.[4] This framework is in turn traced in origin to the Peace of Westphalia which brought an end to the Thirty Years' War and is generally regarded as providing the constitutional foundations for the emerging state system. Indeed, it is almost an article of faith amongst international lawyers that the origins of their discipline can be traced to the Peace of Westphalia as a founding, original moment.[5] David Kennedy (1988) comments on this story of origins:

> International legal scholars are particularly insistent that their discipline began in 1648 with the Treaty of Westphalia closing the Thirty Years' War. The originality of 1648 is important to the discipline, for it situates public international law as a rational philosophy, handmaiden of statehood, the cultural heir to religious principle. As part of the effort to sustain this image, public international law historians have consistently treated earlier work as immature and incomplete – significant only as a precursor for what followed. Before 1648 were facts, politics, religion, in some tellings a "chaotic void" slowly filled by sovereign states. Thereafter, after the establishment of peace, after the "rise of states," after the collapse of "religious universalism," after the chaos of war, came law – as philosophy, as idea, as word. (14)

As Kennedy notes, law came as philosophy into a void. There it established state sovereignty as the fundamental ordering principle of the state system, placing the state at the center as the unambiguous

3 For limitations to the use of the domestic analogy, see Suganami (1989). This next section is adapted from Cutler (2001 a).

4 For the view that international society is a constitutional order characterized by norms and rules see Chapter 3, Cutler (1991), and the references cited therein relating to the English School and the works of Martin Wight, Hedley Bull, and Sir Hirsch Lauterpacht. And see Jackson (2000) and Kratochwil (1989).

5 For a classic statement of this position see Gross (1948) and for more contemporary texts that date the history of modern international law to the Peace of Westphalia, see Falk (1985) and Malanczuk (1997).

locus of authority.[6] As a story of origins, it marks the birth of modern international law, anticipating the moves from natural to positive law conceptions more in keeping with notions of sovereign consent. According to Kennedy (1988: 22) the "traditional intellectual story of international law's evolution from 1648 to 1918 is familiar. Begun as a series of disassociated doctrines about navigation, war, and relations with aboriginals within a 'natural law' philosophy, international law slowly matured as a comprehensive doctrinal fabric rendered coherent by a set of 'general principles' and authoritative by its 'positivist' link to sovereign consent. The shift from fragmentation to coherence is accompanied, then, by a shift from 'natural law' to a combination of 'principles' and 'positivism.' " As previous chapters have argued, the entire edifice of modern international law came to be crafted on the foundation of the state and positive acts of sovereign consent, evidenced explicitly in treaty law and implicitly in customary international law. The doctrine of international legal personality identified states as the legal "subjects" of the constitutional order, while treaty and customary law came to be regarded as the primary legal sources of the order. Indeed, for most of the history of modern international law, states have been considered to be the sole legitimate subjects of the law. While there has been a slow recognition of the legal personality of other corporate bodies, such as international organizations, the general orientation of the law has been state-centered. However, there are problems with this story of origins. To begin, historically, other nonstate entities such as the Holy See, chartered companies, and belligerents have been treated as having some legal capacities (see M. N. Shaw, 1991: 137). As Stephen Krasner (1993) notes, Westphalia did not provide an unambiguous determination of the state as the sole or exclusive locus of authority.

> The view that the Westphalian system implies that sovereignty has a taken-for-granted quality is wrong. The actual content of sovereignty, the scope of authority that states can exercise, has always been contested. The basic organizing principle of sovereignty – exclusive control over territory – has been persistently challenged by the creation of new institutional forms that better meet specific material needs. (235)

Today, challenges to the state authority emanate from supranational regional associations, such as the European Union, while the developing international human rights regime challenges the domestic authority of states and a globalizing modernity or postmodernity, of ubiquitous

[6] See Bull (1977), but see Krasner (1993).

influence economically and culturally, is challenging the authority of national governments (see Fried, 1997; Twining, 1996: Koskenniemi, 1991). Claims for recognition under international law are increasingly emanating from individuals, international organizations, business enterprises, human rights and environmental movements, ethnic minorities, and indigenous peoples. Individuals are acquiring significant attributes of international legal personality through the operation of international human rights agreements that provide individual claimants direct access to human rights tribunals and courts in order to challenge the conduct of states.[7] Moreover, through their practices and legal arrangements, states are endowing a number of nonstate entities such as international organizations and regional associations with elements of legal personality.[8]

In addition, private, nongovernmental organizations, such as Amnesty International, Greenpeace, and Médecins Sans Frontières, and international business corporations and their private associations, including the International Chamber of Commerce, International Air Transport Association, and international federations of trade unions and employers, are increasingly participating in the international legal system.[9] Finally, as we have seen, governments are endowing multi- and transnational corporations with many of the elements of international legal personality required in order to assert their rights against states. Bilateral investment treaties entered into by states under the auspices of the World Bank's International Centre for the Settlement of Investment Disputes, the Canada–US Free Trade Agreement, the North American Free Trade Agreement, and the failed Multilateral Agreement on Investment all provide corporations with the legal personality required to sue states directly under international law.[10] These developments point to significant reordering of authority relations, both locally and globally.

However, the problem goes much deeper than ambiguity over the exclusivity of state claims to authority and relates to status of the state as the "subject" of law and politics. This is referred to as the "problem of the subject." Pierre Schlag (1991) formulates the problem of the subject

[7] See Chapters 2 and 6 and see Higgins (1985); Janis (1984 a); and Keohane, Moravcsik, and Slaughter (2000).
[8] See Chapters 2 and 6 and see Malanczuk (1997: 92–6) and Brownlie (1990: 63 and 1998).
[9] See Malanczuk (1997: 96–7); Cutler, Haufler, and Porter (1999 a); and Higgott, Underhill, and Bieler (2000).
[10] See Chapter 6 and see Eden (1996); Cutler (2000 a; 2001 a).

in the context of the objectification and sublimation of the subject as a formalistic move to give law the appearance of neutrality and objectivity and, hence, to render law stable and legitimate. The problem runs something as follows. The problem of the subject involves the tendency to "avoid confronting the question of who or what thinks or produces law" (ibid.: 1629). Schlag (ibid., n. 6) notes that it can be stated in different ways: "Just who or what is it that thinks about or produces law?" or "What must be true or potentially true about the character of the agents that construct the law, in order for the law to be a legitimate or a viable enterprise?" or "What conception of subject–object relations is implicit in the rhetorical and social forces that are constructing us?" Schlag (ibid., 1640) argues that the tendencies to avoid these issues result in a fetishized understanding of law. Earlier chapters have already considered the nature of fetishized law and the reversal that occurs between the law and its creators. Fetishized law takes on an objective form that eclipses and obscures the significance of the "subject" in its creation. In Schlag's terms this involves a sublimation of the subject into the order of the object:

> [t]he sublimation of the subject into the order of the object and the resulting fetishism is a move that is replayed endlessly in American legal thought. This self-effacement of the subject to the order of the object is precisely what enables legal thinkers to keep believing in their objectified thought-structures as off the shelf, stand-alone, self-sufficient, self-sustaining systems, completely independent of the activity of the subjects. This sublimation of the subject is precisely the kind of process targeted by the reification critique of liberal legal thought offered by cls [critical legal studies].
> (Ibid)

In international law, the problem of the subject appears in the designation of states as "subjects" of the law, while individuals and corporations are regarded as "objects" of the law. As such, whatever rights or duties individuals and corporations have are derivative of and enforceable only by states who as subjects conferred these rights and duties on them. Conceptualizing the state as the subject thus performs a valuable function. Schlag (ibid., 1,726) notes that the subject is a "concierge" and as "the keeper of artifacts is a kind of bailee" whose role it is to conserve and avoid change. But the subject is more than conservative of the existing order, for the concierge also functions as a gatekeeper. In international law, the state functions to keep out antistatist tendencies and personalities. This is achieved through a process of differentiating between subject and object, associating the former with states and the latter with individuals and corporations and then objectifying this condition by allowing the subject to drop out of sight and enabling the law to stand alone as the embodiment of sovereign will, authority, and legitimacy. Under positive international law the law became the embodiment of the sovereign will; it was abstracted, objectified, and related to the state as thought relates to action or as legal theory relates to state practice. Most importantly, the state was both reified as a "subject" and deified through objectification of the law. For David Kennedy (1988) "[d]octrinally, the development of a territorial jurisdiction, so crucial to the image of a disembodied state, was first and foremost a religious notion – replacing and instantiating a disembodied deity as state" (25). He further notes that "[i]ronically, at the very moment of religion's disappearance, international law appears as a universalist ideology of its own – temporally freed from its origins and context" (ibid.). Moreover, law, like religion before, came to operate as a "mechanism of exclusion," excluding and suppressing "actual social difference" (ibid.: 25). Kennedy's observation that international law is not characterized by tolerance and liberality, but by intolerance and exclusionary practices has been noted in earlier chapters, but is worth emphasizing. Paradoxically, it highlights both the pretension of international law's claims to universality and inclusivity and the success that the law has in presenting itself in objective terms as a universal and embracing order. The law suppressed or sublimated the subjective identity of business corporations, which are regarded as analogous to individuals as "objects" of the legal order. Together with individuals, corporations were thus excluded as part of the reification and deification of the state. Moreover, the law came to operate dialectically with the state. The law both constituted the state as "subject" and mirrored the state through laws governing legal personality and legal sources. But, the law also stood outside the state and, through the process of objectification described above, policed, measured, and disciplined state action. Kennedy describes this as a dialectical or double movement:

> The move is paradoxical. We need to read it very slowly. On the one hand, international law is a matter of ideas, born in the move from state to law, instantiating law to facilitate the state. On the other, maturity is achieved at each stage through a double reversal of this order – first by a movement from thought to action, and second, exactly at the moment of law's movement from principle toward practice, law is set up *against* the state, separated from the sovereign it facilitates and mirrors. (Ibid.: 23)

Legal formalism then solidified this move by providing the analytical, theoretical, and ideological frameworks for the objectification of law and its unproblematized and *a priori* acceptance as simply out "there" (Shklar, 1964).

The implications of treating corporations and individuals as objects and not as subjects are deeply troubling empirically and normatively. Previous chapters have argued that, while transnational corporations and private business associations may be objects at law (*de jure*), they are, in fact, operating as subjects (*de facto*). Indeed, the problem of the subject is becoming increasingly more acute in the context of contemporary developments that are reconfiguring state–society relations, in some cases causing a contraction of state authority and an expansion of private, corporate authority in the world. Susan Strange (1996: 184) has posed the problem of the subject in the context of "Who or what is responsible for change?" and "Who, or what, exercises authority – the power to alter outcomes and redefine options for others – in the world economy or world society?" She calls it Pinocchio's problem, for, like Pinocchio upon his transformation from a puppet into a boy with no strings to guide him, it involves making choices over "allegiance, loyalty, and identity" in "a world of multiple, diffused authority."

The problem of the subject is a problem of the growing disjunctions between theory and practice. The *de jure* insignificance of business corporations and associations in the face of their *de facto* significance reflects a disjunction between theory and practice. In the context of the problem of the "subject," it marks disjunctions between both law and state and law and society. The law has ceased to constitute, mirror, and, in some cases to discipline state practice and bears only a remote relationship to the demands for recognition coming from emerging social forces. This portends a legitimacy crisis for both law and state. Moreover, these disjunctions provide important insight into the dialectical operation of international law and its potential as a source of transformative and emancipatory praxis.

The Disjunction Between Theory and Practice: International Law as Dialectic

All constitutional orders require some measure of conformance between their principles and practices. Whether conformance is assured through H. L. A. Hart's (1961) "rules of recognition" or Stephen Krasner's (1983 b) "convergent expectations of the participants," the legitimacy of a constitutional order is predicated upon some measure of identity between its constitutive and founding principles and the practices of its participants. A disjunction between constitutional theory and the practices of participants, more often than not, portends a crisis of legitimacy.[11]

However, the nature of the relationship between theory and practice, as of those between law and politics, and law and society, more generally, is not without controversy. Theorists of international society, for example, note an inverse relationship between international law and diplomatic practice: "international law seems to follow an inverse movement to that of international politics. When diplomacy is violent and unscrupulous, international law soars into the regions of natural law; when diplomacy acquires a certain habit of co-operation, international law crawls in the mud of legal positivism" (Wight, 1966: 29). For Martin Wight (ibid.) a correspondence between constitutional theory and political practices is conceivable and attainable only within the confines of domestic constitutional orders where there is a body politic capable of fashioning the unity between political theory and political activity. In contrast, in international relations there is a "tension between international theory and diplomatic practice [that] can be traced to the heart of international society itself" (ibid., 30). This is evident in the "disharmony between international theory and diplomatic practice, and a kind of recalcitrance of international politics to being theorized about" (ibid., 33). Basically, the realist preoccupation with international anarchy thwarts any attempt to infuse the politics of "necessity" with moral or legal content. This is the familiar realist predisposition to limit the recognition of the historical effectivity and constitutive nature of international law that we considered in earlier chapters. Moreover, as Wight (ibid., 26) acknowledges explicitly, this position is premised upon the belief that the character of international politics is "incompatible with progressivist theory." The separations of law, politics, and morality preclude attributing any emancipatory quality to the law. International lawyers are doomed to their fate as "futile metaphysicians among practical men," while international politics remains the "realm of recurrence and repetition" and political necessity (ibid., 18 and 26).

It is possible, however, to read this tension between legal theory and political practices critically, as a dialectical relationship that gives rise to significant potential for revolutionary applications and understandings

[11] See Cutler (2001 a).

of international law.[12] This book has argued that conventional approaches to international law and international relations reify an unhistoric understanding of world order by freezing the Westphalian moment in time. International law and international relations are all about states: the state is naturalized as the primordial entity. The present is thus "sealed off," appearing as a "static and reified entity" (Hobson, 2002: 6). In another equally important move, conventional theories are then "extrapolated backwards through time" positing the past to be much like the present (ibid., 7). The way in which the state has created its own subjectivity under international law and given authority to its own voice as a source of the law is lost in presumptions of the timelessness and enduring character of the Westphalian order. Thus the Westphalian moment stands frozen and transfixed for all time, while sources and subject doctrines discipline antistatist tendencies in what appears to be an objectively rational state of affairs and the best-of-all-possible-worlds.

However, previous chapters have also argued that there has been increasing pluralism, heterogeneity, and differentiation in both legal subjects and sources over time. The *de facto* subjectivity of transnational corporations and private business associations and new claims to subjectivity coming from a variety of nonstate identities are rivaling the adequacy of subject doctrine. New and expanding sources of nonstate law are similarly pushing beyond the confines of sources doctrine. A critical understanding views these transformations as manifestations of the nature and operation of international law as an historically specific dialectical process. Through movements of legal doctrine the law operates dialectically in a number of dimensions. In one dimension, it operates as both a constitutive and a regulative influence. It creates and constitutes the state as "subject," mirroring the sovereign subject through subject and sources doctrines. Then it steps outside and "the law is set up *against* the state" to objectively police, measure, and regulate state action (David Kennedy, 1988: 23). Through processes of objectification and fetishization we have already considered, the law is objectified and fetishized, becoming the embodiment of sovereign will, whilst letting the subjective nature of the state-based order slip from sight. The objectification and sublimation of the subject, as noted above, are thus formalistic moves to give the law the appearance of neutrality and objectivity and, hence, to render law stable and legitimate (Schlag, 1991: 1627). This enables theorists to believe in their "objectified thought-structures

12 The following is an adaptation of Cutler (2002 a).

as off the shelf, stand-alone, self-sufficient, self-sustaining systems, completely independent of the activity of the subjects" (ibid., 1640). The state is no longer responsible for legal doctrines governing who matters as a subject and what counts as a source, because subject and sources doctrines step in and do the job as embodiments of rationality and objectivity. The fairness or equity or inclusivity or even accuracy of subject and sources doctrines simply cannot be raised in this analytical, theoretical, and normative framework. Subject and sources doctrines are quite simply placed beyond consideration and contention.

These moves to objectify and fetishize the law are of crucial significance to our understanding of contemporary transformations in world order. By attributing objective status to statist subject and sources doctrines, both the law and the state are removed from the subjective determination of who counts and who does not count in the global polity. It results in the fetishism of international law whereby the law becomes "an 'independent,' 'autonomous' reality to be explained according to its own 'internal dynamics,' i.e., conceives it as an independent subject, on whose creativity the survival of the society depends ... individuals [or states] affirm that they owe their existence to the law, rather than the reverse, inverting the real causal relationship between themselves and their product" (Balbus, 1977: 583; and see Chapter 5). As a result, the possibility for human intervention to challenge and displace conventional theories becomes ontologically infeasible.

Of equal significance is the way in which another dimension of the dialectical operation of the law also slips from view. This is the dialectical tension between positive law theory and state practice built right into sources and subject doctrines. This book argues that international law reifies a state-centric ontology through legal doctrines governing subjects and sources. However, international law simultaneously empowers antistatist tendencies by recognizing attributes of legal personality possessed by nonstate actors, such as individuals, corporate entities, and a potentially growing list of aspiring subjects, such as indigenous people and women. Paradoxically, it is international law that gave voice to revolutionary aspirations for subjectivity and voice coming from women, indigenous people, colonized people, individuals, and a host of social movements. Interestingly, many of these aspirations eventually materialized through state practice and customary sources of law, as articulated in resolutions of the United Nations General Assembly and other international organizations. The right to national self-determination, permanent sovereignty over natural resources, the condemnation of apartheid, the recognition of war crimes, crimes against humanity, the crime of genocide, and the imposition of individual responsibility for such crimes under international law all emerged in part through the mechanism of customary sources of law (see Malanczuk, 1997: 326–7 and 354). However, their recognition is potentially disruptive of, if not revolutionary for, statist orthodoxy. Thus conventional theories have written customary law (and its agents or subjects) out of sources (and subject) doctrines thus obscuring the internal tension between consent-based positive law and extraconsensual customary law.[13] In this sense, law operates dialectically, moving between formal consent-based law and law emerging through the evolution of state practice. But by collapsing practice into formal law, the revolutionary potential of emerging practice is lost and the orthodoxy of consent-based state law prevails. Conventional theories thus arrest the dialectical movement of law between consensual theory and state practice, excluding the agency of nonstate subjects in the face of statist orthodoxy. The fetishism of international law then renders this state of affairs and the law to be unproblematic, by definition, for "when Society is said to be a result of the Law, rather than the law to be a result of one particular type of society, then the Law by definition is unproblematical" (Balbus, 1977: 583).

The disjunction between legal theory and state practice is part of a larger disjunction associated with globalization more generally. As Philip Cerny (1995) observes:

> globalization leads to a growing disjunction between the democratic, constitutional, and social aspirations of people – which continue to be shaped by and understood through the framework of the territorial state – and increasingly problematic potential for collective action through state political processes. Certain possibilities for collective action through multilateral regimes may increase, but these operate at least one remove from democratic accountability. Indeed, the study of international regimes is expanding beyond intergovernmental institutions or public entities *per se* toward "private regimes" as critical regulatory mechanisms. New nodes of private quasi-public economic power are crystallizing that, in their own partial domains, are in effect more sovereign than the state.[14] (618)

[13] Cutler (2002 c) addresses how conventional legal scholarship in actuality collapses the tests of customary law into that for positive law. Because positivists prefer treaty law as a source of law, customary law is reinterpreted in a manner more consistent with consent-based positive law. As a result, the distinction between positive and customary international law is emptied of meaning. See also, David Kennedy (1987 c).

[14] On the disjunction between law and practice see also Held (1995: ch. 5).

The disjunction between law and practice is not lost on corporate actors. Indeed, it is the transnational corporate elite that is pushing vociferously for the establishment of a global business regulatory order (see Johns, 1994: 896; Vagts, 1970: 764). But it is an order of a particular sort – one consistent with a renewed emphasis on neoliberal values concerning the superiority of the private ordering of global corporate relations.[15] Global corporate actors are not trying to undo the "liberal art of separation" that draws the "map of the social and political world" by separating the economy and civil society from the political community and was meant to "mark off" "free exchange" from "coercive decision making" (Walzer, 1984: 315 and 321). They are not trying to harness private power through state regulatory controls. Rather, driven by intensified global competition, corporations and states are attempting to reposition themselves in a manner consistent with the move from the welfare to the competition state. Philip Cerny (1990: 230) notes that states can no longer focus on welfare as a purely domestic problem. "As the world economy is characterized by increasing interpenetration and the crystallization of transnational markets and structures, the state itself is having to act more and more like a market player, that shapes its policies to promote, control, and maximize returns from market forces in an international setting." Furthermore, "[i]n a globalizing world, the competition state is more likely to be involved in a process of competitive deregulation and creeping liberalization" (Cerny, 1997: 273). In the corporate law world, this trend is evident in what is variously referred to as the "race to the bottom," "lowest common denominator," and "regulatory meltdown" as states engage in competitive deregulation of corporate activities.[16] Moreover, Robert Cox (1995) suggests that "economic globalization ... may prove to be the underlying factor in the constitution of future political authorities and future world order" (39). He further observes that:

> [t]he key criterion today is competitiveness; and derived from that are universal imperatives of deregulation, privatization, and the restriction of public intervention in economic processes. Neoliberalism is transforming states from being buffers between external economic

[15] This is evident in terms of the failed Multilateral Agreement on Investment that was being negotiated in the Organization for Economic Cooperation and Development (OECD), which restricts the regulatory ambit of states over foreign investment activities. It is also evident in the shift in corporate legal preferences for "soft law" agreements over "hard law" ones.

[16] See Chapter 6 and for European deregulation see Charny (1991).

> forces and the domestic economy into agencies for adapting domestic economies to the exigencies of the global economy. So now the market appears to be bursting free from the bonds of national societies, to subject global society to its laws. (ibid.)

In a similar vein, Stephen Gill (1995 b: 85) identifies the globalization of the state with the "restructuring of state and capital on a world stage towards a more globally integrated and competitive market-driven system" which transforms the state "so as to give greater freedom to the private aspects of capital accumulation in the extended state at the local, national and transnational levels." But the enhanced power of private capital is rendered virtually "invisible" by the dominant ways of thinking about political authority. This portends a legitimacy crisis that is empirical, theoretical, and normative. From an empirical point of view, the law governing international legal personality tells us very little about the nature of the corporate world, the authority wielded by corporations, or their complex relationships with states, both national and foreign. Theoretically, international law is unable to theorize about its "subject" in any but the most formalistic and artificial ways. The corporation is undertheorized, while the state is overtheorized. Finally, and probably most importantly, the normative implications of the problem of the "subject" are obscured by the same moves suppressing the corporate subject. States, in "guaranteeing the economic *res* public for capitalism" are causing shifts in power relations within and between states (Panitch, 1996: 86). Robert Cox (1996 d: 27) refers to a "decomposition of civil society," in terms of "a fragmentation of social forces and a growing gap between the base of society and political leadership." He identifies the alienation of people from their political institutions and a loss of confidence in the abilities of politicians to deal with contemporary problems as contradictions generated by globalization. To Cox (ibid.), "globalization has undermined the authority of conventional political structures and accentuated the fragmentation of societies." Stephen Gill (1997: 205) reminds us that "the question of globalization raises the issue of globalization for whom and for what purposes." Echoing Cox's view that theory always serves some purpose, Gill (ibid., 206) notes increasing social polarization, "a sense of political indifference, government incompetence, and a decay of public and private responsibility and accountability" as aspects of the contemporary crisis. The basic contradiction between globalization and democratization portends a legitimacy crisis wherein "the ruling class has lost its consensus, i.e. is no longer 'leading' but only 'dominant'... The crisis consists precisely in the fact that the old is dying and the new cannot be born" (Gramsci, 1971: 275–6). The problem of the subject is so deeply embedded in international thought that it creates a blind spot for changes in practices resulting from changing material conditions. Moreover, neoliberal ideology compounds the problem by reasserting the values of enhanced private authority and the continuing significance of the distinction between the public and private spheres. Liberal thinking works against recognizing the authority of private corporations. The liberal faith in free economic markets and in representative democracy presents barriers to conceiving private relations or entities as politically authoritative or representative. Fleur Johns (1994: 912) notes that "both of these institutions require international law to abdicate responsibility for the TNC... The TNC is a creature of private law – 'a typically democratic method of lawmaking... characterised as the sphere of private autonomy.' "[17] To impute political authority and accountability to private, market activity, as noted before, would be to turn representative democracy on its head. It would be "inconsistent with the liberal belief that the processes of democratically-elected government ought to be the only legitimate means of curtailing individual liberty" (Johns, 1994: 913). Liberalism and public notions of authority thus preclude the recognition of corporate legal personality. They are incapable of conceptualizing *de facto* corporate authority and control, for this would upset the logic of the liberal representative state and consent-based notions of international law. Moreover, such recognition would threaten the state as the "subject" of international law and, hence, challenge law's claims to objectivity, neutrality, and legitimacy. In a word, the recognition of corporate personality comes up against the "problem of the subject." Disciplinary neoliberalism reinscribes the problem of the subject as a seemingly objective and, ultimately, legitimate state of affairs that is removed from individual challenge. This suggests that for international law there is only one story and one problem. "The story is the story of formalism and the problem is the problem of the subject. The story of formalism is that it never deals with the problem of the subject. The problem of the subject is that it's never been part of the story" (Schlag, 1991: 1628).

What is needed is a new type of theory that captures the integral role of international law in the constitution of political practices and restores the role of human agency to effect change. In a word, what is required is

[17] Johns here quotes Hans Kelsen (1967: 282).

the reengagement of law and politics. Conventional theories have lost sight of the symbiotic nature of the relationship between law and politics in the effort to create law in the form of a rational and objective order. The resulting fetishism of law produces analytical and theoretical paralysis, while undue formalism blinds the dominant modes of thought to major transformations in the subjects and sources of law. Both prevent inquiry into the practical and normative implications of these developments for democracy and the future viability of an inclusive and democratic rule of law. The discussion will now turn to consider how we might remedy this situation by imagining international law as praxis.

Recasting the Story: Imagining International Law as Praxis

At the beginning of this inquiry into the conditions of global authority it was noted that a new sense of historical agency is required in order to capture the historical effectivity of international law in the global political economy. This new sense must be attuned to the national, transnational, and subnational dimensions of authority. The impetus and the rationale are at once empirical, theoretical, and normative. The pressing problem is to reconceive the story. This involves recasting the story to include a broader array of actors and agents as part of our understanding of global authority. However, the real challenge is more than broadening notions of agency, empirically and theoretically. More crucially, what is involved is a reconsideration of the very notions of agency and of change *for what ends and for what purposes*. Recalling the sentiment of Robert Cox that all theory serves some purpose, one must begin by asking what "the story" is all about: who writes it, who benefits from it, and who loses. The story about global authority is the story about power and the relations and structures in which power is embedded. There is a public and a private face to this story; one involving states and nonstate, corporate and institutional actors. Moreover, this story is an historical one, bound up with the history of the state system and the materiality of the dominant modes of production. But the story as an engagement of critical theory and emancipatory politics must go further to inquire into the conditions of the possible – the prospects for "radical politics" (Giddens, 1994 a). In this regard, Gramsci is instructive for, as noted above, hegemony based upon fraud is unsustainable. Also noted in earlier chapters is the Gramscian insight that hegemony operates somewhere between consent and coercion (see also, Cutler 1999 a). Arguably, fraud marks the transition from hegemonic to coercive authority. Moreover, as Anthony Giddens (1994 a: 5) notes, globalization is not a monolithic process, "but a complex mixture of processes, which often act in contradictory ways, producing conflicts, disjunctures and new forms of stratification." Others echo this view and identify a major disjuncture or asymmetry between globalization as a neoliberal economic project and globalization as a political project. Globalization is "a partial, incomplete and contradictory process – an uneasy correlation of economic forces, power relations and social structures . . . globalisation's hegemonic project is neoliberalism," but "liberal democracy cannot keep pace with its spread" (Chin and Mittelman, 1997: 26). It is at the points of disjuncture and asymmetry and at the interstices of social relations where resistance becomes possible. Importantly, "we have to realize that the consensual institutions of which Gramsci spoke are not only among international elites, but largely still embedded within what is usually seen as 'national society' or civil society. It is the task of movements grounded in civil society to change the direction of state practice in a manner that counters the neoliberal globalisation trend" (Amoore, et al., 1997: 192). This raises a question about the mercatocracy's ability to maintain neoliberal discipline and to deliver on the promise and the rhetoric of globalization. More specifically, the issue turns on the ability of global private legal ordering to produce the efficiencies, economic wealth, and justice that proponents of the new law merchant claim as its virtues.

Clearly, the first step is to begin to wage Gramsci's war of position, which builds slowly by creating alternate institutions, laws, and practices (see Cox, 1993 b: 128–9). The prospects for transformation will become more apparent if there is a greater understanding of the inequities embedded in the rules, processes, and institutions of private legal ordering. Better understandings of the problem of the subject, of the nature and function of the public/private law distinction, and of the power relations embedded in neoliberal commercial law are preconditions for the generation of emancipatory practices. This is the first step in the effort to realign theory with democratic practices. Giddens (1994 a) speaks of increasing the "transparency" of governments as a means for democratizing politics through dialogue, as opposed to through relations of violence.[18] Gramsci encouraged the development

[18] And see Giddens (1994 b).

of counterhegemonic resistance through the development of "common sense," combining national popular movements with revolutionary notions of praxis, through the agency of the organic intellectual (see Rupert, 1997 a; 1997 b; 2000: ch. 6). However, the translation of understanding and dialogue into practice is deeply problematic. As Perry Anderson (1994: 43) cautions, the "danger of conceiving democratic life as dialogue is that we may forget that its primary reality remains strife." Faith in democratic dialogue reflects belief that "reason will answer to reason," which Anderson observes is the most utopian legacy of the Enlightenment. Indeed, reason may not answer to reason and so violence remains an ever-present possibility. Moreover, the locus of agency remains problematic. The mercatocracy functions much like the organic intellectual, but its membership is diverse and arguably fraught with multiple and competing interests and purposes. The unity of purpose evident in its commitment to neoliberal discipline may be quite fragile if its members begin to experience disappointments with the system of private ordering. Identifying potential agents of change is thus as difficult as locating authority in the global political economy, where this inquiry began. However, difficult as it might be, this is where the story must begin in order to embrace the challenge of critical theory and to take seriously the view that theory is always "*for* someone and *for* some purpose" and cannot be "divorced from a standpoint in time and space" (Cox, 1996 a: 87).

To this end, critical theory must begin to build where instrumental Marxist theories of law have failed to theorize the historical effectivity of law. This requires a looser historical materialism that, in addition to exploring the material dimensions of law, analyzes the historical significance of its ideological and institutional dimensions. Here the work of people like Robert Cox is instructive and assists in understanding the historical permutations of the law merchant order in terms of changing material, ideological, and institutional forces. The Marxist notion of the symbiotic and reciprocal relationship between theory and practice in praxis alerts us to the mutual constitution of the material and ideational worlds and assists in developing a critical understanding of law. International lawmaking is thus to be understood in dynamic terms as a process giving rise to material, institutional, and ideological conditions embodying both oppressive and potentially emancipatory social relations. Gramsci's insights into the material and ideological significance of the law and the nature of legal hegemony are also helpful in developing critical international law (see Chapter 3).

There is also a further need to review the analytical foundations of historical materialist analysis in order to broaden notions of human agency beyond class-based associations (see generally, Rupert and Smith, 2002). Class-based analysis alone, just like state-based analysis, simply does not comprehend the complexity of the social forces implicated in the new constitutionalism and neoliberal discipline. At present, sources and subject doctrines control the lawmaking process by determining who counts as a legal subject and who has voice as a source of law. As noted before, they function as mechanisms of exclusion, repressing and excluding actual social difference in the face of statist orthodoxy (David Kennedy, 1988: 25). However, it does not have to be this way, for the lawmaking process also provides opportunities for reconceiving subject and sources doctrines to create a more inclusive and equitable order. This requires recognizing the inadequacy of unhistoric appeals to Westphalia as definitive of contemporary political practices and recognizing the historical differentiation in legal subjects and sources as an empirical reality. It also requires analyzing and incorporating into legal doctrines and lawmaking institutions the claims to subjectivity and voice coming from a multiplicity of identities. The materiality of the law must be critically analyzed in the context of the representativeness and inclusiveness of the interests and rights promoted by contemporary law. For example, the claims made by women that international legal doctrines in the area of development operate to disadvantage women must be taken seriously and examined with a view to equalizing their distributional impact.[19] Similarly, claims for the recognition of indigenous peoples' property rights as protected rights under the World Intellectual Property Law regime must also be examined in the context of the continuing relevance of traditional property law regimes.[20] Progressive law and practices must extend into the institutional framework of international law. For example, the inclusion of women and the representatives of human rights and environmental groups and other people claiming recognition as subjects and a voice in the operations of international organizations and other bodies involved in lawmaking, such as the meetings of the World Trade Organization and the Organization of Economic Cooperation and Development, must be addressed. Finally, critical analysis of the ways in which legal doctrines, such as subject and sources doctrines, have historically operated to exclude marginalized and repressed peoples and developing countries by favoring existing

[19] See Chapter 3. [20] See Chapter 3; Doucas (1995); Cutler (2002 d).

positive law over potentially destabilizing, if not revolutionary, customary law is a necessary step in beginning to understand the ideological operation of the law.[21] These are modest but necessary beginnings for the development of a theory of international law as praxis.

Imagining international law as praxis is not just an intellectual engagement, but a very material one upon which turns the future viability, relevance, and, indeed, the desirability of the rule of law in international relations. A critical understanding of international law requires recognition of its consensual and coercive faces and its dialectical nature as a source of both conservatism and transformation. While unquestionably a challenging undertaking, "to engage in praxis is not to tread on alien ground, external to the theory [of historical materialism]," because revolutionary theory is already contained in historical materialist theory: "The theory itself is already a practical one; praxis does not only come at the end but is already present in the beginning of the theory" (Marcuse, 1972 a: 5).

Reconceiving transnational merchant law as praxis thus involves recognizing the historical effectivity of the law in its material, ideological, and institutional dimensions. Transnational merchant law has served different interests and purposes over its history. Initially a customary order, the medieval law merchant provided a deterritorialized and delocalized self-disciplinary system that functioned outside the ambit of local politico-legal systems and local political economies. The medieval law merchant anticipated what would later become the private sphere of capital accumulation under nationally-based capitalist societies. Its customary nature reflected the feudal organization of society and contrasts sharply with the systematic and rationalized system that evolved with the juridification of commercial relations during the phase of state-building and the establishment of nationally-based capitalist activities. These developments served to localize and territorialize the law, whilst simultaneously isolating and neutralizing it within a protected sphere of the economy and civil society. The important and enduring link between law and capitalism was forged and constitutionalized in an international legal order that placed the state at the center of the order. Today this link is intensifying with the deepening of juridified commercial relations. However, significant transformations in political economy and authority are resulting in the pluralization and privatization

[21] In this regard the work of Boaventura de Sousa Santos (1995) on the systems of law regulating indigenous peoples is, indeed, foundational.

of commerce. These transformations are expanding the private sphere and reworking the relationships between law and state and between law and society. The mercatocracy plays a central role in the reconfiguration of public and private authority, functioning as the organic intellectuals of a nascent transnationalized historic bloc. The modern law merchant operates dialectically, both deterritorializing/delocalizing and reterritorializing/localizing commercial relations. Recognizing the dialectical nature of the law is a crucial insight offered by critical theory for it identifies the locus of transformative potential. It is the local societies, where the laws are ultimately enforced, as well as the international institutions and the private transnational associations and networks, where the law is created and interpreted, that must be the focus for critical and emancipatory politics. As the mediator of local and global juridico-political relations, transnational commercial law provides fertile possibilities for societies to assert or reassert claims to identity, rights, and representation through law with a view to ensuring that the rule of law really is in *both* theory and practice an unqualified human good.[22]

[22] As E. P. Thompson (1975) argued law to be.

References

Abbott, Alden F. 1976, "Latin America and International Arbitration Conventions: The Quandary of Non-ratification," *Harvard International Law Journal* 17 (1): 131–40.

Abbott, Frederick M. 2000, "NAFTA and the Legalization of World Politics: A Case Study," *International Organization* 54 (3): 519–47.

Abbott, Kenneth 1992, "International Law and International Relations Theory: Building Bridges – Elements of a Joint Discipline," *Proceedings of the American Society of International Law* 86: 167–72.

Abbot, Kenneth and Duncan Snidal 2000, "Hard and Soft Law in International Governance," *International Organization* 54 (3): 421–56.

Abbot, Kenneth, Robert Keohane, Andrew Moravcsik, Anne-Marie Slaughter, and Duncan Snidal 2000, "The Concept of Legalization," *International Organization* 54 (3): 401–20.

Agnew, John 1994, "The Territorial Trap: The Geographical Assumptions of International Relations Theory," *Review of International Political Economy* 1 (1): 53–80.

Agnew, John and Stuart Corbridge 1995, *Mastering Space: Hegemony, Territory and the International Political Economy*, London: Routledge.

Ago, Roberto 1957, "Positive Law and International Law," *American Journal of International Law* 51 (4): 691–733.

Akehurst, Michael 1987, *A Modern Introduction to International Law*, 6th edn, London and New York: Routledge.

Aksen, Gerald 1984, "The Need to Utilize International Arbitration," *Vanderbilt Journal of Transnational Law* 17 (1): 11–17.

1990, "Arbitration and Other Means of Dispute Settlement," in David Goldsweig and Roger Cummings (eds.), *International Joint Ventures: A Practical Approach to Working with Foreign Investors in the U.S. and Abroad*, Chicago: American Bar Association, pp. 203–10.

Alter, Karen J. 2000, "The European Union's Legal System and Domestic Policy: Spillover or Backlash?" *International Organization* 54 (3): 489–518.

Althusser, Louis 1971, "Ideology and Ideological State Apparatuses," in *Lenin and Philosophy and Other Essays*, New York: Monthly Review Press, pp.127–86.

and Étienne Balibar 1970, *Reading Capital*, London: New Left Books.

Amin, Ash and Ronen Palan 1996, "Editorial: The Need to Historicize IPE," *Review of International Political Economy* 3 (2): 209–15.

Amin, Samir 1974, *Accumulation on a World Scale: A Critique of the Theory of Underdevelopment*, vols. I and II, London: Monthly Review Press.

1990, *Maldevelopment: Anatomy of a Global Failure*, London: Zed Books.

Amoore, Louise, Richard Dodgson, Barry K. Gills, Paul Langley, Don Marshall, and Iain Watson 1997, "Overturning 'Globalisation': Resisting the Teleological, Reclaiming the 'Political'," *New Political Economy* 2 (1): 179–95.

Amoore, Louise, Richard Dodgson, Randal D. Germain, Barry K. Gills, Paul Langley, and Iain Watson 2000, "Paths to a Historicized International Political Economy," *Review of International Political Economy* 7 (1): 53–71.

Anderson, Perry 1974 a, *Lineages of the Absolutist State*, London: Verso Editions.

1974 b, *Passages from Antiquity to Feudalism*, London: Verso Editions.

(1976–7) "The Antinomies of Antonio Gramsci,' *New Left Review* 100: 5–94.

1994, "Comment: Power, Politics and the Enlightenment," in David Miliband (ed.), *Reinventing the Left*, Cambridge: Polity Press, pp. 39–44.

Arend, Anthony 1998, "Do Legal Rules Matter? International Law and International Politics," *Virginia Journal of International Law* 38 (2): 107–54.

Arrighi, Giovanni 1993, "The Three Hegemonies of Historical Capitalism," in Gill, 1993 a, pp. 148–85.

Arzt, Donna E. and Igor I. Lukashuk 1998, "Participants in International Legal Relations," in Charlotte Ku and Paul F. Diehl (eds.), *International Law: Classic and Contemporary Readings*, Boulder, CO: Westview Press, pp. 155–76.

Ashley, Richard 1983, "Three Modes of Economism," *International Studies Quarterly* 27 (4): 463–96.

1988, "Untying the Sovereign State: A Double Reading of the Anarchy Problematique," *Millennium: Journal of International Studies* 17 (2): 227–62.

Ashley, Richard and R. B. J. Walker 1990, "Speaking the Language of Exile," *International Studies Quarterly* 34 (3): 259–68.

Asser Institute 1988, "List of Arbitral Institutions," *Yearbook of Commercial Arbitration* 13: 713–37.

Atiyah, Patrick 1979, *The Rise and Fall of Freedom of Contract*, Oxford: Clarendon Press.

Augelli, Enrico and Craig Murphy 1988, *America's Quest for Supremacy and the Third World: A Gramscian Analysis*, London: Pinter Publishers.

1993, "Gramsci and International Relations: A General Perspective with Examples from Recent US Policy Toward the Third World," Gill, 1993 a, pp. 127–47.

Austin, John (1832) 1954, *The Province of Jurisprudence Determined, and the Uses of the Study of Jurisprudence*, London: Weidenfeld and Nicolson.

Azzi, John 1994, "Historical Development of Australia's International Taxation Rules," *Melbourne University Law Review* 19 (4): 793–813.

Baer, Marvin, Joost Bloom, Elizabeth Edinger, Nicholas Rafferty, Geneviève Saumier, and Catherine Walsh 1997, *Private International Law in Common Law Canada: Cases, Texts, and Materials*, Toronto: Emond Montgomery Publications Ltd.

Bagner, Hans 1982, "Enforcement of International Commercial Contracts by Arbitration: Recent Developments," *Case Western Reserve Journal of International Law* 14 (3): 573–89.

Bainbridge, Stephen 1984, "Trade Usages in International Sales of Goods: An Analysis of the 1964 and 1980 Sales Conventions," *Virginia Journal of International Law* 24 (3): 619–65.

Baker, J. H. 1990, *An Introduction to English Legal History*, 3rd edn, London: Butterworths.

Balbus, Isaac 1977, "Commodity Form and Legal Form: An Essay on the 'Relative Autonomy' of the Law," *Law and Society* 11 (3): 571–88.

Baldwin, David A. (ed.) 1993, *Neorealism and Neoliberalism: The Contemporary Debate*, New York: Columbia University Press.

Bannicke, Leonard B. 1985, "International Chamber of Commerce Court of Arbitration," *Alberta Law Review* 23 (1): 51–61.

Barker, J. Craig 2000, *International Law and International Relations*, London and New York: Continuum.

Bartelson, Jens 1995, *A Genealogy of Sovereignty*, Cambridge University Press.

Batt, Francis R. (ed.) 1947, *Chalmers' Digest of the Law of Bills of Exchange, Promissory Notes, Cheques and Negotiable Instruments*, 11th edn, London: Stevens & Sons.

Bauman, Zygmunt 2000, *Liquid Modernity*, Cambridge: Polity Press.

Beck, Robert J., Anthony C. Arend, and Robert Vander Lugt (eds.) 1996, *International Rules: Approaches from International Law and International Relations*, New York: Oxford University Press.

Bedjaoui, Mohammed 1979, *Towards a New International Economic Order*, Paris: UNESCO.

Beirne, Piers 1982, "Ideology and Rationality in Max Weber's Sociology of Law," in Beirne and Quinney (eds.), 1982, pp. 44–62.

Beirne, Piers and Richard Quinney (eds.) 1982, *Marxism and Law*, New York: John Wiley & Sons.

Bellamy, Richard 1990, "Gramsci, Croce and the Italian Political Tradition," *History of Political Thought* 11 (2): 313–37.

Benedict, Robert D. 1909, "The Historical Position of the Rhodian Law," *Yale Law Journal* 18 (4): 223–42.

Benney, Mark 1983, "Gramsci on Law, Morality, and Power," *International Journal of Sociology of Law* 11(2): 191–208.

Benson, Bruce 1988–89, "The Spontaneous Evolution of Commercial Law," *Southern Economic Journal* 55 (3): 644–61.

1999, "To Arbitrate or to Litigate: That Is the Question," *European Journal of Law and Economics* 8 (2): 91–151.

Berger, Klaus, P. 1997, "The *Lex Mercatoria* Doctrine and the UNIDROIT Principles of International Commercial Contracts," *Law and Policy in International Business* 28 (4): 943–90.

Berman, Harold 1977, "The Origins of Western Legal Science," *Harvard Law Review* 90 (5): 894–943.

1983, *Law and Revolution: The Formation of the Western Legal Tradition*, Cambridge, MA: Harvard University Press.

Berman, Harold and Colin Kaufman 1978, "The Law of International Commercial Transactions (*Lex Mercatoria*)", *Harvard International Law Journal* 19 (1): 221–78.

Bewes, Wyndham 1923, *The Romance of the Law Merchant*, London: Sweet & Maxwell.

Blackburn, Terence 1994, "The Unification of Corporate Laws: The United States, the European Community and the Race to Laxity," *George Mason Independent Law Review* 3 (1): 1–95.

Boka, E. 1964, "The Sources of the Law of International Trade in the Developing Countries of Africa," in Schmitthoff, 1964 b, pp. 227–54.

Bonell, Michael J. 1978, "The UNIDROIT Initiative for the Progressive Codification of International Trade Law," *International and Comparative Law Quarterly* 27: 413–41.

1995, "The UNIDROIT Principles of International Commercial Contracts and CISG – Alternatives or Complementary Instruments?" in Ziegel (ed.), 1995, pp. 62–77.

Booth, Ken and Steve Smith (eds.) 1995, *International Relations Theory Today*, University Park: Pennsylvania University Press.

Bourdieu, Pierre 1987, "The Force of Law: Toward a Sociology of the Juridical Field," *The Hastings Law Journal* 38 (5): 805–53.

Bowett, Derek W. 1986, "Claims Between States and Private Entities: The Twilight Zone of International Law," *Catholic University Law Review* 35 (4): 929–60.

Boyle, James 1985, "Ideas and Things; International Legal Scholarship and the Prison-House of Language," *Harvard International Law Journal* 26 (2): 327–59.

1996, *Shamans, Software, and Spleens: Law and the Construction of the Information Society*, Cambridge, MA: Harvard University Press.

Braithwaite, John and Peter Drahos 2000, *Global Business Regulation*, Cambridge University Press.

Bratton, William, Joseph McCahery, Sol Picciotto, and Colin Scott (eds.) 1996, *International Regulatory Competition and Coordination: Perspectives on Economic Regulation in Europe and the United States*, Oxford: Clarendon Press.

Brewer, Anthony 1990, *Marxist Theories of Imperialism: A Critical Survey*, 2nd edn, London: Routledge.

Broches, Aaron 1987, "The 1985 UNCITRAL Model Law on International Commercial Arbitration: An Exercise in International Legislation," *Netherlands Yearbook of International Law* 18: 3–69.

Brodhurst, Bernard E. S. 1909, "The Merchants of the Staple," in *Select Essays in Anglo-American Legal History*, vol. III, 16–33.

Brown, Chris 1992, *International Relations Theory: New Normative Approaches*, Harlow: Prentice Hall.

1995, "International Theory and International Society: The Viability of the Middle Way?" *Review of International Studies* 21 (2): 183–96.

Brownlie, Ian 1990, *Principles of Public International Law*, 4th edn, Oxford: Clarendon Press.

1998, *Principles of Public International Law*, 5th edn, Oxford: Clarendon Press.

Buchanan, Mark 1988, "Public Policy and International Commercial Arbitration," *American Business Law Journal* 26 (3): 511–33.

Bull, Hedley 1966, "The Grotian Conception of International Society," in Butterfield and Wight (eds.), 1966, pp. 51–73.

1977, *The Anarchical Society: A Study of Order in World Politics*, New York: Columbia University Press.

Bull, Hedley and Adam Watson (eds.) 1985, *The Expansion of International Society: A Comparative Analysis*, New York: Oxford University Press.

Bull, Hedley, Benedict Kingsbury, and Adam Roberts (eds.) 1990, *Hugo Grotius and International Relations*, Oxford University Press.

Burch, Kurt 1998, *Property and the Making of the International System*, Boulder, CO, and London: Lynne Rienner Publishers.

Burdick, Francis M. 1909, "Contributions of the Law Merchant to the Common Law," in *Select Essays in Anglo-American Legal History*, vol. III, pp. 34–50.

Butterfield, Herbert and Martin Wight (eds.) 1966, *Diplomatic Investigations*, London: Allen & Unwin.

Buzan, Barry 1993, "From International System to International Society: Structural Realism and Regime Theory Meet the English School," *International Organization* 47 (3): 327–52.

Buzan, Barry, Charles Jones, and Richard Little 1993, *The Logic of Anarchy: Neorealism to Structural Realism: New Directions in World Politics*, New York: Columbia University Press.

Byers, Michael 2000, *The Role of International Law in International Politics: Essays in International Relations and International Law*, New York: Oxford University Press.

Byrnes, Andrew 1992, "Women, Feminism and International Human Rights Law – Methodological Myopia, Fundamental Flaws or Meaningful Marginalisation? Some Current Issues," *Australian Yearbook of International Law* 12: 205–41.

Cafruny, Alan 1987, *Ruling the Waves: The Political Economy of International Shipping*, Berkeley: University of California Press.

Cain, Maureen and Alan Hunt 1979, *Marx and Engels on Law*, London and New York: Academic Press.

Campbell, C. M. and Paul Wiles 1980, *Marx and Engels on Law and Laws*, Oxford: Martin Robertson.

Campbell, David 1998, *Writing Security: United States Foreign Policy and the Politics of Identity*, rev. edn, Manchester University Press.

Carbonneau, Thomas E. 1984, "Arbitral Adjudication: A Comparative Assessment of Its Remedial and Substantive Status in Transnational Commerce," *Texas International Law Journal* 19 (1): 33–114.

Carbonneau, Thomas E. (ed.) 1990, *Lex Mercatoria and Arbitration: A Discussion of the New Law Merchant*, Dobbs Ferry, New York: Transnational Juris Publications.

Cardoso, Fernando Henrique and Enzo Faletto 1979, *Dependency and Development in Latin America*, trans. Marjory Mattingly Urquidi, Berkeley: University of California Press.

Carr, E. H. 1939, *The Twenty Years' Crisis: 1919–1939*, London: Macmillan.

Carty, Anthony 1986, *The Decay of International Law? A Reappraisal of the Limits of the Legal Imagination in International Affairs*, Manchester University Press.

1991 a, " 'Liberalism's Dangerous Supplements': Medieval Ghosts of International Law," *Michigan Journal of International Law* 13 (1): 161–71.

1991 b, "Critical International Law: Recent Trends in the Theory of International Law," *European Journal of International Law* 2 (1): 66–96.

Castel, J.-G. 1967, "Canada and the Hague Conference on Private International Law: 1893–1967," *Canadian Bar Review* 45 (1): 1–34.

1989, "The Settlement of Disputes Under the 1988 Canada–United States Free Trade Agreement," *American Journal of International Law* 83 (1): 118–28.

Cerny, Philip 1990, *The Changing Architecture of Politics: Structure, Agency and the Future of the State*, London: Sage Publications.

1995, "Globalization and the Changing Logic of Collective Action," *International Organization* 49 (4): 595–625.

1997, "Paradoxes of the Competition State: The Dynamics of Political Globalization," *Government and Opposition* 32 (2): 251–74.

2000, "Embedding Global Financial Markets: Securitization and the Emerging Web of Governance," in Karsten Ronit and Volker Schneider (eds.), *Private Organizations in Global Politics*, London: Routledge, pp. 59–82.

Cerny, Phillip (ed.) 1993, *Finance and World Politics: Markets, Regimes and States in the Post-hegemonic Era*, Cheltenham, and Brookfield, VT: Edward Elgar.

Charlesworth, Hilary 1992 a, "The Public/Private Distinction and the Right to Development in International Law," *Australian Yearbook of International Law* 12: 190–204.

1992 b, "Subversive Trends in the Jurisprudence of International Law," *Proceedings of the Annual Meetings of the American Society of International Law* 86, pp. 125–30.

Charlesworth, Hilary and Christine Chinkin 1993, "The Gender of *Jus Cogens*," *Human Rights Quarterly* 15 (1): 63–76.

Charlesworth, Hilary, Christine Chinkin, and Shelley Wright 1991, "Feminist Approaches to International Law," *American Journal of International Law* 85 (4): 613–45.

Charny, David 1991, "Competition Among Jurisdictions in Formulating Corporate Law Rules: An American Perspective on the 'Race to the Bottom' in the European Communities," *Harvard International Law Journal* 32 (2): 423–56.

Charney, Jonathan 1983, "Transnational Corporations and the Developing Public International Law," *Duke Law Journal* 4: 748–88.

Chase-Dunn, Christopher 1989, *Global Formation: Structures of the World Economy*, Oxford: Blackwell.

Chaudhuri, K. N. 1991, "Reflections on the Organizing Principle of Premodern Trade," in Tracy (ed.), 1991, pp. 421–42.

Chayes, Abram and Antonia Chayes 1995, *The New Sovereignty: Compliance with International Regulatory Agreements*, Cambridge, MA: Harvard University Press.

Chen, Lung-Chu 1989, *An Introduction to Contemporary International Law: A Policy-Oriented Perspective*, New Haven, CT and London: Yale University Press.

Chimni, B. S. 1993, *International Law and World Order: A Critique of Contemporary Approaches*, Newbury Park, CA: Sage Publications.

Chin, Christine B. N. and James H. Mittelman 1997, "Conceptualising Resistance to Globalisation," *New Political Economy* 2 (1): 25–37.

Chinkin, Christine 1991, "A Gendered Perspective to the International Use of Force," *Australian Yearbook of International Law* 12: 279–93.

2000, "Human Rights and the Politics of Representation: Is There a Role for International Law?" in Byers, 2000, pp. 131–48.

Clough, Shepard B. 1959, *The Economic Development of Western Civilization*, New York: McGraw-Hill Book Co. Inc.

Clough, Shepard B. and Charles W. Cole 1946, *Economic History of Europe*, rev. edn, Boston, MA: D. C. Heath & Co.

Cohen, Benjamin 1998, *The Geography of Money*, Ithaca, NY and London: Cornell University Press.

Cohen, Morris 1927–8, "Property and Sovereignty," *The Cornell Law Quarterly* 13 (1): 8–30.

1950, *Reason and Law*, New York: Collier Books.

Cohn, Theodore H. 2000, *Global Political Economy: Theory and Practice*, New York: Longman.

Connolly, William 1993, *Political Theory and Modernity*, 2nd edn, Ithaca: Cornell University Press.

Coulson, Robert 1982, "A New Look at International Commercial Arbitration," *Case Western Reserve Journal of International Law* 14 (2): 359–71.

Cox, Robert 1987, *Production, Power, and World Order: Social Forces in the Making of History*, New York: Columbia University Press.

1989, "Production, the State, and Change in World Order," in Ernst-Otto Czempiel and James N. Rosenau (eds.) 1989, *Global Changes and Theoretical*

Challenges, Lexington, MA: Lexington Books, D. C. Heath and Co., pp. 37–50.

1993 a, "Structural Issues of Global Governance: Implications for Europe," in Gill, 1993 a, pp. 259–89.

1993 b, "Gramsci, Hegemony and International Relations: An Essay in Method," in Gill, 1993 a, pp. 49–66.

1995, "Critical Political Economy," in Hettne (ed.), 1995, pp. 31–45.

1996 a, "Social Forces, States, and World Orders: Beyond International Relations Theory," in Cox with Sinclair, 1996, pp. 85–123.

1996 b "The Global Political Economy and Social Choice," in Cox with Sinclair 1996, pp. 191–208.

1996 c, "Realism, Positivism and Historicism," in Cox with Sinclair, 1996, pp. 49–59.

1996 d, "A Perspective on Globalization," in Mittelman (ed.), 1996, pp. 21–30.

1999, "Civil Society at the Turn of the Millennium: Prospects for Alternative World Order," *Review of International Studies* 25 (1): 3–28.

Cox, Robert W. with Timothy J. Sinclair 1996, *Approaches to World Order*, Cambridge University Press.

Craig, W. Laurence 1995, "Some Trends and Developments in the Laws and Practice of International Commercial Arbitration," *Texas International Law Journal* 30 (1): 1–58.

Crawford, James 1993, "Democracy and International Law," *British Yearbook of International Law* 64: 113–33.

Cremades, Bernado M. and Steven L. Plehn 1984, "The New Lex Mercatoria and the Harmonization of the Laws of International Commercial Transactions," *Boston University International Law Journal* 2 (3): 317–48.

Crouch, Colin 1986, "Sharing Public Spaces: States and Organized Interests in Western Europe," in John A. Hall (ed.), *States in History*, Oxford and New York: Basil Blackwell, pp. 177–210.

Cutler, A. Claire 1991, "The 'Grotian' Tradition in International Relations," *Review of International Studies* 17(1): 41–65.

1992, "Canada and the Private International Trade Law Regime," in A. Claire Cutler and Mark W. Zacher (eds.)1997, *Canadian Foreign Policy and International Economic Regimes*, Vancouver: University of British Columbia Press, pp. 89–112.

1995, "Global Capitalism and Liberal Myths: Dispute Settlement in Private International Trade Relations," *Millennium: Journal of International Studies* 24 (3): 377–97.

1997, "Artifice, Ideology and Paradox: The Public/Private Distinction in International Law," *Review of International Political Economy* 4 (2): 261–85.

1999 a, "Locating 'Authority' in the Global Political Economy," *International Studies Quarterly* 43 (1): 59–81.

1999 b, "Public Meets Private: The International Unification and Harmonisation of Private International Trade Law," *Global Society* 13 (1): 25–48.

1999 c, "Private Authority in International Trade Relations: The Case of Maritime Transport," in Cutler, Haufler, and Porter, 1999 a, pp. 283–329.

2000 a, "Globalization, Law and Transnational Corporations : A Deepening of Market Discipline," in Theodore H. Cohn, Stephen McBride, and John Wiseman (eds.), *Power in the Global Era: Grounding Globalization*, Basingstoke: The Macmillan Press and New York: St. Martin's Press, pp. 53–66.

2000 b, "Theorizing the 'No-Man's Land' Between Politics and Economics," in Thomas C. Lawton, James N. Rosenau, and Amy C. Verdun (eds.), *Strange Power: Shaping the Parameters of International Relations and International Political Economy*, Aldershot and Burlington, USA: Ashgate, pp. 159–74.

2001 a, "Critical Reflections on the Westphalian Assumptions of International Law and Organization: A Crisis of Legitimacy," *Review of International Studies* 27 (2): 133–50.

2001 b, "Globalization, the Rule of Law and the Modern Law Merchant: Medieval or Late Capitalist Associations?" in the Special Issue on Law in the Global Polity, *Constellations: An International Journal of Critical and Democratic Theory* 8 (4): 480–502.

2002 a, "Critical Historical Materialism and International Law: Imagining International Law as Praxis," in Hobden and Hobson (eds.), 2002, pp. 181–99.

2002 b, "The Privatization of Global Governance and the New Law Merchant," in Adrienne Héritier (ed.), *Common Goods: Reinventing European and International Governance*, Lanham, MD: Rowman & Littlefield, pp. 127–57.

2002 c, "Law in the Global Polity," in Richard Higgott and Morten Ougaard (eds.), *Towards a Global Polity*, London: Routledge, pp. 58–77.

2002 d, "Historical Materialism, Globalization, and Law: Competing Conceptions of Property," in Rupert and Smith (eds.), 2002: 230–56.

forthcoming, "Global Governance and the Modern *Lex Mercatoria*" in Claire Turenne-Sjolander and Jean-François Thibault (eds.), *Of Global Governance: Culture, Economics and Politics*, University of Ottawa Press.

Cutler, A. Claire, Virginia Haufler, and Tony Porter (eds.) 1999 a, *Private Authority and International Affairs*, Albany, NY: SUNY Press.

1999 b, "Private Authority and International Affairs," in Cutler, Haufler, and Porter, 1999 a, pp. 3–30.

1999 c, "The Contours and Significance of Private Authority in International Affairs," in Cutler, Haufler, and Porter, 1999 a, pp. 333–76.

D'Amato, Anthony 1985, "The Moral Dilemma of Positivism," *Valparaiso University Law Review* 20 (1): 43–54.

1989, "Is International Law Part of Natural Law?" *Vera Lex* 9 (1): 8–25.

Date-Bah, S. K. 1981, "The Convention on the International Sale of Goods from the Perspective of the Developing Countries," in A. Guiffré (ed.), *La Vendita Internationale*, Milan: A. Guiffré, pp. 25–38.

David, René 1972 a, "The International Unification of Private Law," in *International Encyclopedia of Comparative Law: The Legal Systems of the World, Their Comparison and Unification*, vol. II, ch. 5, Tübingen: J.C.B. Mohr (Paul

Siebeck); The Hague, Boston, and London: Martinus Nijhoff Publishers, pp. 3–218.

1972 b "Different Conceptions of Law," in *International Encyclopedia of Comparative Law: The Legal Systems of the World, Their Comparison and Unification*, vol. I, ch. 2, pp. 1–25.

1972 c, "The Movement in Favour of the Unification of Private Law," in *International Encyclopedia of Comparative Law*, vol. II, ch. 5, pp. 123–208.

1972 d, "Sources of Law," in *International Encyclopedia of Comparative Law*, vol. II, ch. 3, pp. 3–404.

David, René, and J. E. C. Brierley 1978, *Major Legal Systems in the World Today: An Introduction to the Comparative Study of Law*, 2nd edn, London: Stevens & Sons.

De Enterría, Javier García 1990, "The Role of Public Policy in International Commercial Arbitration," *Law and Policy in International Business* 21 (3): 389–440.

Delaume, Georges R. 1989, "Comparative Analysis as a Basis of the Law in State Contracts: The Myth of the Lex Mercatoria," *Tulane Law Review* 63: 575–611.

Derains, Yves 1981, "New Trends in the Practical Application of the ICC Rules of Arbitration," *Northwestern Journal of International Law and Business* 3 (1): 35–55.

Der Derian, James and Michael Shapiro (eds.) 1989, *International/Intertextual Relations: Postmodern Readings of World Politics*, MA: Lexington Books.

De Roover, Florence 1945, "Early Examples of Marine Insurance," *Journal of Economic History* 5 (2): 172–200.

Devlin, Viscount Kilmuir 1961, "The Future of the Commercial Court," *Journal of Business Law* (1961): 8–11.

Dezalay, Yves 1995, "Introduction: Professional Competition and the Social Construction of Transnational Markets," in Dezalay and Sugarman (eds.), 1995, pp. 1–21.

Dezalay, Yves and Bryant G. Garth 1996, *Dealing in Virtue: International Commercial Arbitration and the Construction of a Transnational Legal Order*, University of Chicago Press.

Dezalay, Yves and David Sugarman (eds.) 1995, *Professional Competition and Professional Power: Lawyers, Accountants and the Social Construction of Markets*, London and New York: Routledge.

Dicey, A.V. 1967, *Introduction to the Study of the Constitution*, London: Macmillan; first published 1885.

Dolzer, Rudolf 1982, "International Agencies for the Formulation of Transnational Economic Law," in Horn and Schmitthoff (eds.), 1982, pp. 61–80.

Donovan, Donald Francis 1995, "International Commercial Arbitration and Public Policy," *New York University Journal of International Law and Politics* 27 (3): 645–57.

Dore, Isaac 1983, "Peaceful Settlement of International Trade Disputes: Analysis of the Scope of Application of the UNCITRAL Conciliation Rules," *Columbia Journal of Transnational Law* 21: 339–53.

Doucas, Margaret 1995, "Intellectual Property Law – Indigenous Peoples' Concerns," *Canadian Intellectual Property Review* 12 (1): 1–5.

Droz, Georges A. L. and A. Dyer 1981, "The Hague Conference and the Main Issues of Private International Law for the Eighties," *Northwestern Journal of International Law and Business* 3 (1): 155–211.

Eden, Lorraine 1996, "The Emerging North American Investment Regime," *Transnational Corporations* 5 (3): 61–98.

Ellinger, E. P. 1970, *Documentary Letters of Credit: A Comparative Study*, University of Singapore Press.

Enein, M. I. M. Aboul 1986, "Arbitration under the Auspices of the Cairo Regional Centre for Commercial Arbitration," *International Tax and Business Lawyer* 4: 256–65.

Engering, Frans 1996, "The Multilateral Investment Agreement," *Transnational Corporations* 5 (3): 147–61.

Enloe, Cynthia 1989, *Bananas, Beaches and Bases: Making Feminist Sense of International Politics*, London: Pandora.

1993, *The Morning After: Sexual Politics at the End of the Cold War*, Berkeley: University of California Press.

Eörsi, Gyula 1977, "Contracts of Adhesion and the Protection of the Weaker Party in International Trade Relations," in UNIDROIT, *New Directions in International Trade Law*, vol. I, New York: Oceana Publications, pp. 155–76.

Evans, Peter 1979, *Dependent Development: The Alliance of Multinational State, and Local Capital in Brazil*, Princeton University Press.

Falk, Richard 1970, *The Status of Law in International Society*, Princeton University Press.

1985, "The Interplay of Westphalia and Charter Conceptions of International Legal Order," in Richard Falk, Friedrich Kratochwil, and Saul Mendolvitz (eds.), *International Law: A Contemporary Perspective*, Boulder, CO: Westview Press, pp. 116–42.

1992, *Explorations at the Edge of Time: The Prospects for World Order*, Philadelphia: Temple University Press.

Falk, Richard and Samuel Kim (eds.) 1982, *Toward a Just World Order*, Boulder, CO: Westview Press.

,Friedrich Kratochwil, and Saul Mendolvitz (eds.) 1985, *International Law: A Contemporary Perspective*, Boulder, CO: Westview Press.

Farnsworth, E. Allan 1969, "The Past of Promise: An Historical Introduction to Contract," *Columbia Law Review* 69 (3): 576–607.

1979, "Developing International Trade Law," *California Western International Law Journal* 9: 461–71.

1984, "Unification of Sales Law: Usage and Course of Dealing," in Aubrey Diamond (ed.), *Unification and Comparative Law in Theory and Practice*, Deventer: Kluwer, pp. 81–9.

1995, "Unification and Harmonization of Private Law," in Ziegel (ed.), 1995, pp. 78–101.

Feeley, Malcolm 1976, "The Concept of Laws in Social Science: A Critique and Notes on an Expanded View," *Law and Society Review* 10 (4): 497–524.

Finnis, J. M. 1990, "Authority," in Raz (ed.), 1990 a, pp. 174–202.

Fisher, William III, Morton J. Horwitz, and Thomas A. Reed (eds.) 1993, *American Legal Realism*, Oxford University Press.

Foucault, Michel 1979 a, *Discipline and Punish: The Birth of the Prison*, trans. Alan Sheridan, New York: Vintage Books.

1979 b, "Governmentality," *Ideology and Consciousness, Governing the Present* 6: 5–21.

1980, *The History of Sexuality, Volume I: An Introduction*, trans. Robert Hurley, NY: Vintage Books.

Fox, James 1992, *Dictionary of International and Comparative Law*, Dobbs Ferry, NY: Oceana Publications.

Franck, Thomas 1990, *The Power of Legitimacy Among Nations*, New York: Oxford University Press.

Frank, André Gunder 1966,"The Development of Underdevelopment," *Monthly Review* 18 (4): 17–31.

1979, *Dependent Accumulation and Underdevelopment*, New York: Monthly Review Press.

Fraser, Andrew 1976, "Legal Theory and Legal Practice," *Arena* 44–5: 123–56.

1978, "The Legal Theory We Need Now," *Socialist Review* 8(4–5): 147–87.

Freedberg, J. A. 1995, "The Role of the International Council for Commercial Arbitration in Providing Source Material in International Commercial Arbitration," *International Journal of Legal Information* 23 (3): 272–83.

Fried, Jonathan 1997, "Globalization and International Law – Some Thoughts for States and Citizens," *Queen's Law Journal* 23 (1): 259–76.

Friedman, R. B. 1990, "On the Concept of Authority in Political Philosophy," in Raz (ed.), 1990 a, pp. 56–91.

Gabel, Peter 1977, "Intentions and Structure in Contractual Conditions: Outline of a Method for Critical Legal Theory," *Minnesota Law Review* 61: 601–43.

Gabor, Francis A. 1986, "Emerging Unification of Conflict of Laws Rules Applicable to the International Sale of Goods: UNCITRAL and the New Hague Conference on Private International Law," *Northwestern Journal of International Law and Business* 7(4): 538–70.

Galtung, Johan 1971, "A Structural Theory of Imperialism," *Journal of Peace Research* 8 (2): 81–117.

Gardam, Judith 1991, "A Feminist Analysis of Certain Aspects of International Humanitarian Law," *Australian Yearbook of International Law* 12: 265–78.

Garro, Alejandro M. 1989, "Reconciliation of Legal Traditions in the UN Convention on Contracts for the International Sale of Goods," *The International Lawyer* 23 (2): 443–83.

Germain, Randall and Michael Kenny 1998, "Engaging Gramsci: International Relations Theory and the New Gramscians," *Review of International Political Economy* 24 (3): 3–21.

Giannuzzi, Karen B. 1997, "The Convention on Contracts for the International Sale of Goods: Temporarily Out of 'Service'?" *Law and Policy in International Business* 28 (4): 991–1035.

Giddens, Anthony 1971, *Capitalism and Modern Social Theory: An Analysis of Marx, Durkheim and Max Weber*, Cambridge University Press.

1981, *A Contemporary Critique of Historical Materialism, vol. I: Power, Property and the State*, Berkeley and Los Angeles: University of California Press.

1987, *The Nation-State and Violence*, vol. II, Berkeley and Los Angeles: University of California Press.

1990 a, *The Consequences of Modernity*, Cambridge: Polity Press.

1990 b, *New Rules of Sociological Method: A Positive Critique of Interpretive Sociology*, Oxford: Polity Press.

1994 a, *Beyond Left and Right: The Future of Radical Politics*, Stanford University Press.

1994 b, "Brave New World: The New Context of Politics," in David Miliband (ed.), *Reinventing the Left*, Cambridge: Polity Press, pp. 21–38.

Gilchrist, J. 1969, *The Church and Economic Activity in the Middle Ages*, London: Macmillan.

Gill, Stephen 1990, *American Hegemony and the Trilateral Commission*, Cambridge University Press.

1993 a, *Gramsci, Historical Materialism and International Relations*, Cambridge University Press.

1993 b, "Gramsci and Global Politics: Towards a Post-hegemonic Research Agenda," in Gill, 1993 a, pp. 1–18.

1995 a, "Globalisation, Market Civilisation, and Disciplinary Neoliberalism," *Millennium: Journal of International Studies* 24 (3): 399–423.

1995 b, "Theorizing the Interregnum: The Double Movement and Global Politics in the 1990s," in Hettne (ed.), 1995, pp. 65–99.

1997, "Globalisation, Democratization and the Politics of Indifference," in Mittelman (ed.), 1996, pp. 205–28.

1998, "New Constitutionalism, Democratisation and the Global Political Economy," *Pacifica Review* 10 (1): 23–38.

Gill, Stephen and David Law 1988, *The Global Political Economy: Perspectives, Problems and Policy*, Baltimore: Johns Hopkins University Press.

1993, "Global Hegemony and the Structural Power of Capital," in Gill, 1993 a, pp. 93–126.

Gill, Stephen and James Mittelman (eds.) 1997, *Innovation and Transformation in International Studies*, Cambridge University Press.

Gold, Edgar 1981, *Maritime Transport: The Evolution of International Marine Policy and Shipping Law*, Lexington Books and Toronto: D. C. Heath and Company.

Goldman, Berthold 1983, "Lex Mercatoria," *Forum Internationale* 3: 3–24.

1986, "The Applicable Law: General Principles of Law – The Lex Mercatoria," in J. Lew (ed.), *Contemporary Problems in International Arbitration*, London: School of International Arbitration, Centre for Commercial Studies, pp. 113–25.

Goldstajn, A. 1981 "The New Law Merchant," *Journal of Business Law*: 17–42.

Goldstein, Judith, and Robert Keohane 1986, "Usages of Trade and Other Autonomous Rules of International Trade According to the U. N. (1980) Sales Convention," in Petar Sarcevic and Paul Volken (eds.), *Dubrovnik Lectures*, New York: Oceana Publications, pp. 55–110.

Goldstein, Judith, and Robert Keohane (eds.) 1993, *Ideas and Foreign Policy: Beliefs, Institutions and Political Change*, Ithaca: Cornell University Press.

Gottlieb, Gidon 1968, "The Conceptual World of the Yale School of International Law," *World Politics* 21 (1): 120–9.

Gramsci, Antonio 1971, *Selections from Prison Notebooks*, ed. and trans. Quentin Hoare and Geoffrey Nowell Smith, London: Lawrence and Wishart.

2000, "Philosophy, Common Sense, Language and Folklore," from *Prison Writings 1929–1935* in David Forgacs (ed.), *The Antonio Gramsci Reader: Selected Writings 1916–1935*, New York University Press, pp. 323–62.

Graving, Richard. J. 1989, "The International Commercial Arbitration Institutions: How Good a Job Are They Doing?" *American University Journal of International Law and Policy* 4 (2): 319–76.

Green, L. 1990, "Commitment and Community," in Raz (ed.), 1990 a, pp. 240–67.

Greenwalt, K. 1990, "Promissory Obligation: The Theme of Social Contract," in Raz (ed.), 1990 a, pp. 268–99.

Greif, Avner 1993, "Contract Enforceabliity and Economic Institutions in Early Trade: The Maghribi Traders' Coalition," *The American Economic Review* 83 (3): 525–48.

Greif, Avner, Paul Milgrom, and Barry Weingast 1994, "Coordination, Commitment, and Enforcement: The Case of the Merchant Guild," *Journal of Political Economy* 102 (4): 745–76.

Grieco, Joseph 1988, "Anarchy and the Limits of Cooperation: A Realist Critique of the Newest Liberal Institutionalism," *International Organization* 42 (3): 485–507.

Gross, Leo 1948, "The Peace of Westphalia, 1648–1948," *American Journal of International Law* 42 (1): 20–41.

Habermas, Jürgen 1994, *The Structural Transformation of the Public Sphere: An Inquiry into a Category of Bourgeois Society*, trans. T. Burger, Cambridge, MA: MIT Press.

1998, *Between Facts and Norms: Contributions to a Discourse Theory of Law and Democracy*, trans. William Rehg, Cambridge, MA: MIT Press.

Haggard, Stephan and Beth Simmons 1987, "Theories of International Regimes," *International Organization* 41 (3): 491–517.

Hall, Rodney and Thomas Biersteker (eds.) 2002, *The Emergence of Private Authority in Global Governance*, Cambridge University Press.

Halliday, Fred 1994, *Rethinking International Relations*, London: Macmillan.

Hamilton, Walton H. 1931, "The Ancient Maxim *Caveat Emptor*," *Yale Law Journal* 40 (8): 1,133–87.

Hanson, Donald 1970, *From Kingdom to Commonwealth: The Development of Civic Consciousness in English Political Thought*, Cambridge, MA: Harvard University Press.

Hart, H. L. A. 1958, "Positivism and the Separation of Law and Morals," *Harvard Law Review* 71 (4): 593–629.

1961, *The Concept of Law*, Oxford: Clarendon Press.

1962, *Law, Liberty, and Morality*, Stanford University Press.

Harvey, David 1990, *The Condition of Postmodernity: An Enquiry into the Origins of Cultural Change*, Cambridge, MA, and Oxford: Basil Blackwell.

Heckscher, Eli 1955, *Mercantilism*, New York: Macmillan.

Heilbroner, Robert and William Milberg 1995, *The Crisis of Vision in Modern Economic Thought*, Cambridge University Press.

Held, David 1995, *Democracy and the Global Order: From the Modern State to Cosmopolitan Governance*, Stanford University Press.

Henkin, Louis 1968, *How Nations Behave: Law and Foreign Policy*, New York: Praeger.

Herrmann, Gerold 1982, "The Contribution of UNCITRAL to the Development of International Trade Law," in Horn and Schmitthoff (eds.), 1982, pp. 35–50.

Hettne, Björn (ed.) 1995, *International Political Economy: Understanding Global Disorder*, Halifax: Fernwood Publishing.

Higgins, Rosalyn 1963, *The Development of International Law Through the Political Organs of the United Nations*, London: Oxford University Press.

1968, "Policy Considerations and the International Judicial Process," *International and Comparative Law Quarterly* 17: 58–84.

1985, "Conceptual Thinking About the Individual in International Law," in Falk, Kratochwil, and Mendolvitz, 1985, pp. 476–93.

1994, *Problems and Process: International Law and How We Use It*, Oxford: Clarendon Press.

Higgott, Richard, Geoffrey Underhill, and Andreas Bieler (eds.) 2000, *Non-State Actors and Authority in the Global System*, London: Routledge.

Highet, Keith 1989, "The Enigma of the Lex Mercatoria," *Tulane Law Review* 63 (3): 613–28.

Hirsch, Joachim 1995, "Nation-State, International Regulation and the Question of Democracy," *Review of International Political Economy* 2 (2): 267–84.

Hirst, Paul 1979, *On Law and Ideology*, London and Basingstoke: The Macmillan Press.

1997, "The Global Economy – Myths and Realities," *International Affairs* 73 (3): 409–25.

Hirst, Paul and Grahame Thompson 1996, *Globalization in Question: The International Economy and the Possibilities of Governance*, Cambridge: Polity Press.

Hobden, Stephen and John Hobson (eds.) 2002, *Historical Sociology of International Relations*, Cambridge University Press.

Hobson, J. A. 1965, *Imperialism: A Study*, Ann Arbor: University of Michigan Press.

Hobson, John 2002, "What's At Stake in 'Bringing Historical Sociology *Back* into International Relations: Beyond 'Chronofetishism' and 'Tempocentrism' in International Relations," in Hobden and Hobson (eds.), 2002, pp. 3–41.

Hoellering, Michael F. 1986, "The UNCITRAL Model Law on International Commercial Arbitration," *The International Lawyer* 20 (1): 327–41.

Holdsworth, William S. 1907 "The Development of the Law Merchant and Its Courts," in *Select Essays in Anglo-American Legal History*, vol. I, pp. 289–331.

Hollingsworth, J. Rogers and R. Boyer (eds.) 1997, *Contemporary Capitalism: The Embeddedness of Institutions*, Cambridge University Press.

Holloway, John and Sol Picciotto 1978, "Introduction: Towards a Materialist Theory of the State," in Holloway and Picciotto (eds.), *State and Capital: A Marxist Debate*, London: Edward Arnold, pp. 1–31.

Holton, R. J. 1985, *The Transition from Feudalism to Capitalism*, New York: St. Martin's Press.

Holzgrefe, J. L. 1989, "The Origins of Modern International Relations Theory," *Review of International Studies* 15 (1): 11–26.

Honnold, John 1964, "The Influence of the Law of International Trade on the Development and Character of English and American Commercial Law," in Schmitthoff, 1964 b, pp. 70–87.

1982, "Uniform Law and Uniform Trade Terms – Two Approaches to Common Goals," in Horn and Schmitthoff (eds.), 1982, pp. 161–74.

1984, "The New Uniform Law for International Sales and the UCC: A Comparison," *The International Lawyer* 18 (1): 21–8.

1991, *Uniform Law on International Sales Under the 1980 United Nations Convention*, Deventer: Kluwer, 1991.

1995, "International Unification of Private Law," in Oscar Schachter and Christopher C. Joyner (eds.), *United Nations Legal Order*, vol. II, Cambridge: Grotius Publications, pp. 1025–56.

Horn Norbert, 1982, "Uniformity and Diversity in the Law of International Commercial Transactions," in Horn and Schmitthoff (eds.), 1982, pp. 3–18.

and Clive Schmitthoff (eds.) 1982, *The Transnational Law of International Commercial Transactions*, Deventer: Kluwer.

Horwitz, Morton 1974, "The Historical Foundations of Modern Contract Law," *Harvard Law Review* 87 (5): 917–56.

1975, "The Rise of Legal Formalism," *American Journal of Legal History* 19: 251–64.

1979–80, "Law and Economics: Science or Politics?" *Hofstra Law Review* 8 (4): 905–12.

1982, "The History of the Public/Private Distinction," *University of Pennsylvania Law Review* 130 (6): 1423–8.

Hunt, Alan 1982 a, "Emile Durkheim: Towards a Sociology of Law," in Beirne and Quinney (eds.), 1982, pp. 27–43.

1982 b, "Dichotomy and Contradiction in the Sociology of Law," in Beirne and Quinney (eds.), 1982, pp. 74–97.

1993, *Explorations in Law and Society: Toward a Constitutive Theory of Law*, New York and London: Routledge.

Hunt, Alan and Gary Wickham, 1994, *Foucault and Law: Towards a Sociology of Law as Governance*, London and Boulder, CO: Pluto Press.

Hurrell, Andrew 1993, "International Society and the Study of International Regimes: A Reflective Approach," in Volker Rittberger (ed.), *Regime Theory and International Relations*, Oxford: Clarendon Press, 49–72.

Ismail, Hilmy 1991, "Forum Non Conveniens: United States Multinational Corporations, and Personal Injuries in the Third World: Your Place or Mine?" *Boston College Third World Law Journal* 11(2): 249–76.

Jackson, Robert H., 2000, *The Global Covenant: Human Conduct in a World of States*, Oxford University Press.

James, Alan 1978, "International Society," *British Journal of International Studies* 4 (2): 91–106.

Jameson, Fredric 1991, *Postmodernism, or the Cultural Logic of Late Capitalism*, Durham, NC: Duke University Press.

Janis, M. W. 1983, "The Ambiguity of Equity in International Law," *Brooklyn Journal of International Law* 9 (1): 7–34.

1984 a, "Individuals as Subjects of International Law," *Cornell International Law Journal* 17 (1): 61–78.

1984 b, "Jeremy Bentham and the Fashioning of 'International Law'," *American Journal of International Law* 78 (2): 405–18.

Jenks, Edward 1909, "The Early History of Negotiable Instruments," in *Select Essays in Anglo-American Legal History*, vol. III, pp. 50–71.

Jessop, Bob 1980, "On Recent Marxist Theories of Law, the State, and Juridico-Political Ideology," *International Journal of the Sociology of Law* 8 (4): 339–68.

Johns, Fleur 1994, "The Invisibility of the Transnational Corporation: An Analysis of International Law and Legal Theory," *Melbourne University Law Review* 19 (4): 893–923.

Jones, Glower W. 1989, "Warranties in International Sales: UN Convention on Contracts for the International Sale of Goods Compared to the US Uniform Commercial Code on Sales," *International Business Lawyer* 17 (11): 497–500.

Jones, William C. 1958, "An Inquiry into the History of the Adjudication of Mercantile Disputes in Great Britain and the United States," *University of Chicago Law Review* 25 (3): 445–64.

Kahler, Miles 1997, "Inventing International Relations: International Relations Theory After 1945," in M. W. Doyle and G. J. Ikenberry (eds.), *New Thinking in International Relations Theory*, Boulder, CO: Westview Press, pp. 20–53.

Kearney, Neil 1999, "Corporate Codes of Conduct: The Privatized Application of Labour Standards," in Picciotto and Mayne (eds.), 1999, pp. 205–220.

Keller, William and Louis W. Pauly 1997, "Globalization at Bay," *Current History* 96 (613): 370–6.

Kelsen, Hans 1952, *Principles of International Law*, New York: Rinehart.
1961, *General Theory of Law and the State*, New York: Russell & Russell.
1967, *Pure Theory of Law*, Berkeley: University of California Press.
Kennedy, David 1980, "Theses About International Law Discourse," *German Yearbook of International Law* 23: 353–91.
1985, "International Legal Education," *Harvard International Law Journal* 26 (2): 361–84.
1985–86,"Critical Theory, Structuralism and Contemporary Legal Scholarship," *New England Law Review* 21 (2): 209–89.
1987 a, *International Legal Structures*, Baden-Baden: Nomos.
1987 b, "The Move to Institutions," *Cardozo Law Review* 8 (5): 841–988.
1987 c, "The Sources of International Law," *American University Journal of International Law and Policy* 2 (1): 1–96.
1988, "A New Stream of International Law Scholarship,"*Wisconsin International Law Journal* 7 (1): 1–49.
1991, "Turning to Market Democracy: A Tale of Two Architectures," *Harvard International Law Journal* 32 (2): 373–96.
Kennedy, Duncan 1982, "The Stages of the Decline of the Public/Private Distinction," *University of Pennsylvania Law Review* 130 (6): 1,349–57.
1985, "The Role of Law in Economic Thought: Essays on the Fetishism of Commodities," *The American University Law Review* 34 (4): 939–1001.
Keohane, Robert O. 1984, *After Hegemony*, Princeton University Press.
1989, *International Institutions and State Power: Essays in International Relations Theory*, Boulder, CO: Westview Press.
and Lisa Martin 1995, "The Promise of Institutionalist Theory," *International Security* 20 (1): 39–51.
Keohane, Robert O, Andrew Moravcsik, and Anne-Marie Slaughter 2000, "Legalized Dispute Resolution: Interstate and Transnational," *International Organization* 54 (3): 457–88.
Kim, Nancy 1993, "Toward a Feminist Theory of Human Rights: Straddling the Fence Between Western Imperialism and Uncritical Absolutism," *Columbia Human Rights Law Review* 25 (1): 49–105.
Kindred, Hugh M., J.-G. Castel, W. Graham, A. De Mestral, L. Reif, I. Vlasic, and S. Williams 1993, *International Law: Chiefly as Interpreted and Applied in Canada*, 5th edn, Toronto: Emond Montgomery Publishers Ltd.
Klare, Karl 1979, "Law-Making as Praxis," *Telos* 40: 123–35.
1982, "The Public/Private Distinction in Labor Law," *University of Pennsylvania Law Review* 130: (6): 1,358–422.
Kopelmanas, Lazare 1964, "International Conventions and Standard Contracts as Means of Escaping from the Application of Municipal Law – II," in Schmitthoff, 1964 b, pp. 118–26.
Koskenniemi, Martti 1989, *From Apology to Utopia: The Structure of International Legal Argument*, Helsinki: Finnish Lawyers' Publishing CO.
1991, "The Future of Statehood," *Harvard International Law Journal* 32 (2): 397–410.

Krasner, Stephen (ed.) 1983 a, *International Regimes*, Ithaca: Cornell University Press.

Krasner, Stephen 1983 b, "Structural Causes and Regime Consequences: Regimes as Intervening Variables," in Krasner (ed.), *International Regimes*, pp. 1–21.

1993, "Westphalia and All That," in Goldstein and Keohane, 1993, pp. 235–64.

1995, "Power Politics, Institutions, and Transnational Relations," in Risse-Kappen, 1995 b, pp. 257–79.

1997, "Pervasive Not Perverse: Semi-Sovereigns as the Global Norm," *Cornell International Law Journal* 30 (3): 651–80.

Kratochwil, Friedrich 1989, *Rules, Norms, and Decisions: On the Conditions of Practical and Legal Reasoning in International Relations and Domestic Affairs*, Cambridge University Press.

2000, "How Do Norms Matter?" in Byers, 2000, pp. 35–68.

Kratochwil, Friedrich and John Ruggie 1986, "A State of the Art on the Art of the State," *International Organization* 40 (4): 753–76.

Kronstein, Heinrich 1963, "Arbitration is Power," *New York University Law Review* 38 (June): 661–700.

Kymlicka, Will 1992, "Liberal Individualism and Liberal Neutrality," in James Sterba (ed.), *Justice: Alternative Political Perspectives*, 2nd edn, Belmont, CA: Wadsworth Publishing Company., pp. 252–72.

Lando, Ole 1985, "The *Lex Mercatoria* in International Commercial Arbitration," *International and Comparative Law Quarterly* 34 (October): 747–68.

Langen, Eugen 1973, *Transnational Commercial Law*, Leiden: A. W. Sijthoff.

Lansing, Paul 1980, "The Change in American Attitude to the International Unification of Sales Law Movement and UNCITRAL," *American Business Law Journal* 18 (4): 269–81.

Lasswell, Harold and Myres McDougal 1943, "Legal Education and Public Policy: Professional Training in the Public Interest," *Yale Law Journal* 52 (2): 203–95.

Lasswell, Harold and Michael Reisman 1968, "Theories About International Law: Prologue to a Configurative Jurisprudence," *Virginia Journal of International Law* 8 (2): 188–299.

Lauterpacht, Sir Hirsch 1946, "The Grotian Tradition in International Law," *British Yearbook of International Law* 23: 1–53.

Lecuyer-Thieffry, Christine and Patrick Thieffry 1990, "Negotiating Settlement of Disputes Provisions in International Business Contracts: Recent Developments in Arbitration and Other Processes," *The Business Lawyer* 45 (February): 577–623.

Leebron, David W. 1995, "Lying Down with Procrustes: An Analysis of Harmonization Claims," in Ziegel (ed.), 1995, pp. 1–61.

Lenin, V. I. 1939, *Imperialism: The Highest Stage of Capitalism*, New York: International Publishers.

Lincoln, Bruce 1991, *Authority: Construction and Corrosion*, University of Chicago Press.

Linklater, Andrew 1982, *Men and Citizens in the Theory of International Relations*, London: The Macmillan Press.

1990, *Beyond Realism and Marxism: Critical Theory and International Relations*, London: Macmillan.

Liu, Ge and Alexander Lourie 1995, "International Commercial Arbitration in China: History, New Developments, and Current Practice," *The John Marshall Law Review* 28 (3): 539–66.

Lopez, R. 1971, *The Commercial Revolution of the Middle Ages, 950–1350*, Cambridge University Press.

Lorenzen, Ernest G. 1919, "Causa and Consideration in the Law of Contracts," *Yale Law Journal* 28 (7): 621–46.

Loucaides, L. G. 1990, "Personality and Privacy Under the European Convention on Human Rights," *The British Yearbook of International Law* 61: 175–97.

Lukes, Stephen 1990, "Perspectives on Authority," in Raz (ed.), 1990 a, pp. 203–17.

Mabey, Nick 1999, "Defending the Legacy of Rio: The Civil Society Campaign against the MAI," in Picciotto and Mayne (eds.), 1999, pp. 60–81.

McCahery, Joseph and Sol Picciotto 1995, "Creative Lawyering and the Dynamics of Business Regulation," in Dezalay and Sugarman (eds.), 1995, pp. 238–74.

McClendon, J. Stewart (ed.) 1993, *Survey of International Arbitration Sites*, New York: American Arbitration Association.

McConnaughay, Philip 1999, "The Risks and Virtues of Lawlessness: A 'Second Look' at International Commercial Arbitration," *Northwestern University Law Review* 93 (2): 453–523.

McDougal, Myres 1953, "International Law, Power, and Policy: A Contemporary Conception," *Recueil des Cours* 82: 137–258.

McDougal, Myres and Harold Lasswell 1959, "The Identification and Appraisal of Diverse Systems of Public Order," *American Journal of International Law* 53 (1): 1–29.

McNair, Lord 1970, "A Note on the History of the Commercial Court," *Law Quarterly Review* 86 (343): 313–17.

Macpherson, Crawford Brough 1962, *The Political Theory of Possessive Individualism*, New York: Oxford University Press.

Maine, Sir Henry Sumner 1885, *Ancient Law: Its Connection with the Early History of Society and Its Relations to Modern Ideas*, London: John Murray.

Malanczuk, Peter (ed.) 1997, *Akehurst's Modern Introduction to International Law*, 7th rev. edn, London and New York: Routledge.

Malynes, Gerard de 1981, *Consuetudo, vel Lex Mercatoria: or, Ancient Law Merchant* (1686), vol. I, reprinted, Abingdon: Professional Books.

Mann, Michael 1986, *The Sources of Social Power*, vol I, New York: Cambridge University Press.

Marchand, M and A. Runyan (eds.) 1999, *Gender and Global Restructuring*, London: Routledge.

Marcuse, Herbert 1972 a, "The Foundation of Historical Materialism," in Herbert Marcuse, *Studies in Critical Philosophy* (1932), trans. Joris de Bres, London: New Left Books, pp. 1–48.

1972 b,"Industrialization and Capitalism in the Work of Max Weber," in Herbert Marcuse, *Negations: Essays in Critical Theory*, London: Penguin University Books, pp. 201–26.

Marx, Karl 1976, *Capital: A Critique of Political Economy*, vol. I, trans. Ben Fowkes, London: Penguin Books.

Marx, Karl and F. Engels 1965, *The Communist Manifesto*, New York: Washington Square Press.

Matteucci, Mario 1960, "The Unification of Commercial Law," *Journal of Business Law* 137–43.

1977, "UNIDROIT: The First Fifty Years," in UNIDROIT, *New Directions in International Trade Law*, New York: Oceana Publications, pp. xvii–xxv.

Mayer, Carl J. 1990, "Personalizing the Impersonal: Corporations and the Bill of Rights," *The Hastings Law Journal* 41 (3): 577–667.

Mayne, Ruth 1999, "Regulating TNCs: The Role of Voluntary and Governmental Approaches," in Picciotto and Mayne (eds.), 1999, pp. 235–54.

Mears, Thomas L. 1908, "The History of the Admiralty Jurisdiction," in *Select Essays in Anglo-American Legal History*, vol. II, pp. 312–64.

Mearsheimer, John 1994–95, "The False Promise of International Institutions," *International Security* 19 (3): 5–49.

Mendolvitz, Saul 1975, *On the Creation of a Just World Order: Preferred Worlds for the 1990s*, New York: The Free Press.

Michalet, C. A. 1991, "Strategic Partnerships and the Changing Internationalization Process" in Lynn Mytelka (ed.), *Strategic Partnerships: States, Firms and International Competition*, London: Pinter, pp. 35–50.

1994, "Transnational Corporations and the Changing International Economic System," *Transnational Corporations* 3 (1): 9–21.

Milgrom, Paul R., Douglass C. North, and Barry R. Weingast 1990, "The Role of Institutions in the Revival of Trade: The Law Merchant, Private Judges, and the Champagne Fairs," *Economics and Politics* 2 (1): 1–23.

Mitchell, William 1904, *An Essay on the Early History of the Law Merchant*, Cambridge University Press.

1909, "Early Forms of Partnerships," in *Select Essays in Anglo-American Legal History*, vol. III, pp. 183–94.

Mittelman, James H. (ed.) 1996, *Globalization: Critical Reflections*, Boulder, CO: Lynne Rienner Press.

Monaco, Riccardo 1977, "The Scientific Activity of UNIDROIT," in UNIDROIT, *New Directions in International Trade Law*, New York: Oceana Publications, pp. xvii–xxxix.

Morgenthau, Hans 1948, *Politics Among Nations: The Struggle for Power and Peace*, New York: Knopf.

Muchlinski, Peter T. 1995, *Multinational Enterprises and the Law*, Oxford: Blackwell.

1997, "'Global Bukowina' Examined: Viewing the Multinational Enterprise as a Transnational Law-Making Community," in Teubner (ed.), 1997 a, pp. 79–108.

Murphy, Cornelius F. 1961–2, "Medieval Theory and Products Liability," *Boston College Industrial and Commercial Law Review* 3 (1): 29–37.

Murphy, Craig 1994, *International Organization and Industrial Change: Global Governance Since 1850*, New York: Oxford University Press.

Murphy, Kent 1981, "The Traditional View of Public Policy and *Ordre Public* in Private International Law," *Georgia Journal of International and Comparative Law* 11 (3): 591–615.

Naón, Horacio A. Grigera 1982, "The UN Convention on Contracts for the International Sale of Goods," in Horn and Schmitthoff (eds.), 1982, pp. 89–124.

1993, "ICC Arbitration and Developing Countries," *ICSID Review – Foreign Investment Law Journal* 8: 116–22.

Nardin, Terry 1983, *Law, Morality, and the Relations of States*, Princeton University Press.

Neufeld, Mark 1995, *The Restructuring of International Relations Theory*, Cambridge University Press.

North, Douglass C. 1981, *Structure and Change in Economic History*, New York: Norton.

1990, *Institutions, Institutional Change and Economic Performance*, Cambridge University Press.

1991, "Institutions, Transaction Costs, and the Rise of Merchant Empires," in Tracy (ed.), 1991, pp. 22–40.

North, Douglass C., and Robert P. Thomas 1973, *The Rise of the Western World: A New Economic History*, Cambridge University Press.

Notes 1986, "Liability of Parent Corporations for Hazardous Waste Cleanup and Damages," *Harvard Law Review* 99 (5): 986–1,003.

Notes of Cases 1984, "The Multinational and the Antiquities of Company Law," *The Modern Law Review* 47(1): 87–92.

O'Neill, John 1986, "The Disciplinary Society: From Weber to Foucault," *British Journal of Sociology* 37 (1): 42–60.

Owen, Roger and Bob Sutcliffe (eds.) 1972, *Studies in the Theory of Imperialism*, London: Longman.

Panitch, Leo 1996, "Rethinking the Role of the State," in Mittelman (ed.), 1996, pp. 83–113.

Pashukanis, Evgenii 1978, *Law and Marxism: A General Theory*, trans. Barbara Einhorn, ed. Chris Arthur, London: Pluto Press.

Patchel, Kathleen 1993, "Interest Group Politics, Federalism, and the Uniform Laws Process: Some Lessons from the Uniform Commercial Code," *Minnesota Law Review* 78 (1): 83–164.

Patterson, Elizabeth 1986, "United Nations Convention on Contracts for the International Sale of Goods: Unification and the Tension Between Compromise and Domination," *Stanford Journal of International Law* 22 (2): 263–303.

Paul, Joel 1988, "The Isolation of Private International Law," *Wisconsin International Law Journal* 7 (1): 149–78.

1991, "Comity in International Law,' *Harvard International Law Journal* 32 (1): 1–79.

Paulsson, Jan 1981, "Arbitration Unbound: Award Detached from the Law of Its Country of Origin," *International and Comparative Law Quarterly* 30 (2): 358–87.

Pauly, Louis W. and Simon Reich 1997, "National Structures and Multinational Corporate Behavior: Enduring Differences in the Age of Globalization," *International Organization* 51 (1): 1–30.

Pearson, M. N. 1991, "Merchants and States," in Tracy (ed.), 1991, pp. 41–116.

Perillo, Joseph 1994, "UNIDROIT Principles of International Commercial Contracts: The Black-Letter Test and a Review," *Fordham Law Review* 63 (2): 281–344.

Perraton, Jonathan, David Goldblatt, David Held, and Anthony McGrew 1997, "The Globalisation of Economic Activity," *New Political Economy* 2 (2): 257–77.

Peterson, V. S. and A. Runyan 1993, *Global Gender Issues*, Boulder, CO: Westview Press.

Pettman, J. 1996, *Worlding Women: A Feminist International Politics*, London: Routledge.

Pfund, Peter and G. Taft 1986, "Congress' Role in the International Unification of Private Law," *Georgia Journal of International and Comparative Law* 16 Supp: 671–86.

Picciotto, Sol 1979, "The Theory of the State, Class Struggle and the Rule of Law," in Bob Fine, Richard Kinsey, John Lea, Sol Picciotto, and Jock Young (eds.), *Capitalism and the Rule of Law: From Deviancy Theory to Marxism*, London: Hutchinson & Co, pp. 164–77.

1988, "The Control of Transnational Capital and the Democratisation of the International State," *Journal of Law and Society* 15 (1): 58–76.

1996, "The Regulatory Criss-Cross: Interaction between Jurisdictions and the Construction of Global Regulatory Networks," in Bratton, McCahery, Picciotto, and Scott (eds.), 1996, pp. 89–123.

1999 a, "Introduction: What Rules for the World Economy?" in Picciotto and Mayne (eds.), 1999, pp. 1–26.

1999 b, "A Critical Assessment of the MAI," in Picciotto and Mayne (eds.), 1999, pp. 82–105.

2001, "Democratizing Globalism," in Daniel Drache (ed.), *The Market or the Public Domain: Global Governance and the Asymmetry of Power*, London: Routledge, pp. 335–59.

Picciotto, Sol and Ruth Mayne (eds.) 1999, *Regulating International Business: Beyond Liberalization*, Basingstoke: The Macmillan Press; and New York: St. Martin's Press.

Pirenne, Henri 1937, *Economic and Social History of Medieval Europe*, London: Kegan Paul.

Polanyi, Karl 1944, *The Great Transformation: The Political and Economic Origins of Our Time*, Boston, MA: Beacon Press.

Pollock, Frederick 1901, "The Early History of the Law Merchant in England," *The Law Quarterly Review* 67 (3): 232–51.

Pollock, Frederick and Frederic W. Maitland 1898, *History of English Law*, vol. I, Cambridge University Press.

Posner, R. A. 1980 a, "The Ethical and Political Basis of the Efficiency Norm in Common Law Adjudication," *Hofstra Law Review* 8 (3): 487–507.

1980 b, "A Theory of Primitive Society, with Special Reference to Law," *Journal of Law and Economics* 23 (1): 1–54.

1986, *Economic Analysis of Law*, Toronto: Little Brown.

Potter, Patrick J. 1989, "Note, International Commercial Arbitration in the United States: Considering Whether to Adopt UNCITRAL's Model Law," *Michigan Journal of International Law* 10 (3): 912–34.

Poulantzas, Nicos 1973, *Political Power and Social Classes*, London: New Left Books and Sheed and Ward.

Powell, Robert 1994, "Anarchy in International Relations Theory: The Neorealist–Neoliberal Debate," *International Organization* 48 (2): 313–44.

Price, Jacob M. 1991, "Transaction Costs: A Note on Merchant Credit and the Organization of Private Trade," in Tracy (ed.), 1991, pp. 276–97.

Purvis, Nigel 1991, "Critical Legal Studies in Public International Law," *Harvard International Law Journal* 32 (1): 81–127.

Ramberg, Jan 1982, "Incoterms 1980," in Horn and Schmitthoff (eds.), 1982, pp. 137– 52.

2000, *ICC Guide to Incoterms 2000*, Paris: ICC, Pub. No. 620.

Raz, Joseph (ed.) 1990 a, *Authority*, Oxford: Basil Blackwell.

(ed.) 1990 b, "Introduction," Raz (ed.), 1990 a, pp. 1–19.

Reese, Willis L. M. 1985, "The Hague Conference on Private International Law: Some Observations," *International Lawyer* 19 (3): 881–6.

Risse-Kappen, Thomas (ed.) 1995 a, *Bringing Transnational Relations Back In: Non-State Actors, Domestic Structures and International Institutions*, Cambridge University Press.

Risse-Kappen Thomas 1995 b, "Structures of Governance and Transnational Relations: What Have We Learned?" in Risse-Kappen, 1995 a, pp. 280–313.

Robé, Jean-Phillipe 1997, "Multinational Enterprises: The Constitution of a Pluralist Legal Order," in Teubner (ed.), 1997 a, pp. 45–78.

Roberts, Adam and Benedict Kingsbury (eds.) 1993, *United Nations, Divided World: The UN's Roles in International Relations*, Oxford: Clarendon Press.

Robertson, Roland 1992, *Globalization: Social Theory and Global Culture*, London and Thousand Oaks, CA: Sage.

Robinson, William 1996, "Globalisation: Nine Theses On Our Epoch," *Race and Class* 38 (2): 13–31.

1998, "Beyond the Nation-State Paradigms: Globalization, Sociology, and the Challenge of Transnational Studies," *Sociological Forum* 13 (4): 561–94.

Rochester, J. Martin 1986, "The Rise and Fall of International Organization as a Field of Study," *International Organization* 40 (4): 777–813.

1995, "The United Nations in a New World Order: Reviving the Theory and Practice of International Organization," in Charles W. Kegley (ed.), *Controversies in International Relations Theory: Realism and the Neoliberal Challenge*, New York: St. Martin's Press, pp. 199–221.

Romany, Celina 1993, "Women as *Aliens*: A Feminist Critique of the Public/Private Distinction in International Human Rights Law," *Harvard Human Rights Journal* 6: 87–125.

Ronit, Karsten and Volker Schneider (eds.) 2000, *Private Organizations in Global Politics*, London: Routledge.

Rose, Nikolas 1977, "Fetishism and Ideology: A Review of Theoretical Problems," *Ideology and Consciousness* 2 (Autumn): 27–54.

Rosenberg, Justin 1994, *The Empire of Civil Society: A Critique of the Realist Theory of International Relations*, London: Verso.

Rosett, A. 1984, "Critical Reflections on the United Nations Convention on Contracts for the International Sale of Goods," *Ohio State Law Journal* 45 (2): 265–305.

Rowe, Michael C. 1982, "The Contribution of the ICC to the Development of International Trade Law," in Horn and Schmitthoff (eds.), 1982, pp. 51–60.

Ruggie, John G. 1982, "International Regimes, Transactions, and Change: Embedded Liberalism in the Post-war Order," *International Organization* 36 (4): 379–415.

1993 a, "Territoriality and Beyond: Problematizing Modernity in International Relations," *International Organization* 47 (1): 139–74.

Ruggie, John G. (ed.) 1993 b, *Multilateralism Matters: The Theory and Praxis of an Institutional Form*, New York: Columbia University Press.

Ruggie, John G. 1994, "Trade, Protectionism and the Future of Welfare Capitalism," *Journal of International Affairs* 48 (1): 1–11.

1995 a, "At Home Abroad, Abroad at Home: International Liberalisation and Domestic Stability in the New World Economy," *Millennium: Journal of International Studies* 24 (3): 507–26.

1995 b, "The False Premise of Realism," *International Security* 20 (1): 62–70.

Rupert, Mark 1993, "Alienation, Capitalism and the Inter-state System: Toward a Marxian/Gramscian Critique," in Gill, 1993 a, pp. 67–92.

1995, *Producing Hegemony: The Politics of Mass Production and American Global Power*, Cambridge University Press.

1997 a, "Globalisation and American Common Sense: Struggling to Make Sense of a Post-hegemonic World," *New Political Economy* 2 (1): 105–16.

1997 b, "Globalization and Contested Common Sense in the United States," in Gill and Mittelman (eds.), 1997, pp. 138–52.

2000, *Ideologies of Globalization: Contending Visions of World Order*, London and New York: Routledge.

Rupert, Mark and Hazel Smith (eds.) 2002, *Historical Materialism and Globalization*, New York and London: Routledge.

Sanborn, Frederic R. 1930, *Origins of the Early English Maritime and Commercial Law*, London: Century Co.
Santos, Boaventura de Sousa 1982 a, "Law and Community: The Changing Nature of State Power in Late Capitalism," in Richard L. Abel (ed.), *The Politics of Informal Justice, Vol. I: The American Experience*, New York: Academic Press, pp. 249–66.
1982 b, "Popular Justice, Dual Power, and Socialist Strategy," in Beirne and Quinney (eds.), 1982, pp. 364–75.
1985, "On Modes of Production of Law and Social Power," *International Journal of Sociology of Law* 13: 295–336.
1987, "Law: A Map of Misreading: Toward a Postmodern Conception of Law," *Journal of Law and Society* 14 (3): 279–302.
1993, "The Postmodern Transition: Law and Politics," in Austin Sarat and Thomas R. Kearns, *The Fate of Law*, Ann Arbor: University of Michigan Press, pp. 79–118.
1995, *Toward a New Common Sense: Law, Science, and Politics in the Paradigmatic Transition*, London and New York: Routledge.
Sassoon, David M. 1975, *British Shipping Laws: C.I.F. and F.O.B. Contracts*, London: Stevens & Sons.
Sauders, Pieter 1979, "Procedures and Practices Under the UNCITRAL Rules," *American Journal of Comparative Law* 27: 453–68.
Schachter, Oscar 1977,"The Twilight Existence of Nonbinding International Agreements", *The American Journal of International Law* 71 (2): 296–304.
1985, "Sharing the World's Resources," in Falk, Kratochwil, and Mendolvitz (eds.), 1985, pp. 525–46.
Schall, James 1991–2, "Natural Law and the Law of Nations: Some Theoretical Considerations," *Fordham International Law Journal* 15 (4): 997–1030.
Scheuerman, William (ed.) 1996, *The Rule of Law Under Siege: Selected Essays of Franz L. Neumann and Otto Kirchheimer*, Berkeley: University of California Press.
1999, "Economic Globalization and the Rule of Law," *Constellations: An International Journal of Critical and Democratic Theory* 6 (1): 3–25.
2000,"Global Law in Our High Speed Economy," in Volkmar Gessner (ed.), *Rules and Networks: The Legal Culture of Global Business Transactions*, Oxford: Hart Publishing.
2001, "Reflexive Law and the Challenge of Globalization," *The Journal of Political Philosophy* 9 (1): 81–102.
Schlag, Pierre 1991, "The Problem of the Subject," *Texas Law Review* 69 (7): 1,627–1,744.
Schmitthoff, Clive M. 1961, "International Business Law: A New Law Merchant," *Current Law and Social Problems* 2: 129–53.
1964 a, "The Law of International Trade, Its Growth, Formulation, and Operation," in Schmitthoff (ed.), 1964 b, pp. 3–38.
Schmitthoff, Clive M. (ed.) 1964 b, *The Sources of the Law of International Trade*, New York: Praeger.

Schmitthoff, Clive M. 1968, "The Unification or Harmonization of Law by Means of Standard Contracts and General Conditions," *International and Comparative Law Quarterly* 17 (July): 551–70.

1981, *Commercial Law in a Changing Economic Climate*, London: Sweet & Maxwell.

1982, "Nature and Evolution of the Transnational Law of International Commercial Transactions," in Horn and Schmitthoff (eds.), 1982, pp. 19–31.

Scholte, Jan 1997, "Global Capitalism and the State," *International Affairs* 73 (3): 427–52.

Schwartz, Alan and Robert Scott 1995, "The Political Economy of Private Legislatures," *University of Pennsylvania Law Review* 143 (3): 595–654.

Scrutton, Thomas, E. 1907, "Roman Law Influence in Chancery, Church Courts, Admiralty, and the Law Merchant," in *Select Essays in Anglo-American Legal History*, vol. I, pp. 209–47.

1909, "General Survey of the History of the Law Merchant," in *Select Essays in Anglo-American Legal History* (1909), vol. III, pp. 7–15.

Seidl-Hohenveldern, I. 1979, "International Economic 'Soft Law'," in *Recueil Des Cours II, Collected Courses of the Hague Academy of International Law* 163: 165–246.

Selden Society 1892, *Leet Jurisdiction in Norwich*, ed. William Hudson, London: Bernard Quaritch.

1908, *Select Cases Concerning the Law Merchant*, ed. C. Gross, vol. I, London: Bernard Quaritch.

Select Essays in Anglo-American Legal History, 3 vols., 1907–1909, Boston: Little, Brown and Co.

Sempasa, Samson 1992, "Obstacles to International Commercial Arbitration in African Countries," *International and Comparative Law Quarterly* 41 (April): 387–413.

Seward, Allin C. 1987, "After Bhopal: Implications for Parent Company Liability," *The International Lawyer* 21 (3): 695–707.

Shaw, M. N. 1991, *International Law*, 3rd edn, Cambridge University Press.

1997, *International Law*, 4th edn, Cambridge University Press.

Shaw, Martin 1994, *Global Society and International Relations: Sociological Concepts and Political Perspectives*, Cambridge: Polity Press.

Shklar, Judith 1964, *Legalism*, Cambridge, MA: Harvard University Press.

Silbey, Susan 1997, "Let Them Eat Cake: Globalization, Postmodern Colonialism, and the Possibilities of Justice," *Law and Society Review* 31 (2): 207–35.

Simpson, A. W. B. 1975, *A History of the Common Law of Contract*, Oxford: Clarendon Press.

Sklair, Leslie 2001, *The Transnational Capitalist Class*, Oxford: Blackwell Publishers.

Slaughter, Anne-Marie 1994, "The Liberal Agenda for Peace: International Relations Theory and the Future of the United Nations," *Transnational Law and Contemporary Problems* 4 (2): 377–419.

Slaughter-Burley, Anne-Marie 1993, "International Law and International Relations: A Dual Agenda," *American Journal of International Law* 87 (2): 205–39.

Slaughter, Anne-Marie, Andrew S. Tulumello, and Stepan Wood 1998, "International Law and International Relations Theory: A New Generation of Interdisciplinary Scholarship," *American Journal of International Law* 92 (3): 367–97.

Smit, Hans 1986, "The Future of International Commercial Arbitration: A Single Transnational Institution?" *Columbia Journal of Transnational Law* 25 (1): 9–34.

Smith, Hazel 1996, "The Silence of the Academics: International Social Theory, Historical Materialism and Political Values," *Review of International Studies* 22: 191–212.

Smith, Steve 1995, "The Self-images of a Discipline: A Genealogy of International Relations Theory" in Booth and Smith (eds.), 1995, pp. 1–37.

Sono, Kazuaki 1988, "Restoration of the Rule of Reason in Contract Formation: Has There Been a Civil and Common Law Disparity?" *Cornell International Law Journal* 21(3): 477–86.

Special Issue on the Legalization of World Politics 2000, *International Organization* 54 (3).

Spitzer, Steven 1983, "Marxist Perspectives in the Sociology of Laws," *Annual Review of Sociology* 9: 103–24.

Spruyt, Hendrick 1994, "Institutional Selection in International Relations: State Anarchy as Order," *International Organization* 48 (4): 527–57.

Staker, Christopher 1990, "Diplomatic Protection of Private Business Companies: Determining Corporate Personality for International Law Purposes," *The British Yearbook of International Law* 61: 155–74.

Starke, J. G. 1936, "The Relation Between Private and Public International Law," *The Law Quarterly Review* 207: 395–401.

Steans, J. 1998, *Gender and International Relations*, Oxford: Polity Press.

Stevenson, J. 1952, "The Relationship of Private International to Public International Law," *Columbia Law Review* 52 (5): 561–88.

Stoecker, Christoph 1990, "The *Lex Mercatoria*: To What Extent Does It Exist?" *Journal of International Arbitration* 7 (1): 101–25.

Story, Joseph 1834, *Commentaries on the Conflict of Laws, Foreign and Domestic in Regard to Contracts, Rights and Remedies, Especially in Regard to Marriages, Divorces, Wills, Successions and Judgments*, Boston: Hill and Gray and Co.

Strange, Susan 1983, "*Cave! Hic dragones*: A Critique of Regimes Analysis," in Krasner, 1983 a, pp. 337–54.

1994, "Global Government and Global Opposition," in *Politics in an Interdependent World: Essays Presented to Ghita Ionescu*, Aldershot: Edward Elgar, pp. 20–33.

1995 a, "The Defective State," *Daedalus* 124 (2): 55–74.

1995 b, "Political Economy and International Relations," in Booth and Smith (eds.), 1995, pp. 154–74.

1996, *The Retreat of the State: The Diffusion of Power in the World Economy*, Cambridge University Press.

Sturley, M. F. 1987, "International Uniform Laws in National Courts: The Influence of Domestic Law in Conflicts of Interpretation," *Virginia Journal of International Law* 27 (4): 729–803.

Suganami, Hidemi 1989, *The Domestic Analogy and World Order Proposals*, Cambridge University Press.

Sylvester, Christine 1994, *Feminist Theory and International Relations in a Postmodern Era*, Cambridge University Press.

Tallon, Denis 1983, "Civil Law and Commercial Law," in *International Encyclopedia of Comparative Law: Specific Contracts*, vol, III, ch. 2, Tübingen: Mohr; The Hague, Boston, and London: Martinus Nijhoff, pp. 103–14.

Tawney, R. H. 1962, *Religion and the Rise of Capitalism: A Historical Study*, Gloucester, MA: Peter Smith.

Tesón, Fernando 1990, "International Obligation and the Theory of Hypothetical Consent," *Yale Journal of International Law* 15 (1): 84–120.

Tetley, William 1978, *Marine Cargo Claims*, 2nd edn, Toronto: Butterworths.

Teubner, Gunther (ed.) 1997 a, *Global Law Without a State*, Aldershot, England and Brookfield, USA: Dartmouth Publishing Company Ltd.

(ed.) 1997 b, "'Global Bukowina:' Legal Pluralism in the World Society," in Teubner (ed.), 1997 a, pp. 3–30.

Thayer, Philp W. 1936, "Comparative Law and the Law Merchant," *Brooklyn Law Review* 6 (2): 139–54.

Thompson, E. P. 1971, "The Moral Economy of the English Crowd in the Eighteenth Century," *Past and Present* 50 (February): 76–136.

1975, *Whigs and Hunters: The Origin of the Black Act*, London: Penguin Books.

Tickner, Ann 1992, *Gender in International Relations*, New York: Columbia University Press.

Tollefson, Chris 1993, "Corporate Constitutional Rights and the Supreme Court of Canada," *Queens Law Journal* 19 (1): 309–49.

2002, "Games Without Frontiers: Investor Claims and Citizen Submissions Under the NAFTA Regime," *The Yale Journal of International Law* 27 (1): 141–91.

Tracy, James D. (ed.) 1991, *The Political Economy of Merchant Empires*, Cambridge University Press.

Trakman, Leon E. 1983, *The Law Merchant: The Evolution of Commercial Law*, Littleton, CO: Fred B. Rothman and Co.

Trimble, Phillip 1985, "International Trade and the 'Rule of Law'," *Michigan Law Review* 83 (February): 1,016–32.

1990, "International Law, World Order and Critical Legal Studies," *Stanford Law Review* 42 (February): 811–45.

Twining, William 1996, "Globalization and Legal Theory: Some Local Implications," *Current Legal Problems* 49 (2): 1–42.

Udovitch, Abraham 1962, "At the Origins of the Western Commenda: Islam, Israel, Byzantium?" *Speculum* 37 (2): 198–207.

Unger, Roberto 1976, *Law in Modern Society: Toward a Criticism of Social Theory*, New York: Free Press.

Vagts, Detlev F. 1970, "The Multinational Enterprise: A New Challenge for Transnational Law," *Harvard Law Review* 83 (4): 739–92.

Vance, William R. 1909, "Early History of Insurance Law," in *Select Essays in Anglo-American Legal History*, vol. III, pp. 98–116.

Van der Pijl, Kees 1998, *Transnational Classes and International Relations*, London and New York: Routledge.

Verdross, Alfred and Heribert F. Koeck 1983, "Natural Law: The Tradition of Universal Reason and Authority," in Ronald St. J. Macdonald and Douglas M. Johnston (eds), *The Structure and Process of International Law: Essays in Legal Philosophy, Doctrine and Theory*, The Hague: Martinus Nijhoff, pp. 17–50.

Vincent, Andrew 1993, "Marx and Law," *Journal of Law and Society* 20 (4): 371–97.

Viner, Jacob 1978, *Religious Thought and Economic Society*, Durham, NC: Duke University Press.

Von Caemmerer, Ernst 1964, "The Influence of the Law of International Trade on the Development and Character of Commercial Law in the Civil Law Countries," in Schmitthoff, 1964 b, pp. 88–100.

Von Glahn, Gerhard 1996, *Law Among Nations: An Introduction to Public International Law*, 7th edn, Boston, MA: Allyn and Bacon.

Walker, R.B.J. 1987, *One World, Many Worlds: Struggles for a Just World Peace*, London: Zed Books.

1993, *Inside/Outside: International Relations as Political Theory*, Cambridge University Press.

Wallerstein, Immanuel 1974, 1980, 1989, *The Modern World-System*, vols. I–III, San Diego, CA: Academy Press.

Waltz, Kenneth 1979, *Theory of International Politics*, Reading, MA: Addison Wesley.

Walzer, Michael 1984, "Liberalism and the Art of Separation," *Political Theory* 12 (3): 315–30.

Waring, Marilyn 1991, "Gender and International Law: Women and the Right to Development," *Australian Yearbook of International Law* 12: 177–89.

Watson, Adam 1992, *The Evolution of International Society: A Comparative Analysis*, New York: Routledge.

Weber, Cynthia 1995, *Simulating Sovereignty: Intervention, the State and Symbolic Exchange*, Cambridge University Press.

Weber, Max 1966, *Law and Economy in Society*, ed. Max Rheinstein, Cambridge, MA: Harvard University Press.

1978 a, *Economy and Society*, vols. I and II, ed. Guenther Roth and Claus Wittich, Berkeley: University of California Press.

1978 b, *The Protestant Ethic and the Spirit of Capitalism*, London: Allen and Unwin.

Weiss, Andrew Glenn 1986, "The Status of the UNCITRAL Model Law on International Commercial Arbitration Vis-à-Vis the ICC, LCIA, and UNCITRAL Arbitration Rules: Conflict or Complement?" *Syracuse Journal of International Law and Commerce* 13 (2): 367–90.

Wendt, Alexander 1992, "Anarchy is What States Make of It: The Social Construction of Power Politics," *International Organization* 46 (2): 391–425.

1994, "Collective Identity Formation and the International State," *American Political Science Review* 88 (2): 384–96.

1995, "Constructing International Politics," *International Security* 20 (1): 71–81.

Whitworth, Sandra 1994, *Feminism and International Relations: Towards a Political Economy of Gender in Interstate and Non-governmental Institutions*, London: Macmillan.

Wiener, Jarrod 1999, *Globalisation and Harmonisation of Laws*, New York: Pinter.

Wight, Martin 1966, "Why is There No International Theory?" in Butterfield and Wight (eds.), 1966, pp. 17–34.

Winship, Peter 1988, "Private International Law and the UN Sales Convention," *Cornell International Law Journal* 21 (3): 487–534.

Wolff, R. P. 1990, "The Conflict Between Authority and Autonomy," in Raz (ed.), 1990 a, pp. 20–31.

Wood, Ellen Meiksins 1995, *Democracy Against Capitalism: Renewing Historical Materialism*, Cambridge University Press.

Wright, Shelly 1991, "Economic Rights and Social Justice: A Feminist Analysis of Some International Human Rights Conventions," *Australian Yearbook of International Law* 12: 242–64.

Yasuaki, Onuma (ed.) 1993, *Normative Approaches to War: Peace, War, Justice in Hugo Grotius*, Oxford University Press.

Yakovlev, Andrei 1996, "International Commercial Arbitration Proceedings and Russian Courts," *Journal of International Arbitration* 13 (1): 37–63.

Young, Gary 1979, "Marx on Bourgeois Law," *Research in Law and Sociology* 2: 133–67.

Young, Oran 1979, *Compliance and Public Authority: A Theory with International Implications*, Baltimore: Johns Hopkins University Press.

Zacher, Mark W. with Brent Sutton 1996, *Governing Global Networks: International Regimes for Transportation and Communications*, Cambridge University Press.

Zalewski, Marysia and J. Parpart 1998, *The "Man Question" in International Relations*, Oxford: Westview Press.

Ziegel, Jacob (ed.) 1995, *Twenty-fifth Annual Workshop on Commercial and Consumer Law "Harmonization and Change" Workshop Papers and Other Materials*, Toronto: S. N.

Cases cited

Earl of Oxford's Case (1615) 1 Rep. Ch. 1.
Lochner v. New York 198 US 45 (1905).
Mitsubishi v. Soler Chrysler-Plymouth, Inc. 473 US 614 (1985).
Pillans v. van Mierop 3 Burr. 1663, 97 Eng. Rep. 1035 (KB 1765).
Reparations for Injuries Suffered in the Service of the United Nations Case [1949] ICJ Rep. 174, 180.

International treaties and United Nations documents

General Assembly Resolutions

General Assembly Resolution 2205 (21) December 17, 1966 *Official Records of the General Assembly*, Twenty-first Session, Annexes, agenda item 88, UN Doc. A/6396 and Add. 1 and 2, reprinted in *UNCITRAL Yearbook*, vol. I, 65–6.

Significant United Nations reports

Development of Guidelines on the Role and Social Responsibilities of the Private Sector, Report of the Secretary General of the United Nations 24 February, A/AC. 253/21, February 24, 2000.

Report of the Secretary-General on the Progressive Development of the Law of International Trade, UN Doc. A/6396, reprinted in *UNCITRAL Yearbook* 1968–70, vol I, pp. 18–45.

Report of the United Nations Commission on International Trade Law on the Work of its Ninth Session, UN Doc. A/Conf. 31/17, reprinted in *UNCITRAL Yearbook* 1978, vol. IX, pp. 3–9.

Report of the United Nations on the Progressive Development of the Law of International Trade, UN Doc. A/6396, reprinted in *UNCITRAL Yearbook* 1968–70, vol. I, pp. 58–65.

"Unification of the Law of International Trade: Note by the Secretariat," *Official Records of the General Assembly, Twentieth Session*, Annexes, agenda item 92, UN Doc. A/C. 6/L.572, reprinted in *UNCITRAL Yearbook* 1968–73, vol. I, p. 17.

"Working Methods of the Commission: Note by the Secretariat," UN Doc. A/Conf. 9/299, reprinted in *UNCITRAL Yearbook* 1988, vol. XIX, pp. 165–69.

International conventions and model laws

Charter of the United Nations, June 26, 1945, Canada Treaty Series, 1945, No. 7, International Legislation IX, No. 327.

Convention on the Execution of Foreign Arbitral Awards, September 26, 1927, LNTS 92: 301.

Convention on the Limitation Period in the International Sale of Goods (New York, 1974), UN Doc. A/ Conf. 63/15, reprinted in *ILM* 13 (1974): 952–61.

Free Trade Agreement (Can–US), January 2, 1988, Canada Treaty Series, 1989, 3.

General Agreement on Tariffs and Trade, October 30, 1947, 61 Stat. A-11, 55 UNTS: 194.

Guidelines for Procurement under World Bank Loans and IDA Credits, Washington, DC: World Bank, 1992.

ICC Uniform Customs and Practice for Documentary Credits, April 29, 1994, UN Doc. A/CN.9/395.

ICC Uniform Rules for a Combined Transport Document, October 1975, Paris: ICC, Pub. No. 298.

Incoterms 1980, Paris: ICC Series, SARL, 1980.

Incoterms 2000, Paris: ICC, 2000, Pub. No. 620.

Multilaterally Agreed Equitable Principles and Rules for the Control of Restrictive Business Practices, UN Doc. A/Conf.2/35/6.

North American Free Trade Agreement, December 17, 1992, US–Can–Mex; repr. 1993 *ILM* 32: 296.

Protocol on Arbitration Clauses, 24 September 1923, LNTS 27: 158.

Statute of the International Court of Justice, signed 1945; reproduced in Hugh Kindred, Jean-Gabriel Castel, Donald Fleming, William Graham, Armand de Mestral, Linda Reif, Ivan Vlasic, and Sharon Williams 1993, *International Law: Chiefly as Interpreted and Applied in Canada*, Documentary Supplement, Toronto: Emond Montgomery Publications Ltd, pp. 33–44.

UNCITRAL Arbitration Rules, UN Doc. A/31/17.

UNCITRAL Conciliation Rules, UN Doc. A/Conf. 35/17, reprinted in *ILM* 20 (1) (1981): 300–6.

UNCITRAL Model Law on Electronic Commerce, November 11, 1996, UN Doc./A/C.6/51/L8.

UNCITRAL Model Law on International Commercial Arbitration, UN Doc. A/ Conf. A/40/17, reprinted in *UNCITRAL Yearbook* 1986, 16: 393.

UNCITRAL Model Law on Procurement of Goods, Construction and Services, December 9, 1993, UN Doc. A/RES/48/33.

UNCTAD Convention on a Code of Conduct for Liner Conferences, November 30, 1984, UN Doc. TD/B/C.4/Dec/50/XI.

UNCTAD International Code on the Transfer of Technology, June 3, 1970, UN Doc. TD/DEC/113 (6).

UNIDROIT 1994, Principles of International Commercial Contracts, Paris: UNIDROIT.

United Nations Convention on the Carriage of Goods by Sea, 1978 (Hamburg Rules), UN Doc. A/Conf.89/13, Annex 1, reprinted in *ILM* 17 (1978): 603–31.

United Nations Convention on Contracts for the International Sale of Goods (Vienna Sales Convention), UN Doc. A/Conf. 97/19, 178–90, Annex I, reprinted in *ILM* 19 (1980): 668–99.

United Nations Convention on International Bills of Exchange and International Promissory Notes, December 9, 1988, UN Doc. A/RES/43/165; repr. *ILM* 28 (1989): 170.

United Nations Convention on the Liability of Operators of Transport Terminals in International Trade, April 19, 1991, UN Doc. A/Conf. 152/13; repr. *ILM* 30 (1991): 1503.

United Nations Convention on the Recognition and Enforcement of Foreign Arbitral Awards (New York Convention), June 10, 1958, UN Doc. A/Conf.9/22, reprinted in *ILM* 7 (1968): 1,042–62.

Vienna Convention on the Law of Treaties, 1969, 155 UNTS: 331.

York-Antwerp Rules in the General Average 1994, available online: http://www.usaveragadjusters.org/Yorkantwerp.htm

Index

CAMBRIDGE STUDIES IN INTERNATIONAL RELATIONS

Series list continued from page iv

79 *Richard Shapcott*
Justice, community and dialogue in international relations

78 *Phil Steinberg*
The social construction of the ocean

77 *Christine Sylvester*
Feminist international relations
An unfinished journey

76 *Kenneth A. Schultz*
Democracy and coercive diplomacy

75 *David Houghton*
US foreign policy and the Iran hostage crisis

74 *Cecilia Albin*
Justice and fairness in international negotiation

73 *Martin Shaw*
Theory of the global state
Globality as an unfinished revolution

72 *Frank C. Zagare* and *D. Marc Kilgour*
Perfect deterrence

71 *Robert 0' Brien, Anne Marie Goetz, Jan Aart Scholte and Marc Williams*
Contesting global governance
Multilateral economic institutions and global social movements

70 *Roland Bleiker*
Popular dissent, human agency and global politics

69 *Bill McSweeney*
Security, identity and interests
A sociology of international relations

68 *Molly Cochran*
Normative theory in international relations
A pragmatic approach

67 *Alexander Wendt*
Social theory of international politics

66 *Thomas Risse, Stephen C. Ropp and Kathryn Sikkink (eds.)*
The power of human rights
International norms and domestic change

65 *Daniel W. Drezner*
The sanctions paradox
Economic statecraft and international relations

64 *Viva Ona Bartkus*
The dynamic of secession

63 *John A. Vasquez*
The power of power politics
From classical realism to neotraditionalism

62 *Emanuel Adler and Michael Barnett (eds.)*
Security communities

61 *Charles Jones*
E. H. Carr and international relations
A duty to lie

60 *Jeffrey W. Knopf*
Domestic society and international cooperation
The impact of protest on US arms control policy

59 *Nicholas Greenwood Onuf*
The republican legacy in international thought

58 *Daniel S. Geller and J. David Singer*
Nations at war
A scientific study of international conflict

57 *Randall D. Germain*
The international organization of credit
States and global finance in the world economy

56 *N. Piers Ludlow*
Dealing with Britain
The Six and the first UK application to the EEC

55 *Andreas Hasenclever, Peter Mayer and Volker Rittberger*
Theories of international regimes

54 *Miranda A. Schreurs and Elizabeth C. Economy (eds.)*
The internationalization of environmental protection

53 *James N. Rosenau*
Along the domestic–foreign frontier
Exploring governance in a turbulent world

52 *John M. Hobson*
The wealth of states
A comparative sociology of international economic and political change

51 *Kalevi J. Holsti*
The state, war, and the state of war

50 *Christopher Clapham*
Africa and the international system
The politics of state survival

49 *Susan Strange*
The retreat of the state
The diffusion of power in the world economy

48 *William I. Robinson*
Promoting polyarchy
Globalization, US intervention, and hegemony

47 *Roger Spegele*
Political realism in international theory

46 *Thomas J. Biersteker and Cynthia Weber (eds.)*
State sovereignty as social construct

45 *Mervyn Frost*
Ethics in international relations
A constitutive theory

44 *Mark W. Zacher with Brent A. Sutton*
Governing global networks
International regimes for transportation and communications

43 *Mark Neufeld*
The restructuring of international relations theory

42 *Thomas Risse-Kappen (ed.)*
Bringing transnational relations back in
Non-state actors, domestic structures and international institutions

41 *Hayward R. Alker*
Rediscoveries and reformulations
Humanistic methodologies for international studies

40 *Robert W. Cox with Timothy J. Sinclair*
Approaches to world order

39 *Jens Bartelson*
A genealogy of sovereignty

38 *Mark Rupert*
Producing hegemony
The politics of mass production and American global power

37 *Cynthia Weber*
Simulating sovereignty
Intervention, the state and symbolic exchange

36 *Gary Goertz*
Contexts of international politics

35 *James L. Richardson*
Crisis diplomacy
The Great Powers since the mid-nineteenth century

34 *Bradley S. Klein*
Strategic studies and world order
The global politics of deterrence

33 *T. V. Paul*
Asymmetric conflicts: war initiation by weaker powers

32 *Christine Sylvester*
Feminist theory and international relations in a postmodern era

31 *Peter J. Schraeder*
US foreign policy toward Africa
Incrementalism, crisis and change

30 *Graham Spinardi*
From Polaris to Trident: The development of US Fleet Ballistic Missile technology

29 *David A. Welch*
Justice and the genesis of war

28 *Russell J. Leng*
Interstate crisis behavior, 1816–1980: realism versus reciprocity

27 *John A. Vasquez*
The war puzzle

26 *Stephen Gill (ed.)*
Gramsci, historical materialism and international relations

25 *Mike Bowker and Robin Brown (eds.)*
From Cold War to collapse: theory and world politics in the 1980s

24 *R. B. J. Walker*
Inside/outside: international relations as political theory

23 *Edward Reiss*
The Strategic Defense Initiative

22 *Keith Krause*
Arms and the state: patterns of military production and trade

21 *Roger Buckley*
US–Japan alliance diplomacy 1945–1990

20 *James N. Rosenau and Ernst-Otto Czempiel (eds.)*
Governance without government: order and change in world politics

19 *Michael Nicholson*
Rationality and the analysis of international conflict

18 *John Stopford and Susan Strange*
Rival states, rival firms
Competition for world market shares

17 *Terry Nardin and David R. Mapel (eds.)*
Traditions of international ethics

16 *Charles F. Doran*
Systems in crisis
New imperatives of high politics at century's end

15 *Deon Geldenhuys*
Isolated states: a comparative analysis

14 *Kalevi J. Holsti*
Peace and war: armed conflicts and international order 1648–1989

13 *Saki Dockrill*
Britain's policy for West German rearmament 1950–1955

12 *Robert H. Jackson*
Quasi-states: sovereignty, international relations and the Third World

11 *James Barber and John Barratt*
South Africa's foreign policy
The search for status and security 1945–1988

10 *James Mayall*
Nationalism and international society

9 *William Bloom*
Personal identity, national identity and international relations

8 *Zeev Maoz*
National choices and international processes

7 *Ian Clark*
The hierarchy of states
Reform and resistance in the international order

6 Hidemi Suganami
The domestic analogy and world order proposals

5 *Stephen Gill*
American hegemony and the Trilateral Commission

4 *Michael C. Pugh*
The ANZUS crisis, nuclear visiting and deterrence

3 *Michael Nicholson*
Formal theories in international relations

2 *Friedrich V. Kratochwil*
Rules, norms, and decisions
On the conditions of practical and legal reasoning in international relations and domestic affairs

1 *Myles L.C. Robertson*
Soviet policy towards Japan
An analysis of trends in the 1970s and 1980s